DATE DUE

OCT 2 4 2014

Brodart Co.   Cat. # 55 137 001   Printed in USA

Learning and the Infant Mind

LEARNING AND THE INFANT MIND

Edited by

Amanda Woodward
and Amy Needham

UNIVERSITY PRESS

2009

OXFORD
UNIVERSITY PRESS

Oxford University Press, Inc., publishes works that further
Oxford University's objective of excellence
in research, scholarship, and education.

Oxford   New York
Auckland   Cape Town   Dar es Salaam   Hong Kong   Karachi
Kuala Lumpur   Madrid   Melbourne   Mexico City   Nairobi
New Delhi   Shanghai   Taipei   Toronto

With offices in
Argentina   Austria   Brazil   Chile   Czech Republic   France   Greece
Guatemala   Hungary   Italy   Japan   Poland   Portugal   Singapore
South Korea   Switzerland   Thailand   Turkey   Ukraine   Vietnam

Published by Oxford University Press, Inc.
198 Madison Avenue, New York, New York 10016
www.oup.com

Library of Congress Cataloging-in-Publication Data

Learning and the infant mind / edited by Amanda Woodward and Amy Needham.
       p.   cm.
  Includes bibliographical references and index.
  ISBN 978-0-19-530115-1   1. Learning, Psychology of.   2. Infant psychology.
3. Cognition in infants.   I. Woodward, Amanda.   II. Needham, Amy.
  BF318.L3856 2008
  155.42'2315—dc22   2008003856

9 8 7 6 5 4 3 2 1

Printed in the United States of America
on acid-free paper

*We dedicate this book to Sophia, Abbey, and J.D.,
who helped us see the power of young minds.*

Acknowledgments

This book began over breakfast at Duke University's Washington Duke Inn. There, the two of us started a conversation about the challenges posed by having one foot on either side of the gap between infant learning and infant cognition. That conversation led to a wonderfully stimulating conference, held at Duke University's David Thomas Center in May of 2005. The conference was made possible by the generous support of the National Science Foundation, the National Institute of Child Health and Human Development, and Duke University. The meeting could not have happened without the help of Stephanie DiGuiseppi, who dealt with countless practical challenges in the planning of the meeting and did everything possible to make the conference itself go smoothly (including arranging for delightful weather!).

During the early phases of this project, Amanda Woodward received invaluable sabbatical support from the James McKeen Cattell fund and the University of Chicago, and Amy Needham received a sabbatical leave granted by Duke University.

Along the way, our efforts benefited immensely from our conversations with Dedre Gentner, Dick Aslin, Rachel Keen, Judy DeLoache, Susan Goldin-Meadow, Tina Williams, and Renée Baillargeon. We are grateful to them for their support and guidance. We also thank our colleagues and departments at Duke University, the University of Chicago, and the University of Maryland for their many contributions to our intellectual and material survival. We are grateful to Catharine Carlin, Nicholas Liu, and Rachel Mayer at Oxford University Press for their support and patience as the project has grown to fruition.

Finally, we thank each of the authors in this volume and everyone who came to the Duke conference. We had a larger group than is officially represented in these pages, including Dedre Gentner, Rachel Keen, Steve Reznick, Melanie Spence, and Wallace Dixon, and a great collection of rising stars who were invited to give posters. This group included Elizabeth Brannon, Marianella Casasola, Leslie Carver, Patricia Ganea, Lisa Gershkoff-Stowe, Rebecca Gomez, Susan Graham, Susan Hespos, George Hollich, Jordy Kaufman, Natasha Kirkham, Lori Markson, Jessica Maye, Michael McCarty, Bob McMurray, Donna Mumme, Kevin Pelphrey, Megan Saylor, Eric Thiessen, Betty Repacholi, and Peter Vishton. We invited all of these researchers to consider the challenges we identified at that first breakfast meeting. The real contributions of this project are the result of their wisdom, energy, and insight in addressing them.

Contents

Contributors

Karen E. Adolph, Department of Psychology, New York University

Richard N. Aslin, Brain and Cognitive Sciences, University of Rochester

Renée Baillargeon, Department of Psychology, University of Illinois at Urbana-Champaign

Patricia J. Bauer, Department of Psychology, Emory University

Judy S. DeLoache, Department of Psychology, University of Virginia

Patricia A. Ganea, Department of Psychology, Boston University

Jessica S. Horst, Department of Psychology, University of Iowa

Amy S. Joh, Department of Psychology and Neuroscience, Duke University

Scott P. Johnson, Department of Psychology, University of California, Los Angeles

Kristine A. Kovack-Lesh, Department of Psychology, University of Iowa

Jie Li, Department of Psychology, University of Illinois at Urbana-Champaign

Laura L. Namy, Department of Psychology, Emory University

Amy Needham, Department of Psychology and Neuroscience, Duke University

Weiting Ng, Department of Psychology, University of Illinois at Urbana-Champaign

Lisa M. Oakes, Department of Psychology, University of California–Davis

Sammy Perone, Department of Psychology, University of Iowa

Jenny R. Saffran, Department of Psychology, University of Wisconsin–Madison

Teresa Wilcox, Department of Psychology, Texas A&M University

Amanda Woodward, Department of Psychology, University of Maryland, College Park

Rebecca Woods, Department of Psychology, Texas A&M University

Sylvia Yuan, Department of Psychology, University of Illinois at Urbana-Champaign

Introduction

AMY NEEDHAM, DUKE UNIVERSITY; AND
AMANDA WOODWARD, UNIVERSITY OF MARYLAND

This book is the product of a small conference that the two of us organized in May 2005. The conference, on the Duke University campus, consisted of a wonderfully stimulating two days of talks and posters. Our goals in organizing the conference were many, and they are now the goals that we have for anyone (student, faculty, or others) who might pick up this book. We set out as our goals:

1. Encouraging those investigating infants' conceptual knowledge to focus on the mechanisms that give rise to this knowledge, and, in particular, to consider the role of learning in this process.
2. Encouraging those investigating infant learning to focus on the implications of these processes for questions of infants' conceptual structure.
3. Opening and enriching lines of communication among researchers who are conducting cutting-edge investigations into infant learning and infants' conceptual structure.
4. Achieving consensus on appropriate terminology, and, more generally, grounding discussions in a common set of questions so as to work toward productive debates.
5. Encouraging young researchers and students to consider these questions in their own work.
6. Communicating to the broader research community the insights gleaned from this effort.

Thus, our goals were to bring together researchers from diverse areas in the study of infant learning and infant cognition in order to move toward a more general understanding of the role of learning in infant cognitive development. Much of the work on infant cognition has focused on investigating infants' knowledge in core domains but has not thoroughly investigated the factors that contribute to the growth of this knowledge. Recent research elucidating rich learning processes in infants offers a vantage point from which to address this gap and thereby address a number of unresolved issues concerning the nature of the infant mind.

BACKGROUND AND RATIONALE FOR STUDYING INFANT LEARNING

Psychologists have long understood the importance of learning to the human mind. The hallmarks of human thought—among them cognitive flexibility, scientific discovery, and the existence of variations in systems of belief across cultures—are clear demonstrations that the mind is structured, and restructured, by information gleaned from the environment. Learning is evident at all levels of information processing, from the fine-grained dynamic tuning of perceptual and motor systems to the environment (e.g., Gibson & Gibson, 1955) to the acquisition of knowledge in abstract domains, including language, cultural beliefs, and both folk and formal scientific systems (e.g., Gentner & Medina, 1998). It is also evident at all points in the human lifespan.

It seems obvious to consider learning when asking how cognition comes to take its mature form. And, indeed, developmental psychologists have long considered this issue. However, until very recently, there has been limited exploration of learning as a mechanism of conceptual development during infancy. One major line of research on infant cognition has focused on the basic knowledge systems that subserve human thought, investigating infants' conceptual knowledge in these domains. To illustrate, investigators have asked whether infants apprehend the physical permanence of objects, the causal relations between objects, and the intentions that give rise to actions. These researchers are deeply concerned with conceptual structure in infants, but they often have not considered the ways in which learning may contribute to this structure. Another major line of research has focused on infants' perceptual and motor learning. These researchers have focused on how infants extract information from the environment, tune their behavior patterns according to this information, and generalize learning to new situations. These researchers have been deeply concerned with elucidating learning mechanisms but often do not consider the potential effects of these mechanisms on conceptual structure. We held this conference to promote the integration of investigations of infant conceptual structure and infant learning, facilitating communication between these two groups of researchers and thereby moving toward a unified framework for understanding infant cognition.

THE ROLE OF LEARNING IN DEVELOPMENT

Adaptability is a hallmark of human cognition, setting our species apart from others. This adaptability results, in part, from the complexity of human learning.

Therefore, understanding the process and contents of learning is critical for understanding human nature. We believe that a full understanding of a process is possible only after examining its origins and development.

In the context of development, learning has been considered from two vantage points. One classic theoretical position has considered learning to be the backbone of development (e.g., Munn, 1946; Siegler, 2000). In this view, the complexity, flexibility, and variability of mature functioning are directly explainable as the products of learning. Learning is evident from the earliest points in human ontogeny, and research has long underscored the uniformity of processes that contribute to learning across the lifespan (Munn, 1946; Rovee-Collier & Barr, 2001). Indeed, researchers have made important strides in elucidating the learning mechanisms that contribute to conceptual development during childhood (e.g., Gentner & Medina, 1998; Samuelson & Smith, 2000; Siegler, 2000; McClelland & Siegler, 2001).

In contrast, a second classic position points out the insufficiency of learning as a mechanism to explain the emergence of mature cognition (e.g., Piaget, 1954). There are two main arguments in favor of this position. First, it has been suggested that the information available to children is in principle insufficient to support the extraction of regularities that children come to represent (Spelke, Breinlinger, Macomber, & Jacobson, 1992; Pinker, 1994). Second, it has been noted that there are strong limits on what children can learn at particular points in development (e.g., Piaget, 1954). For these reasons, it is argued that the complexity, generality, and flexibility of mature cognition exist, in large part, because of internal constraints on how children represent information.

Resolutions between these two driving intuitions are possible. Indeed, most researchers believe that development is the product of interactions between structure in the organism and structure in the environment, and the real questions concern the nature and unfolding of these interactions. What can be learned at any point in development is constrained by structure in the learner. Learning could, in principle, render changes in this structure, thereby constraining subsequent learning. However, in the field of infancy research, there has been an unfortunate tendency to polarize these two views about the explanatory power of learning. Moreover, these two views have been conflated with assumptions about the nature of cognition in infants. Researchers who posit little explanatory power for learning also tend to posit the existence of rich and relatively abstract systems of knowledge in infants. Researchers who posit a great deal of explanatory power for learning also tend to posit the absence of rich and relatively abstract knowledge in infants. This conflation has led to a neglect of the role that learning plays in infant cognitive development, and, more generally, to a neglect of the complex organism–environment interactions that contribute to cognitive development in infancy.

INFANT COGNITION

Twenty years of research has provided strong evidence that infants possess structured knowledge that informs their responses to novel events. This knowledge is evident in studies of infants' representations of objects (Clifton, Rochat, Litovsky, & Perris, 1991; Spelke et al., 1992; Xu & Carey, 1996; S. Johnson, 1997; Wilcox, 1999; Baillargeon, 2002), causal relations (Leslie, 1982, 1984; Leslie & Keeble, 1987; Oakes & Cohen, 1990; Kotovsky & Baillargeon, 1998; Schlesinger & Langer, 1999; Kotovsky & Baillargeon, 2000), quantity (Wynn, 1992; Brannon, 2002; Feigenson, Carey, & Spelke, 2002; Mix, Huttenlocher, & Levine, 2002), space (Hermer, & Spelke, 1994; Kaufman & Needham, 1999; Newcombe & Learmonth, 1999), categories (Mandler, 1998, 2000; Quinn & M. Johnson, 2000; see Rakison & Oakes 2003), and intentional action (Gergely, Nadasdy, Csibra, & Biro, 1995; Meltzoff, 1995; Woodward, 1998; Baldwin & Baird, 2001; Kuhlmeier, Wynn, & Bloom, 2003). In each case, infants have been shown to perceive and respond to the components of an event in terms of conceptually important dimensions. These findings emerge from studies using a range of methodologies, including paradigms assessing infants' visual attention and paradigms assessing infants' organized actions on objects and their interactions with social partners.

In almost all cases, these studies investigate what infants know but not how they come to this knowledge. Indeed, especially when researchers uncover systematic responding in very young infants, the conclusion is often drawn that this responding reflects innately specified knowledge. Researchers have been deeply concerned with gaining a clear view of infants' knowledge at a particular point in time and, therefore, typically test "snapshots" of infants' representations at a point in time rather than assessing how these representations may change as a function of experience. This is an important first step in a developmental research program because it can establish a skeletal outline of the shape of development and nominate certain kinds of experiences as likely contributors to developmental change. But this is only the first step in understanding development.

Moreover, considering learning may help resolve current debates concerning the nature of infant cognition. For one, there is not yet a general consensus about the processes that give rise to infants' attention to the conceptually relevant aspects of experimentally presented events or how these processes and the resulting knowledge develop. One debated issue is the extent to which infants' mental representations are limited to stored perceptual regularities rather than including forms of knowledge that are more abstract. A second set of issues concerns the extent to which infants' knowledge is tied to particular behavioral contexts rather than being accessible across response modalities, and the related question of when and whether there are dissociations between the knowledge expressed in different kinds of actions (e.g., in the deployment of visual attention versus in motor behavior). In addition, there are open questions concerning the developmental mechanisms that underlie infant cognitive development. Developmental mechanisms include the emergence of symbolic thought, perhaps a result of the emergence of language; the strengthening of initially weak representations; and the integration of previously isolated pockets of knowledge.

Considering the role of learning in infant cognitive development will provide a foothold for addressing the following issues. How infants extract information from experience and generalize it to new instances directly informs conclusions about how abstract and modality-general infants' knowledge is. The acquisition of new or novel information may be particularly informative in this regard. By discovering what infants *can* learn based on particular kinds of experiences, we can elucidate the processes that likely contribute to cognitive development. Moreover, by discovering what infants *can't* learn as readily, we can begin to determine how the structure of the learner constrains development at particular moments in ontogeny. The extents to which infants generalize information along some dimensions and not others, resist learning violations of entrenched regularities, and acquire some kinds of information more quickly than others all provide insight into the potential constraints (established either during phylogeny or ontogeny, in the latter case, perhaps by prior learning) that govern development. Concordance between changes in learning and other potentially important developmental events (e.g., the emergence of language or the development of inhibitory mechanisms) will inform theories of how these changes might contribute to cognitive development. More generally, to really understand infants' cognitive functioning, we need to understand the process(es) by which they acquired their knowledge. This requires making connections between what infants seem to know and how they acquired that knowledge. Making these connections is important because we may well find commonalities across domains of study that have typically not been integrated.

For these reasons, we believe there is much insight yet to be gained about infant cognitive development by taking a closer look at the processes by which cognitive abilities change with development. As a result, we wish to bring learning to the forefront of thinking for researchers who are interested in infants' conceptual knowledge and to highlight questions concerning infants' conceptual knowledge for those who study infant learning. Because debates about the nature of infant cognition have often been expressed in disagreements about the terms that are used to describe infant knowledge (compare Baillargeon, 1999, and Smith, 1999; also Haith, 1998, and Spelke, 1998), we hope to get discussion started on the meanings of terms that are often used to refer to cognitive functions in infants.

PLAN FOR THE BOOK

Historically, infant learning was studied in the context of classical and operant conditioning (e.g. Brackbill, 1958; Lipsitt, 1967; Clifton, 1974; Rovee-Collier, 1986). In part, infant-cognition researchers turned away from learning because these mechanisms seemed unlikely to yield insights into cognitive development. However, researchers of various aspects of infant development have begun to take a new look at learning and have documented that infants' repertoire of learning tools is richer than once thought. The relevant research is spread across diverse domains. In each case, researchers have begun to document infant learning in the laboratory. These experimenters introduce infants to new information and then track the ways this information is encoded and subsequently integrated into infants' cognitive functioning.

SUPPORTING LEARNING: ATTENTION, PERCEPTION, MEMORY, AND NEURAL PROCESSES

Learning occurs in a system in which perception, attention, and memory interact. Much has been learned in recent years about the development of these processes during infancy. We know that even fetuses have some capabilities in each of these areas, although many improvements do occur during the first several years of life. Research has investigated the characteristics of objects and events that tend to draw and keep infants' attention, and the relation between shifts in attention and changes in heart rate (Ruff, 1984; Richards & Casey, 1991). Perception of objects is reasonably accurate but non-inferential during the newborn period, with major improvements in acuity, color vision, and interpretive functions between birth and six months of age (for reviews, see S. Johnson, 1997; Kellman & Banks, 1998; Needham, 1998; Slater, 1998; Teller, 1998). Memory is also improving dramatically during the first year of life, although even fetuses show evidence of learning and remembering for short periods of time, with retention intervals systematically increasing with gestational age both before and after birth (e.g., Slater, Mattock, Brown, Burnham, & Young, 1991; DeCasper, Lecanuet, Busnel, Granier-Deferre, & Maugeais, 1994; Krueger, Holditch-Davis, Quint, & DeCasper, 2004). There is good evidence for implicit, "pre-explicit," and explicit memory developing during the first year of life, with the nature of the event (is there a clear causal structure or not) and language (language-based representations are thought to be qualitatively different from pre-linguistic representations) exerting important influences. Recent work has begun to shed light on the brain structures responsible for each of these advances (M. Johnson, 1997; Diamond, 2000; Nelson, 2002; Bauer, 2004). Infants must be capable of perceiving and remembering objects, and of integrating their experiences into knowledge structures if they are to learn from their prior experiences and apply this learning to novel circumstances. Chapter 1 addresses issues of learning, memory, and consolidation, and Chapter 3 discusses the early development of object perception.

LEARNING ABOUT OBJECTS AND ACTIONS

How do infants come to understand and predict the physical movements that the objects in the world, including their own body, will undergo? This question has motivated various lines of research, with investigators asking how infants perceive and represent objects, focusing on what sources of information are useful in these tasks, and considering how we should think about the interactions between more concrete and more conceptual kinds of information in these tasks (Xu & Carey, 1996; S. Johnson, 1997; Needham, 1998, 1999; Wilcox, 1999).

Infants' expectations about how objects interact with each other have been studied somewhat extensively although, as noted earlier, much more is known about what infants know at a variety of ages than about how infants go from one kind of understanding to another. However, there are some notable exceptions. For example, Baillargeon (1999, 2002) has shown that contrastive evidence—seeing the results of a violation and a fulfillment of a physical principle—is particularly important to infants' learning of physical principles.

Also important in this area of research is specificity in infants' learning: Infants seem to learn separately about the movements of physical objects and the movements of a very complicated "object": the infant's own body (Adolph, 1997). Infants learn separately about occlusion and containment events involving inanimate objects, and they learn separately about the limits of their own body while crawling and while walking (Adolph, 1997; Hespos & Baillargeon, 2001). Other findings on motor development support these general claims (Goldfield, Kay, & Warren, 1993; Thelen, Corbetta, Kamm, Spencer, Schneider, & Zernicke, 1993; Diamond, 2000).

Together, these two lines of research suggest that learning from the environment about the movements of objects or people is a grassroots effort in which experiences may be grouped together based on critical but superficial similarities between them (e.g., removal of support leads to an object's falling down; crawling versus standing posture creates very different vantage points on the situation). Over time, generalization across different pockets of knowledge must occur and is an important process to understand for both of these kinds of learning about the world.

In this volume, Chapter 4, Chapter 5, Chapter 7, and Chapter 8 discuss the relations between objects and actions in a learning context. Chapters 4, 5, and 8 discuss how infants learn about the physical world (i.e., the world of objects) and how their own experiences and other cognitive processes (e.g., categorization, judgments of perceptual similarity) play a role in this learning. Chapters 7 and 8 discuss the ways in which infants' learning to move their bodies looks very much like other kinds of learning that infants do.

LANGUAGE LEARNING

In many ways, the language domain is a model for the productive study of infant learning. Recent research has brought many aspects of language learning into the infant laboratory—from the extraction of the phonemic categories of one's native language (Kuhl, 2000; Maye, Werker, & Gerken, 2002; Werker & Tees, 2002) to the extraction of linguistic units from the speech stream (Saffran, Aslin, & Newport, 1996), to the linking of form with meaning (Woodward, Markman, & Fitzsimmons, 1994; Stager & Werker, 1997; Gogate, Walker-Andrews, & Bahrick, 2001; Smith, Jones Landau, Gershkoff-Stowe, & Samuelson, 2002; Booth & Waxman, 2003), to the acquisition of grammar (Gomez & Gerken, 1999; Marcus, Vijayan, Bandi Rao, & Vishton, 1999; Gomez & Gerken, 2000). For each of these diverse aspects of language learning, researchers have established paradigms for directly investigating learning in the laboratory. These experiments have revealed that a range of learning processes contribute to language acquisition, including perceptual learning—the refinement of perceptual categories based on the distributional properties of the input; statistical learning—the extraction of units from unsegmented speech via the computation of transitional probabilities; rule learning—the acquisition of rules from observed regularities, and associative learning.

Across these processes, researchers find that the products of learning can be relatively abstract in nature. To illustrate, Marcus and colleagues (1999) report that eight-month-old infants who are exposed to the pattern A-B-A in a series of nonsense syllables recognize this pattern when they later encounter it in novel sequences. That is, infants seemed to have stored not just the particular sound sequences they had heard but also the abstract pattern that gave rise to them. The products of learning can also be generative, providing the basis for future acts of learning. For example, statistical segmentation of speech sounds yields units that can be co-opted for word learning (Saffran, 2001), and an infant's prior experiences mapping words to meanings shapes their expectations about the likely meanings of new words (Smith et al., 2002).

A cross-cutting debate concerns the extent to which infants' language learning can be explained via general mechanisms rather than via language-specific learning mechanisms (e.g., Tomasello, 2001; Lidz et al., 2003). Indeed, several of the learning processes initially identified in the context of infant language learning seem likely to have much broader application. To illustrate, Baldwin and Baird (2001) suggested that statistical-unit extraction may provide the basis for infants' detecting behavioral regularities in the actions of social partners.

Chapter 2 and Chapter 10 describe different perspectives on the learning mechanisms underlying language development, including statistical learning mechanisms and situational factors that may support word learning.

CONCEPTUAL LEARNING

Central to any act of learning and generalization is (1) the detection of differences across individual instances and (2) the identification of correspondences or commonalities across these instances. Several decades of research have elucidated infants' ability both to extract differences and to notice at least some commonalities that allow for the formation of perceptual categories. Across these studies, infants manifest a sensitivity to category structure in their patterns of attention (see Quinn, 2002; Rakison & Oakes, 2003). Like adults, infants appear to structure their categories around a prototype. And over the course of the first year of life, infants come to attend not only to individual features but also to correlations among features in doing so (Cohen, Chaput, & Cashon, 2002). Infants, like adults, categorize more efficiently when given the opportunity to compare members of a category to one another or to members of a contrasting category (Oakes & Madole, 2003). By the end of the first year, infants have moved beyond the perceptual commonalities that unite categories. They infer that members of a kind share properties that are not immediately observable. By the end of the first year, infants begin to understand the link between conceptual categories and language: Hearing diverse members of a kind labeled with the same name leads infants to seek out commonalities among them (Waxman, 2003).

In recent years, researchers have asked about the relation between perceptual and conceptual representations of categories. Some have proposed strong discontinuities between perceptual and conceptual categories, either because the two systems are proposed to exist independently from early in life (Mandler, 1998) or because conceptual representations are proposed to depend on the emergence of new cognitive capacities and/or language (Xu & Carey, 1996; Quinn, 2002). However, others have proposed that increasingly abstract category knowledge grows from early perceptual categories and the processes that give rise to them (Oakes & Madole, 2003; Rakison, 2003). In this view, learning contributes centrally to the formation of conceptual knowledge in infants.

Although even infants have been shown to identify commonalities across different instances of a category that has at least some perceptual support, other commonalities are more difficult to appreciate. For instance, the correspondence between a symbol and its referent (e.g., a room and a scale model of that room) are not understood until sometime between two and three years of age (DeLoache, 1987, 2004). A genuine appreciation of the relation between a symbol and its referent (perhaps especially the unique relation between a model and the space it represents) may require more conceptual ability than most infants and very young children typically possess. As we write, the perceptual and conceptual contributions to the ability to symbolize are still being investigated, with many interesting questions yet to be answered.

Chapter 6 and Chapter 11 discuss the role of learning in categorization and symbolization abilities early in life. Both chapters highlight the importance of perceptual support, especially early in the development of these skills.

SOCIAL LEARNING

Researchers have long understood the foundational role of social partners in structuring development (e.g., Harlow & Zimmerman, 1959), and recent studies have begun to bring infant social learning into the laboratory to investigate the processes by which it occurs. One process, initially identified by Bandura, Ross, and Ross (1963) in older children, is learning by reproducing the observed actions of social partners. Forms of imitative learning are present from birth (Meltzoff & Moore, 1977; Heimann, 2002). By 9 to 12 months, imitative learning is robust across a range of situations, and the products of learning can be sustained for weeks or even months, even when infants lack the opportunity to reproduce the observed action in the intervening period (Collie & Hayne, 1999; Meltzoff, 2002; Bauer, 2004). Imitative learning yields a range of cognitive products, including not only procedural knowledge but also conceptual representations of the relevant objects and events (Bauer, Hayne) and possibly information about the goals that drive action (Meltzoff, 2002). Recent findings documenting neurocognitive mirroring systems in adults suggest a possible basis for imitative learning in infants (see Meltzoff & Prinz, 2002), but it is also clear that general memorial processes, and top-down constraints on event representation, contribute to infants' learning from the observed actions of other people (Bauer & Mandler, 1992; Meltzoff, 1995; Gergely, Bekkering, & Kiraly, 2002). Critically, infants' learning from social partners is mediated by their emerging knowledge about the intentional structure of action, not only in the case of imitative learning (Meltzoff, 1995;

Gergely et al., 2002) but also in language learning (Tomasello, 1999; Baldwin & Moses, 2001; Woodward, 2003) and social referencing (Moses, Baldwin, Rosicky, & Tidball, 2001). To illustrate, by 14 to 18 months, infants use behavioral evidence of a speaker's attention and purposefulness to determine which of several objects is the intended referent (see Tomasello, 1999; Baldwin & Moses, 2001, for reviews). Thus, in this domain, researchers have begun to investigate the ways that social knowledge is generative, building on itself in development.

In this volume, Chapter 9 delves into intriguing new ideas about how infants learn about people, knowledge that helps infants understand what people are doing in the present and predict what they will do in the future.

INTEGRATION

At the conference, we were very fortunate to have the involvement of a number of senior scholars who provided a valuable integrative force to our discussions. This was especially important because we had solicited presentations about a wide range of topics. In this volume, our last chapter is an integrative piece written by Dick Aslin. Dick was one of our advisers during the conference, and he agreed to reprise his role in written form here in our book. He read all of the chapters and crafted a beautiful document that helps us see both where we have been and where we need to go.

CONCLUSIONS

Across all of these domains, three trends indicate that the time is right to move to a more general understanding of the role of learning in infant cognition.

1. Researchers have begun to consider whether and how the products of learning "go beyond" the input, in several senses. First, they have begun to investigate whether infants derive relatively abstract representations from experience. Second, they have begun to investigate the extent to which infants generalize (or fail to generalize) information learned in one behavioral context to a new behavioral context. Third, they have begun to investigate the extent to which learning is generative—constraining and informing subsequent learning.
2. Researchers have begun to elucidate the general and the more specific processes that subserve or contribute to learning and cognitive development, and the ways in which these processes may change with development.
3. There is now a more generally recognized need for consistency in terminology across domains. When this research was in its earliest stages, researchers tended to use terms that were idiosyncratic to their own domains of study. Now the field has progressed to the point that more consistency in the ways in which cognitive terms are used to refer to infant development are absolutely necessary if the field hopes to move forward constructively.

Whether you are a beginning student, an advanced student, or a researcher, we hope you will gain a new appreciation for the relations between what we know about infant cognition and what we are discovering about infant learning. Specifically, we are very excited about the ways in which learning can help transform our snapshot-based characterization of infant development into a vivid Technicolor movie of the infant mind. At present, we can only speculate about how the infant, the learning processes, the structured physical world, and the people in that environment work together to produce the fascinating movie that is the developing infant mind.

References

Adolph, K. E. (1997). Learning in the development in infant locomotion. *Monographs of the Society for Research in Child Development, 62* (3, Serial No. 251).

Baillargeon, R. (1999). Young infants' expectations about hidden objects: A reply to three challenges. *Developmental Science, 2,* 115–133.

Baillargeon, R. (2002). The acquisition of physical knowledge in infancy: A summary in eight lessons. In P. K. Smith & C. H. Hart (Eds.), *Blackwell handbook of childhood cognitive development* (pp. 47–83). Oxford, UK: Blackwell.

Baldwin, B. A., & Baird, J. A. (2001). Discerning intentions in dynamic human action. *Trends in Cognitive Sciences, 5,* 171–178.

Baldwin, B. A., & Moses, L. J. (2001). Links between social understanding and early word learning: Challenges to current accounts. *Social Development, 10,* 309–329.

Bandura, A., Ross, D., & Ross, S. A. (1963). Imitation of film-mediated aggressive models. *Journal of Abnormal and Social Psychology, 66,* 3–11.

Bauer, P. J. (2004). Getting explicit memory off the ground: Steps toward construction of a neuro-developmental account of changes in the first two years of life. *Developmental Review, 24,* 347–373.

Bauer, P. J., & Mandler, J. M. (1992). Putting the horse before the cart: The use of temporal order in recall of events by one-year-old children. *Developmental Psychology, 28,* 441–452.

Booth, A. E., & Waxman, S. R. (2003). Mapping words to the world in infancy: Infants' expectations for count nouns and adjectives. *Journal of Cognition & Development, 4,* 357–381.

Brackbill, Y. (1958). Extinction of the smiling response in infants as a function of reinforcement schedule. *Child Development, 29,* 114–124.

Brannon, E. M. (2002). The development of ordinal numerical knowledge in infancy. *Cognition, 83,* 223–240.

Clifton, R. K. (1974). Heart rate conditioning in the newborn infant. *Journal of Experimental Child Psychology, 18,* 9–21.

Clifton, R. K., Rochat, P., Litovsky, R. Y., & Perris, E. E. (1991). Object representation guides infants' reaching in the dark. *Journal of Experimental Psychology: Human Perception and Performance, 17,* 323–329.

Cohen, L. B., Chaput, H. H., & Cashon, C. H. (2002). A constructivist model of infant cognition. *Cognitive Development, 17,* 1323–1343.

Collie, R., & Hayne, H. (1999). Deferred imitation by 6- and 9-month-old infants: More evidence for declarative memory. *Developmental Psychobiology, 35,* 83–90.

DeCasper, A. J., Lecanuet, J. P., Busnel, M. C., Granier-Deferre, C., & Maugeais, R. (1994). Fetal reactions to recurrent maternal speech. *Infant Behavior and Development, 17,* 159–164.

DeLoache, J. S. (1987). Symbolic functioning in very young children: Understanding of pictures and models. *Child Development, 62,* 736–752.

DeLoache, J. S. (2004). Becoming symbol-minded. *TRENDS in Cognitive Sciences, 8,* 66–70.

Diamond, A. (2000). Close interrelation of motor development and cognitive development and of the cerebellum and prefrontal cortex. *Child Development, 71,* 44–56.

Feigenson, L., Carey, S., & Spelke, E. (2002). Infants' discrimination of number vs. continuous extent. *Cognitive Psychology, 44,* 33–66.

Gentner, D., & Medina, J. (1998). Similarity and the development of rules. *Cognition, 65,* 263–297.

Gergely, G., Bekkering, H., & Kiraly, I. (2002). Rational imitation in preverbal infants. *Nature, 415,* 755–761.

Gergely, G., Nadasdy, Z., Csibra, G., & Biro, S. (1995). Taking the intentional stance at 12 months of age. *Cognition, 56,* 165–193.

Gibson, J. J., & Gibson, E. J. (1955). Perceptual learning: Differentiation or enrichment? *Psychological Review, 62,* 32–41.

Gogate, L. J., Walker-Andrews, A. S., & Bahrick, L. E. (2001). The intersensory origins of word-comprehension: An ecological-dynamic systems view. *Developmental Science, 4,* 1–18.

Goldfield, E. C., Kay, B. A., & Warren, W. H. (1993). Infant bouncing: The assembly and tuning of action systems. *Child Development, 64,* 1128–1142.

Gomez, R. L., & Gerken, L. (1999). Artificial grammar learning by 1-year-olds leads to specific and abstract knowledge. *Cognition, 70,* 109–135.

Gomez, R. L., & Gerken, L. (2000). Infant artificial language learning and language acquisition. *Trends in Neurosciences, 4,* 178–181.

Haith, M. M. (1998). Who put the cog in infant cognition? Is rich interpretation too costly? *Infant Behavior and Development, 21,* 167–179.

Harlow, H. F., & Zimmerman, P. R. (1959). Affectional responses in the infant monkey. *Science, 130,* 421–432.

Heimann, M. (2002). Notes on individual differences and the assumed elusiveness of the neonatal imitation. In A. N. Meltzoff & W. Prinz (Eds.), *Imitative mind: Development, evolution, and brain bases* (pp. 74–84). Cambridge, UK: Cambridge University Press.

Hermer, L., & Spelke, E. S. (1994). A geometric process for spatial reorientation in young children. *Nature, 370,* 57–59.

Hespos, S. J., & Baillargeon, R. (2001). Infants' knowledge about occlusion and containment events: A surprising discrepancy. *Psychological Science, 12,* 141–147.

Johnson, M. H. (1997). *Developmental cognitive neuroscience: An introduction.* Oxford, UK: Blackwell.

Johnson, S. P. (1997). Young infants' perception of object unity: Implications for development of attentional and cognitive skills. *Current Directions in Psychological Science, 6,* 5–11.

Kaufman, J., & Needham, A. (1999). Objective spatial coding by 6.5-month-old infants in a visual dishabituation task. *Developmental Science, 2,* 432–442.

Kellman, P. J., & Banks, M. S. (1998). Infant visual perception. In D. Kuhn & R. S. Siegler (Eds.), *Handbook of child psychology, volume 2: Cognition, perception and language* (pp. 103–146). New York: John Wiley & Sons.

Kotovsky, L., & Baillargeon, R. (1998). The development of calibration-based reasoning about collision events in young infants. *Cognition, 67,* 311–351.

Kotovsky, L., & Baillargeon, R. (2000). Reasoning about collisions involving inert objects in 7.5-month-old infants. *Developmental Science, 3,* 344–361.

Krueger, C., Holditch-Davis, D., Quint, S., & DeCasper, A. (2004). Recurring auditory experience in the 28- to 34-week-old fetus. *Infant Behavior and Development, 27*, 537–543.

Kuhl, P. K. (2000). A new view of language acquisition. *Proceedings of the National Academy of Sciences, 97*, 11,850–11,857.

Kuhlmeier, V., Wynn, K., & Bloom, P. (2003). Attribution of dispositional states by 12-month-olds. *Psychological Science, 14*, 402–408.

Leslie, A. M. (1982). Discursive representation in infancy. In B. de Gelder (Ed.), *Knowledge and representation* (pp. 80–93). London: Routledge & Kegan Paul.

Leslie, A. M. (1984). Spatiotemporal continuity and the perception of causality in infants. *Perception, 13*, 287–305.

Leslie, A. M., & Keeble, S. (1987). Do six-month-old infants perceive causality? *Cognition, 25*, 265–288.

Lidz, J., Gleitman, H. & Gleitman, L. (2003). Understanding how input matters: verb learning and the footprint of universal grammar. *Cognition, 87*, 151–178.

Lipsitt, L. P. (1967). Learning in the human infant. In H. W. Stevenson, E. H. Hess, & H. L. Rheingold (Eds.), *Early behavior: Comparative and developmental approaches* (pp. 225–247). New York: John Wiley & Sons.

Mandler, J. M. (1998). On developing a knowledge base in infancy. *Developmental Psychology, 34*, 1274–1288.

Mandler, J. M. (2000). Perceptual and conceptual processes in infancy. *Journal of Cognition and Development, 1*, 3–36.

Marcus, G. F., Vijayan, S., Bandi Rao, S., & Vishton, P. M. (1999). Rule learning by seven-month-old infants. *Science, 283*, 77–80.

Maye, J., Werker, J. F., & Gerken, L. (2002). Infant sensitivity to distributional information can affect phonetic discrimination. *Cognition, 82*, B101–B111.

McClelland, J. L., & Siegler, R. S. (2001). *Mechanisms of cognitive development*. Mahwah, NJ: LEA.

Meltzoff, A. N. (1995). Understanding the intentions of others: Re-enactment of intended acts by 18-month-old children. *Developmental Psychology, 31*, 838–850.

Meltzoff, A. N. (2002). Elements of a developmental theory of imitation. In A. N. Meltzoff & W. Prinz (Eds.), *Imitative mind: Development, evolution, and brain bases* (pp. 19–41). Cambridge, UK: Cambridge University Press.

Meltzoff, A. N., & Moore, M. K. (1977). Imitation of facial and manual gestures by human neonates. *Science, 198*, 74–78.

Meltzoff, A. N., & Prinz, W. (2002.). *Imitative mind: Development, evolution, and brain bases*. Cambridge, UK: Cambridge University Press.

Mix, K. C., Huttenlocher, J., & Levine, S. C. (2002). Multiple cues for quantification in infancy: Is number one of them? *Psychological Bulletin, 128*, 278–294.

Moses, L. J., Baldwin, D. A., Rosicky, J. G., & Tidball, G. (2001). Evidence for referential understanding in the emotions domain at twelve and eighteen months. *Child Development, 72*, 718–736.

Munn, N. (1946). Learning in children. In L. Carmichael (Ed.), *Manual of child psychology* (pp. 374–458). New York: John Wiley & Sons.

Needham, A. (1998). Infants' use of featural information in the segregation of stationary objects. *Infant Behavior and Development, 21*, 47–76.

Needham, A. (1999). The role of shape in 4-month-old infants' object segregation: A boundary-based method for obtaining object parts. *Infant Behavior and Development, 22*, 161–178.

Nelson, C. A. (2002). The ontogeny of human memory: A cognitive neuroscience perspective. In Mark H. Johnson, Yuko Munakata, & Rick O Gilmore (Eds.), *Brain development and cognition: A reader* (pp. 151–178). Blackwell Publishing.

Newcombe, N. S., & Learmonth, A. (1999). Change and continuity in early spatial development: Claiming the "radical middle." *Infant Behavior and Development, 22,* 457–474.

Oakes, L. M., & Cohen, L. B. (1990). Infant perception of a causal event. *Cognitive Development, 5,* 193–207.

Oakes, L. M., & Madole, K. L. (2003). Principles of developmental change in infants' category formation. In D. H. Rakison & L. M. Oakes (Eds.), *Early category and concept development: Making sense of the blooming, buzzing confusion* (pp. 132–158). New York: Oxford University Press.

Piaget, J. (1954). *The construction of reality in the child.* New York: Ballantine.

Pinker, S. (1994). *The language instinct: The new science of language and mind.* Harmondsworth, Middlesex, UK: Penguin.

Quinn. P. C. (2002). Category representation in infants. *Current Directions in Psychological Science, 11,* 66–70.

Quinn, P. C., & Johnson, M. H. (2000). Global-before-basic object categorization in connectionist networks and 2-month-old infants. *Infancy, 1,* 31–46.

Rakison, D. H. (2003). Parts, categorization, and the animate-inanimate distinction in infancy. In D. H. Rakison & L. M. Oakes (Eds.), *Early category and concept development: Making sense of the blooming, buzzing confusion* (pp. 159–192). New York: Oxford University Press.

Rakison, D. H., & Oakes, L. M. (2003). *Early category and concept development: Making sense of the blooming, buzzing confusion.* New York: Oxford University Press.

Richards, J. E., & Casey, B. J. (1991). Heart-rate variability during attention phases in young infants. *Psychophysiology, 28,* 43–53.

Rovee-Collier, C. (1986). The rise and fall of infant classical conditioning research: Its promise for the study of early development. In L. P. Lipsitt & C. Rovee-Collier (Eds.), *Advances in infancy research* (pp. 139–159). Norwood, NJ: Ablex.

Rovee-Collier, C. & Barr, R. (2001). Infant learning and memory. In J. G. Bremner & A. Fogel (Eds.), *Blackwell Handbook of Infant Development* (pp. 139–168). Oxford, UK: Blackwell.

Ruff, H. A. (1984). Infants' manipulative exploration of objects: Effects of age and object characteristics. *Developmental Psychology, 20,* 9–20.

Saffran, J. R. (2001). Words in a sea of sounds: The output of infant statistical learning. *Cognition, 81,* 149–169.

Saffran, J. R., Aslin, R. N., & Newport, E. L. (1996). Statistical learning by 8-month-old infants. *Science, 274,* 1926–1928.

Samuelson, L. K., & Smith, L. B. (2000). Grounding development in cognitive processes. *Child Development, 71,* 98–107.

Schlesinger, M., & Langer, J. (1999). Infants' developing expectations of possible and impossible tool-use events between ages 8 and 12 months. *Developmental Science, 2,* 195–206.

Siegler, R. S. (2000). The rebirth of children's learning. *Child Development, 71,* 26–35.

Slater, A. (1998). Visual perception and its organization in early infancy. In J. Gavin Bremner, Alan Slater, & George Butterworth (Eds.), *Infant Development: Recent advances* (pp. 31–53). Hove, UK: Psychology Press.

Slater, A., Mattock, A., Brown, E., Burnham, D., & Young, A. (1991). Visual processing of stimulus compounds in newborn infants. *Perception, 20,* 29–33.

Smith, L. B. (1999). Do infants possess innate knowledge structures? The con side. *Developmental Science, 2,* 133–145.

Smith, L. B., Jones, S. S., Landau, B., Gershkoff-Stowe, L., & Samuelson, L. (2002). Object name learning provides on-the-job training for attention. *Psychological Science, 13,* 13–20.

Spelke, E. S. (1998). Nativism, empiricism, and the origins of knowledge. *Infant Behavior and Development, 21,* 181–200.

Spelke, E. S., Breinlinger, K., Macomber, J., & Jacobson, K. (1992). Origins of knowledge. *Psychological Review, 99,* 605–632.

Stager, C. L., & Werker, J. F. (1997). Infants listen for more phonetic detail in speech perception than in word-learning tasks. *Nature, 388,* 381–382.

Teller, D. Y. (1998). Spatial and temporal aspects of infant color vision. *Vision Research, 38,* 3275–3282.

Thelen, E., Corbetta, D., Kamm, K., Spencer, J. P., Schneider, K., & Zernicke, R. F. (1993). The transition to reaching: Mapping intention and intrinsic dynamics. *Child Development, 64,* 1058–1098.

Tomasello, M. (1999). *The Cultural Origins of Human Cognition.* Cambridge, MA: Harvard University Press.

Tomasello, M. (2001). Perceiving intentions and learning words in the second year of life. In M. Bowerman & S. Levinson (Eds.), *Language acquisition and conceptual development* (pp.132–158). Cambridge, UK: Cambridge University Press.

Waxman, S. R. (2003). Links between object categorization and naming: Origins and emergence in human infants. In D. H. Rakison & L. M. Oakes (Eds.), *Early category and concept development: Making sense of the blooming, buzzing confusion* (pp. 213–241). New York: Oxford University Press.

Werker, J. F., & Tees, R. C. (2002). Cross-language speech perception: Evidence for perceptual reorganization during the first year of life. *Infant Behavior and Development, 25,* 121–133.

Wilcox, T. (1999). Object individuation: Infants' use of shape, size, pattern, and color. *Cognition, 72,* 125–166.

Woodward, A. L. (1998). Infants selectively encode the goal object of an actor's reach. *Cognition, 69,* 1–34.

Woodward, A. L. (2003). Infants' developing understanding of the link between looker and object. *Developmental Science, 6,* 287–311.

Woodward, A. L., Markman, E. M., & Fitzsimmons, C. M. (1994). Rapid word learning in 13- and 18-month-olds. *Developmental Psychology, 30,* 553–566.

Wynn, K. (1992). Addition and subtraction by human infants. *Nature, 358,* 749–750.

Xu, F., & Carey, S. (1996). Infants' metaphysics: The case of numerical identity. *Cognitive Psychology, 30,* 111–153.

Learning and the Infant Mind

1

Learning and Memory
Like a Horse and Carriage

PATRICIA J. BAUER, EMORY UNIVERSITY

The lyrics of James van Heusen and Sammy Cahn's 1955 song, "Love and Marriage" (written for the musical version of *Our Town,* by Thornton Wilder), advise that the emotion of love and the institution of marriage are linked such that "you can't have one without the other." So it is with learning and memory. We assess learning by testing memory; memory is essential for learning to occur. Yet in myriad ways, what we remember is not what we learned. The purpose of this chapter is to explore some of the multifaceted relations between learning and memory early in life, as the knowledge base is being established and as the memory system that permits accrual of declarative or explicit knowledge is being constructed. The chapter features discussion of some of the methods used to test learning and memory in infancy and of the characteristics of the cognitive products that result from participation in the tasks. Also featured is discussion of some of the mnemonic processes that occur after learning and discussion of their neural substrate. The chapter ends with examination of the implications of these processes for the otherwise tight relations between learning and memory. The carriage ride begins with a brief historical note that helps explain why work on relations between these foundational cognitive processes is still in its own infancy.

CHANGING PERSPECTIVES ON LEARNING AND MEMORY

Regardless of where one stands on the issue of the nature of the starter set (whether it is rich or lean), the role of learning in cognitive development is not to be denied. Basic facts—such as the rising of the sun in the eastern sky—and esoteric bits— such as the names of the writers of the song "Love and Marriage"—all require that information be entered into the knowledge base. For the entries to be maximally useful, they should be encoded in a manner that enables their later explicit recollection. Historically, this fundamental ability was thought beyond the capabilities of the human infant. The most prominent proponent of this perspective, Jean Piaget (1926, 1952), recognized that human infants learn and remember. Piaget (with the aid of his wife, Valentine Châtenay) carefully chronicled the modifications of sensory and motor schemes that constituted the infants' tools for constructing knowledge about the world. For Piaget, the learning process was slow and the resulting products were not accessible outside the context in which the objects and events were experienced. Rather, knowledge was tied to the sensory systems that gave rise to experience and to the muscles and joints that determined how an object was grasped or held, for example. The capacity to form explicit, symbolic knowledge that was "transportable" and sharable through language was thought to be achieved by the middle to the end of the second year of life.

The 1970s and early 1980s were full of challenges to the Piagetian perspective on cognitive development (see Gelman & Baillargeon, 1983, for a review). It seemed that everywhere one looked there was evidence of competence not predicted by the structural aspects of the theory. One exception was infant memory. Whereas some tools for studying infant memory were available, they did not provide compelling evidence of the capacity to *re*-present objects or events in their absence. For example, looking at a novel stimulus for a longer period after visual exposure to a different stimulus (as in the visual paired comparison task introduced by Fantz, 1956) provided experimental evidence of recognition memory (although see Snyder, 2006, for a different interpretation). Yet the recognition behaviors were similar to those Piaget (1952) had described in his own infants, for which he saw no need to invoke representational ability. Similarly, differential rates of kicking before and after experience of contingent movement of a mobile attached to an infant's leg (as in the mobile conjugate reinforcement task) (see Rovee-Collier & Gerhardstein, 1997, for a review) provided strong evidence of learning and memory. However, the type of learning apparent in the paradigm did not differ from that shown by a variety of nonhuman animals in the context of operant conditioning tasks. The result was that, amid a revolution in the way the field thought about the mental life of infants and children, infants' abilities to recall the past remained in question for lack of convincing methods.

Behavioral Measures of Recall

A serious challenge to the assumption that infants were unable to represent the past came with the development of elicited and deferred imitation as experimental tests of recall memory. Piaget (1952) himself had identified deferred imitation as one of the hallmarks of the development of symbolic thought: He used his daughter Jacqueline's deferred imitation of a cousin's temper tantrum as an illustration of her developing representational capacity. Meltzoff (1985, 1988a), Bauer and Shore (1987), and Bauer and Mandler (1989) brought the behavior into the laboratory by having models (typically adult experimenters) use props to demonstrate individual actions or sequences of actions that the infant or child was permitted to

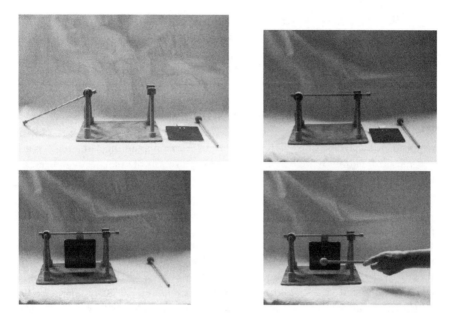

Figure 1–1. Three-step sequence of making a gong. The sequence consists of folding a bar across a support, handing a metal plate from the bar, and striking the plate with a mallet to make a ringing sound.

imitate either immediately (in elicited imitation), after a delay (in deferred imitation), or both immediately and after a delay. For example, in a 3-step sequence, the objects pictured in Figure 1–1 can be combined to create a gong.

Originally, the argument that imitation-based paradigms provide a means of testing recall memory was based in Piaget's (1952) observations. Routine use of the technique has provided a range of evidence that supports the claim. Because the argument has been developed in detail elsewhere (e.g., Bauer, 2005b, 2006), I present only three components of it. First, the paradigm passes the "amnesia test." Whereas intact adults accurately imitate sequences after a delay, patients with amnesia due to hippocampal lesions perform no better than naïve controls (McDonough, Mandler, McKee, & Squire, 1995). Adolescents and young adults who sustained hippocampal damage early in life also exhibit deficits in performance on the task (Adlam, Vargha-Khadem, Mishkin, & de Haan, 2005). Deficits in performance also are apparent in infants with suspected hippocampal damage associated with maternal gestational diabetes (which in animal models impairs hippocampal function) (Georgieff & Rao, 2001; DeBoer, Wewerka, Bauer, Georgieff, & Nelson, 2005). These observations suggest that the paradigm taps the type of memory (declarative or explicit) that gives rise to recall.

The second component of the argument that imitation-based tasks tap recall memory comes from the observation that once children acquire the requisite language, they talk about events that they experienced as preverbal infants, in the context of imitation tasks (e.g., Bauer, Kroupina, Schwade, Dropik, & Wewerka,

1998; Bauer, Wenner, & Kroupina, 2002; Bauer, Van Abbema, Wiebe, Cary, Phill, & Burch, 2004; Cheatham & Bauer, 2005). This is strong evidence that the format in which the memories are encoded is declarative or explicit, as opposed to implicit, procedural, or sensorimotor (formats inaccessible to language). Third, performance on imitation tasks in infancy is correlated with later performance on experimental tests of deliberate memory, such as sort-recall (Larkina & Bauer, 2005), and standardized tests, such as the Children's Memory Scale (DeBoer, Cheatham, Stark, & Bauer, 2005). The most straightforward interpretation of these cross-lag relations is that the various measures tap the same underlying mnemonic function, namely, the capacity to re-present the past as evidenced by recall of it.

Electrophysiological Measures of Recognition

Development of elicited and deferred imitation as experimental tests of recall memory permitted challenging the assumption that infants were unable to re-present the past. Converging and complementary evidence of the mnemonic abilities of infants and young children comes from event-related potentials or ERPs. ERPs are scalp-recorded electrical oscillations associated with excitatory and inhibitory postsynaptic potentials. Because they are noninvasive and make no performance demands on the participant (e.g., ERPs to auditory stimuli can be recorded while the participant sleeps), they are ideal for use with human infants. Moreover, because they are time-locked to a stimulus, differences in the latency and amplitude of the response to various classes of stimuli—familiar and novel, for example—can be interpreted as evidence of differential neural processing. For example, in Bauer et al. (2006), differences in amplitude in response to photographs of familiar stimuli at 9 months versus 10 months of age related to differences in recall at the two ages (with infants showing more robust ERP responses and more robust recall at the older relative to the younger age). In Bauer, Wiebe, Carver, Waters, and Nelson (2003), the latency to peak amplitude of response to familiar stimuli after a 1-week delay predicted 28% of the variance in recall of sequences 1 month later.

WHAT KIND OF LEARNING IS APPARENT?

The techniques of elicited and deferred imitation and ERP have revealed a great deal about the mnemonic life of infants in the first two years. Importantly, for present purposes, they reveal that the learning that infants do shares two important characteristics with learning among older children and adults. Specifically, infants and very young children learn quite quickly and they can apply the lessons that they have learned in a flexible manner. Neither feature is consistent with a characterization of infants as being restricted to sensorimotor or procedural learning. After describing the speed with which information is acquired and the flexibility of new learning, I turn to a discussion of the pronounced changes in learning and memory that we see over the first two years of life.

Learning Is Fast

The speed with which infants acquire new information is readily apparent by comparing their behavior toward the same stimuli before and after exposure to a modeled sequence of actions using the stimuli (such as the gong pictured in Fig. 1–1). In Figure 1–2, Panel a, are plotted the number of individual target actions and the number of pairs of actions in the target order produced by 16- and 20-month-olds (1) in a premodeling or baseline period (before exposure to a modeled sequence of actions), (2) immediately after two demonstrations of the modeled sequence, and (3) 2 weeks after experiencing the sequence (Bauer & Mandler, 1989). The sequences were novel to the infants, per parental report. Nevertheless, after brief exposure to the sequences (modeling a 3-step sequence two times in a row requires approximately 15 s), the infants learned an average of 2.39 of the 3 target actions. They also learned about the order in which the actions should be produced. They retained a substantial amount of the information over a 2-week delay. Learning and remembering novel sequences, such as how to make a gong, was on par with learning and remembering sequences based on routine events such as bathing and making breakfast (Fig. 2, Panel b).

The behavioral measures just described actually underestimate the speed with which even young infants extract information from a model or display. In Wiebe, Cheatham, Lukowski, Haight, Muehleck, and Bauer (2006), nine-month-old infants viewed an adult demonstrate a 2-step sequence two times in a row. The infants were then fitted with a 32-channel electrode cap and were tested for their ERP responses to three classes of photograph stimuli pictured in Figure 1–3: (1) the objects used to produce the modeled sequence, presented repeatedly for 30 trials (familiar event); (2) the objects used to produce a novel 2-step sequence, presented repeatedly for 30 trials (novel repeated event); and (3) stimuli that were unique for each of 30 trials (novel trial–unique event). Each picture was displayed for 500 milliseconds. To determine the speed with which infants extracted information about the stimuli presented in the ERP portion of the experiment, we examined ERP responses to the first and second half of the trials for each class of stimuli (i.e., the first and second 7500 ms of exposure). As is apparent in Figure 1–4, for the familiar stimuli, ERP responses changed over trials: The amplitude of responses was reduced in the second relative to the first half of trials. The change in response was not a function of practice or fatigue because for the novel trial–unique stimuli there was no change in amplitude of response on the first and second half of trials. Tellingly, for the novel repeated sequence, the amplitude of response changed between halves of the task, with responses decreasing in magnitude as infants presumably learned about the stimuli from the displays. Thus, after only 7.5 seconds of exposure, the neural representation of repeated stimuli was already "educated," recruiting a smaller population of neurons as experience accrued.

Whereas even young infants learn quite rapidly, there are developmental differences in the speed with which learning occurs. For example, there are changes in the number of exposures to material that infants seem to require in order to learn and remember it. Six-month-olds require six demonstrations of a sequence in order to encode and retain it over a 24-hour delay, whereas nine-month-olds

A

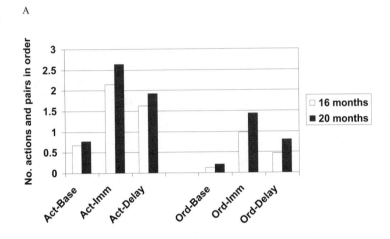

B

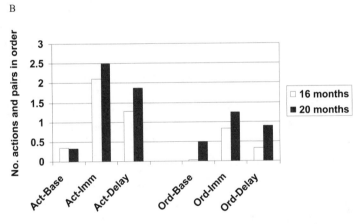

Figure 1–2. Number of actions ("act") and pairs of actions produced in target order ("ord") by infants 16 and 20 months of age in a premodeling or baseline period ("base"), immediately after two demonstrations of the modeled sequence ("imm"), and 2 weeks after experience of the sequences ("delay"). Panel *a* illustrates performance on novel sequences such as making a gong (see Figure 1–1); Panel *b* illustrates performance on sequences based on routine events such as bathing and making breakfast. Based on data from Bauer, P. J., & Mandler, J. M. (1989). One thing follows another: Effects of temporal structure on one- to two-year-olds' recall of events. *Developmental Psychology, 25,* 197–206. Reprinted with permission.

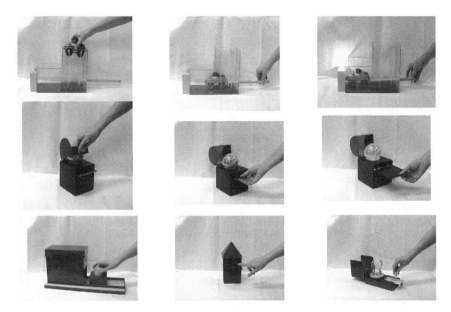

Figure 1–3. Three classes of stimuli tested in Wiebe et al. (2006). In the top row are photographs of objects used to produce a sequence modeled for an infant. In the middle row are objects used in a novel sequence the infant had never seen before. In the bottom row are trial-unique objects: The objects were different on each of 30 trials.

require only three (Barr, Dowden, & Hayne, 1996). There also are age-related differences in the amount of information infants learn from the same amount of experience. In Bauer and Mandler (1989), for example, after watching a model demonstrate a 3-step sequence two times in a row, 16-month-olds reproduced 2.15 of the steps immediately after modeling, whereas 20-month-olds reproduced 2.63 of the steps.

Learning Is Flexible

One of the hallmarks of explicit or declarative knowledge is its flexibility. I can learn something in one context and "transport" my knowledge to a new context. For example, I can learn how to defeat the *autocorrect* features on my personal computer at home and then apply the knowledge to my laptop and my office computer. The specific applications are different in each case, yet the underlying structure of the problem is the same. Because traditionally infants' knowledge was thought to be tied to a particular sensorimotor context, infants were not expected to flexibly apply knowledge across situations. This expectation was proven wrong: There are reports of robust generalization from encoding to test by infants across a wide age range.

Imitation-based tasks have shown that infants generalize their knowledge in a number of ways. For example, they have been shown to extend their knowledge

Familiar Event

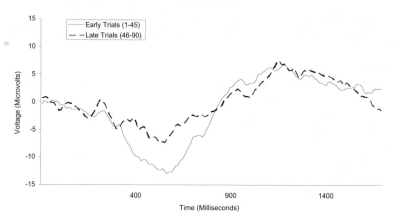

Novel Trial-Unique Event

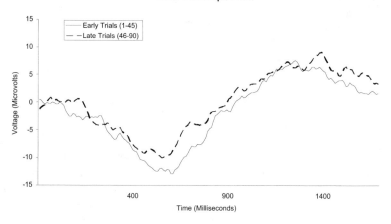

Novel Repeated Event

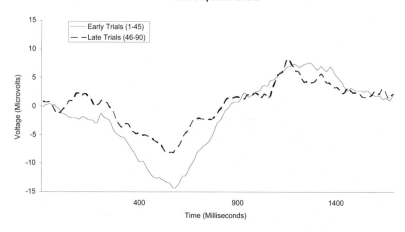

across changes in the size, shape, color, and/or material composition of the objects used in demonstration versus test (e.g., Bauer & Fivush, 1992; Bauer & Dow, 1994; Lechuga, Marcos-Ruiz, & Bauer, 2001). Infants generalize across changes in the appearance of the room at the time of demonstration of modeled actions and at the time of memory test (e.g., Barnat, Klein, & Meltzoff, 1996; Klein & Meltzoff, 1999). Infants also generalize across the setting for demonstration of the modeled actions and the test of memory for them (e.g., Hanna & Meltzoff, 1993; Klein & Meltzoff, 1999), and between the individual who demonstrated the actions and the individual who tested for memory for the actions (e.g., Hanna & Meltzoff, 1993). Infants are even able to use three-dimensional objects to pro-duce events that they have only seen modeled on a television screen (Meltzoff, 1988c; although see Barr & Hayne, 1999). Evidence of flexible extension of event knowledge is apparent in infants as young as 9 to 11 months of age (e.g., Bald-win, Markman, & Melartin, 1993; McDonough & Mandler, 1998). Thus, there is substantial evidence that from an early age, infants' memories survive changes in context and stimuli.

There also are age-related differences in the flexibility of learning and memory across the infancy period. In research by Hayne, MacDonald, and Barr (1997), 18- and 21-month-olds were exposed to a 3-step puppet sequence that involved taking a mitten off a puppet's hand, shaking the mitten (which at the time of the demonstration held a bell that rang), and replacing the mitten. When 18-month-olds experienced the sequence demonstrated on a cow puppet and then were tested with the same puppet, they showed robust retention over 24 hours. However, when they experienced the sequence modeled on a cow puppet and then were tested with a duck puppet, they did not show evidence of memory. Twenty-one-month-olds remembered the sequence whether tested with the same or a different puppet (see also Hayne, Boniface, & Barr, 2000; Herbert & Hayne, 2000). In summary, from an early age, learning and memory are flexible, surviving changes in context and stimuli. Nevertheless, there is evidence that with age, infants' memories as tested in imitation-based paradigms become more flexible (e.g., Herbert & Hayne, 2000).

AGE-RELATED CHANGES IN MEMORY IN THE FIRST TWO YEARS OF LIFE

The characterization of learning just provided highlighted two age-related differ-ences in the first two years of life. Within this age period, older infants, relative to younger infants, seem to acquire new information more rapidly and to extend their

---

Figure 1–4. ERP responses to three classes of stimuli tested in Wiebe et al. (2006). For familiar stimuli (top row), the amplitude of ERP responses was smaller in the second rela-tive to the first half of trials. For trial-unique stimuli (middle row), ERP amplitude in the first and second half of trials did not differ significantly. For novel stimuli (bottom row), as was the case for familiar stimuli, the amplitude of ERP responses was smaller in the second relative to the first half of trials.

knowledge more flexibly. Developments in the speed of learning and in its flexible application no doubt are related to two especially salient changes in memory in the same space of time: changes in the length of time over which memory is apparent and changes in the reliability with which it is observed in the population. After reviewing the evidence of these changes in long-term memory, I turn to discussion of relations between learning and memory, and of whether the former explains the latter.

Changes in the Length of Time over Which Memory Is Apparent

One of the most salient changes in memory over the first 2 years of life is in the length of time over which memories are retained. Importantly, because as with any complex behavior, the length of time an event is remembered is multiply determined, there can be no "growth chart" mapping how long infants and children of a given age should remember. Nonetheless, as summarized in Table 1, Panel a, data from a number of studies provide evidence that, with increasing age, infants retain the products of learning over longer delays. In research by Barr and her colleagues

Table 1   Age-Related Changes in Memory in the First Two Years of Life

Panel a: Length of time over which memory is apparent

Age Group	Length of Delay	References
6-month-olds	24 hours	Barr et al. (1996); Collie & Hayne (1999)
9-month-olds	24 hours 1 month	Meltzoff (1988b) Carver & Bauer (1999, 2001)
10–11-month-olds	3 months	Mandler & McDonough (1995); Carver & Bauer (2001)
13–14-month-olds	4–6 months	Meltzoff (1995); Bauer et al. (2000)
20-month-olds	12 months	Bauer et al. (2000)

Panel b: Changes in the reliability with which memory is observed

Age Group	Percentage of Infants Showing Ordered Recall	References
6-month-olds	25% for 24 hours	Barr et al. (1996)
9-month-olds	~50% for 1 month	Carver & Bauer (1999); Bauer et al., 2001, 2003
13-month-olds	75% for 1 month; 40% for 6 months	Bauer et al. (2000)
20-month-olds	100% for 1 month; 80% for 6 months	Bauer et al. (2000)

(1996), six-month-old infants retained an average of 1 action of the 3-step puppet sequence for 24 hours. Collie and Hayne (1999) found that six-month-olds remembered an average of 1 out of 5 possible actions over a 24-hour delay. These findings of six-month-olds' memories for a specific event after 24 hours are remarkable in the context of traditional conceptualizations of a late-developing capacity for re-presentation. The glass is also half-empty, however: Such low levels of performance after 24 hours have not compelled tests of retention over longer intervals.

By 9 to 11 months of age, the length of time over which memory for laboratory events is apparent has increased substantially. Nine-month-olds remember individual actions over delays from 24 hours (Meltzoff, 1988b) to 1 month (Carver & Bauer, 1999, 2001). By 10 to 11 months of age, infants remember over delays as long as 3 months (Mandler & McDonough, 1995; Carver & Bauer, 2001). Thirteen- to 14-month-olds remember actions over delays of 4 to 6 months (Meltzoff, 1995; Bauer, Wenner, Dropik, & Wewerka, 2000). By 20 months of age, children remember the actions of multi-step sequences over as many as 12 months (Bauer et al., 2000).

Changes in the Reliability with Which Memory Is Observed

As summarized in Table 1, Panel b, with age, a larger percentage of infants in a given sample show evidence of recall. The trend is especially apparent in the ability to learn and remember the temporal order of multi-step sequences. Although 67% of the six-month-olds Barr et al. (1996) studied remembered some of the actions associated with the puppet sequence over 24 hours, only 25% of them remembered actions in the correct temporal order. Collie and Hayne (1999, Experiment 1) reported no ordered recall after 24 hours by six-month-olds (the infants were exposed to three target events, two of which required two steps to complete). Among nine-month-olds, approximately 50% of infants exhibit ordered reproduction of sequences after a 1-month delay (Carver & Bauer, 1999; Bauer, Wiebe, Waters, & Bangston, 2001; Bauer et al., 2003). By 13 months of age the substantial individual variability in ordered recall has resolved: Three quarters of 13-month-olds exhibit ordered recall after 1 month; fully 100% of 20-month-olds show ordered recall over the same interval. Over longer delays, however, the memories of younger infants are less reliable relative to those of older infants. After 6 months, for example, whereas more than 80% of 20-month-olds show evidence of ordered recall, only roughly 40% of 13-month-olds do (Bauer et al., 2000).

RELATIONS BETWEEN LEARNING AND MEMORY: DOES THE HORSE EXPLAIN THE CARRIAGE?

It is likely that changes in learning account at least in part for changes in memory. For instance, because older infants learn more rapidly than younger infants, they may encode more information about an event and thus enter a delay period with a stronger, more complete memory representation. As a result, older infants may remember for a longer period of time, relative to younger infants. Greater flexibility in application of new learning may also be expected to influence memory in that a more flexible memory representation may be easier to cue at the time of retrieval, relative to a representation that is more tightly bound to the original context of experience. However, a link—even a potentially strong one—between learning and memory does not imply that age-related differences in memory are explained by age-related differences in learning. A clear demonstration that not all of the variance in memory is explained by learning is available in Bauer (2005a). Thirteen-, 16-, and 20-month-old infants were matched for levels of learning (as measured by immediate imitation) before imposition of delay intervals ranging from 1 to 6 months. Although the age groups entered the delay periods having achieved equal learning, they did not emerge with equal remembering after the delays. The older infants remembered more than the younger infants; age differences in remembering were especially apparent at the longer delay intervals. Moreover, age differences persisted even after relearning trials (i.e., the sequences were modeled and infants were invited to imitate), suggesting that the age effects were not due to retrieval failure.

The findings just described make clear that whereas learning is intimately related to memory, the former does not explain the latter. To understand how newly learned material becomes differentially accessible after a delay we must consider cognitive processes that occur after learning. At the turn of the twentieth century, the post-learning process of *consolidation* was hypothesized to explain changes in knowledge representations that occur "off line," after material has been learned or encoded (Müller & Pilzecker, 1900). Nearly 70 years later, the concept of *reconsolidation* was hypothesized to explain further changes to knowledge representations that occur each time a memory is reactivated (Misanin, Miller, & Lewis, 1968). The concepts of consolidation and reconsolidation have substantial developmental significance because the neural structures implicated in them undergo pronounced development in the first years of life. The processes thus have the potential to explain age-related variance in learning and memory.

POST-LEARNING PROCESSES OF CONSOLIDATION AND RECONSOLIDATION

We typically think of learning as something that we do in the moment, as we are experiencing an event, listening to a lecture, reading material, and so forth. Yet we also understand the importance of rehearsal and repetition of new information in order to keep it alive and available. The processes of consolidation and reconsolidation can be thought of as "neural rehearsal." They are hypothesized neural processes that keep newly learned material alive long enough for it to become integrated into memory.

Consolidation

There is strong evidence that for newly learned information to be maintained over the long term, it must undergo additional processing subsequent to initial registration. The processing that turns immediate perceptual experience into an enduring memory trace is described as involving integration and stabilization of the inputs from different cortical regions. These tasks, collectively termed *consolidation*, are thought to be performed by medial temporal structures (including the hippocampus), in concert with cortical areas. Whereas consolidation processes begin upon registration of a stimulus, they do not end there: They continue for hours, days, months, and even years.

The Phenomenon of Consolidation

Consolidation was originally hypothesized by Müller and Pilzecker (1900) to explain retroactive interference in list-learning experiments. In a typical such experiment, subjects in one condition studied one list of words, and then, some time later, studied a second list of words, followed by tests of both lists. In another condition, subjects studied List 1 and then very shortly thereafter studied List 2, followed by tests of both lists. When the study periods were a distance apart, recall of both lists was high. When the study periods were close in timer, subjects' recall of List 1 was impaired, relative to their recall of List 2. Müller and Pilzecker suggested that in the short-spacing condition, List 2 retroactively interfered with List 1 because at the time the second list was learned, memory for the first list had not yet consolidated or stabilized.

Müller and Pilzecker (1900) illustrated two principles of consolidation— (1) that it takes time; and (2) that while newly learned information is being consolidated, it is vulnerable to forgetting. Additional evidence of both principles is apparent in the phenomenon of temporally graded retrograde amnesia. In a pattern precisely the opposite of normal forgetting, memory for recently learned material is impaired, relative to memory for information learned long ago. Temporally graded retrograde amnesia is well documented in humans with lesions and disease of medial temporal structures (e.g., Brown, 2002), and can be produced in animal models (e.g., Kim & Fanselow, 1992). As illustrated in Figure 1–5, rats lesioned 1 day after trace eye-blink conditioning (a form of learning that is dependent on medial temporal lobe structures) had impaired memory (relative to rats in a cortical lesion control group). With increasing delay between training and surgery, memory performance improved such that when the lesion was induced 30 days after training, performance was unimpaired (Takehara, Kawahara, & Kirino, 2003). Thus, when the lesion was induced early in the consolidation period, memory for the learned association was impaired. Lesions induced later, when learning was more fully consolidated, did not disrupt performance. Similar patterns, across a variety of paradigms, have been observed in rabbits, mice, and nonhuman primates (see Squire & Alvarez, 1995, and Eichenbaum & Cohen, 2001, for reviews).

The Substrate and Process of Consolidation

Both the human participants in the studies of Müller and Pilzecker (1900) and the rat subjects tested by Takehara and colleagues (2003) were mature adults. In the developing organism, the consolidation period may be even more susceptible to

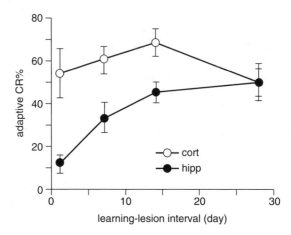

Figure 1–5. Temporally graded retrograde amnesia in rats in a trace eye-blink conditioning paradigm. Reflected are the percentages of adaptive conditioned responses in rats with hippocampal lesions (filled circles) and rats with cortical control lesions (open circles). From Takehara, K., Kawahara, S. & Kirino, Y. Time-dependent reorganization of the brain components underlying memory retention in trace eye-blink conditioning. *Journal of Neuroscience, 23,* 9897–9905. Copyright (2003) by the Society for Neuroscience. Used with permission.

disruption because aspects of the neural network implicated in the process are late to develop. As implied by the association between impairments in consolidation and medial temporal lobe damage, it is thought that medial temporal structures, including the hippocampus, parahippocampus, and entorhinal and perirhinal cortices, do the work of binding into a single memory trace the distributed neocortical representation of an event or experience (e.g., Kandel & Squire, 2000; Zola & Squire, 2000; Eichenbaum & Cohen, 2001). Cortical association areas also assume some of the burden of the effort by associating new learning with the products of earlier experience already stored in the cortex. Critically, aspects of the hippocampus and prefrontal cortex, in particular, are late to develop.

In the early phases of consolidation, information is processed in the hippocampus and other medial temporal structures. The information that is being processed is that received from the various cortical areas that are responsible for initial registration and encoding of experience. Different unimodal and polymodal cortical association areas contribute different elements of experience (e.g., what objects look like, sound like) much the way that individual balloons contribute to a balloon bouquet. As illustrated in the schematic diagram of the input and output pathways of the hippocampal formation (Fig. 1–6, adapted from Squire & Zola, 1996, and Kandel, Schwartz, & Jessell, 2000), the inputs from the unimodal and polymodal cortical association areas (the strings of the balloons) are projected to the perirhinal and parahippocampal structures in the medial temporal lobes. The perirhinal and parahippocampal cortices in turn project the information

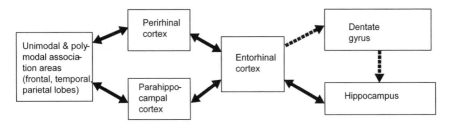

Figure 1–6. Schematic representation of the input and output pathways of the hippocampal formation. Adapted from Kandel, E. R., Schwartz, J. H., and Jessell, T. M. *Principles of neural science,* Fourth Edition (2000, Figure 62–5, p. 1232), and Zola, S. M., and Squire, L. R. (2000, Figure 30.1, p. 487), The medial temporal lobe and the hippocampus. In E. Tulving and F.I.M. Craik (Eds.), *The Oxford handbook of memory* (pp. 485–500).

(the strings) to the entorhinal cortex, which in turn projects to the hippocampus. Processing in these medial temporal lobe structures ties the strings of the individual balloons together into a bouquet that remains bound even when no longer held in the hand. In information-processing terms, processing in the medial temporal lobe structures creates linkages among the separate elements of the distributed cortical representation, allowing the representation to persist beyond the physical presence of the stimulus.

The means by which the medial temporal lobe structures create an enduring memory representation is a sort of "neural rehearsal." The perirhinal and parahippocampal cortices serve as intermediate-term stores. Through repeated firings of neurons, they maintain the pattern of activation associated with experience, much like repeating the individual words on a to-be-remembered list. While the pattern of activation (the individual words) is maintained, the hippocampus is engaged in the elaborative processing that encodes conjunctions and relations among current stimuli (i.e., those that are held in the intermediate-term medial temporal cortical stores) and between current stimuli and previously processed stimuli (i.e., representations of stimuli and events already in long-term neocortical stores). As a result of hippocampal processing, the individual elements of experience become linked into a single event or episode, and current episodes are associated with previous episodes (see Eichenbaum & Cohen, 2001, for extended discussion). Eventually, intracortical connections between the various elements of the event or experience are strengthened to the point that medial temporal lobe activity is no longer required to maintain the representation.

The Development of the Substrate of Consolidation

Whereas there is still much work to do to map developmental changes in the network responsible for consolidation of new learning, it is clear that some components of the temporal-cortical network undergo pronounced development over the first years of life. These developments can be expected to have implications for the efficiency and efficacy of memory-trace consolidation. As discussed in detail in Bauer (2006; see also Nelson, 1995, 1997, 2000; Bauer, 2004), there are a number of indicators that, in the human, many of the medial temporal lobe components of the temporal-cortical network develop early. For instance, as reviewed by Seress (2001), the cells that comprise most of the hippocampus are formed in the first half of gestation and virtually all are in their adult locations by the end of the prenatal period. The neurons in most of the hippocampus also begin to connect early in development: Synapses are present as early as 15 weeks gestational age. Both the number and density of synapses increase rapidly after birth and reach adult levels by approximately six postnatal months. Perhaps as a consequence, glucose utilization in the temporal cortex reaches adult levels at the same time (i.e., by about six months) (Chugani, 1994; Chugani & Phelps, 1986). Thus, there are numerous indices of early maturity of major portions of the medial temporal components of the network.

In contrast to early maturation of most of the hippocampus, development of the dentate gyrus of the hippocampus is protracted (Seress, 2001). At birth, the dentate gyrus includes only about 70% of the adult number of cells. Thus, roughly 30% of the cells are produced postnatally. It is not until 12 to 15 postnatal months that the morphology of the structure appears adult-like. Maximum density of synaptic connections in the dentate gyrus is also delayed, relative to that in the other regions of the hippocampus. In humans, synaptic density increases dramatically (to well above adult levels) beginning at 8 to 12 postnatal months and reaches its peak at 16 to 20 months. After a period of relative stability, excess synapses are pruned until adult levels are reached at about four to five years of age (Eckenhoff & Rakic, 1991).

Although the functional significance of later development of the dentate gyrus is not clear, there is reason to speculate that it affects behavior. As already noted, upon experience of an event, information from distributed regions of the cortex converges on the entorhinal cortex (see Fig. 1–6). From there, it makes it way into the hippocampus in one of two ways: via a "long route" or a "short route." The long route involves projections from the entorhinal cortex into the hippocampus, by way of the dentate gyrus; the short route bypasses the dentate gyrus. Whereas the short route may support some forms of memory (Nelson, 1995, 1997), it seems, based on data from rodents, that adult-like memory behavior depends on the passage of information through the dentate gyrus (Nadel & Willner, 1989; Czurkó, Czéh, Seress, Nadel, & Bures, 1997). This implies that maturation of the dentate gyrus of the hippocampus may be a rate-limiting variable in the development of explicit memory early in life (Nelson, 1995, 1997, 2000; Bauer, 2002; Bauer et al., 2003; Bauer, 2004, 2006). It is not until adult levels of synapses are reached at four to five years of age that we would expect fully effective and efficient medial temporal processing (Goldman-Rakic, 1987).

Like the dentate gyrus of the hippocampus, the association areas develop slowly (Bachevalier, 2001). For example, it is not until the seventh prenatal month that all six cortical layers are apparent. The density of synapses in the prefrontal cortex increases dramatically at 8 postnatal months and peaks between 15 and 24 months. Pruning to adult levels is delayed until adolescence (Huttenlocher, 1979; Huttenlocher & Dabholkar, 1997; see Bourgeois, 2001, for discussion). Although the maximum density of synapses may be reached as early as 15 postnatal months, it is not until 24 months that synapses develop adult morphology (Huttenlocher, 1979). There also are changes in glucose utilization and blood flow over the second half of the first year and into the second year: Blood flow and glucose utilization increase to exceed adult levels by 8 to 12 and 13 to 14 months of age, respectively (Chugani, Phelps, & Mazziotta, 1987). Other maturational changes in the prefrontal cortex, such as myelination, continue into adolescence, and adult levels of some neurotransmitters are not seen until the second and third decades of life (Benes, 2001).

Consolidation Processes in Infancy

What are the consequences for consolidation processes of the slow course of development of the neural network implicated in them? At the most general level, we may expect that the relative immaturity of the association cortices and dentate gyrus of the hippocampus implies that consolidation processes may be less effective and less efficient in the first years of life. As a result, even after new material is successfully learned, it remains vulnerable to forgetting, as illustrated in Bauer et al. (2003). In this study we combined behavior and ERP to examine long-term recall. To minimize initial learning as a source of variability, we exposed nine-month-olds to sequences (Sequences A, B, & C) at each of three sessions, spaced 24 to 48 hours apart. At the third session, we tested learning via ERP (familiar Sequence A versus novel Sequence D). One week later we tested consolidation and storage by administering another ERP test (Sequences B & E). We then tested recall of the sequences 1 month later (along with three novel sequences, as a within-subjects control).

As a group, the nine-month-old infants in Bauer et al. (2003) showed evidence of learning the sequences (differential responses to Sequences A & D), yet there was differential long-term recall that in turn related to differential consolidation and storage. Infants who did not recall the sequences after 1 month also did not recognize them after 1 week (exhibiting similar responses to Sequences B & E). In contrast, infants who recalled the sequences showed successful consolidation and storage. The subgroups did not differ at the first ERP and thus did not differ in their level of initial learning. Nor was individual variability in initial learning a significant predictor of long-term recall. In contrast, successful consolidation and storage over 1 week accounted for 28% of the variance in recall after 1 month. Although Bauer et al. is an illustration of individual differences in consolidation, we may also expect developmental differences such that the younger the infant, the more vulnerable the trace.

Reconsolidation

The necessity that newly learned material be consolidated for long-term storage, and the fact that the neural network implicated in consolidation processes is immature in infancy, present challenges for learning and memory early in life. To make matters "even worse," there is strong evidence at both the cellular and systems levels that traces undergo *reconsolidation* each time they are reactivated. That is, each time a stored trace is cued—typically by elements of the present situation that overlap with elements that are part of the stored trace (cueing may be either intentional or unintentional)—it is reactivated and undergoes consolidation all over again. The process of reactivation and reconsolidation is a double-edged sword. On the negative side, each time a memory trace is reconsolidated, it becomes vulnerable all over again (though for a shorter period of time, as will be seen). On the positive side, reconsolidation affords the opportunity to integrate new learning with old learning. After describing some of the recent data on reconsolidation at the cellular and systems levels, I turn to discussion of the implications of reconsolidation for learning and memory in infancy.

Cellular Reconsolidation

There is evidence that the cellular events involved in establishing new long-term memories are repeated whenever old traces are reactivated. Briefly, the long-term storage of information depends on new protein synthesis, which supports structural changes that enhance functional connectivity, including changes in the morphology of and growth of new dendritic spines on postsynaptic neurons. This process occurs the first time a memory is stored and, as suggested by the results of a study by Debiec, LeDoux, and Nader (2002), is repeated when memories are reactivated.

The procedure used by Debiec and colleagues is represented schematically in Table 2, Panel a. Rats were conditioned to expect a shock when placed in a distinctive context, a type of learning that is known to be dependent on the hippocampus. Three days after learning, different subgroups of trained rats underwent different treatments. One subgroup had their memories of the contingency reactivated: They were placed back in the distinctive context, though no shocks were administered. The other subgroup did not have their memories reactivated. Rats in both subgroups then were injected with anisomycin, a compound known to block the new protein synthesis necessary for long-term memory. Four hours later both subgroups of rats were tested for short-term memory. Maintenance of information over this space of time does not depend on new protein synthesis and thus should not have been affected by reactivation or anisomycin. Consistent with this expectation, the performance of the subgroups did not differ after this brief delay. Both subgroups showed evidence of retention of the conditioned response. When they were placed in the conditioning chamber, they froze, an indication of fear induced by the distinctive environment (see Fig. 1–7). Twenty hours later the rats were tested for long-term memory of the contingency by placing them in the conditioning chamber once again. The rats that had not had their memories reactivated showed evidence of retention of the conditioned response by once again freezing upon experiencing the distinctive environment. In contrast, the rats whose memories had been reactivated showed little evidence of memory, as indicated by high mobility and low freezing. These results strongly suggest that memory traces undergo protein synthesis–dependent reconsolidation after reactivation. When reactivation occurs, the processes that originally converted a temporary pattern of

Table 2 Schematic Representation of Protocol Used by Debiec, LeDoux, and Nader (2002) to Examine Reconsolidation at the Cellular (Panel a) and Systems (Panel b) Levels

	Treatment Groups	
Phase	Reactivation	No Reactivation

Panel a: Cellular Reconsolidation

Learning	Contextual fear conditioning	Contextual fear conditioning
Delay	(3 days)	(3 days)
Treatment	Reactivation—infuse anisomycin	No reactivation—infuse anisomycin
Delay	(4 hours)	(4 hours)
Test 1	Short-term memory	Short-term memory
Delay	(20 hours)	(20 hours)
Test 2	Long-term memory	Long-term memory

Panel b: Systems Reconsolidation

Learning	Contextual fear conditioning	Contextual fear conditioning
Delay	(45 days)	(45 days)
Treatment	Reactivation—lesion hippocampus	No reactivation—lesion hippocampus
Delay	(7 days)	(7 days)
Test	Long-term memory	Long-term memory

activation into an enduring trace must recur. If they are blocked, the memory is, in effect, functionally erased.

Systems Reconsolidation

As evidenced by the work of Takehara et al. (2003; see also Kim & Fanselow, 1992), memories eventually become independent of the hippocampus. Yet the work of Debiec and colleagues (2002) indicates that hippocampal dependence is reinstated by reactivation of the memory. Evidence of a return to hippocampal dependence at the neural-systems level comes from another study of contextual fear conditioning, represented schematically in Table 2, Panel b. Debiec and his colleagues conditioned rats to fear a particular context and then waited 45 days to allow the memory to fully consolidate and become independent of the hippocampus. Half of the rats then had their memories reactivated by being reexposed to the distinctive context. All of the rats then underwent hippocampal surgery. Seven days later the rats were once again placed in the distinctive context and their behavior was observed. The rats that had not had their memories reactivated exhibited retention of the contingency, as evidenced by the fact that they spent about half of their time immobile. In contrast, the rats that had had their memories reactivated before the hippocampal lesion spent only about 10% of their time freezing, suggesting loss of memory for the contingency. These results indicate that even memories that have been safely tucked away for long-term storage are, when reactivated, vulnerable all over again.

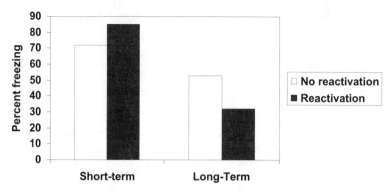

Figure 1–7. Short- and long-term memory performance by rats after contextual fear conditioning. Reflected is the percentage of time spent immobile (freezing) in the distinctive, fear-conditioned context. Rats that did not have their memories reactivated (open bars) before infusion of anisomycin spent the majority of time freezing in both short- and long-term memory tests. Rats that had their memories reactivated (filled bars) before infusion of anisomycin spent the majority of time freezing in short-term testing but not in long-term testing. Data from Debiec et al. (2002). Values are approximate.

Fortunately, although memories that are reactivated return to a labile state, they do not remain there for long. In another experiment in Debiec and colleagues (2002), rats underwent contextual fear conditioning and were allowed to consolidate their memories for 45 days. The rats were then placed in the distinctive context, which reactivated the memories. Different groups then received hippocampal lesions 4 hours, 24 hours, and 48 hours after the reactivation treatment. Seven days later, long-term memory for the contingency was tested. Animals that received the lesion 4 hours and 24 hours after the reactivation treatment evidenced amnesia: They spent little time freezing. The rats whose reactivated memories were allowed 48 hours to reconsolidate showed no impairment, relative to control rats. Thus, whereas memories initially may require 45 days to consolidate (Kim & Fanselow, 1992; Takehara et al., 2003), reconsolidation seemingly occurs in as few as 48 hours.

Summary and Implications

It is clear that learning and memory are intimately related. Yet learning does not explain remembering. The fact that these two foundational processes cannot be reduced to one another is made clear by the finding that there are age-related differences in memory in the face of equivalent levels of learning. To explain the differences, we must consider cognitive processes that occur after learning. An excellent candidate process is consolidation: the means by which initially labile memory traces become stabilized for long-term storage. Work with animal models makes clear that memory traces are vulnerable throughout the period of consolidation. In the developing human, consolidation may be especially perilous because the neural structures implicated in it (medial temporal and cortical structures) are relatively immature. As a result, newly learned information may never make it to long-term storage. Further complicating the matter is the apparent fact that even once they have been successfully stored, memory traces may return to a period of lability (and thus, vulnerability) when they are reactivated by exposure to some element that cues the stored trace.

Whereas reconsolidation represents a period of vulnerability, it also provides an opportunity for growth and cognitive development. Learning involves storing new facts and experiences and also relating them to old facts and experiences. Reconsolidation provides a means by which new elements of experience become added to old and a means by which various learning episodes become linked with one another. With the experience of an event, the process of stabilizing a memory trace begins. Hours later or days later, the event can be reactivated by a cue. The cue can be reexperience of the same or a similar event or experience of something reminiscent of it by virtue of shared elements. Once reactivated, the memory trace is open to incorporating new elements. Thus, with each reconsolidation, initially "sparse" memory representations can become augmented with additional information. The new elements become part of the reconsolidated trace, leaving it "new and improved," relative to the original. Various learning episodes may be linked to one another through the same process on the basis of shared elements.

CONCLUSIONS

Learning and memory are tightly linked. Like "love and marriage," it seems that you cannot have one without the other. The study of memory has revealed that, even in the first years of life, learning is fast and flexible. Infants learn about new objects and events in a matter of milliseconds. They can use what they have learned to guide their behavior (their imitation) both immediately and after delays. They extend knowledge from one exemplar to another, across changes in the settings in which learning occurs and memory is tested, and from one medium to another. Yet during the same time, learning and memory undergo significant developmental changes. In the first year of life, only a minority of infants retains information over limited periods of time. By the end of the second year, long-term recall is both reliable and robust.

It is clear that changes in learning explain some of the age-related variance in memory. After the same number of learning trials, older infants show more robust learning relative to younger infants. They subsequently show more robust long-term memory as well. Yet not all of the variance in memory is explained by learning. Older and younger infants matched for level of learning nevertheless show differential levels of memory after a delay. The differences cannot be explained by older infants' more successful retrieval. Even after re-exposure to sequences, older infants show more robust recall. These patterns implicate the post-learning processes of consolidation and reconsolidation as sources of difference in cognitive performance. While new learning is being consolidated into a stable memory trace, it is vulnerable to interference and disintegration. The vulnerability is repeated each time the trace is reactivated and thus reconsolidated.

Consolidation and reconsolidation have been observed in a variety of species (e.g., rodents, chicks, crabs, garden slugs) and tested with various behavioral paradigms (both appetitive and aversive) after induction through a number of amnesic agents (e.g., electroconvulsive shock, anisomycin) (Sara, 2000). However, relatively little is known about the parameters of these processes in humans. Virtually nothing is known about the parameters of consolidation and reconsolidation in human infants. In fact, although we can speculate that the memories of human infants may be especially vulnerable while new traces are being consolidated and old ones reconsolidated, we do not even know whether these periods are longer, shorter, or of the same duration in infants and adults. Our impoverished state of knowledge presents a number of challenges to understanding these foundational processes. Given their central role in learning and memory, it is imperative that we begin to investigate them.

Acknowledgments   Much of the work discussed in this chapter was supported by grants from the National Institute of Child Health and Human Development (HD-28425, HD-42483) to the author. The author thanks the infants and families who participated in this research that makes possible the discovery of new knowledge about the relations between learning and memory.

References

Adlam, A.-L. R., Vargha-Khadem, F., Mishkin, M., & de Haan, M. (2005). Deferred imitation of action sequences in developmental amnesia. *Journal of Cognitive Neuroscience, 17,* 240–248.

Bachevalier, J. (2001). Neural bases of memory development: Insights from neuropsychological studies in primates. In C. A. Nelson & M. Luciana (Eds.), *Handbook of developmental cognitive neuroscience* (pp. 365–379). Cambridge, MA: MIT Press.

Baldwin, D. A., Markman, E. M., & Melartin, R. L. (1993). Infants' ability to draw inferences about nonobvious properties: Evidence from exploratory play. *Child Development, 64,* 711–728.

Barnat, S. B., Klein, P. J., & Meltzoff, A. N. (1996). Deferred imitation across changes in context and object: Memory and generalization in 14-month-old children. *Infant Behavior and Development, 19,* 241–251.

Barr, R., Dowden, A., & Hayne, H. (1996). Developmental change in deferred imitation by 6- to 24-month-old infants. *Infant Behavior and Development, 19,* 159–170.

Barr, R., & Hayne, H. (1999). Developmental changes in imitation from television during infancy. *Child Development, 70,* 1067–1081.

Bauer, P. J. (2002). Long-term recall memory: Behavioral and neuro-developmental changes in the first 2 years of life. *Current Directions in Psychological Science, 11,* 137–141.

Bauer, P. J. (2004). Getting explicit memory off the ground: Steps toward construction of a neuro-developmental account of changes in the first two years of life. *Developmental Review, 24,* 347–373.

Bauer, P. J. (2005a). Developments in declarative memory: Decreasing susceptibility to storage failure over the second year of life. *Psychological Science, 16,* 41–47.

Bauer, P. J. (2005b). New developments in the study of infant memory. In D. M. Teti (Ed.), *Blackwell handbook of research methods in developmental science* (pp. 467–488). Oxford, UK: Blackwell.

Bauer, P. J. (2006). *Remembering the times of our lives: Memory in infancy and beyond.* Mahwah, NJ: Lawrence Erlbaum.

Bauer, P. J., & Dow, G. A. A. (1994). Episodic memory in 16- and 20-month-old children: Specifics are generalized, but not forgotten. *Developmental Psychology, 30,* 403–417.

Bauer, P. J., & Fivush, R. (1992). Constructing event representations: Building on a foundation of variation and enabling relations. *Cognitive Development, 7,* 381–401.

Bauer, P. J., Kroupina, M. G., Schwade, J. A., Dropik, P. L., & Wewerka, S. S. (1998). If memory serves, will language? Later verbal accessibility of early memories. *Development and Psychopathology, 10,* 655–679.

Bauer, P. J., & Mandler, J. M. (1989). One thing follows another: Effects of temporal structure on one- to two-year-olds' recall of events. *Developmental Psychology, 25,* 197–206.

Bauer, P. J., & Shore, C. M. (1987). Making a memorable event: Effects of familiarity and organization on young children's recall of action sequences. *Cognitive Development, 2,* 327–338.

Bauer, P. J., Van Abbema, D. L., Wiebe, S. A., Cary, M. S., Phill, C., & Burch, M. M. (2004). Props, not pictures, are worth a thousand words: Verbal accessibility of early memories under different conditions of contextual support. *Applied Cognitive Psychology, 18,* 373–392.

Bauer, P. J., Wenner, J. A., Dropik, P. L., & Wewerka, S. S. (2000). Parameters of remembering and forgetting in the transition from infancy to early childhood. *Monographs of the Society for Research in Child Development, 65* (4, Serial No. 263).

Bauer, P. J., Wenner, J. A., & Kroupina, M. G. (2002). Making the past present: Later verbal accessibility of early memories. *Journal of Cognition and Development, 3,* 21–47.

Bauer, P. J., Wiebe, S. A., Carver, L. J., Lukowski, A. F., Haight, J. C., Waters, J. M., & Nelson, C. A. (2006). Electrophysiological indices of encoding and behavioral indices of recall: Examining relations and developmental change late in the first year of life. *Developmental Neuropsychology, 29,* 293–320.

Bauer, P. J., Wiebe, S. A., Carver, L. J., Waters, J. M., & Nelson, C. A. (2003). Developments in long-term explicit memory late in the first year of life: Behavioral andelectrophysiological indices. *Psychological Science, 14,* 629–635.

Bauer, P. J., Wiebe, S. A., Waters, J. M., & Bangston, S. K. (2001). Reexposure breeds recall: Effects of experience on 9-month-olds' ordered recall. *Journal of Experimental Child Psychology, 80,* 174–200.

Benes, F. M. (2001). The development of prefrontal cortex: The maturation of neurotransmitter systems and their interaction. In C. A. Nelson & M. Luciana (Eds.), *Handbook of developmental cognitive neuroscience* (pp. 79–92). Cambridge, MA: MIT Press.

Bourgeois, J.-P. (2001). Synaptogenesis in the neocortex of the newborn: The ultimate frontier for individuation? In C. A. Nelson & M. Luciana (Eds.), *Handbook of developmental cognitive neuroscience* (pp. 23–34). Cambridge, MA: MIT Press.

Brown, A. S. (2002). Consolidation theory and retrograde amnesia in humans. *Psychonomic Bulletin and Review, 9,* 403–425.

Carver, L. J., & Bauer, P. J. (1999). When the event is more than the sum of its parts: Nine-month-olds' long-term ordered recall. *Memory, 7,* 147–174.

Carver, L. J., & Bauer, P. J. (2001). The dawning of a past: The emergence of long-term explicit memory in infancy. *Journal of Experimental Psychology: General, 130,* 726–745.

Cheatham, C. L., & Bauer, P. J. (2005). Construction of a more coherent story: Prior verbal recall predicts later verbal accessibility of early memories. *Memory, 13,* 516–532.

Chugani, H. T. (1994). Development of regional blood glucose metabolism in relation to behavior and plasticity. In G. Dawson & K. Fischer (Eds.), *Human behavior and the developing brain* (pp. 153–175). New York: Guilford.

Chugani, H. T., & Phelps, M. E. (1986). Maturational changes in cerebral function determined by 18FDG positron emission tomography. *Science, 231,* 840–843.

Chugani, H. T., Phelps, M., & Mazziotta, J. (1987). Positron emission tomography study of human brain functional development. *Annals of Neurology, 22,* 487–497.

Collie, R., & Hayne, H. (1999). Deferred imitation by 6- and 9-month-old infants: More evidence of declarative memory. *Developmental Psychobiology, 35,* 83–90.

Czurkó, A., Czéh, B., Seress, L., Nadel, L., & Bures, J. (1997). Severe spatial navigation deficit in the Morris water maze after single high dose of neonatal X-ray irradiation in the rat. *Proceedings of the National Academy of Science, 94,* 2766–2771.

Debiec, J., LeDoux, J. E., & Nader, K. (2002). Cellular and systems reconsolidation in the hippocampus. *Neuron, 36,* 527–538.

DeBoer, T., Cheatham, C. L., Stark, E., & Bauer, P. J. (2005). *Beyond the gong: Relations between elicited imitation performance at 20–40 months of age and memory at 6 years.* Poster presented at the biennial meeting of the Society for Research in Child Development, Atlanta, GA.

DeBoer, T., Wewerka, S., Bauer, P. J., Georgieff, M. K., & Nelson, C. A. (2005). Explicit memory performance in infants of diabetic mothers at 1 year of age. *Developmental Medicine and Child Neurology, 47,* 525–531.

Eckenhoff, M., & Rakic, P. (1991). A quantitative analysis of synaptogenesis in the molecular layer of the dentate gyrus in the rhesus monkey. *Developmental Brain Research, 64,* 129–135.

Eichenbaum, H. & Cohen, N. J. (2001). *From conditioning to conscious recollection: Memory systems of the brain.* New York: Oxford University Press.

Fantz, R. L. (1956). A method for studying early visual development. *Perceptual and Motor Skills, 6,* 13–15.

Gelman, R., & Baillargeon, R. (1983). A review of some Piagetian concepts. In J. H. Flavell & E. M. Markman (Eds.), *Handbook of child psychology—Volume III: Cognitive development* (pp. 167–230). New York: Wiley.

Georgieff, M. K., & Rao, R. (2001). The role of nutrition in cognitive development. In C. A. Nelson & M. Luciana (Eds.), *Handbook of developmental cognitive neuroscience* (pp. 491–504). Cambridge, MA: MIT Press.

Goldman-Rakic, P. S. (1987). Circuitry of primate prefrontal cortex and regulation of behavior by representational memory. In F. Plum (Ed.), *Handbook of physiology, the nervous system, higher functions of the brain* (Vol. 5, pp. 373–417). Bethesda, MD: American Physiological Society.

Hanna, E., & Meltzoff, A. N. (1993). Peer imitation by toddlers in laboratory, home, and day-care contexts: Implications for social learning and memory. *Developmental Psychology, 29,* 702–710.

Hayne, H., Boniface, J., & Barr, R. (2000). The development of declarative memory in human infants: Age-related changes in deferred imitation. *Behavioral Neuroscience, 114,* 77–83.

Hayne, H., MacDonald, S., & Barr, R. (1997). Developmental changes in the specificity of memory over the second year of life. *Infant Behavior and Development, 20,* 233–245.

Herbert, J., & Hayne, H. (2000). Memory retrieval by 18- to 30-month-olds: Age-related changes in representational flexibility. *Developmental Psychology, 36,* 473–484.

Huttenlocher, P. R. (1979). Synaptic density in human frontal cortex: Developmental changes and effects of aging. *Brain Research, 163,* 195–205.

Huttenlocher, P. R., & Dabholkar, A. S. (1997). Regional differences in synaptogenesis in human cerebral cortex. *Journal of Comparative Neurology, 387,* 167–178.

Kandel, E. R., Schwartz, J. H., & Jessell, T. M. (2000). *Principles of neural science* (4th ed.). New York: McGraw-Hill.

Kandel, E. R., & Squire, L. R. (2000). Neuroscience: Breaking down scientific barriers to the study of brain and mind. *Science, 290,* 1113–1120.

Kim, J. J., & Fanselow, M. S. (1992). Modality-specific retrograde amnesia of fear. *Science, 256,* 675–677.

Klein, P. J., & Meltzoff, A. N. (1999). Long-term memory, forgetting, and deferred imitation in 12-month-old infants. *Developmental Science, 2,* 102–113.

Larkina, M., & Bauer, P. J. (2005). *Continuity in recall memory: Links between infancy and middle childhood.* Poster presented at the biennial meeting of the Society for Research in Child Development, Atlanta, GA.

Lechuga, M. T., Marcos-Ruiz, R., & Bauer, P. J. (2001). Episodic recall of specifics and generalisation coexist in 25-month-old children. *Memory, 9,* 117–132.

Mandler, J. M., & McDonough, L. (1995). Long-term recall of event sequences in infancy. *Journal of Experimental Child Psychology, 59,* 457–474.

McDonough, L., & Mandler, J. M. (1998). Inductive generalization in 9- and 11-month-olds. *Developmental Science, 1,* 227–232.

McDonough, L., Mandler, J. M., McKee, R. D., & Squire, L. R. (1995). The deferred imitation task as a nonverbal measure of declarative memory. *Proceedings of the National Academy of Sciences, 92,* 7580–7584.

Meltzoff, A. N. (1985). Immediate and deferred imitation in fourteen- and twenty-four-month-old infants. *Child Development, 56,* 62–72.

Meltzoff, A. N. (1988a). Infant imitation after a 1-week delay: Long-term memory for novel acts and multiple stimuli. *Developmental Psychology, 24,* 470–476.

Meltzoff, A. N. (1988b). Infant imitation and memory: Nine-month-olds in immediate and deferred tests. *Child Development, 59,* 217–225.

Meltzoff, A. N. (1988c). Imitation of televised models by infants. *Child Development, 59,* 1221–1229.

Meltzoff, A. N. (1995). What infant memory tells us about infantile amnesia: Long-term recall and deferred imitation. *Journal of Experimental Child Psychology, 59,* 497–515.

Misanin, J. R., Miller, R. R., & Lewis, D. J. (1968). Retrograde amnesia produced by electroconvulsive shock after reactivation of a consolidated memory trace. *Science, 160,* 203–204.

Müller, G. E., & Pilzecker, A. (1900). Experimentalle Beitrage zur Lehre vom Gedachtnis. *Zeitschrift fur Psychologie, 1,* 1–300.

Nadel, L., & Willner, J. (1989). Some implications of postnatal maturation of the hippocampus. In V. Chan-Palay & C. Köhler (Eds.), *The hippocampus—New Vistas* (pp. 17–31). New York: Alan R. Liss.

Nelson, C. A. (1995). The ontogeny of human memory: A cognitive neuroscience perspective. *Developmental Psychology, 31,* 723–738.

Nelson, C. A. (1997). The neurobiological basis of early memory development. In N. Cowan (Ed.), *The development of memory in childhood* (pp. 41–82). Hove East Sussex: Psychology Press.

Nelson, C. A. (2000). Neural plasticity and human development: The role of early experience in sculpting memory systems. *Developmental Science, 3,* 115–136.

Piaget, J. (1926). *The language and thought of the child.* New York: Harcourt, Brace.

Piaget, J. (1952). *The origins of intelligence in children.* New York: International Universities Press.

Rovee-Collier, C., & Gerhardstein, P. (1997). The development of infant memory. In N. Cowan (Ed.), *The development of memory in childhood* (pp. 5–39). Hove East Sussex: Psychology Press.

Sara, S. J. (2000). Retrieval and reconsolidation: Toward a neurobiology of remembering. *Learning and Memory, 7,* 73–84.

Seress, L. (2001). Morphological changes of the human hippocampal formation from midgestation to early childhood. In C. A. Nelson & M. Luciana (Eds.), *Handbook of developmental cognitive neuroscience* (pp. 45–58). Cambridge, MA: MIT Press.

Snyder, K. A. (2006). Neural mechanisms of attention and memory in preferential-looking tasks. In L. M. Oakes and P. J. Bauer (Eds.), *Short- and long-term memory in infancy and early childhood: Taking the first steps toward remembering.* New York: Oxford University Press.

Squire, L. R., & Alvarez, P. (1995). Retrograde amnesia and memory consolidation: A neurobiological perspective. *Current Opinion in Neurobiology, 5,* 169–177.

Squire, L. R., & Zola, S. M. (1996). Structure and function of declarative and nondeclarative memory systems. *Proceedings of the National Academy of Sciences, 93,* 13515–13522.

Takehara, K., Kawahara, S., & Kirino, Y. (2003). Time-dependent reorganization of the brain components underlying memory retention in trace eye-blink conditioning. *The Journal of Neuroscience, 23,* 9897–9905.

Wiebe, S. A., Cheatham, C. L., Lukowski, A. F., Haight, J. C., Muehleck, A. J., & Bauer, P. J. (2006). Infants' ERP responses to novel and familiar stimuli change over time: Implications for novelty detection and memory. *Infancy, 9,* 21–44.

Zola, S. M., & Squire, L. R. (2000). The medial temporal lobe and the hippocampus. In E. Tulving and F.I.M. Craik (Eds.), *The Oxford handbook of memory* (pp. 485–500). New York: Oxford University Press.

2

What Can Statistical Learning Tell Us About Infant Learning?

JENNY R. SAFFRAN, UNIVERSITY
OF WISCONSIN–MADISON

Infants possess many extraordinary capacities that allow them to make sense of their worlds. The ontogenesis of their remarkable knowledge base has been the focus of debates across all aspects of developmental psychology and developmental cognitive science. How do babies know what they know? Where does their exquisitely detailed and rich knowledge base come from? Across these many debates, two broad controversies have emerged. One concerns the origins of knowledge: do infants arrive in the world possessing "factory-installed" information about how their environment (linguistic, physical, social, affective, etc.) is structured, or is this information gleaned through experience? The other question concerns the mechanisms that gather and instantiate this knowledge: Are these mechanisms domain-specific—that is, tied to a particular domain of knowledge, such as words, numbers, objects, or emotions—or are these mechanisms shared across domains? Like all such two-sided issues, the answers to both questions presumably lie somewhere in the middle. Nevertheless, understanding how these factors may be teased apart and how they interact is a pressing scientific issue in developmental psychology.

In this chapter, I will take a new look at these issues through the lens of learning. In particular, I will focus on statistical learning as a model system within which to consider broader issues and implications pertaining to the role of learning in development. Statistical learning is an old idea, with roots in mid-twentieth-century fields of inquiry as diverse as structural linguistics (e.g., Bloomfield, 1933; Harris, 1955), early neuroscience (e.g., Hebb, 1949), and operant conditioning paradigms (e.g., Rescorla, 1968). Like many old ideas in psychology, statistical learning has received renewed attention over the past decade. Two broad claims underlie the statistical learning literature. First, important structures in the environment are mirrored by surface statistics. Second, organisms are in fact sensitive to these patterns in their environments. This combination of environmental structure and learning mechanisms that can exploit this structure is the central tenet of theories focused on learning—in this case, the potent combination of informative statistics in the input paired with processes that can make use of such statistics. This pairing is arguably non-accidental. In cases where the pertinent environmental structures predate the learning mechanisms that capture their structure, such as physical information (e.g., objects), our learning mechanisms have presumably evolved to best fit this structure. However, in cases where the environmental structures likely emerged after the learning mechanisms in question, such as human language, we might find cases where the environmental structures evolved to best fit our learning mechanisms.

Much of the recent work in the statistical learning tradition has focused on language acquisition (e.g., Saffran, Newport, & Aslin, 1996; Maye, Werker, & Gerken, 2002; Saffran, 2003a; Newport & Aslin, 2004). Importantly, these ideas are explicitly linked to studies in other areas of perceptual and cognitive development (e.g., Saffran, Johnson, Aslin, & Newport, 1999; Fiser & Aslin, 2002; Kirkham, Slemmer, & Johnson, 2002; Baldwin, Andersson, Saffran, & Meyer, 2008). There are also many more implicit links between statistical language learning and research in other domains (e.g., Canfield & Haith, 1991; Kelly & Martin, 1994; Hannon & Trehub, 2005). Interest in this area has been fueled by the rise of connectionist models of development, in which learning is driven by statistical patterns of covariation in the input (e.g., Elman, Bates, Johnson, & Karmiloff-Smith, 1996; Munakata & McClelland, 2003; Elman, 2005).

Learning may be a particularly informative arena of cognition within which to investigate classic developmental issues, such as the relative roles of innate structure and experience. One might imagine that learning is relevant to this debate because evidence for learning supports the experience "side" of these debates. However, we take a more nuanced view: Learning serves as a critical *bridge* between innate structure and environmental input. One cannot learn in the absence of internal mechanisms that serve to track patterns in the environment; such mechanisms are likely to be available from a very early age (e.g., Kirkham et al., 2002). One also cannot learn in the absence of relevant experience. Learning provides the link between these two factors; studying the architecture of human learning mechanisms is thus one way to bridge the venerable nature/nurture divide.

There are, of course, many classes of potential learning mechanisms operating in infancy (e.g., Marcus, 2000). In this chapter, we will explore some of statistical learning's implications for thinking about the architecture of learning in infancy. In particular, we will argue that learning is not a unitary construct and that substantial progress can occur when investigators consider the components of any given learning process separately. There are multiple interleaved aspects of learning, and the instantiation of each of these components may have implications for issues of innateness and domain-specificity. For any given learning problem, we must consider the input to learning and how it is represented, the output representations that emerge from learning and how these are integrated with extant knowledge, and the mechanisms that operate over the input to create the output.

The complexity of this problem is multiplied greatly when one realizes that, at any given moment, the child is presumably tracking multiple levels of regularities across multiple domains, and the output of any given learning process likely changes how the input to subsequent learning episodes is represented.

To highlight the importance of breaking learning down into its parts, we will consider two quite different learning problems. The first will be drawn from the area of statistical learning of tone sequences. In this discussion, we will focus on the importance of considering input representations by examining the interaction between pitch perception and statistical learning. In the second example, we will consider issues of domain-specificity and species-specificity in learning syntax. Here, we will focus on constraints on learning that affect the operation of learning mechanisms.

STATISTICAL LEARNING AS A MODEL SYSTEM: COMPONENTS OF LEARNING

Broadly speaking, any given learning episode consists of three interrelated components. First, there must be some sort of input. Input can be divided into two overlapping classes: external input and internal input. External input is most typically what we think of when we think about input to learners—it is derived from the environment and can be approximated by analyses of the structure of the external world. However, learners also receive what I will call internal input. This is input to learning that is derived from prior learning episodes, which involves a reanalysis of previously gleaned external input. For example, consider this simple example of a learner who is exposed to sound sequences in which words are organized into categories as a function of their relative position (e.g., "A" words precede "B" words precede "C" words). Initially, the learner must track patterns of words from the external input. Part of the output of this learning process will presumably include the categories into which the words of the input were organized (e.g., initial words, medial words, final words). Now, the learner can begin to discover the patterns that interrelate the categories themselves (e.g., that "A" words precede "B" words). This requires an analysis of internal input, derived initially from the external input but incorporating the results of prior analyses of the external input.

Often, analyses of internal and external input will serve to inform one another. For example, infants engaged in the process of discovering the boundaries between words are able to use words that they already know, such as their names, as potent cues to discover new words (Bortfeld, Morgan, Golinkoff, & Rathbun, 2005). In this case, the output of prior learning events—such as one's name—alters the landscape of the subsequent input. Similarly, prior learning experiences in the lab, including exposure to novel phonotactic, phonological, and grammatical regularities, influence how infants incorporate previous learning with subsequent analyses of the input (e.g., Saffran & Thiessen, 2003; Gómez, 2006; Thiessen & Saffran, 2007).

An important consideration when thinking about the input to learning is how it is represented in the minds of learners. Indeed, much of the power of computational models rests on input representations; when the representations are a good match to the problem at hand, models are more likely to converge on solutions. Unfortunately, relatively little is known about the contents of infants' representations of the input. One area of interest in this regard is how infants represent speech sounds—do they focus more on smaller units like phonemes, larger units like syllables, or something in between that does not match our adult intuitions about speech (e.g., Newport, Weiss, Wonnacott, & Aslin, 2004)? Later in this chapter, we will consider our own work on nonlinguistic tone perception as an approach to the problem of studying the contents of learners' input representations.

The input must then be analyzed by some set of computations—the mechanism itself. This is the heart of what we are usually talking about when we discuss learning—what are the algorithms or computations that operate over the input? Researchers in infant cognition in general, and infant language in particular, have primarily focused on computations considered to be "statistical"—that is involving the use of probabilistic information in the input, and on computations considered to be "rules"—that is, involving the use of deterministic information in the input. Because of the relative paucity of infant studies in this domain, the distinction between the two classes of learning remains substantially blurry (though see Marcus, 2000, for a different view). This problem is not limited to infant studies; even adult studies that attempt to carefully control their stimuli do not always clearly distinguish between rule-based or statistical-based learning accounts (e.g., Seidenberg, MacDonald, & Saffran, 2002).

With respect to statistical learning, several subclasses of learning mechanisms have been proposed. Infants can detect the probabilities of co-occurrence of elements in a sequence: the likelihood that X is followed by Y (e.g., Aslin, Saffran, & Newport, 1998). In addition, infants can detect nonadjacent probabilities: the likelihood that X is followed by Y when A intervenes, at least under certain circumstances (e.g., Gómez, 2002; Newport & Aslin, 2004). Infants can use frequency distributions to categorize elements, as when determining whether two sounds are examples of the same phoneme or of two different phonemes (Maye, Werker, & Gerken, 2002). Finally, as discussed below, infants can find patterns of predictability over categories of words, a process equivalent to noticing that the presence of determiners (words like "a" or "the") predicts the presence of nouns.

The third component of learning is the output of learning. Like input, output has received relatively little attention in the literature on infant learning. The kinds of questions one might ask about output concern such issues as whether the output is a veridical representation of the input, and how these output representations are integrated with prior knowledge in a given domain. Understanding the output is particularly important because, as intimated above, the output of one learning episode may serve as input to another. For example, consider the following study by Saffran & Wilson (2003). Twelve-month-old infants heard fluent speech—sequences of nonsense words—that were organized into a simple finite-state grammar. This task is unusual because most infant experiments concentrate on a single learning task, such as word segmentation or grammar learning. Here, infants were faced with a multitask problem that is more similar to natural language learning; they were required to segment the sound stream into words *and* to find the patterns organizing those words into sentences. To do so, infants presumably began by representing the input in speech units—syllables, or possibly phonemes. They then tracked the statistics of those speech units and located the boundaries between words. The output of this process was presumably word-like units. Next, the infants had to reanalyze the same corpus of speech, now using word-like units as input representations, in order to find the grammar, which was opaque before they discovered the words. In this dynamic fashion, infants took a learning problem at the syllables-to-word level, found the words, and then solved a learning problem at the words-to-sentences level using knowledge gained earlier in the task.

STATISTICAL LEARNING AND DOMAIN-SPECIFICITY

Now that we have attempted to parse the learning process into three distinct but interrelated components—input, computation, and output—we can begin to recast the question of "is statistical learning domain-specific" somewhat more narrowly. The punch line, of course, is that this type of learning, like all learning, is likely to be both general and specific at the same time.

There is evidence to suggest that the input representations to learning encompass domain-specific properties. At some level, this is trivially true. Input that comes from language is vastly different in structure from input coming from any other domain; nobody will ever confuse a symphony with a newscast. There is also evidence to suggest that there may be domain-specific constraints on how the input is represented. For example, Newport, Weiss, Wonnacott, & Aslin (2004) suggest that the same computations operate more readily over segments (consonants and vowels) than over syllables. Some speech segments may be privileged in input representations relative to others, at least with adult learners (e.g., Bonatti, Peña, Nespor, & Mehler, 2005; for related arguments about statistics versus rules, see Peña, Bonatti, Nespor, & Mehler, 2002). The studies on tone learning discussed in more detail below were explicitly designed to examine how our perceptual systems influence input representations. Whether or not one wants to consider this "domain-specific" is not clear, but it is certainly the case that different domains of knowledge place distinct demands on perception. On this view, the input is domain-specific to the extent that perceptual constraints linked to a given domain determine the primitives over which computations are performed. Music and language are both auditory, but they make use of different perceptual primitives for the most part (pitch and rhythm being notable exceptions).

Similarly, there is evidence to suggest that the output of statistical learning is domain-specific in the sense that infants attempt to integrate what they have just learned with prior knowledge about a given domain. For example, infants treat the output of statistical word segmentation tasks as possible English words (Saffran, 2001a).[1] These output representations facilitate the process of mapping sound to meaning in word learning (Graf Estes, Evans, Alibali, & Saffran, 2007). Similarly, infants appear to treat the output of tone sequence segmentation tasks as "melodies" (Saffran, 2003b). Although little is known about this process, it appears that this learning process is sufficiently nuanced to ensure that the output of learning is appropriately "dumped" into the right system of knowledge.

What about the statistical learning mechanisms themselves? Here, there is no evidence to suggest *any* domain-specific learning algorithms. There are some suggestions that statistical learning may be easier in some domains than in others (Conway & Christiansen, 2005). However, it seems likely that the quality of input representations, as mitigated by perceptual salience and prior experience in a given domain, interacts in important ways with the learning mechanisms to produce some qualitative and quantitative differences in ease of learning (for similar arguments about infant rule learning, see Saffran, Pollak, Seibel, & Shkolnik, 2007).

Statistical learning of adjacent units works over a wide variety of primitives, including speech, tone sequences, shape sequences, visual-spatial patterns, visuo-motor patterns, action patterns, and textures (e.g., Saffran et al., 1999; Fiser & Aslin, 2001, 2002; Kirkham et al., 2002; Conway & Christiansen, 2005; Baldwin et al., 2008). Similarly, statistical learning of nonadjacent regularities also operates over a variety of primitives, possibly governed by Gestalt heuristics, including consonants, vowels, tones, and noise (e.g., Creel, Newport, & Aslin, 2004). Higher-level statistical learning (e.g., grammatical patterns) is also observed across domains (Saffran, 2002; McMullen & Saffran, submitted). For these reasons, we suggest that whereas the input and output appear to be tied to particular domains, the computations are not.

With these considerations in mind, we will turn to our "case studies": tones and input representations, and grammar and learning mechanisms. Throughout, our focus will be on how the input and the computations constrain learning. It may be that how learning unfolds in infancy can help us understand a number of critical questions: How do infants solve the "richness of the stimulus" problem—honing in on the important regularities while not being sidetracked by the infinite other patterns lurking in the input? Does the structure of the input drive learning? Why do some patterns but not others emerge across human languages? If learning is so important, why are nonhuman animals relatively poor at language learning? Although it will take decades to answer these questions, some of the insights derived from taking learning seriously may help focus the questions in fruitful ways.

EXAMPLE PROBLEM 1: STATISTICAL LEARNING OF TONE SEQUENCES

This line of research has its roots in an interesting issue that emerged from our initial forays into statistical language learning. In our earliest studies, we used the problem of word segmentation—discovery of word boundaries in fluent speech—as a domain in which to explore statistical learning (Saffran, Aslin, & Newport, 1996; Saffran, Newport, & Aslin, 1996; Saffran, Newport, Aslin, Tunick, & Barrueco, 1997; Aslin, Saffran, & Newport, 1998). To test the hypothesis that learners might use the co-occurrence statistics of syllables to discover word boundaries, we exposed learners (adults, children, and eight-month-old infants) to sequences like the following: *golabupabikututibugolabupabiku*. These streams lasted anywhere from 2 min (infants) to 21 min (adults), and ranged in their internal complexity (4 versus 6 words, simpler versus more complex statistics, etc.). Our learners' task was to find the "words" in these sequences, where word-ness was determined by the statistics of the sounds. For example, in the preceding example, *golabu* was a word because *go* was consistently followed by *la* and *la* was consistently followed by *bu*. Across these age groups, and using a variety of techniques appropriate to each age group, we found that learners readily distinguished words from novel orders of the same syllables (nonwords) and, more challengingly, sequences that spanned a word boundary and were thus familiar but were not themselves words (part-words).

These results suggest the presence of a powerful learning mechanism that operates implicitly across multiple age groups. The next pressing question concerned whether this mechanism was specialized for language or available more generally for learning across domains. There were many reasons to suspect the latter. While studies had not explored sequential statistical learning of this kind, particularly in infancy, several other literatures suggested the presence of statistical learning mechanisms in other domains. For example, studies from several decades ago suggested that rats in conditioning experiments compute conditional probabilities (e.g., Rescorla, 1968). There is also a large literature on incidental learning, showing that mere exposure results in detection of such statistics as base frequency (e.g., Hasher & Zacks, 1984). Infants appear to be attuned to correlation and covariation across domains (e.g., Younger & Cohen, 1983; Canfield & Haith, 1991). Moreover, within the field of psycholinguistics, some researchers were beginning to speculate on common underpinnings for language and other types of structured information, based largely on the use of probabilistic information (e.g., Elman, 1990; Kelly & Martin, 1994; Seidenberg, 1997). Given that the brain is attuned to detecting predictability, it seemed reasonable to hypothesize that the learning mechanism we had observed in a language-learning task was also useful for learning in nonlinguistic tasks.

With these ideas in mind, we designed a parallel task using quasi-musical stimuli. Despite obvious differences, music and language possess important similarities, both structurally and in terms of developmental trajectories (see McMullen & Saffran, 2004, for discussion). We took our adult and infant statistical language learning tasks and translated the speech streams into nonlinguistic tones. Each syllable (e.g., *bu*) was replaced by a particular note (e.g., C#), to generate a fluent stream of tones: e.g., AC#EDGFCBG#A#F#D#. The question of interest was whether learners could segment "tone words" like AC#E based on the same statistical distributions used in our prior linguistic studies (Saffran et al., 1999). Adults and eight-month-old infants both succeeded at this task, suggesting that sequential statistical learning is not domain-specific to language. This conclusion has been bolstered by numerous findings in statistical learning tasks across a number of domains, using adults and, in some cases, infants: These include sequential visual learning tasks (e.g., Kirkham et al., 2002; Turk-Browne, Junge, & Scholl, 2005), visuo-spatial tasks (e.g., Fiser & Aslin, 2001, 2002), visuo-motor tasks (Hunt & Aslin, 2001), texture tasks (Conway & Christiansen, 2005), and action sequence tasks (Baldwin et al., 2008). The hypothesis that sequential statistical learning is domain general has also been supported by studies showing that cotton-top tamarin monkeys and rats can perform our linguistic statistical learning task, suggesting that the learning mechanism in question is not specialized for language acquisition (Hauser, Newport, & Aslin, 2001; Toro & Trobalón, in press).

These results suggest that the computation in question—detecting transitional probabilities (the probability of Y, given X) between elements—is not specific to language. But other factors influence performance on these tasks. In particular, there are real differences between the tone-sequence task and the syllable-sequence task that have implications for musical statistical learning. Consider the tone sequences used in our experiment, for example, AC#EDGFCBG#A#F#D#. By translating each syllable from the linguistic experiments into a distinct musical tone, we implicitly assumed that learners would represent tones in the same way as syllables and would perform their computations accordingly. However, it is critical to ask which units enter into learners' computations. There are multiple perceptual primitives that might have been tracked in these experiments. Consider AC#E. Learners could have tracked the probabilities with which the *absolute pitches* A, C#, and E co-occurred, just as they tracked the probabilities with which the syllables *go, la,* and *bu* co-occurred. Alternatively, learners might have tracked the probabilities with which the *relative pitches,* or the intervals between those pitches, co-occurred. In this case, learners would be tracking the probability of an ascending major third (the interval between A and C#), followed by an ascending minor third (the interval between C# and E).

The design of the original Saffran et al. (1999) experiment did not distinguish between statistical learning of absolute pitches versus relative pitches. Learners in other tasks appear to have access to both types of cues across development (e.g., Levitin, 1994; Trehub, Schellenberg, & Hill, 1997; Schellenberg & Trehub, 2003). However, humans may be predisposed to use one type of pitch information in some tasks relative to others. We reasoned that the statistical learning task was a good domain within which to assess the role of perception in statistical learning. To do so, we manipulated the materials used in our tone statistical learning tasks so that, in some conditions, successful test discrimination required the use of absolute pitch cues during learning, whereas in other conditions, successful test discrimination required the use of relative-pitch cues during learning (Saffran & Griepentrog, 2001). The results suggested that learners of different ages capitalized on different perceptual primitives to perform our task: Eight-month-old infants tracked absolute pitch cues, whereas adults tracked relative-pitch cues. In this case, our adult and infant participants heard identical stimuli, but they appear to have learned something quite different about them.

In some ways, these results were rather puzzling because infants in other types of tasks are demonstrably quite skilled at detecting relative-pitch information (for review, see Trehub et al., 1997). One possibility was that infants failed to make use of relative-pitch cues in our task because the tone-sequence materials were quite unmusical. In particular, the materials used by Saffran and Griepentrog (2001) were atonal (that is, not in a key but rather in a random distribution of notes) and did not conform to any of the conventions of Western tonal music. The lack of melodic structure may have led infants to a focus on absolute pitch information rather than on the melodic information carried by relative pitch. To test this hypothesis, we exposed infants and adults to a tone-sequence segmentation task that was somewhat more musical: The materials conformed to the key of C major (Saffran, 2003b). However, the infants continued to succeed only when absolute pitch cues facilitated the test discrimination, and not when relative-pitch cues distinguished the test items.

Why might our statistical learning task have led infants to show one type of perceptual processing when other tasks have shown that infants use a different set of perceptual cues? One possibility concerns an interaction between learners' existing perceptual sensitivities and the structure of the tasks in question. Interestingly, research with birds suggests that stimulus design plays a critical role in pitch processing when applied to learning tasks (MacDougall-Shackleton & Hulse, 1996). European starlings were presented with a pitch discrimination task that could be performed using either absolute or relative-pitch cues. Initially, the birds solved the task using absolute pitches. However, when the researchers changed the task to require transfer of the pitch sequences, rendering the absolute pitch cues useless, the birds began to use relative-pitch cues instead. These results show that although the birds had access to both types of pitch cues, task demands determined which pitch dimensions were used to perform the test discriminations.

Perceptual learning in human infants may be similarly influenced by task demands. That is, infants may have access to both types of pitch cues; the structure of the learning task and/or test discrimination determines which aspects of pitch enter into a particular learning experience. If this hypothesis is correct, then when absolute pitch cues are rendered unreliable, infants should track relative-pitch cues instead. We thus created tone sequences that no longer contained consistent absolute pitch sequences; this was accomplished by continually transposing the "tone words" (Saffran, Reeck, Niehbur, & Wilson, 2005). Relative-pitch sequences, however, remained highly predictable. Given these materials, infants were able to capitalize on relative-pitch cues, which they failed to do when absolute pitch information was also reliable and predicable. With absolute pitch cues essentially removed as a signal of structure in the input, infants began to take advantage of the available relative-pitch cues. In this study, the structure of the input presented affected infants' choices about which perceptual cues to track during learning.

We can extend these suggestions about how infants determine which cues to use beyond our laboratory experiments. How might infants learn to take advantage of the various pitch cues in their native environments? Infants appear to have access to absolute pitch cues in the same "dumb" way that nonhuman animals do: Our auditory systems automatically code the pitches of incoming stimuli. However, given the informational structure of our environment, absolute pitch is not highly predictive of structure; both speech and music rely instead on ratios between pitches and on the contours of pitches. Thus, while we remain able to track absolute pitches throughout life, this is not the most important facet of our auditory environment to represent and remember, at least for most people (for discussion, see Saffran & Griepentrog, 2001). The broader point is that although infants possess powerful learning mechanisms, the learning process is constrained both by infants' perceptual capabilities and by the structure of the material to be learned.

In addition, these findings raise the possibility that statistical learning may contribute to how we learn to understand music. Detecting sequences of notes may help us discover melodies in music. Moreover, as reviewed in Jonaitis & Saffran (submitted), other types of statistics may underlie other aspects of musical knowledge, including harmony. Notably, Jonaitis and Saffran demonstrated that adult knowledge of harmony is predicted by the sequential statistics of chords, and that adults can learn novel harmonic systems via their statistical structure. It thus seems that, as with language, detecting statistical information may provide important structural knowledge to learners acquiring musical knowledge.

EXAMPLE PROBLEM 2: LEARNING LINGUISTIC PHRASE STRUCTURE

The second "case study" concerns how infants learn syntactic structure. Two kinds of research have focused on how infants come to understand the ways in which words and word classes interrelate to form grammar. One type focused on what infants know about how their native language syntax works. These studies provide clear evidence that infants possess nuanced knowledge about the ways in which words can combine, and that infants understand grammatical structures months or years before they can produce them (e.g., Golinkoff, Hirsh-Pasek, & Gordon, 1987; Naigles, 1990). Some of these linguistic structures are argued to be highly abstract and unavailable in the input to children, thereby unlearnable and thus part of the presumed innate linguistic knowledge possessed by humans (e.g., Crain & Nakayama, 1987; Lidz, Waxman, & Freedman, 2003). Other studies, by exposing infants to "sentences" drawn from small artificial grammars and exploring the conditions under which infants subsequently generalize to novel sentences, have focused more heavily on learning (e.g., Gómez & Gerken, 1999; Marcus, Vijayan, Bandi Rao, & Vishton, 1999; Saffran & Wilson, 2003).

In the work discussed here, we chose a different strategy, one drawn from the sizable literature on artificial grammar learning in adults. In this literature, researchers have attempted to develop miniature languages that nevertheless capture some critical features of natural languages (e.g., Moeser & Bregman, 1972; Morgan & Newport, 1981; Morgan, Meier, & Newport, 1987, 1989; Braine et al., 1990). These studies are designed to uncover the kinds of learning mechanisms operating in language learning by carefully manipulating experimental materials. For example, these studies, from the 1970s and 1980s, have drawn conclusions about what kinds of cues are needed to help learners discover linguistic phrases by creating languages that either do or do not contain the relevant cues (e.g., semantic reference worlds, correlated prosodic cues, movement transformations, case endings, and other such cues).

We took advantage of this strategy to begin to explore a possible role for statistical cues in the acquisition of grammatical phrase structure. Although words occur serially in speech, they are grouped into phrases that carry important grammatical information. It is not obvious how learners might discover phrase structure, given that it is not transparently mirrored in the surface structure that we hear; there are not reliable prosodic markers of phrase structure even in speech to infants (e.g., Fisher & Tokura, 1996; Morgan & Demuth, 1996). We reasoned that, as with cues to word boundaries, there may be statistical information in the input that could point to phrasal units. Indeed, when one considers the distributions of word categories (e.g., nouns and verbs) in sentences, phrases contain unidirectional dependency relations: The presence of some word categories requires others, which conjointly make up a phrase. For example, nouns can occur without articles like *the* and *a,* but articles cannot occur without nouns. This provides a cue to noun-phrase structures in many languages. Similarly, noun phrases can occur without prepositions, but prepositions cannot occur without noun phrases; this pairing provides a cue to prepositional-phrase structure. Studies with adults and children demonstrate that these predictive-dependency relationships provide a statistical cue that highlights phrasal units for learners, even in the absence of any surface (e.g., prosodic) cues to phrase boundaries (Saffran, 2001b).

Why do we see predictive dependencies within phrases across many human languages? One possibility is that the presence of predictive dependencies helps learners discover phrases and thus facilitate language acquisition. To test this hypothesis, Saffran (2002) compared the acquisition of two artificially created languages. In one of these languages, the Predictive language, predictive dependencies linked members of a phrase together. For example, "A phrases" contained "A words" and "D words." An "A" word could occur with or without a "D" word, but the presence of a "D" word required that an "A" word also be present. Importantly, the direction of these predictions was the opposite of English, the native language of the participants. In the second grammar, the Nonpredictive language, the presence of one word type within a phrase did *not* predict the presence of the other word type. For example, "A" words could occur with or without "D" words, and "D" words could occur with or without "A" words. Learners—adults and seven-year-old children—exposed to languages containing predictive dependencies outperformed learners exposed to languages lacking predictive dependencies. Interestingly, the same constraint on learning emerged in comparable tasks using nonlinguistic materials, including computer alert sounds, drum and bell sounds, and simultaneously presented visual shape arrays (Saffran, 2002).

These results are interesting because they suggest that the structures that tend to recur across human languages are the very structures that facilitate learning. At the same time, this learning ability does not appear to be specifically designed for language learning. One intriguing possibility is that human languages have been shaped by constraints on human learning. According to this view, the kinds of patterns that are generally easier for human learners to detect and use should be most likely to recur across languages. In this way, general constraints on learning could affect the structures present in a specific system such as language.

The claim that human languages exemplify exactly those structures that human learners are best able to track and compute has been previously investigated using the nonadjacent sequence-learning task (Newport & Aslin, 2004). Given transitional probabilities computed over nonadjacent syllables (with other syllables intervening between the target syllables), human adults and cotton-top tamarin monkeys show quite different patterns of performance (Newport, Hauser, Spaepen, & Aslin, 2004). Both species are limited in the types of patterns they easily detect. Critically, however, the kinds of limitations observed in humans map onto natural language structures. Adults in laboratory learning paradigms can learn segmental nonadjacency patterns; these patterns also occur in human languages, as when consonants predict other consonants despite intervening vowels (as in Semitic languages, such as Arabic and Hebrew), and vowels predict other vowels despite intervening consonants (as in languages that use vowel harmony, such as Turkish). However, adults in laboratory tasks fail to learn patterns where nonadjacent syllables predict one another; this sort of pattern does not occur in natural languages. Interestingly, tamarin monkeys' learning abilities in this domain appear to be unrelated to the kinds of structures observed in natural languages. These results support the hypothesis that the interface between our computational systems and the phonological representations over which they operate may have shaped the structure of human languages (see Saffran & Thiessen, 2003, for a similar argument). Importantly, constraints on this learning process do not appear to be specific to language but are instead a function of perceptual factors that cut across domains (Creel et al., 2004).

The predictive dependency task used by Saffran (2002) raises similar questions about the relationship between human learning mechanisms and language structure. In particular, is there a relationship between the kinds of statistical patterns that humans readily learn and the kinds of statistical patterns exhibited in natural language grammars? To address this question, we designed a set of comparative experiments in which we compared human infants and cotton-top tamarind monkeys, using identical stimuli and methods designed to be as similar as possible (Saffran, Hauser et al., 2008). We used the Predictive and Non-predictive languages from Saffran (2002) to explore the use of predictive dependencies in learning by these two species. Our broader goal was to investigate the relationship between the structure of human languages and the learning capacities that underlie its acquisition.

In our first experiment (Saffran, Hauser et al., 2008), we exposed 12-month-old infants and adult cotton-top tamarin monkeys to stimuli derived from the Predictive and Non-predictive grammars from Saffran (2002). Because these languages are more complex than those used in prior studies with either population, we simplified the task by decreasing the languages' vocabularies, and writing the grammatical rules so that they operated over individual words, rather than categories of words. This simplification makes these materials quite unlike human languages, where the pertinent regularities occur over word classes, not individual words. Nevertheless, these stimuli maintained the contrast between having predictive dependencies (in the Predictive language) and not having them (in the Non-predictive language). Both species successfully distinguished the ungrammatical sentences used during testing from the grammatical sentences, but only after exposure to the Predictive language; there was no evidence of learning after exposure to the otherwise comparable Non-predictive language. These findings replicate the data from adults and older children from Saffran (2002), and suggest that both infants and tamarins can make use of predictive dependencies, at least in relatively simple linguistic environments.

In the second experiment (Saffran, Hauser et al., 2008), we tested the infants and tamarins on the stimuli previously used by Saffran (2002). Because these grammars were written over categories of words, not individual words, these languages were far larger and more complex than those used in our first experiment. Under these circumstances, the tamarins failed to learn, given exposure to either the Predictive or the Non-predictive grammars. However, the infants showed the same pattern of performance as seen with the simpler languages in Experiment 1: Successful learning given exposure to the Predictive grammar, but not the Non-predictive grammar.

This pattern of results suggests some intriguing cross-species differences. Tamarins were able to learn the smaller Predictive language in Experiment 1, suggesting that they are able to make use of predictive dependencies in relatively simple linguistic environments. Indeed, stimulus analyses presented in Saffran, Hauser et al. (2008) suggest that the presence/absence of predictive dependencies was a primary factor influencing performance in this experiment, rather than other statistical regularities in the stimuli. Interestingly, even the simpler languages from Experiment 1 were sufficiently difficult to learn that the tamarins failed to learn when predictive dependencies were absent in the Non-predictive language.

The tamarins and infants diverged, given the larger languages used in Experiment 2, which possess some of the expressive power of natural languages. Here, the tamarins failed to show evidence of learning, even when predictive dependencies were present. The infants, however, continued to successfully exploit the predictive dependency cues in these materials to learn the Predictive language. These results are striking because the infants also failed to learn the Non-predictive language, suggesting that predictive dependencies do in fact influence the acquisition of complex artificial grammars by human infants.

What is clear from these results is that infants are able to learn complex grammatical structure rapidly and implicitly. Of course, at some level this is obvious, because infants learn their native language, which is vastly more complex than any stimuli we can develop for laboratory use. The more subtle point is that infants learn some grammars more easily than other ones. When predictive dependencies were present, infant learners successfully learned basic features of the grammar. When predictive dependencies were not present, they failed to show evidence of any learning. This result is predicted by the constrained statistical learning hypothesis (Saffran, 2003a): Human learning mechanisms are one factor that shaped (and continues to shape) the structure of natural languages. Importantly, the learning mechanism itself does not appear to be specific to language, at least given our adult findings (Saffran, 2002), which await replication in the infants. The theory that emerges from these findings, and also from the nonadjacent sequence-learning studies by Newport and Aslin (2004; Newport, Hauser et al., 2004), suggests the following set of ideas. Human learners are endowed with a perceptual and cognitive system that builds on those possessed by our nonhuman forebears. This system is not designed specifically for language acquisition, processing, or production. As humans developed systems of communication, these emerging languages were shaped by perceptual and cognitive constraints on learning, processing, and production. In this way, languages are a very specific instantiation of a cohort of nonspecific constraints on how humans perceive, process, and use information. This view allows us to integrate findings that suggest that statistical learning is both general and specific: A class of general mechanisms has had very specific effects on how humans learn in different domains.

CONCLUSIONS

It should be evident, given the foregoing discussion, that learning is not a unitary construct. Each instance of learning requires input, computations, and output. Each component of learning in a given task can be, and should be, examined separately. Hot-ticket issues such as the role of experience versus preexisting knowledge, and general versus specific processes entailed in learning may come into clearer focus as we tease apart the multifaceted features of knowledge acquisition. Then, when the pieces are put back together, we can expect a fuller understanding of how learning works.

It should also be evident from this treatment of learning that describing a mechanism as "general" does not imply a blank-slate process, where experience holds all the cards. Indeed, statistical learning appears to be subject to many constraints, including how the input is perceived, how the input is structured, the computations performed by learners, and existing perceptual and cognitive constraints that delimit what is learnable. Some of these constraints likely come from brain structures. Although the neural underpinnings of infant learning are not well understood, we can speculate that distinct architectures present in various brain regions, distinct computations performed in various brain regions, and connectivity both among cortical areas and the input and output from the cortex to other neural structures all influence how learning proceeds and how it is constrained. For example, a recent adult study suggests that various brain regions underlie associative learning (hippocampus) and frequency-based learning (striatum), highlighting the importance of considering the many varied processes that enter into various types of learning episodes, including working memory, stimulus binding, and executive control (Amso, Davidson, Johnson, Glover, & Casey, 2005). Investigations of statistical learning by individual neurons, as in a recent study showing that cortical neurons appear to process the probabilities with which particular sounds occur, may also illuminate constraints on statistical learning (e.g., Ulanovsky, Las, & Nelken, 2003).

Finally, there is a tendency to assume that "general mechanism" means "not innate." The statistical learning research supports a very different view. These learning mechanisms have all the hallmarks of innateness: They are available early in life and observed across species. The important observation is that developing humans presumably *use* these general mechanisms quite differently than nonhuman animals do. Consider detecting probabilities in fluent speech streams, a task that both infants and monkeys can perform (e.g., Hauser et al., 2001). It seems likely that while monkeys might behave in ways that *look* as though they are segmenting words in this task, the monkeys presumably do not treat these newly segmented sequences as "words," integrating them into an existing language-knowledge base (e.g., Saffran, 2001a). Also, unlike infants, the monkeys probably do not attempt to link the words they have just segmented to novel meanings (Graf Estes, Evans, Alibali, & Saffran, 2007). We might expect to see more overlap in the use of mechanisms when they are applied to domains of knowledge shared across species, such as knowledge about physical objects. The broader point is that closer examinations of how learning unfolds, both within and across species, are likely to yield much information about where knowledge comes from. Understanding what is *not* learnable by infants may be just as useful as documenting their many prodigious feats of learning.

Acknowledgments   Preparation of this manuscript was supported by grants to JRS from NICHD (R01HD37466) and NSF (BCS-9983630).

Note

1. Note that our use of "word" here presumes that infants younger than one year of age are representing these sound sequences as units of some sort but does not presume that infants possess full-fledged adult-like lexical representations. For discussion of the sound representations that make up early words, see Saffran & Graf Estes, 2006.

References

Amso, D., Davidson, M. C., Johnson, S. P., Glover, G., & Casey, B. J. (2005). Contributions of the hippocampus and the striatum to simple association and frequency-based learning. *NeuroImage, 27,* 291–298.

Aslin, R. N., Saffran, J. R., & Newport, E. L. (1998). Computation of conditional probability statistics by 8-month-old infants. *Psychological Science, 9*(4), 321–324.

Baldwin, D., Andersson, A., Saffran, J. R., & Meyer (2008). Segmenting dynamic human action via statistical structure. *Cognition, 106,* 1382–1407.

Bloomfield, L. (1933). *Language.* New York: Henry Holt.

Bonatti, L. L., Peña, M., Nespor, M., & Mehler, J. (2005). Linguistic constraints on statistical computations. *Psychological Science, 6*(6), 451–459.

Bortfeld, H., Morgan, J. L., Golinkoff, R. M., & Rathbun (2006). Mommy and me: Familiar names help launch babies into speech stream segmentation. *Psychological Science, 16*(4), 298–304.

Braine, M.D.S., Brody, R. E., Brooks, P. J., Sudhalter, V., Ross, J. A., Catalano, L., & Fisch, S. (1990). Exploring language acquisition in children with a miniature artificial language: Effects of item and pattern frequency, arbitrary subclasses, and correction. *Journal of Memory and Language, 29,* 591–610.

Canfield, R. L., & Haith, M. M. (1991). Active expectations in 2- and 3-month-old infants: Complex event sequences. *Developmental Psychology, 27,* 198–208.

Conway, C., & Christiansen, M. H. (2005). Modality constrained statistical learning of tactile, visual, and auditory sequences. *Journal of Experimental Psychology: Learning, Memory & Cognition, 31,* 24–39.

Crain, S., & Nakayama, M. (1987). Structure dependence in grammar formation. *Language, 63,* 522–543.

Creel, S. C., Newport, E. L., & Aslin, R. N. (2004). Distant melodies: Statistical learning of nonadjacent dependencies in tone sequences. *Journal of Experimental Psychology: Learning, Memory, & Cognition, 30*(5), 1119–1130.

Elman, J. L. (1990). Finding structure in time. *Cognitive Science, 14,* 179–211.

Elman, J. L. (2005). Connectionist models of cognitive development: Where next? *Trends in Cognitive Science, 9,* 111–117.

Elman, J., Bates, E., Johnson, M., & Karmiloff-Smith, A. (1996). *Rethinking innateness: A connectionist perspective on development.* Cambridge, MA: MIT Press.

Fiser, J., & Aslin, R. N., (2001). Unsupervised statistical learning of higher-order spatial structures from visual scenes. *Psychological Science, 12,* 499–504.

Fiser, J., & Aslin, R. N. (2002). Statistical learning of new visual feature combinations by infants. *Proceedings of the National Academy of Sciences, 99,* 15822–15826.

Fisher, C., & Tokura, H. (1996). Acoustic cues to grammatical structure in infant-directed speech: Cross-linguistic evidence. *Child Development, 67,* 3192–3218.

Golinkoff, R. M., Hirsh-Pasek, K., & Gordon, L. (1987). The eyes have it: Lexical and syntactic comprehension in a new paradigm. *Journal of Child Language, 14,* 23–45.

Gómez, R. L. (2002). Variability and detection of invariant structure. *Psychological Science, 13*(5), 431–436.

Gómez, R. L. (2006). Dynamically guided learning. In Y. Munakata & M. Johnson (Eds.) *Attention & performance XXI: Processes of change in brain and cognitive development.* Oxford, UK: Oxford University Press.

Gómez, R. L., & Gerken, L. (1999). Artificial grammar learning by 1-year-olds leads to specific and abstract knowledge. *Cognition, 70*(2), 109–135.

Graf Estes, K. M., Evans, J., Alibali, M. W., & Saffran, J. R. (2007). Can infants map meaning to newly segmented words? Statistical segmentation and word learning. *Psychological Science, 18,* 254–260.

Harris, Z. S. (1955). From phoneme to morpheme. *Language, 31,* 190–222.

Hannon, E. E., & Trehub, S. E. (2005). Tuning in to musical rhythms: Infants learn more readily than adults. *Proceedings of the National Academy of Science, 102,* 12639–12643.

Hasher, L., & Zacks, R. T. (1984). Automatic processing of fundamental information: The case of frequency of occurrence. *American Psychologist, 39,* 1372–1388.

Hauser, M. D., Newport, E. L., & Aslin, R. N. (2001). Segmentation of the speech stream in a non-human primate: Statistical learning in cotton top tamarinds. *Cognition, 78*(3), B53–B64.

Hebb, D. O. (1949). *The organization of behavior: A neuropsychological theory.* New York: Wiley.

Hunt, R. H., & Aslin, R. N. (2001). Statistical learning in a serial reaction time task: Simultaneous extraction of multiple statistics. *Journal of Experimental Psychology: General, 130*(4), 658–680.

Jonaitis, E. M., & Saffran, J. R. (2008). Learning harmony: The role of serial statistics. Manuscript under editorial review.

Kelly, M. H., & Martin, S. (1994). Domain-general abilities applied to domain-specific tasks: Sensitivity to probabilities in perception, cognition, and language. *Lingua, 92,* 105–140.

Kirkham, N. Z., Slemmer, J. A., & Johnson, S. P. (2002). Visual statistical learning in infancy: Evidence for a domain general learning mechanism. *Cognition, 83,* B35–B42.

Levitin, D. J. (1994). Absolute memory for musical pitch: Evidence from the production of learned melodies. *Perception & Psychophysics, 56,* 414–423.

Lidz, J., Waxman, S., & Freedman, J. (2003). What infants know about syntax but couldn't have learned: Experimental evidence for syntactic structure at 18-months. *Cognition, 89,* B65–B73.

MacDougall-Shackleton, S., & Hulse, S. H. (1996). Concurrent absolute and relative pitch processing by European starlings (*Sturnus vulgaris*). *Journal of Comparative Psychology, 110,* 139–146.

Marcus, G. F. (2000). Pa bi ku and ga ti ga: Two mechanisms children could use to learn about language and the world. *Current Directions in Psychological Science, 9,* 145–147.

Marcus, G. F., Vijayan, S., Bandi Rao, S., & Vishton, P. (1999). Rule learning by seven-month-old infants. *Science, 283,* 77–80.

Maye, J., Werker, J. F., & Gerken, L. (2002). Infant sensitivity to distributional information can affect phonetic discrimination. *Cognition, 82*(3), B101–B111.

McMullen, E., & Saffran, J. R. (2004). Music and language: A developmental comparison. *Music Perception, 21,* 289–311.

Moeser, S. D., & Bregman, A. S. (1972). The role of reference in the acquisition of a miniature artificial language. *Journal of Verbal Learning and Verbal Behavior, 11,* 759–769.

Morgan, J. L., & Demuth, C. (Eds.) (1996). *Signal to syntax: Bootstrapping from speech to grammar in early acquisition.* Mahwah, NJ: Lawrence Erlbaum.

Morgan, J. L., Meier, R. P., & Newport, E. L. (1987). Structural packaging in the input to language learning: Contributions of prosodic and morphological marking of phrases to the acquisition of language. *Cognitive Psychology, 19,* 498–550.

Morgan, J. L., Meier, R. P., & Newport, E. L. (1989). Facilitating the acquisition of syntax with cross-sentential cues to phrase structure. *Journal of Memory and Language, 28,* 360–374.

Morgan, J. L., & Newport, E. L. (1981). The role of constituent structure in the induction of an artificial language. *Journal of Verbal Learning and Verbal Behavior, 20,* 67–85.

Munakata, Y., & McClelland, J. L. (2003). Connectionist models of development. *Developmental Science, 6,* 413–429.

Naigles, L. (1990). Children use syntax to learn verb meanings. *Journal of Child Language, 17,* 357–374.

Newport, E. L., & Aslin, R. N. (2004). Learning at a distance: I. Statistical learning of non-adjacent dependencies. *Cognitive Psychology, 48,* 127–162.

Newport, E. L., Hauser, M. D., Spaepen, G., & Aslin, R. N. (2004). Learning at a distance: II. Statistical learning of non-adjacent dependencies in a non-human primate. *Cognitive Psychology, 49,* 85–117.

Newport, E. L., Weiss, D., Wonnacott, E., & Aslin, R. N. (2004). Statistical learning in speech: Syllables or segments? Talk presented at the 29th annual meeting of the Boston University Conference on Language Development, Boston, MA.

Peña, M., Bonatti, L. L, Nespor, M., & Mehler, J. (2002). Signal-driven computations in speech processing. *Science, 298*(5593), 604–607.

Rescorla, R. A. (1968). Probability of shock in the presence and absence of CS in fear conditioning. *Journal of Comparative and Physiological Psychology, 66,* 1–5.

Saffran, J. R. (2001a). Words in a sea of sounds: The output of statistical learning. *Cognition, 81,* 149–169.

Saffran, J. R. (2001b). The use of predictive dependencies in language learning. *Journal of Memory and Language, 44,* 493–515.

Saffran, J. R. (2002). Constraints on statistical language learning. *Journal of Memory and Language, 47,* 172–196.

Saffran, J. R. (2003a). Statistical language learning: Mechanisms and constraints. *Current Directions in Psychological Science, 12,* 110–114.

Saffran, J. R. (2003b). Absolute pitch in infancy and adulthood: The role of tonal structure. *Developmental Science, 6,* 37–45.

Saffran, J. R., Aslin, R. N., & Newport, E. L. (1996). Statistical learning by 8-month-old infants. *Science, 274,* 1926–1928.

Saffran, J. R., & Graf Estes, K. M. (2006). Word segmentation and word learning in infancy. In R. Kail (Ed.), *Advances in Child Development and Behavior.* New York: Elsevier (p. 1–38).

Saffran, J. R., & Griepentrog, G. J. (2001). Absolute pitch in infant auditory learning: Evidence for developmental reorganization. *Developmental Psychology, 37,* 74–85.

Saffran, J. R., Hauser, M., Seibel, R., Kapfhamer, J., Tsao, F., & Cushman, F. (2008). Cross-species differences in the capacity to acquire language: Grammatical pattern learning by human infants and monkeys. *Cognition, 107,* 479–500.

Saffran, J. R., Johnson, E. K., Aslin, R. N., & Newport, E. L. (1999). Statistical learning of tone sequences by human infants and adults. *Cognition, 70,* 27–52.

Saffran, J. R., Newport, E. L., & Aslin, R. N. (1996). Word segmentation: The role of distributional cues. *Journal of Memory and Language, 35,* 606–621.

Saffran, J. R., Newport, E. L., Aslin, R. N., Tunick, R. A., & Barrueco, S. (1997). Incidental language learning: Listening (and learning) out of the corner of your ear. *Psychological Science, 8,* 101–105.

Saffran, J. R., Pollak, S. D., Seibel, R. L., & Shkolnik, A. (2007). Dog is a dog is a dog: Infant rule learning is not specific to language. *Cognition, 105,* 669–680.

Saffran, J. R., Reeck, K., Niehbur, A., & Wilson, D. P. (2005). Changing the tune: Absolute and relative pitch processing by adults and infants. *Developmental Science, 8,* 1–7.

Saffran, J. R., & Thiessen, E. D. (2003). Pattern induction by infant language learners. *Developmental Psychology, 39,* 484–494.

Saffran, J. R., & Wilson, D. P. (2003). From syllables to syntax: Multi-level statistical learning by 12-month-old infants. *Infancy, 4,* 273–284.

Schellenberg, E. G., & Trehub, S. E. (2003). Accurate pitch memory is widespread. *Psychological Science, 14,* 262–266.

Seidenberg, M. S. (1997). Language acquisition and use: Learning and applying probabilistic constraints. *Science, 275,* 1599–1604.

Seidenberg, M. S., MacDonald, M. C., & Saffran, J. R. (2002). Does grammar start where statistics stop? *Science, 298,* 553–554.

Thiessen, E. D., & Saffran, J. R. (2007). Learning to learn: Infants' acquisition of stress-based strategies for word segmentation. *Language Learning & Development, 3,* 73–100.

Trehub, S., Schellenberg, G., & Hill, D. (1997). The origins of music perception and cognition: A developmental perspective. In I. Deliege & J. Sloboda (Eds.), *Perception and cognition of music* (pp. 103–128). East Sussex, UK: Psychology Press.

Toro, J. M., & Trobalón, J. B. (in press). Statistical computations over a speech stream in a rodent. *Perception & Psychophysics, 67,* 867–875.

Turk-Browne, N. B., Junge, J. A., & Scholl, B. J. (2005). The automaticity of visual statistical learning. *Journal of Experimental Psychology: General, 34*(4), 552–564.

Ulanovsky, N., Las, L., & Nelken, I. (2003). Processing of low-probability sounds by cortical neurons. *Nature Neuroscience, 6,* 391–398.

Younger, B. A., & Cohen, L. B. (1983). Infant perception of correlations among attributes. *Child Development, 54,* 858–867.

3

Developmental Origins of Object Perception

SCOTT P. JOHNSON, UNIVERSITY OF CALIFORNIA,
LOS ANGELES

Figure 3–1 shows two views of the Chrysler Building in New York City. At left is an aerial view, in which the majority of the northern and eastern faces of the building can be seen. At right is a view from the observation deck of the Empire State Building, over the left shoulder of the author's wife (on a rare day out together). Now, only a relatively small proportion of the southern and western faces of the top of the building can be seen, and from this particular point of observation the mesh fence and other buildings obscure much of the structure so that only a few fragments remain visible. The scene at right is typical of most of our exposure to the Chrysler Building: Rarely do we have the opportunity to board a helicopter and tour New York from above. Yet our subjective experience of this building, and of all solid objects, is inconsistent with the scene at the right, and is in a way inconsistent with the scene at the left because any single vantage point cannot provide full visible access to an object that is not translucent. Even if the reader has never visited New York City, he or she knows that this building, like all objects of its kind, is a solid entity with a back and sides that is stable over time.

This brief discussion of the Chrysler Building illustrates four key steps that the visual system follows in perceiving objects:

1. Segmentation of the visual scene into its components, components that are discriminable by virtue of differences in color, luminance, texture, distance, shape, orientation, and motion.
2. Assembly of the components derived from Step 1 into units.
3. Perception of the units as continuous across space and time.
4. Deduction of the three-dimensional shape of the assembled units from limited views.

Figure 3–1. Two views of the Chrysler Building in New York City. At left is a view from the air, a vantage point that is unusual with respect to this structure. Usually, our view of the Chrysler Building is encumbered by nearer objects, such that we glimpse only portions, as seen at right.

This list is not an exhaustive inventory of all object-relevant perceptual and cognitive skills, which would also include recognition of familiar objects, tracking the identity of objects over time, perceiving affordances for action, and so forth. Nevertheless, when these four steps have been realized, it is possible to perceive the visual world as an organized, coherent, structured environment composed of empty space interspersed with solid objects at various distances from the observer, objects that tend to maintain their properties even when we lose perceptual contact. How it is that the visual system accomplishes this experience has been a subject of intense interest to philosophers and to perceptual and cognitive scientists for decades. How it is that the machinery develops to accomplish this experience is the subject of the present chapter. Less is known about the latter question than about the former, but the gaps that remain in our knowledge of development of object perception are beginning to be filled.

In infants, the first aspect of object perception, visual segmentation, has been addressed in other contexts, such as investigations of the development of sensitivity to depth cues (e.g., Yonas & Granrud, 1985) and the development of object segregation (e.g., Needham, Baillargeon, & Kaufman, 1997). Little is known about the fourth aspect, infants' perception of three-dimensional visual shape, because it has received less attention than the others (Kellman, 1993). I will present data that bear principally on development of the second and third aspects of object perception: assembling visual fragments into units, and perceiving continuity across space and time. To anticipate, I will posit a strong role for learning in achieving veridical object perception in the first several postnatal months: Infants learn by doing (i.e., via development of eye movements) and infants learn by seeing (i.e., via exposure to objects in the environment). Discussion of these data and arguments is presented after a brief history of previous accounts of infants' object perception.

JEAN PIAGET'S THEORY AND MORE RECENT NATIVIST APPROACHES

Piagetian Theory

Piaget (1954/1937) proposed a theory of infant cognitive development organized around *objectification,* a concept of the self and other objects as distinct entities, persisting across time and space, following commonsense causal principles. Objectification is a major cognitive achievement that occurs in the first 2 years (approximately) of postnatal development. During this time, according to Piaget's theory, the infant's thinking is manifest strictly in overt actions. Objectification stems from the recognition of one's body as an independent object and one's movements as movements of objects through space, analogous to movements of other objects. This, in turn, stems from the development and coordination of skilled-action repertoires.

Piaget suggested that, at birth, infants experienced the world as a "tableaux" of disjointed sensory inundation: Inputs were incoherent both within and across perceptual domains. Visual inputs, therefore, consisted of disconnected shapes, not objects, and intermodal inputs were independent, such that a talking face yielded unrelated visual and auditory events. Still, within the first several months, infants exhibited a kind of recognition memory, for example, seeking the mother's breast after losing contact shortly after birth, and continuing to look in the direction of a person's exit from the room. But these behaviors were not systematic, and they were considered more passive than active. For Piaget, active search schemes, initiated by the child, were a critical feature of object concepts, both as evidence for their development, and as a mechanism by which development occurs.

Increasingly active search behavior emerges after 4 months, marking the onset of nascent objectification. Piaget outlined five examples, in roughly chronological order (i.e., the order in which they could be elicited). The first was *visual accommodation to rapid movements,* which occurs when an infant responds to a dropped object by looking down toward the floor, behavior that becomes more systematic when the infant herself drops it. A second behavior, *interrupted prehension,* refers to the infant's attempts to reacquire an object that was dropped or taken from his hand if it is out of sight briefly and within easy reach. (There is no search if the object is fully hidden.) *Deferred circular reactions* describes the child's gestures when interrupted during object-oriented play activity, resuming the game after some delay (involving memory of object, actions, and context). *Reconstruction of an invisible whole from a visible fraction* occurs when, for example, the child retrieves an object from underneath a cover when only a part of the object was visible. Finally, the infant engages in *removal of obstacles preventing perception* when, for example, he pulls a cover away from his face during peek-a-boo, or withdraws a fully hidden toy from beneath a blanket.

Beginning at around eight months of age, the infant will often search actively for a fully hidden object. But search may not be systematic when the object is first hidden at one location, successfully found, then hidden in another location, as the infant watches. Here, the infant often removes the obstacle at the object's first location, even though she subsequently saw it hidden somewhere else, a response commonly known as the A-not-B error. The transition to full objectification is completed across the next year or so as the infant first solves the problem of multiple visible displacements, searching at the last location visited by the object, and then solves the problem of multiple invisible displacements. For Piaget, systematic search revealed a decoupling of the object from the action, and revealed a knowledge of the infant's body itself as merely one object among many, brought into an allocentric system of spatially organized objects and events.

Objections have been raised to Piaget's account of development of object perception, on two grounds. First, some researchers have questioned whether cognitive development is heavily dependent on manual experience, whether infant cognition is purely "sensorimotor," and whether early concepts of objects and people are subjective, not objective. The second objection, related to the first, is based on claims of infant precocity, especially in terms of object representations across occlusion, leading many researchers to abandon Piagetian theory in favor of views of object concepts that deemphasize developmental mechanisms. These views are discussed next.

Nativist Theory

A central tenet of nativist theory is that a limited number of early-emerging kinds of knowledge form a central core around which more diverse, mature cognitive capacities are later elaborated. That is, some kinds of knowledge are innate. Theories of innate object knowledge have been proposed: concepts of objects as obeying physical constraints, such as persistence and solidity across occlusion. Three arguments have been mounted for these hypothesized innate object concepts. First, evidence of object knowledge can be observed in very young infants, perhaps too early for it to have derived from postnatal learning (Spelke, Breinlinger, Macomber, & Jacobson, 1992). Second, infants' detection of apparent violations of physical constraints has been proposed to arise from experience with contrastive evidence, opportunities to observe objects behaving in a manner consistent or inconsistent with a particular concept (Baillargeon, 1994). If this proposal is correct, then a concept of persistence across occlusion must be innate, because it cannot have been acquired from observing contrastive evidence: There simply are no observable events in the real world that demonstrate that an object abruptly ceases to exist. Third, there is evidence from nonhuman animals and anatomical specialization in humans for commonality of function across species, and commonality of structure across individuals, suggesting an inevitability of certain concepts that is "programmed" via evolutionary pressure (Dehaene, 1997).

There is a wealth of evidence from a variety of laboratories and experimental settings for representations of objects as spatiotemporally coherent and persistent for short durations of occlusion, representations that appear to be functional by

3 to 4 months after birth (e.g., Clifton, Rochat, Litovsky, & Perris, 1991; Luo, Baillargeon, Brueckner, & Munakata, 2003). Such evidence is inconsistent with some of the claims of Piagetian theory because it is difficult to reconcile young infants' lack of manual experience, a principal mechanism of development, in Piaget's view, with functional representations of object persistence during brief periods of occlusion. In contrast, such evidence is consistent with the claims of nativist theory.

Nevertheless, unequivocal evidence for innate, unlearned object concepts has not yet been reported. The reasoning underlying the possibility of unlearned knowledge, moreover, would appear to be fallacious: It may not be possible to obtain convincing support for a negative prediction. Evidence *against* functional perception of occlusion in newborn infants, in contrast, is strong, obviating the possibility of object concepts at birth, and evidence in favor of a role for learning in infants' occlusion perception is beginning to emerge. These two lines of evidence are described in subsequent sections.

LEARNING TO PERCEIVE CONTINUITY ACROSS A SPATIAL GAP

Kellman and Spelke (1983) devised a task to examine the perceptual equivalence of two identical forms, one of which was partially occluded; this paradigm exploits the tendency of infants to look longer at a novel visual stimulus relative to a familiar one. After exposure to a partly occluded rod, 4-month-old infants looked longer at two rod parts than at a complete object, implying a representation of unity in the original, partly occluded stimulus (Fig. 3–2). When newborn infants were tested in a similar procedure, however, they responded to a partly occluded object display solely on the basis of its visible parts and did not perceive completion behind the occluder (Slater et al., 1990; Valenza, Zulian, & Leo, 2005). Johnson and Aslin (1995) found that, under some conditions, two-month-olds appeared to perceive

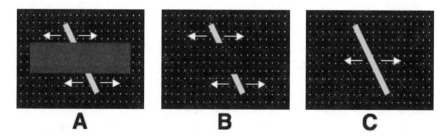

Figure 3–2. Schematic depictions of displays used to examine the development of spatial completion in infancy. (A) A partly occluded rod moves back and forth behind an occluding box. (B) and (C) Broken rod and complete rod test displays. After habituation to (A), a preference for either (B) or (C) is taken as evidence that infants perceived unity of the visible moving surfaces, or disjoint surfaces, respectively.

unity, as when the occluder is made narrow and the distance of perceptual interpolation is reduced, relative to a wide-occluder display in which two-month-olds provided no evidence of unity perception (Johnson & Náñez, 1995). Manipulating proximity of visible surfaces has little effect on neonates' perception of unity, however (Slater, Johnson, Brown, & Badenoch, 1996). Occlusion perception, therefore, presents a substantial challenge to the visual system at birth.

What are the mechanisms of change across the first several postnatal months toward perception of continuity across a spatial gap? Little is known, yet this question is vital to our understanding of object perception. To address this question, I recently examined predictions drawn from two current theoretical perspectives: nativist theory, described previously, and constructivist theory, which is based on principles of information processing.

According to a nativist "core principles" account, infants are predisposed to perceive objects as structured, solid entities, persisting across occlusion (Spelke, 1990). According to a contrasting constructivist account, infants are limited in the capacity to organize simpler components into more complex wholes (Cohen, Chaput, & Cashon, 2003). These two accounts provide opposing views of development of perceptual completion. On the core principles account, young infants respond to objects as coherent solid bodies, and occlusion perception is available early. On the constructivist account, the young infant's visual system processes visible parts before coherent wholes, and occlusion perception emerges with time.

The evidence recounted previously on perceptual completion in neonates (Slater et al. 1990, 1996; Valenza et al., 2005) would appear to be inconsistent with the core principles view, but this account has an explanation. Motion detection is limited in very young infants (Wattam-Bell, 1996; Banton & Bertenthal, 1997), and perceptual completion in static displays has not been observed until six to eight months (Craton, 1996). Moreover, motion-direction discrimination and perceptual completion are first observed at two months, leading to speculation that limits in perceptual completion are rooted in a failure to detect common motion: If common motion is unavailable, either by an inability to see it or by the use of static displays, then perceptual completion is precluded in young infants (Kellman & Arterberry, 1998). Therefore, the visual system is predisposed to view objects as solid and enduring and uses motion as a primary cue to identify unity of objects. Motion-processing mechanisms must develop before this cue is available.

This hypothesis leads to a prediction: Infants should achieve perceptual completion in any occlusion display in which rod parts undergo common motion and in which that motion is detectable. The constructivist account provides an opposing prediction: There will be conditions in which infants detect the motions of visible surfaces that lead to the edge of an occluder, and yet not perceive occlusion, because perceptual completion is a higher order perceptual function than simple registration of visible object parts.

These contrasting predictions were tested by Johnson (2004). Johnson noted that previous experiments with young infants revealed that perceptual completion in rod-and-box displays is facilitated when the moving rod parts are aligned across a narrow occluder, but disrupted when rod parts are misaligned or when

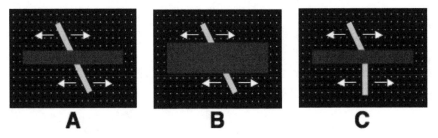

Figure 3–3. Schematic depictions of displays used by Johnson (2004) to investigate spatial completion in two-month-old infants. Infants provided evidence of unity perception in (A), but not in (B) or (C).

the occluder is wide (Johnson & Aslin, 1995, 1996). These effects were replicated in an initial experiment: Two-month-olds provided evidence of completion when the visible rod parts moved in tandem behind a narrow occluder (Fig. 3–3A), but not in a wide-occluder display (Fig. 3–3B), or in a display in which the rod parts were misaligned (Fig. 3–3C). In a second experiment, however, two-month-olds failed to discriminate between two different kinds of rod motion (same phase versus opposite phase) when occluder size and visible rod orientation across the two experiments were held constant (Fig. 3–4). These results indicate that infants register the motions and orientations of object parts prior, in development, to perceiving organized wholes (in the present case, occlusion), as stipulated by a constructivist account.

Yet the outcome of the Johnson (2004) experiments does not provide unequivocal evidence that infants discriminated among various kinds of motion because performance may have stemmed solely from a mechanism sensitive to *changes in position* of visible rod parts, rather than a mechanism sensitive to motion. More broadly, *all* extant studies of infants' perceptual completion in dynamic displays (with a single exception: Johnson & Aslin, 1998) are subject to this interpretation, and so the role of motion sensitivity remains unknown.

Also left open is the central question of precisely what developmental mechanisms might support the ontogeny of perceptual completion. A study described by Johnson, Slemmer, and Amso (2004) begins to provide an answer. Three-month-old infants were tested in a perceptual completion task using the habituation paradigm described previously. The infants' eye movements were recorded with a corneal-reflection eye tracker during the habituation phase of the experiment. We reported differences in scanning patterns between infants whose posthabituation test display preferences indicated unity perception and those infants who provided evidence of perceiving disjoint surfaces: "Perceivers," relative to "non-perceivers," tended to scan more in the vicinity of the two visible rod segments and to scan back and forth between them. Johnson and Johnson (2000) reported as well that there is a shift across 2 to 4 months in the extent to which young infants overcome a "top bias," when visual attention is directed preferentially or exclusively toward the upper portions of a rod-and-box stimulus. Ontogeny of perceptual completion,

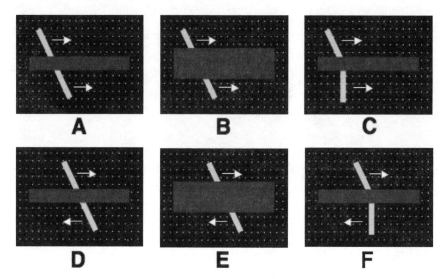

Figure 3–4. Schematic depictions of displays used by Johnson (2004) to investigate discrimination of "corresponding" (top row) from "converse" (bottom row) motion in two-month-old infants. After habituation to either (A) or (D), infants viewed test trials consisting of alternating presentations of both displays, and showed a reliable preference for the novel motion. The same is true for stimulus pairs (B) and (E), and for (C) and (F). This implies that motion discrimination, as tested here, is impaired neither by occluder width nor by edge misalignment, each of which impair unity perception in young infants.

therefore, seems to be accompanied by an inclination to direct visual attention to relevant aspects of a stimulus, in this case, the upper and lower moving rod parts.

What is the relation between infants' visual attention and motion sensitivity, and what are their contributions to perceptual completion? To address this question, Johnson, Davidow, Hall-Haro, and Frank (in press) observed infant performance in four tasks on the same day, asking whether motion sensitivity is related directly to perceptual completion in early development. If it were, we predicted a correlation between performance on motion-direction discrimination and perceptual-completion tasks, in addition to specific patterns of visual attention. If not, we predicted that performance on the motion-direction discrimination task would be independent of both perceptual completion and attention toward rod parts. Motion sensitivity was assessed by recording preferential looking toward a relatively complex region of motion in random-dot kinematograms (Wattam-Bell, 1996; Johnson & Mason, 2002). As a manipulation check to ensure that our measure of motion sensitivity was a valid index of true motion-direction discrimination, and to provide a second index of oculomotor performance, we observed infants' performance on an oculomotor smooth pursuit task. It has been speculated that motion-direction discrimination and smooth pursuit are subserved by the same cortical mechanisms (Johnson, 1990; Kellman & Arterberry, 1998), but this has never been tested directly.

The results were clear. Performance in the motion-sensitivity task was strongly correlated with smooth-pursuit performance: The greater the preference for complex motion in random-dot kinematograms, the higher the smooth-pursuit gain (the ratio of oculomotor pursuit to target speed), a measure that has been thought to rely on cortical motion–sensitive mechanisms (Johnson, 1990). In contrast, motion-sensitivity performance was uncorrelated with a second measure of oculomotor performance: the tendency to scan consistently between regions of rod motion as opposed to demonstrating a top bias. Nor was motion sensitivity related to perceptual completion. However, a measure of a top bias in scanning, provided by recording eye movements as infants viewed an occlusion display, was negatively correlated with the measure of perceptual completion. This corroborates earlier findings in which scanning was found to be related to occlusion perception in rod-and-box stimuli (Johnson et al., 2004).

These results suggest that our tasks tapped into separate visual functions, both undergoing development at two to three months. One function computes direction of motion and motion direction, rather than simple change in position, and supports control of eye movements to track motion of small targets in the environment. The second function identifies objects and supports perception of the unity of the visible portions of a partly occluded surface. Together, these results suggest that development of perceptual completion relies less on cortical maturation and on motion sensitivity than on the infant's own oculomotor behavior. Infants appear to "assemble" surfaces in the visual environment that are spatially segregated via active examination of visible parts: their color and luminance (Johnson & Aslin, 2000), orientation (Johnson & Aslin, 1996), and displacement (Jusczyk, Johnson, Spelke, & Kennedy, 1999), the latter of which might or might not derive from motion sensitivity. The importance of motion to perceptual completion, on this account, is its contribution to segmentation, rather than to unity perception directly.

Recently, Amso and Johnson (2006) investigated in greater detail the nature of the relation between scanning behavior and perceptual completion. We noted that eye movements in the first several months after birth often appear to be relatively more reflexive than deliberate, driven by salient external information. At three to four months of age, infants exhibit more voluntary or endogenous oculomotor control and inhibition of reflexive eye movements, indicating emergence of visual selective attention (Amso & Johnson, 2005). Visual selective attention supports the selection of certain stimuli for further processing while subsequently ignoring or suppressing competing stimuli. Recall that Johnson et al. (2004) recorded eye movements in a group of 3-month-olds during the habituation portion of a perceptual-completion task. Infants who explored the most salient display regions the rod parts and their motion, more effectively were also those whose posthabituation preference indicated unity perception (the perceivers). Non-perceivers, however, tended to be less organized in their orienting, focusing more on the display background or the occluder. The bright blue occluder in these displays was substantially larger than the rod, as was the textured background (see Fig. 3–2), potentially drawing attention away from the moving rod parts. Attending to either of these regions may not provide infants with the information necessary to perceive unity. Gathering the information pertinent to perceptual completion thus requires a mechanism that suppresses, rather than reflexively attends to, these competing display elements.

To examine the operation of this putative mechanism, we replicated the methods of Johnson et al. (2004) with infants at the same age (three months), and added a new visual search task, given in the same testing session. The visual search task was designed to engage, in two conditions, both visual selective attention and reflexive orienting to salient stimuli. The competition condition consisted of a field of static homogeneous vertical bars with a single target bar, tilted from the vertical, at one of three possible orientations. The *control* condition was identical to the competition condition, except the target was vertically oriented and translated laterally at one of three possible speeds (see Fig. 3–5). We reasoned, first, that performance in the competition condition would require visual selective attention, as indexed by increased latency for target selection, whereas the control condition would require simple reflexive orienting. Second, we reasoned that infants who employ visual selective attention should be affected by an increase in target/ distracter similarity in the competition condition by showing the increases in response latency and target selection, relative to infants who rely more on reflexive orienting. Finally, and most critically for purposes of examining developmental mechanism, we reasoned that performance on the visual search and perceptual-completion tasks would be related if completion, as we speculate, arises from the appropriate allocation of visual selective attention.

Our predictions were confirmed. Performance in the control condition, our gauge of reflexive orienting, was near ceiling for all infants. In contrast, there was a range of performance in the competition condition, our gauge of visual

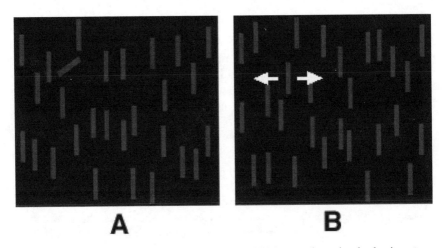

Figure 3–5. Displays used by Amso and Johnson (2006) to explore visual selective attention in three-month-old infants. In each display, a target is set among vertical, static distracters (red bars) that are pseudo-randomly distributed. (A) An orientation-defined target. (B) A motion-defined target.

selective attention, providing evidence that this task was challenging to this age group. In particular, there were reliable differences in the proportion of targets detected (perceivers detected more than non-perceivers did), and in latencies to detect targets (perceivers' latencies were longer than non-perceivers'). These results indicate that visual selective attention undergoes substantial developments in efficiency at selecting some targets and inhibiting others in three-month-olds, and contributes to other perceptual tasks, such as perceptual completion. Most likely, visual selective attention promotes prolonged inspection of display elements relevant for unity perception. That is, developments in oculomotor control, alongside attentional engagement, resulted in superior information acquisition during the habituation phase of the unity experiment. On this view, therefore, perceptual completion is learned and stems from the emergence of a general-purpose ability to efficiently obtain information alongside a time of experience during which to gather pertinent information.

LEARNING TO PERCEIVE CONTINUITY ACROSS A SPATIOTEMPORAL GAP

Johnson, Bremner, Slater, Mason, Foster, and Cheshire (2003) devised a task to examine the perceptual equivalence of two trajectories, one of which was partially occluded; this paradigm, like that one that Kellman and Spelke (1983) employed for similar purposes, exploits infants' tendency to look longer at a novel visual stimulus relative to a familiar one. After exposure to a center-occluded trajectory, six-month-old infants looked longer at two disconnected segments of trajectory than at a continuous trajectory, implying a representation of continuity of the moving object in the original stimulus (Fig. 3–6). In contrast, four-month-olds looked longer at a continuous-trajectory test stimulus relative to the disconnected segments, under identical conditions, implying perception of a discontinuous path of motion

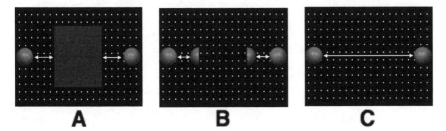

Figure 3–6. Schematic depictions of displays used to examine development of spatiotemporal completion in infancy. (A) A ball moves back and forth, its trajectory partly occluded by a box. (B) and (C) Discontinuous and continuous trajectory test displays. After habituation to (A), a preference for either (B) or (C) is taken as evidence that infants perceived unity of the trajectory, or disconnected segments of trajectory, respectively.

during habituation. However, when tested with a narrow occluder, four-month-olds' test display preferences reversed, indicating that perception of continuity across a spatiotemporal gap (i.e., a gap in perception across both space and time) is available, in fragile form, at this age (Fig. 3–7a). Two-month-olds showed no consistent test display preferences when observed in the narrow-occluder condition.

More recently, Bremner et al. (2005) reported that reducing occlusion time led to continuity perception in four-month-olds, accomplished either by increasing the size of the object, a green ball, such that it was nearly the same size as the occluder, a blue box (Fig. 3–7d), or by speeding up the object when it was occluded, such that it emerged more quickly than when its trajectory speed held steady across the entirety of the event. We also found that four-month-olds' perception of continuity in narrow-occluder displays was not impaired when a temporal delay, equivalent to the time out of view in the wide-occluder event under conditions of steady object speed, was imposed, this time by slowing down the object when it was occluded. In other recent work, Bremner et al. (2007) found that four-month-olds' continuity perception in a narrow-occluder condition was disrupted when the object trajectory

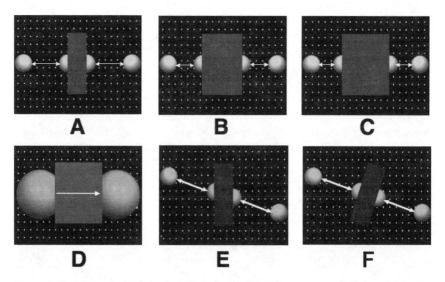

Figure 3–7. Schematic depictions of displays used to examine spatial and temporal attributes of stimuli that influence four-month-olds' spatiotemporal completion. Four-month-olds provide evidence of completion in a narrow-occluder display (A) but appear to perceive trajectory segments as disconnected when the occluder is wide and thus the visible segments of the trajectory are separated across both space and time (C). In (B), the perception of continuity is indeterminate. When a larger object moves behind the occluder, the temporal demands are eased because the object emerges almost immediately after occlusion, and continuity is achieved (D). Four-month-olds provide no evidence of completion of an oblique trajectory (E) unless the occluder, too, is oblique such that the orientations of occluder and trajectory are orthogonal (F).

was oblique relative to the background and the box (Fig. 3–7e). When the box itself was rotated to an angle orthogonal to the trajectory, however, continuity perception obtained (Fig. 3–7f). These results are surprising given that occlusion events in the real world are rarely matched by the precision that characterizes the spatial (e.g., geometric) and temporal parameters of our stimuli; nevertheless, young infants are clearly sensitive to such parameters.

The finding that strict temporal and spatial constraints apply to young infants' perception of object trajectories evokes accounts of infants' responses to occlusion events that are framed in terms of short-term storage of sensory information (e.g., Haith, 1998); accounts framed in terms of concrete knowledge or concepts of object permanence do not explain such results well (e.g., Spelke et al., 1992). At minimum, such "knowledge" appears to be quite inflexible in young infants. But filling in a spatiotemporal gap seems different than the majority of the infant cognition literature concerned with object representations because this literature is concerned predominately with understanding persistence of a static object that was previously viewed and then occluded. In tasks designed to tap spatiotemporal continuity, infants never see the object on the hidden part of its trajectory, and a full account of development of object representations must explain how infants come to interpolate an image of the object during its period behind the screen. This is more than simple storage of a previously perceived event across a particular range of positions (those hidden by the occluder) because the occluded portion of the trajectory was never experienced directly. Instead, it seems more plausible to posit that young infants' visual systems interpolate a continuous trajectory, a kind of spatiotemporal filling-in, and that this mechanism is operative only under short spatial or temporal occlusion periods. A second conclusion from this work is that four months is a pivotal age in the process of perceiving trajectory continuity: Depending on display characteristics, four-month-olds may perceive an occluded trajectory as composed of a single continuous event, as composed of discrete path segments, or as indeterminate.

In the previous section, I presented an argument for learning as a viable developmental mechanism leading to perceptual completion across a spatial gap. Recently, my colleagues and I discovered that learning may also play a role in the development of perceptual completion across a spatiotemporal gap (Johnson, Amso, & Slemmer, 2003). The two kinds of learning differ, however, in important ways. Experiments on learning to perceive spatial completion provide evidence that infants learn from their own actions, via visual selective attention. Experiments on learning to perceive spatiotemporal completion, in contrast, provide evidence that infants learn from passive experience, viewing unoccluded trajectories. These experiments are described next.

Johnson, Amso et al. (2003) used an oculomotor-anticipation paradigm to examine young infants' responses to occluded trajectory displays (Fig. 3–6a). We reasoned that perception of the persistence of a moving object that had recently become occluded would be revealed by a shift of gaze to the place of object reemergence. We recorded gaze shifts in four- and six-month-olds in a "baseline" condition, the goal of which was to examine baseline performance in this type of task. Infants viewed eight 30-second presentations of the moving object event, each presentation consisting of six complete left-right cycles of motion (96 excursions of the object total). We found, not surprisingly, that six-month-olds produced a reliably higher proportion of anticipations, relative to four-month-olds. Baseline anticipation proportions in the younger age group were comparable to those of a separate group of four-month-olds who viewed unpredictable trajectory-occlusion events, in which the place of re-emergence (near or far side) was determined randomly. This corroborates findings from habituation experiments providing evidence of spatiotemporal perceptual completion in six-month-olds, but not four-month-olds (Johnson, Bremner et al., 2003), unless the younger infants view narrow-occluder displays (Johnson, Bremner et al., 2003) or displays in which the object is hidden for only a very short time (Bremner et al., 2005). That is, there is little indication that four-month-olds' spatiotemporal completion is robust, but performance improves within several months.

To examine the effects of learning in the oculomotor anticipation paradigm, separate groups of four- and six-month-olds were provided with "training" in the form of experience viewing unoccluded moving-object trajectories. Infants in the training condition were first presented with four 30-second presentations of an unoccluded moving-object event (i.e., Fig. 3–6c), followed by four 30-second presentations of the occluded-trajectory display (i.e., Fig. 3–6a). Performance was not improved in the six-month-olds in the training condition relative to baseline, but the proportion of anticipations in four-month-olds in the training condition was not statistically different from that of older infants in both the baseline and training conditions. A brief time of training, therefore, was sufficient to facilitate performance levels equivalent to two months of development in the conditions we provided. This effect extended to a second training condition in which four-month-olds were exposed to vertical unoccluded trajectories, followed by the same horizontal occluded trajectories shown to infants in the baseline and training conditions, indicating that the learning effect was not simply a matter of entraining horizontal eye movements. Notably, performance did not improve across trials in either age in any of these conditions, providing evidence that the infants did not learn from repeated exposure to visible motion on either side of the display. Instead, effects of learning were limited to conditions of initial exposure to unoccluded trajectories, followed by viewing of partly occluded trajectory events.

Additional recent work has examined more closely the conditions under which four-month-olds can learn to perceive spatiotemporal completion. In the real world, moving objects often emit sound, and little is known about whether infants can use multimodal information to make predictions about occluded objects. Kirkham and Johnson (2008) investigated the contributions of auditory cues to perception of visual occlusion with methods similar to those of Johnson, Amso et al. (2003), but with displays in which a sound was presented from two speakers on either side of the display monitor. In a "static" sound condition, the sound was emitted from both speakers simultaneously, and in a "dynamic" sound condition, the sound "traveled" between the speakers in tandem with the position of the moving object. As in previous work, oculomotor anticipations provided an index of perception of completion of the object's path. Performance in the static condition was comparable to earlier findings in terms of proportion of eye movements that anticipated the object's re-emergence, but performance in the dynamic condition was facilitated to levels similar to that of the older infants, and trained younger infants, observed by Johnson, Amso et al. (2003). Performance was not simply determined by the direction of the sound source (e.g., the left or right speaker), because during the time at which eye movements were recorded (the period of object occlusion), the sound emanated from both speakers simultaneously. In addition, sensitivity to sound movement alone would predict eye movements that moved *with* the visual display, not eye movements that arrived *ahead* of the visual display. Instead, these results suggest that the infants inferred trajectory continuity by integrating auditory and visual information. Intermodal integration, therefore, may provide a scaffold upon which to build increasingly complex representations in infancy (cf. Bahrick & Lickliter, 2000).

Discussions of experiments presented thus far in this section have portrayed young infants as capable learners whose performance in perceptual-completion tasks is readily facilitated by a variety of sources of information. Recent research is beginning to explore the limits of learning (Johnson & Shuwairi, in press). One important question undertaken by these ongoing experiments concerns how long the training effect might last, a question that bears implications for how occlusion events are perceived and learned in the real world. We have addressed this question with a series of training regimens with four-month-olds, such as imposing a 30-min delay between training (with an unoccluded trajectory, as described previously) and test (with a center-occluded trajectory). In this case, the proportion of oculomotor anticipation reverts to baseline levels; in other cases, such as training with fewer unoccluded trials, the proportion of anticipation does not rise to the levels seen after "full" (i.e., 2 mins) training. Learning in this paradigm, therefore, may be limited by restrictions in encoding or consolidation into long-term memory. These results imply that simply exposing young infants to a few object trajectories is not sufficient to give rise to robust and enduring spatiotemporal completion skills. Such skills likely require months of exposure to dynamic occlusion events in the real world.

CONCLUSIONS

The experiments described in this chapter were designed to fill a void in our knowledge of infant perceptual and cognitive development. Until recently, developmental mechanisms that support the perception of occlusion have remained largely unknown, in favor of viewpoints that ascribe principal responsibility for development to manual activity (the Piagetian view) or to innate knowledge of objects (the nativist view); neither viewpoint is capable of accounting for the findings of experiments that examine young infants' perception of partly occluded objects and object trajectories. I presented evidence for the importance of learning as a viable mechanism of development: learning by doing, as when infants come to perceive the unity of a partly occluded surface by directing visual attention to its visible parts, and learning by seeing, as when infants' oculomotor anticipation of a moving, occluded object is facilitated by previous experience with unoccluded trajectories. This account is explicitly developmental, mechanistic, and process-oriented and seeks to understand how infants assemble visible parts into wholes in real time from existing perceptual and cognitive skills.

The learning account I have described fits well with several related lines of evidence that characterize the young infant's visual system and its development:

- Perception of occlusion arises with the onset of visual experience, as re-counted in the present chapter.
- The human visual system is organized at birth. Neonates tend to direct visual attention toward areas of high contrast (i.e., edges) and motion, providing suitable conditions for extracting information specifying segregated surfaces (Haith, 1980; Slater, 1995).
- Natural scenes are richly structured and characterized by a considerable degree of statistical predictability across space and time (Field, 1994), and there is computational evidence that development of response properties of visual neurons exploits redundancy in the input (Olshausen & Field, 1996).
- Infants clearly are prodigious learners, responding readily to classical and operant conditioning (Bower, 1974) and exhibiting statistical learning soon after birth (Saffran, Aslin, & Newport, 1996; Kirkham, Slemmer, & John-son, 2002).
- Finally, infants receive an abundance of exposure to the visual environment before occlusion perception: Neonates spend 2 to 3 hours per day in a state of quiet alertness (Wolff, 1966), engaged in active scanning of the environment when in this state (Haith, 1980). Like adults, young infants produce 2 to 3 eye movements per second (Bronson, 1974; Johnson et al., 2004). By two months, the proportion of the infant's active and alert state has roughly dou-bled (Roffwarg, Muzio, & Dement, 1966). This provides the infant with sev-eral hundred hours of visual experience, having executed some 2.5 million eye movements prior to functional occlusion perception (Johnson & Aslin, 1995). It is unknown how many instances of object occlusion are available for viewing during this time (this number may be incalculable because occlu-sion is ubiquitous in the visual environment) or how many of those instances attract infants' active attention. Regardless, infants receive ample opportu-nity to examine the visual environment and learn much from it within the first several postnatal months.

Recently, a great deal of progress has been made in understanding the statistics of the visual world, and how visual development may rely on environmental struc-ture (e.g., Simoncelli & Olshausen, 2001). Much of this research effort has been geared toward understanding developing responses to orientation, color, edges, and correlations in the input, using computational models. Characterizing occlusion in the real world in a similar fashion, and its role in human visual development, would go a long way toward advancing current knowledge of the developmental origins of object perception in infancy.

References

Amso, D., & Johnson, S. P. (2005). Selection and inhibition in infancy: Evidence from the spatial negative priming paradigm. *Cognition, 95,* B27–B36.

Amso, D., & Johnson, S. P. (2006). Learning by selection: Visual search and object perception in young infants. *Developmental Psychology, 6,* 1236–1245.

Bahrick, L. E., & Lickliter, R. (2000). Intersensory redundancy guides attentional selectivity and perceptual learning in infancy. *Developmental Psychology, 36,* 190–201.

Baillargeon, R. (1994). How do infants learn about the physical world? *Current Directions in Psychological Science, 3,* 133–140.

Banton, T., & Bertenthal, B. I. (1997). Multiple developmental pathways for motion processing. Optometry and Vision Science, 74, 751–760.

Bower, T. G. R. (1974). *Development in infancy.* San Francisco: Freeman.

Bremner, J. G., Johnson, S. P., Slater, A., Mason, U., Cheshire, A., & Spring, J. (2007). Conditions for young infants' failure to perceive trajectory continuity. *Developmental Science, 10,* 613–624.

Bremner, J. G., Johnson, S. P., Slater, A. M., Mason, U., Foster, K., Cheshire, A., & Spring, J. (2005). Conditions for young infants' perception of object trajectories. *Child Development, 74,* 1029–1043.

Bronson, G. W. (1974). The postnatal growth of visual capacity. *Child Development, 45,* 873–890.

Clifton, R. K., Rochat, P., Litovsky, R. Y., & Perris, E. E. (1991). Object representation guides infants' reaching in the dark. *Journal of Experimental Psychology: Human Perception and Performance, 17,* 323–329.

Cohen, L. B., Chaput, H. H., & Cashon, C. H. (2002). A constructivist model of infant cognition. *Cognitive Development, 17,* 1323–1343.

Craton, L. E. (1996). The development of perceptual completion abilities: Infants' perception of stationary, partly occluded objects. *Child Development, 67,* 890–904.

Dehaene, S. (1997). *The number sense: How the mind creates mathematics.* New York: Oxford University Press.

Field, D. J. (1994). What is the goal of sensory coding? *Neural Computation, 6,* 559–601.

Haith, M. M. (1980). *Rules that babies look by: The organization of newborn visual activity.* Hillsdale, NJ: Erlbaum.

Haith, M. M. (1998). Who put the cog in infant cognition? Is rich interpretation too costly? *Infant Behavior & Development, 21,* 167–179.

Johnson, M. H. (1990). Cortical maturation and the development of visual attention in early infancy. *Journal of Cognitive Neuroscience, 2,* 81–95.

Johnson, S. P. (2004). Development of perceptual completion in infancy. *Psychological Science, 15,* 769–775.

Johnson, S. P., Amso, D., & Slemmer, J. A. (2003). Development of object concepts in infancy: Evidence for early learning in an eye tracking paradigm. *Proceedings of the National Academy of Sciences (USA), 100,* 10,568–10,573.

Johnson, S. P., & Aslin, R. N. (1995). Perception of object unity in 2-month-old infants. *Developmental Psychology, 31,* 739–745.

Johnson, S. P., & Aslin, R. N. (1996). Perception of object unity in young infants: The roles of motion, depth, and orientation. *Cognitive Development, 11,* 161–180.

Johnson, S. P., & Aslin, R. N. (1998). Young infants' perception of illusory contours in dynamic displays. *Perception, 27,* 341–353.

Johnson, S. P., & Aslin, R. N. (2000). Infants' perception of transparency. *Developmental Psychology, 36,* 808–816.

Johnson, S. P., Bremner, J. G., Slater, A., Mason, U., Foster, K., & Cheshire, A. (2003). Infants' perception of object trajectories. *Child Development, 74,* 94–108.

Johnson, S. P., Davidow, J., Hall-Haro, C., & Frank, M. C. (in press). Development of perceptual completion originates in information acquisition. *Developmental Psychology.*

Johnson, S. P., & Johnson, K. L. (2000). Early perception-action coupling: Eye movements and the development of object perception. *Infant Behavior & Development, 23,* 461–483.

Johnson, S. P., & Mason, U. (2002). Perception of kinetic illusory contours by 2-month-old infants. *Child Development, 73,* 22–34.

Johnson, S. P., & Náñez, J. E. (1995). Young infants' perception of object unity in two-dimensional displays. *Infant Behavior and Development, 18,* 133–143.

Johnson, S. P., & Shuwairi, S. M. (in press). Learning and memory facilitate predictive tracking in 4-month-olds. *Journal of Experimental Child Psychology.*

Johnson, S. P., Slemmer, J. A., & Amso, D. (2004). Where infants look determines how they see: Eye movements and object perception performance in 3-month-olds. *Infancy, 6,* 185–201.

Jusczyk, P. W., Johnson, S. P., Spelke, E. S., & Kennedy, L. J. (1999). Synchronous change and perception of object unity: Evidence from adults and infants. *Cognition, 71,* 257–288.

Kellman, P. J. (1993). Kinematic foundations of infant visual perception. In C. E. Granrud (Ed.), *Visual perception and cognition in infancy* (pp. 121–173). Hillsdale, NJ: Erlbaum.

Kellman, P. J., & Arterberry, M. E. (1998). *The cradle of knowledge: Development of perception in infancy.* Cambridge, MA: MIT Press.

Kellman, P. J., & Spelke, E. S. (1983). Perception of partly occluded objects in infancy. *Cognitive Psychology, 15,* 483–524.

Kirkham, N. Z., & Johnson, S. P. (2008). *Sound support: Intermodal information facilitates infants' perception of occlusion.* Revision in preparation.

Kirkham, N. Z., Slemmer, J. A., & Johnson, S. P. (2002). Visual statistical learning in infancy: Evidence for a domain general learning mechanism. *Cognition, 83,* B35–B42.

Needham, A., Baillargeon, R., & Kaufman, L. (1997). Object segregation in infancy. In C. Rovee-Collier and L. Lipsitt (Eds.), *Advances in infancy research* (Vol. 11, pp. 1–44). Greenwich, CT: Ablex.

Luo, Y., Baillargeon, R., Brueckner, L., & Munakata, Y. (2003). Reasoning about a hidden object after a delay: Evidence for robust representations in 5-month-old infants. *Cognition, 88,* B23–B32.

Olshausen, B. A., & Field, D. J. (1996). Emergence of simple-cell receptive field properties by learning a sparse code for natural images. *Nature, 381,* 607–609.

Piaget, J. (1954). *The construction of reality in the child* (M. Cook, Trans.). New York: Basic Books. (Original work published 1937)

Roffwarg, H. P., Muzio, J. N., & Dement, W. C. (1966). Ontogenetic development of the human sleep-dream cycle. *Science, 152,* 604–619.

Saffran. J. R., Aslin, R. N., & Newport, E. L. (1996). Statistical learning by 8-month-old infants. *Science, 274,* 1926–1928.

Simoncelli, E. P., & Olshausen, B. A. (2001). Natural image statistics and neural representation. *Annual Review of Neuroscience, 24,* 1193–1215.

Slater, A. (1995). Visual perception and memory at birth. In C. Rovee-Collier and L. P. Lipsitt (Eds.), *Advances in infancy research* (Vol. 9, pp. 107–162). Norwood, NJ: Ablex.

Slater, A., Johnson, S. P., Brown, E., & Badenoch, M. (1996). Newborn infants' perception of partly occluded objects. *Infant Behavior and Development, 19,* 145–148.

Slater, A., Morison, V., Somers, M., Mattock, A., Brown, E., & Taylor, D. (1990). Newborn and older infants' perception of partly occluded objects. *Infant Behavior & Development, 13,* 33–49.

Spelke, E. S. (1990). Principles of object perception. *Cognitive Science, 14,* 29–56.

Spelke, E. S., Breinlinger, K., Macomber, J., & Jacobson, K. (1992). Origins of knowledge. *Psychological Review, 99,* 605–632.

Valenza, E., Zulian, L., & Leo, I. (2005). The role of perceptual skills in newborns' perception of partly occluded objects. *Infancy, 8,* 1–20.

Wattam-Bell, J. (1996). Visual motion processing in 1-month-old infants: Habituation experiments. *Vision Research, 36,* 1679–1685.

Wolff, P. H. (1966). *Psychological Issues, 5*(1), serial no. 17.

Yonas, A., & Granrud, C. E. (1985). The development of sensitivity to kinetic, binocular, and pictorial depth information in human infants. In D. J. Ingle, M. Jeannerod, & D. N. Lee (Eds.), *Brain mechanisms and spatial vision* (pp. 113–145). Dordrecht: Martinus Nijhoff.

4

An Account of Infants' Physical Reasoning

RENÉE BAILLARGEON, JIE LI, WEITING NG,
AND SYLVIA YUAN, UNIVERSITY OF ILLINOIS
AT URBANA-CHAMPAIGN

Adults possess a great deal of knowledge about the physical world, and developmental researchers have long been interested in uncovering the roots of this knowledge in infancy. Two main questions have guided this research: What expectations do infants possess, at different ages, about physical events, and how do they attain these expectations?

Piaget (1952, 1954) was the first researcher to systematically investigate the development of infants' physical knowledge. He examined infants' actions in various tasks and concluded that young infants understand very little about the physical events they observe. For example, Piaget noted that infants younger than 8 months do not search for objects they have watched being hidden, and concluded that they do not yet realize that objects continue to exist when hidden.

One difficulty with Piaget's (1952, 1954) experimental approach is that action tasks do not test only infants' physical knowledge (e.g., Boudreau & Bushnell, 2000; Berthier et al., 2001; Keen & Berthier, 2004; Hespos & Baillargeon, 2006, 2008). In order to search for a hidden object, for example, infants must not only represent the existence and location of the object but also plan and execute appropriate actions to retrieve it. Because young infants' information-processing resources are sharply limited, they may fail at a search task not because they do not yet understand that objects continue to exist when hidden but because the combined demands of the task overwhelm their processing resources.

Because of the problems inherent in interpreting negative results in action tasks, researchers have developed alternative experimental approaches to study the development of infant's physical knowledge (e.g., Bower, 1974; Baillargeon, Spelke, & Wasserman, 1985; Leslie & Keeble, 1987; Luo, Baillargeon, Brueckner, & Munakata, 2003; Kaufman, Csibra, & Johnson, 2004). The most widely used of these alternative approaches is the violation-of-expectation (VOE) method. In a typical experiment, infants see two test events: an expected event, which is consistent with the expectation being examined in the experiment, and an unexpected event, which violates this expectation. With appropriate controls, evidence that infants look reliably longer at the unexpected than at the expected event is taken to indicate that infants (1) possess the expectation under investigation, (2) detect the violation in the unexpected event, and (3) are "surprised" by this violation. The term "surprise" is used here simply as a shorthand descriptor to denote a state of heightened attention or interest caused by an expectation violation (for discussion of the method, see Wang, Baillargeon, & Brueckner, 2004).

Experiments conducted using the VOE method, in our laboratory and elsewhere, have revealed two main findings: First, and contrary to Piaget's (1952, 1954) claims, even very young infants possess expectations about various physical events; second, infants' expectations undergo significant and systematic developments during the first year of life (for recent reviews, see Baillargeon, 2002, 2004; Baillargeon, Li, Luo, & Wang, 2006).

This chapter is divided into four sections. In the first, we propose an account of the development of infants' physical reasoning that builds on VOE and other findings. In presenting this account, for ease of description, we focus on infants' reasoning about events in which objects become hidden behind, inside, or under other objects. In the second and third sections of the chapter, we describe new lines of research that are designed to test and extend the account. In the final section, we offer a few concluding remarks.

AN ACCOUNT OF INFANTS' PHYSICAL REASONING

We assume that when infants watch a physical event, different computational systems form different representations simultaneously, for distinct purposes (Baillargeon et al., 2006; Li, Baillargeon, & Simons, 2006b; Wang & Baillargeon, 2006, 2008b). In particular, infants' object-representation system encodes information about the properties of the objects in the event, for recognition and categorization purposes. At the same time, infants' physical-reasoning system forms a specialized physical representation of the event, to interpret and predict its outcome. We focus here on this second system.

The information infants include in their physical representation of an event is interpreted in terms of their core knowledge. This knowledge is assumed to be innate and to consist of a few concepts and principles that provide infants with a shallow causal framework for understanding events (e.g., Spelke, Breinlinger, Macomber, & Jacobson, 1992; Carey & Spelke, 1994; Leslie, 1994; Spelke, 1994; Leslie, 1995; Spelke, Phillips, & Woodward, 1995b; Wilson & Keil, 2000; Baillargeon et al., 2006). For example, Leslie (1994) has suggested that, from birth, infants interpret physical events in accord with a primitive concept of force. When watching an object push another object, infants represent a force—like a directional arrow—being exerted by the first object onto the second one. In Leslie's words, infants' physical-reasoning system "takes, as input, descriptions that make explicit the geometry of the objects contained in a scene, their arrangements and their motions, and onto such descriptions paints the mechanical properties of the scenario" (p. 128).

Of most relevance to the present discussion is the *principle of persistence*, which states that objects exist continuously in time and space, retaining their physical properties as they do so (Baillargeon, 2008). The persistence principle has many corollaries; for example, that stationary objects, whether visible or hidden, exist continuously in time; that moving objects, whether visible or hidden, follow continuous paths; that two objects, whether visible or hidden and whether stationary or moving, cannot occupy the same space at the same time; and that an object of a particular size, shape, pattern, and color, whether stationary or moving and whether visible or hidden, cannot spontaneously become an object of a different size, shape, pattern, or color.

The principle of persistence subsumes and extends two of the principles proposed by Spelke and her colleagues (e.g., Spelke et al., 1992; Carey & Spelke, 1994; Spelke, 1994; Spelke et al., 1995b): the principles of continuity (objects exist and move continuously in time and space) and cohesion (objects are connected and bounded entities). According to these principles, infants should be surprised if an object disappears into thin air (continuity) or breaks apart (cohesion), but not if it simply changes size, shape, pattern, or color. According to the persistence principle, in contrast, infants should be surprised by all of these violations (provided, as always, that the infants represent sufficient information to detect them). The principle of persistence thus goes beyond the principles of continuity and cohesion: All other things being equal, objects are expected to retain all of their physical properties as events unfold—to persist, as they are, through time and space.[1] We return to these issues, and to the experimental evidence that led us to adopt the persistence principle, in a later section.

Detecting Basic Violations Through Core Knowledge

In the first few months of life, infants' physical representations tend to be rather sparse. When watching an event, infants typically represent only basic information about the event (see Fig. 4–1) (e.g., Spelke, 1982; Yonas & Granrud, 1984; Kestenbaum, Termine, & Spelke, 1987; Slater, 1995; Needham, 2000; Wu et al., 2006; Luo et al., in press). This basic information specifies primarily (1) how

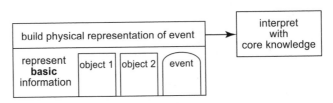

Figure 4–1. An account of infants' physical reasoning: How infants represent and interpret basic information.

many objects are involved in the event; (2) whether these objects are inert or self-propelled; (3) what the distribution of open and closed surfaces in each object is (e.g., is one object open at the top to form a container, open at the bottom to form a cover, or open at both ends to form a tube?); and (4) what the spatial arrangement of the objects is and how it changes over time (e.g., is one object being placed behind, inside, or under the other object?). The basic information infants include in their physical representation of the event thus captures essential aspects of the event but leaves out most of its details; for example, it includes no information about the size, shape, pattern, or color of each object. (Some or all of this information might well be included in infants' object-representation system (e.g., Li et al., 2006b; Wang & Baillargeon, 2008b); our only claim here is that it is not included in the physical-reasoning system and hence cannot be used to interpret and predict the event's outcome.)

Although the basic information young infants represent about events is limited, it is nevertheless sufficient, when interpreted by the persistence principle, to lead them to expect certain outcomes—and hence to detect certain persistence violations when events do not unfold as expected (e.g., Spelke et al., 1992; Wilcox, Nadel, & Rosser, 1996; Lécuyer & Durand, 1998; Aguiar & Baillargeon, 1999; Hespos & Baillargeon, 2001b; Luo & Baillargeon, 2005; Wang, Baillargeon, & Paterson, 2005). As Figures 4–2 and 4–3 illustrate, 2.5- to 3-month-old infants (the youngest tested successfully to date with the VOE method) are surprised when an object rolls behind a large screen, which is then removed to reveal the object resting on the far side of a barrier that should have blocked the object's path (Spelke et al., 1992); when an object is hidden behind one screen and then retrieved from behind a different screen (Wilcox et al., 1996); when an object disappears behind one (asymmetrical or symmetrical) screen and then reappears from behind another screen, without appearing in the gap between them (Aguiar & Baillargeon, 1999; Luo & Baillargeon, 2005); when an object is lowered inside a container through its closed top (Hespos & Baillargeon, 2001b); when an object is lowered into an open container, which is then slid forward and to the side to reveal the object standing in the container's initial position (Hespos & Baillargeon, 2001b); when a cover is lowered over an object, slid to the side, and lifted to reveal no object (Wang et al., 2005); and when a cover is lowered over an object, slid behind the left half of a screen taller than the object, lifted above the screen, moved to the right, lowered behind the right half of the screen, slid past the screen, and finally lifted to reveal the object (Wang et al., 2005).

To succeed in detecting these various persistence violations, infants need only represent the basic information about the events. For example, consider once again the finding that infants are surprised when a cover is lowered over an object, slid to the side, and lifted to reveal no object (Wang et al., 2005; see Fig. 4–3). We would argue that infants represent the following basic information: (1) a cover is held above a closed object; (2) the cover is lowered over the object (the persistence principle would specify at this point that the object continues to exist under the cover); (3) the cover is slid to the side (the persistence principle would specify at this point that the object cannot pass through the sides of the cover and hence must be displaced with the cover to its new location); and (4) the cover is lifted to reveal

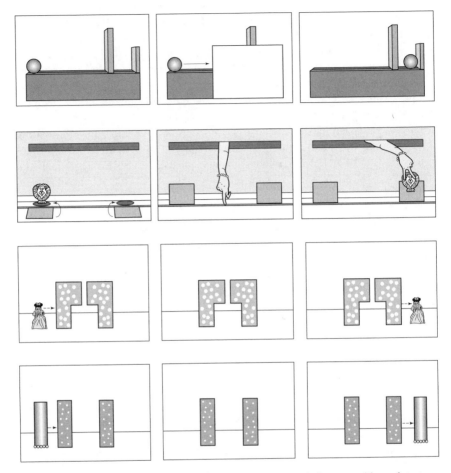

Figure 4–2. Examples of persistence violations that young infants are able to detect, as shown in Spelke et al. (1992), Wilcox et al. (1996), Aguiar and Baillargeon (1999), and Luo and Baillargeon (2005).

no object (the persistence principle would signal at this point that a violation has occurred: The object should have been revealed when the cover was lifted).

Although 2.5- to 3-month-old infants can detect persistence violations that involve only the basic information they represent, they typically fail to detect persistence violations that can be detected only when additional information is represented. To illustrate, as shown in Figure 4–4, current evidence suggests that 3-month-old infants are not surprised when a tall object becomes fully hidden behind a short screen (Baillargeon & DeVos, 1991; Aguiar & Baillargeon, 2002; Luo & Baillargeon, 2005), inside a short container or tube (Hespos & Baillargeon, 2001a; Wang et al., 2005), or under a short cover (Wang & Baillargeon, 2005; Wang et al., 2005; Wang & Baillargeon, 2008a); when an object with a given shape is buried in one location in a sandbox and an object with a different shape is

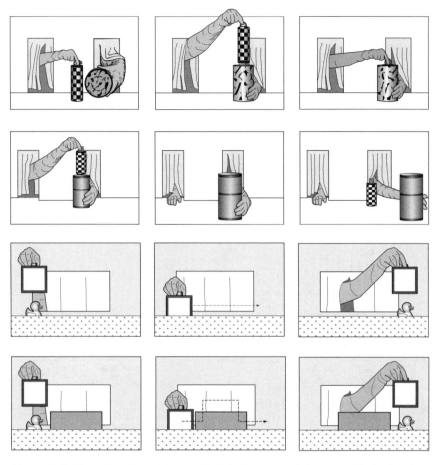

Figure 4–3. Examples of persistence violations that young infants are able to detect, as shown in Hespos and Baillargeon (2001b; top two rows) and Wang et al. (2005; bottom two rows).

retrieved from the same location (Newcombe, Huttenlocher, & Learmonth, 1999); when an object with a given pattern disappears behind a screen (too narrow to hide two objects) and an object with a different pattern reappears from behind it (Wilcox, 1999; Wilcox & Chapa, 2004); and when an object of a given color disappears behind a narrow screen (Wilcox, 1999; Wilcox & Chapa, 2004) or inside a narrow container (Ng & Baillargeon, 2006) and an object of a different color reappears from it.

According to our account, infants fail to detect these and many other persistence violations (as we will see throughout this chapter) because they have not yet learned to include size, shape, pattern, and color information in their physical representations of events. Infants who do not represent an object's physical properties cannot be surprised when the object interacts with other objects in

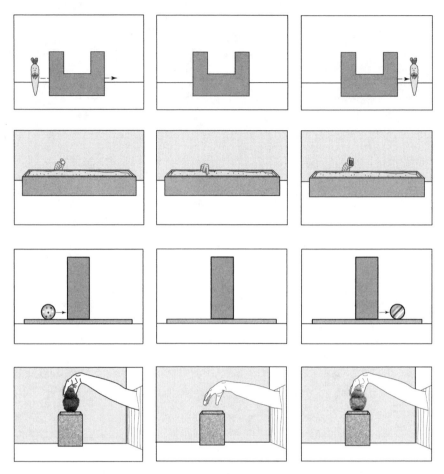

Figure 4–4. Examples of persistence violations that young infants fail to detect, as shown in Aguiar and Baillargeon (2002), Newcombe, Huttenlocher, and Learmonth (1999), Wilcox (1999), and Ng and Baillargeon (2006).

a manner inconsistent with these properties (e.g., when a tall object becomes fully hidden behind a short screen) or when these properties change while the object is out of view (e.g., when a purple toy becomes orange while briefly lowered inside a container). In the next section, we examine how infants come to include additional information in their physical representations of events.

Detecting Variable Violations Through Variable Knowledge

Over time, infants learn to include more and more information in their physical representations; this allows them to form more and more accurate expectations about events' outcomes, and hence to detect more and more violations when shown outcomes inconsistent with these expectations. How do infants come to include this additional information in their physical representations? Research over the past few years has begun to shed light on this process (for recent reviews, see Baillargeon, 2002, 2004; Baillargeon et al., 2006). We briefly review some of the main findings below.

Event Categories, Vectors, and Variables

Recent research suggests that infants form distinct event categories. Many of these categories capture simple spatial relations between objects, such as "object behind other object, or occluder" (occlusion events), "object inside container" (containment events), "object inside tube" (tube events), and "object under cover" (covering events) (e.g., Hespos & Baillargeon, 2001a; Wilcox & Chapa, 2002; Aguiar & Baillargeon, 2003; Casasola, Cohen, & Chiarello, 2003; McDonough, Choi, & Mandler, 2003; Li & Baillargeon, 2005; Wang et al., 2005; Quinn, 2007).

In each event category, infants build one or more vectors, which correspond to distinct problems that must be solved within the category. For example, in the case of occlusion events, infants must learn to predict whether an object will be fully or only partly hidden when behind an occluder, when and where an object that moves behind an occluder will reappear from behind it, and whether an object that reappears from behind an occluder is the same object that disappeared behind it (e.g., Baillargeon & Graber, 1987; Baillargeon & DeVos, 1991; Spelke, Kestenbaum, Simons, & Wein, 1995a; Wilcox, 1999; Hespos & Baillargeon, 2001a; Aguiar & Baillargeon, 2002; Wilcox & Schweinle, 2003; Luo & Baillargeon, 2005; Kochukhova & Gredebäck, 2007; von Hofsten, Kochukhova, & Rosander, 2007). Similarly, in the case of containment events, infants must learn to predict whether an object can be lowered inside a container, how much of an object that is lowered inside a container will protrude above it, and whether the object that is removed from a container is the same object that was lowered into it (e.g., Sitskoorn & Smitsman, 1995; Aguiar & Baillargeon, 1998; Hespos & Baillargeon, 2001a, 2001b; Aguiar & Baillargeon, 2003; Wang et al., 2004; Li & Baillargeon, 2005; Wang et al., 2005; Hespos & Baillargeon, 2006; Ng & Baillargeon, 2006).

For each vector in an event category, infants identify one or more variables that enable them to better predict outcomes (e.g., Sitskoorn & Smitsman, 1995; Wilcox, 1999; Hespos & Baillargeon, 2001a; Aguiar & Baillargeon, 2002; Wang et al., 2005; Luo & Baillargeon, 2008). A variable both calls infants' attention to a certain type of information in an event and provides a causal rule for interpreting this information. In some cases, the rule is akin to a discrete function linking discrete values of the variable to different outcomes. For example, the variable width in containment events specifies that an object can be lowered inside a container if it is narrower, but not wider, than the opening of the container. Each value of the variable (narrower, wider) is thus linked to a different outcome (can be lowered inside, cannot be lowered inside). In other cases, the rule is akin to a continuous function linking continuously changing values of the variable to continuously changing outcomes. For example, the variable height in containment events specifies that an object that is taller than a container not only will protrude above the container when placed inside it but will protrude by an amount identical to the difference in their heights: If the object is 3, 6, or 12 centimeters taller than the container, then the top 3, 6, or 12 centimeters of the object, respectively, should remain visible above the rim of the container.[2] In either case, the principle of persistence provides a ready causal explanation for the rule: For both an object and a container to persist as they are, the two cannot occupy the same space at the time; therefore, the object can be lowered inside the container only if the opening of the container is wide enough for the object to pass through, and the object must retain its height when placed inside the container.

Each variable that is added along a vector revises and refines predictions from earlier variables. This process can be illustrated by a decision tree (for related ideas, see Siegler, 1978; Quinlan, 1993; Mitchell, 1997); with each new variable—or each new partition in the decision tree—infants' predictions slowly approximate those of older children and adults.

As an example, the decision tree in Figure 4–5 depicts some of the variables infants identify as they learn to predict when an object behind an occluder should be hidden or visible. At about 3 months of age, infants identify the variable lower-edge-discontinuity; they now expect an object to be visible when behind an occluder whose lower edge is not continuous with the surface on which it rests, creating an opening between the occluder and the surface (Aguiar & Baillargeon, 2002; Luo & Baillargeon, 2005). Thus, infants expect an object to remain visible when it passes behind a screen shaped like an inverted U, but not one shaped like a U.[3] At about 3.5 to 4 months of age, infants identify height and width as relevant variables; they now expect tall objects to remain partly visible when behind short occluders (Baillargeon & DeVos, 1991), and wide objects to remain partly

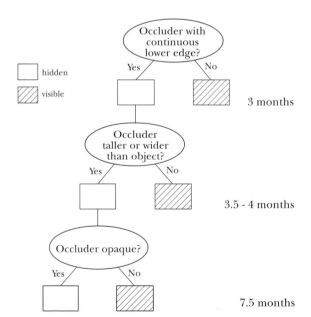

Figure 4–5. A decision tree representing some of the variables infants identify as they learn when an object behind an occluder is hidden or visible.

visible when behind narrow occluders (Wilcox & Baillargeon, 1998b; Wilcox, 1999; Wang et al., 2004).[4] Finally, at about 7.5 months of age, infants identify transparency as a variable; when an object is placed behind a transparent occluder, infants now expect the object to be visible through the front of the occluder and are surprised if it is not (Luo & Baillargeon, 2008).[5]

As another example, the decision tree in Figure 4–6 depicts some of the variables infants identify as they learn to predict, when an object disappears and then reappears from behind an occluder, whether the object that reappears is the same object that disappeared or a different object. Research by Wilcox and her colleagues suggests that, at least by 4.5 months of age, infants have identified size and shape as relevant variables; if a box disappears behind a screen and what reappears is a ball, infants conclude that two distinct objects, a box and a ball, are involved in the event (Wilcox & Baillargeon, 1998b; Wilcox, 1999).[6] At about 7.5 months of age, infants identify pattern as a variable; if a dotted ball disappears behind a screen and what reappears is a striped ball, infants recognize that two different balls, one dotted and one striped, are involved in the event (Wilcox, 1999; Wilcox & Chapa, 2004). Finally, at about 11.5 months, infants identify color as a variable; if a green ball disappears behind a screen and what reappears is a red ball, infants infer that two balls, one green and one red, are involved in the event (Wilcox, 1999; Wilcox & Chapa, 2004; Ng & Baillargeon, 2006).

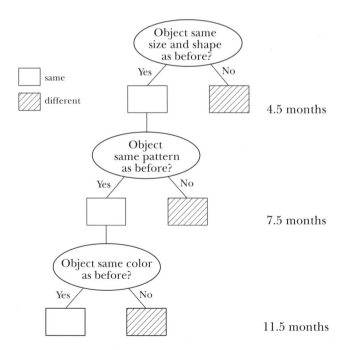

Figure 4–6. A decision tree representing some of the variables infants identify as they learn when an object that reappears from behind an occluder is or is not the same object that disappeared.

We have seen in this section that infants reason and learn in terms of event categories, vectors, and variables. Why would they do so? At a very general level, infants are trying to make sense of the physical events they observe. Infants' physical-reasoning system is designed to break this Herculean task down into small, meaningful components. By sorting events into distinct categories (e.g., containment events) and isolating different vectors within each category (e.g., whether the object can be lowered inside the container, whether the object will protrude above the container, and so on), the physical-reasoning system transforms this Herculean task into a manageable one: that of identifying, one by one, the variables relevant for each vector of each event category.

Reasoning About Variable Information

How does infants' physical reasoning change as they form event categories and identify the vectors and variables relevant for predicting outcomes in each category? According to our account (see Fig. 4–7), when watching an event, infants begin by representing the basic information about the event. Infants then use this information to categorize the event. Next, infants access their knowledge of the category selected; this knowledge specifies the variables that have been identified for the category. Information about each variable is then included in the physical representation and is interpreted in accord with the variable rule. Events whose outcomes are inconsistent with those predicted by the variable rules are flagged as violations.

To illustrate, consider the finding that infants aged 3.5 months and older are surprised when a tall object becomes fully hidden behind a short occluder (Baillargeon & Graber, 1987; Baillargeon & DeVos, 1991; Hespos & Baillargeon, 2001a). When watching this event, infants represent the basic information about

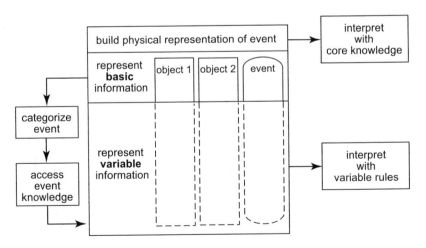

Figure 4–7. An account of infants' physical reasoning: How infants represent and interpret basic and variable information.

the event, categorize it as an occlusion event, and access their knowledge of this category. Because at 3.5 months this knowledge encompasses the variable height (see Fig. 4–5), infants include information about the relative heights of the object and occluder in their physical representation of the event. This information is then interpreted in terms of the variable rule. Because the outcome of the event contradicts this rule—the object is taller than the occluder and yet becomes fully hidden—the event is flagged as a variable violation. Infants younger than 3.5 months, who have not yet identified height as an occlusion variable, typically do not include height information in their physical representations of occlusion events (Baillargeon & DeVos, 1991; Aguiar & Baillargeon, 2002; Luo & Baillargeon, 2005). (This is not to say that young infants watching an occlusion event will represent no information at all about the heights of the object and occluder; as mentioned earlier, infants may include such information in their object-representation system [e.g., Li et al., 2006b; Wang & Baillargeon, 2008b], even if they do not include it in their physical-reasoning system.)

As another illustration, consider the finding that infants aged 11.5 months and older are surprised when a green ball changes into a red ball when passing behind a narrow screen (Wilcox, 1999; Ng & Baillargeon, 2006). When watching the event, infants represent the basic information about the event, categorize it as an occlusion event, and access their knowledge of this category. Because at 11.5 months this knowledge encompasses the variables width (see Fig. 4–5) and color (see Fig. 4–6), infants include information about these variables in their physical representation of the event. This information is then interpreted in accord with infants' width and color rules, and the event is flagged as a variable violation. Infants recognize that the green ball (1) fills most of the space behind the screen and (2) cannot spontaneously change from a green to a red ball. Infants younger than 11.5 months, who have not yet identified color as a relevant variable, do not include color information in their representation of the event. As a result, they assume that the same ball disappeared and reappeared from behind the narrow screen. (Once again, this is not to say that young infants watching an occlusion event represent no information at all about the color of the object that disappears and reappears from behind the occluder; infants may include such information in their object-representation but not their physical-reasoning system.)

Errors of Omission and Commission

If it is true that each new variable in a vector with multiple variables revises predictions from earlier variables, then it should be the case that infants who have acquired only the initial variable(s) in a vector err in systematic ways in their responses to events (Luo & Baillargeon, 2005). First, infants should respond to physically impossible events consistent with their faulty knowledge as though they were expected; we refer to this first kind of error—viewing an impossible event as a non-violation—as an error of omission. Second, infants should respond to physically possible events inconsistent with their faulty knowledge as though they were unexpected; we refer to this second kind of error—viewing a possible event as a violation—as an error of commission.

Do infants produce errors of commission as well as errors of omission in their responses to events? To address this question, Luo and Baillargeon (2005) recently examined 3-month-old infants' responses to physically possible and impossible occlusion events. The experiment focused on the vector in Figure 4–5: When is an object behind an occluder hidden or visible?

The infants were first familiarized with a cylinder that moved back and forth behind a screen; the cylinder was as tall as the screen (see Fig. 4–8). Next, a large portion of the screen's midsection was removed to create a very large opening; a short strip remained above the opening in the discontinuous-lower-edge test event, and below the opening in the continuous-lower-edge test event. For half of the infants, the cylinder did not appear in the opening in either event (CDNA condition); for the other infants, the cylinder appeared (CA condition).

The infants in the CDNA condition were shown two impossible test events. However, because at 3 months infants have identified lower-edge-discontinuity but not height as an occlusion variable (Aguiar & Baillargeon, 2002; see Fig. 4–5), Luo and Baillargeon (2005) predicted that the infants would view only one of these events as unexpected. Specifically, the infants should view the event in which the cylinder failed to appear behind the screen with a discontinuous lower edge as unexpected (a correct response), but they should view the event in which the cylinder failed to appear behind the screen with a continuous lower edge as expected (an error of omission). The infants should therefore look reliably longer at the discontinuous- than at the continuous-lower-edge event.

Unlike the infants in the CDNA condition, those in the CA condition were shown two possible test events. Again, because 3-month-old infants have identified lower-edge-discontinuity but not height as an occlusion variable, Luo and Baillargeon (2005) predicted that the infants would view only one of those events as expected. Specifically, the infants should view the event in which the cylinder appeared behind the screen with a discontinuous lower edge as expected (a correct response), but they should view the event in which the cylinder appeared behind the screen with a continuous lower edge as unexpected (an error of commission). The infants should therefore look reliably longer at the continuous- than at the discontinuous-lower-edge event.

As predicted, the infants in the CDNA condition looked reliably longer at the discontinuous- than at the continuous-lower-edge event, and those in the CA condition showed the opposite looking pattern. Their limited knowledge of occlusion thus (1) led the infants in the CDNA condition to view one of the impossible events they were shown as expected (an error of omission) and (2) led the infants in the CA condition to view one of the possible events they were shown as unexpected (an error of commission). To put it another way, the infants both failed to detect a violation where there was one and perceived a violation where there was none. For infants, as for older children and adults, what is surprising clearly lies in the mind of the beholder (e.g., Karmiloff-Smith & Inhelder, 1975; Siegler, 1978; Caramazza, McCloskey, & Green, 1981; McCloskey, 1983; Carey, 1985; Proffitt, Kaiser, & Whelan, 1990; Keil, 1991; Vosniadou & Brewer, 1992).

Additional experiments have brought to light other errors of commission in infants' responses to occlusion events (e.g., Luo & Baillargeon, 2008). For example,

Cylinder-does-not-appear (CDNA) condition

Familiarization event

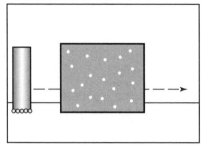

Test events

Discontinuous-lower-edge event

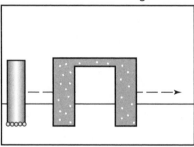

Continuous-lower-edge event

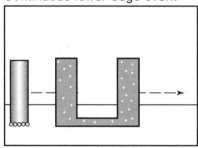

Cylinder-appears (CA) condition

Familiarization event

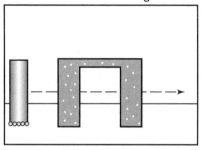

Test events

Discontinuous-lower-edge event

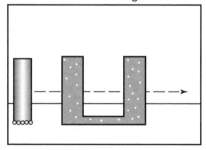

Continuous-lower-edge event

Figure 4–8. Familiarization and test events used in Luo and Baillargeon (2005).

7-month-old infants view as a violation a possible event in which an object placed behind a transparent occluder remains visible through the occluder (Luo & Baillargeon, 2008). At this age, infants have identified lower-edge-discontinuity, height, and width but not yet transparency as occlusion variables (see Fig. 4–5). Thus, when an object is placed behind an occluder that presents no internal or external openings and is taller and wider than the object, infants expect the object to be fully hidden when behind the occluder. Events whose outcomes appear inconsistent with these predictions are flagged as variable violations.

All of the errors of commission discussed above concern the vector in Figure 4–5: When is an object behind an occluder hidden or visible? We have recently completed an experiment (Ng, Baillargeon, & Wilcox, 2007) with 8.5-month-old infants focusing on the vector in Figure 4–6: When is an object that reappears from behind an occluder the same object that disappeared behind it, and when is it a different object? Recall that by 8.5 months of age, infants have identified size, shape, and pattern, but not yet color, as variables in this vector. Thus, it should be the case that infants (1) conclude that two different objects are present when an object is lowered behind a large screen and then an object with the same size and shape, but with a different pattern, is lifted from behind the screen, and (2) conclude that only one object is present when an object is lowered behind a large screen and then an object with the same size, shape, and pattern, but with a different color, is lifted from behind the screen. In the latter case, infants should thus be surprised—an error of commission—when given evidence that there is more than one object behind the screen. Results confirmed these predictions.

Décalages

Recent research suggests that the process by which infants identify variables is event-specific; infants learn separately about each event category. A variable identified in one event category is not generalized to other categories, even when equally relevant; rather, it is learned independently in each category. In some cases, the variable may be identified at about the same age in the different categories. For example, the variable width is identified at about the same age in occlusion and in containment events; 4-month-old infants are surprised when a wide object becomes fully hidden either behind a narrow occluder or inside a narrow container (e.g., Wilcox & Baillargeon, 1998b; Wilcox, 1999; Wang et al., 2004). In other cases, however, there may be marked lags or décalages (to use a Piagetian term) in infants' identification of the same variable in different categories.

As an example, we saw above that infants identify the variable height at about 3.5 months in occlusion events (Baillargeon & DeVos, 1991); they are now surprised when a tall object becomes fully hidden behind a short occluder. However, infants this age are not surprised when a tall object becomes fully hidden inside a short container, under a short cover, or inside a short tube. The variable height is not identified until about 7.5 months in containment events (Hespos & Baillargeon, 2001a, 2006), until about 12 months in covering events (McCall, 2001; Wang et al., 2005; Wang & Baillargeon, 2006), and until about 14 months in tube events (Gertner, Baillargeon, & Fisher, 2005; Wang et al., 2005). Similarly, we saw earlier that the variable transparency is identified at about 7.5 months in occlusion events (Luo & Baillargeon, 2008); infants are now surprised when an object placed behind a transparent occluder is not visible through the occluder. However, it is not until infants are about 9.5 months of age that they identify the same variable in containment events and expect an object placed inside a transparent container to be visible through the container (Luo & Baillargeon, 2008).[7]

When infants of a given age have identified a variable in one event category but not another, striking discrepancies can be observed in their responses to events—even perceptually similar events—from the two categories (see Fig. 4–9). Thus, 4.5-month-old infants, who have identified the variable height in occlusion but not containment events, are surprised when a tall object becomes fully hidden behind but not inside a short container (Hespos & Baillargeon, 2001a). Similarly, 9-month-old infants, who have identified the variable height in containment but not covering events, are surprised when a tall object becomes fully hidden inside a short container but not under a short cover (the short container turned upside down) (Wang et al., 2005). Finally, 12.5-month-old infants, who have identified the variable color in occlusion but not containment events, are surprised when a toy is lowered behind a narrow occluder and then another toy, identical except for color, is removed from behind the occluder; however, they are not surprised when the narrow occluder is replaced with a narrow container—even though the occluder is identical to the front of the container, so that the two events are perceptually highly similar (Ng & Baillargeon, 2006). According to our reasoning account, in each case infants succeed in detecting the variable violation in the first but not the second event category because they have not yet identified the variable as relevant to the second event category. As a result, they include information about the variable in their physical representation of the event from the first but not the second category.

In the findings just described, infants were shown perceptually similar but not identical events: The object was placed behind or inside a container, inside a container or under a cover, and so on. In recent experiments, we asked whether infants might respond differently to *identical* events, if they were led to believe, based on prior information, that the events belonged to two different event categories (Li & Baillargeon, 2005; Wang et al., 2005). The point of departure for these experiments was the finding that the variable height is identified at about 7.5 months in containment events (Hespos & Baillargeon, 2001a, 2006), but only at about 14 months in tube events (Gertner et al., 2005; Wang et al., 2005).

In one experiment, for example, 9-month-old infants watched two test events in which they saw an experimenter lower a tall object inside a container (containment condition) or a tube (tube condition) until it became fully hidden (see Fig. 4–10) (Wang et al., 2005). In one event, the container or tube was slightly taller than the object (tall event); in the other event, the container or tube was only half as tall (short event), so that it should have been impossible for the object to become fully hidden. Before the test session, in an orientation procedure, the experimenter showed the infants each container (containment condition) or tube (tube condition) one at a time, calling attention to its top and bottom. When standing upright on the apparatus floor during the test events, the containers and tubes were indistinguishable. The infants in the containment and tube condition thus saw perceptually identical test events; only the information provided in the orientation procedure could lead them to believe that they were watching events involving containers or tubes.

4.5 months

Occlusion Condition: Success

  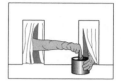

Containment Condition: Failure

 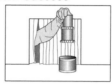 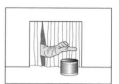

9 months

Containment Condition: Success

 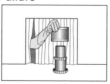 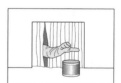

Covering Condition: Failure

 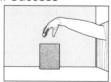 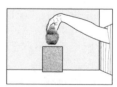

12.5 months

Occlusion Condition: Success

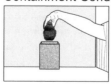  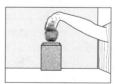

Containment Condition: Failure

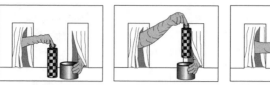 

Figure 4–9. Examples of décalages: height in occlusion and containment events (Hespos & Baillargeon, 2001a), height in containment and covering events (Wang et al., 2005), and color in occlusion and containment events (Ng & Baillargeon, 2006).

Containment and Tube Conditions

Tall Event

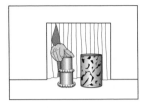 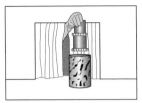 

Short Event

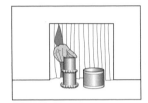 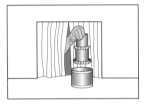 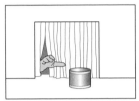

Figure 4–10. Test events used in Wang et al. (2005).

As expected, the infants in the containment condition looked reliably longer at the short than at the tall event, but those in the tube condition tended to look equally at the two events. The infants thus detected the height violation they were shown when they believed they were facing containers, but not tubes.

Identifying Variables

We have seen that, for each event category, infants identify variables, ordered along vectors, which enable them to predict outcomes within the category more and more accurately over time. How do infants identify these variables?

We have proposed that the process by which infants identify a new variable in an event category is one of explanation-based learning (EBL) and involves three main steps (Baillargeon, 2002; Baillargeon et al., 2006; Wang & Baillargeon, 2008a; for a computational description of EBL in the machine-learning literature, see DeJong, 1993). First, infants notice contrastive outcomes relevant to the variable. This occurs when infants watch events, build similar physical representations for the events—and notice that the outcomes of the events differ along some vector (e.g., the object can or cannot be placed inside the container; the object does or does not protrude above the container; and so on). In other words, infants notice contrastive outcomes they cannot predict or interpret; similar physical representations are leading to different outcomes, suggesting that some crucial piece of information is missing from the representations. At this point, infants begin to search for the conditions that map onto the observed contrastive outcomes.

Eventually (research is needed to shed light on the mechanisms at work here), infants identify a possible rule linking conditions and outcomes. Finally, infants attempt to supply an explanation for this condition–outcome rule, using their core knowledge. According to the EBL process, only condition–outcome rules for which causal explanations can be provided are recognized as new variables. After a new variable has been identified, infants begin to routinely include information about the variable in their physical representations of all new events from the category, thus ensuring a powerful, yet appropriate, generalization.

The identification of a new variable is thus described as an EBL process because infants' core knowledge must provide a causal explanation for the variable; it must make clear why one condition, or one value of the variable, would lead to one outcome, and why another condition, or another value of the variable, would lead to a different outcome. The explanations supplied by the core knowledge are no doubt shallow (e.g., Keil, 1995; Wilson & Keil, 2000), but they still serve to integrate new variables with infants' prior causal knowledge.

To illustrate the EBL process, consider the variable height in containment events, which is identified at about 7.5 months of age (Hespos & Baillargeon, 2001a, 2006). We suppose that at some point prior to 7.5 months, infants begin to notice—either as they themselves manipulate objects and containers or as they observe others doing so—that objects that are placed in containers sometimes protrude above the rim and sometimes do not. Because at this time infants include only the information "object placed inside wider, open container" in their physical representations of the events (recall that width is identified at about 4 months as a containment variable) (Wang et al., 2004), they have no way of interpreting these contrastive outcomes. Identical physical representations are leading to different outcomes; sometimes the object protrudes above the rim of the container, and sometimes it does not. Infants then begin to search for the conditions that might be associated with each outcome. By about 7.5 months of age, infants recognize that the relative heights of the object and container are critical; the object protrudes above the rim of the container when it is taller but not shorter than the container. This condition–outcome rule is immediately interpretable by infants' core knowledge: For both a tall object and a short container to exist continuously in time and space, retaining their individual physical properties, the tall object must protrude above the rim of the short container when placed inside it. Infants have thus identified a new vector (when does an object inside a container protrude above it?) and a new variable (height).[8]

From this point on, infants routinely include height information in their representations of containment events and interpret this information in accord with their new variable rule. Thus, infants are surprised whenever a tall object is lowered inside a short container until it becomes fully hidden (e.g., Hespos & Baillargeon, 2001a; Wang et al., 2005). In addition, infants show evidence of attending to height information in simple action tasks involving containers. In a recent experiment (see Fig. 4–11) (Hespos & Baillargeon, 2006), 7.5-month-old infants were shown a tall frog. Next, the frog was placed behind a large screen, which was then removed to reveal a short and a tall container; each container had two frog feet protruding from small holes at the bottom of the container. The

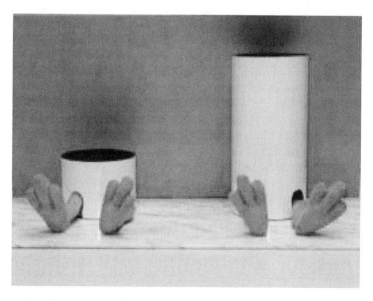

Figure 4–11. Test event used in Hespos and Baillargeon (2006): pretrial (top row) and main trial (bottom row).

infants reached reliably more often for the tall than for the short container, suggesting that they wanted to find the tall frog and realized that it could be hidden inside only the tall container. Control infants who did not see the tall frog tended to reach equally often for the two containers.

In the example discussed above, the identification of the variable height went hand in hand with the creation of a new vector (when does an object placed inside a container protrude above it?). In other cases, the newly identified variable is added to an existing vector. To illustrate, consider the variable transparency in occlusion events, which is identified at about 7.5 months of age (see Fig. 4–5) (Luo & Baillargeon, 2008). As noted earlier, at about 7 months (Johnson & Aslin, 2000), infants become able to detect clear surfaces and begin to include information about the presence—though not the appearance—of these surfaces in their physical representations of events (younger infants presumably simply see and represent openings instead). As a result, infants will now be faced with contrastive outcomes they cannot interpret; they will notice that objects that move behind large occluders sometimes become hidden, as infants' current occlusion knowledge predicts they should be, and sometimes remain visible. Because infants' physical representations of the events include only lower-edge-discontinuity, height, and width information (see Fig. 4–5) (e.g., Baillargeon & DeVos, 1991; Aguiar & Baillargeon, 2002; Wang et al., 2004; Luo & Baillargeon, 2005), they cannot make sense of what they see; the same physical representation "object placed behind taller and wider occluder with no internal or external opening" leads to a predicted (hidden) or an unpredicted (visible) outcome. At this point, infants will begin to look for the condition associated with each observed outcome. By about 7.5 months of age, infants recognize that the opacity or transparency of the occluder is critical; objects become hidden behind opaque but not transparent occluders. Infants' core knowledge allows them to immediately make sense of this information; because an object continues to exist when placed behind a transparent occluder, it must be visible through the occluder. The newly identified variable transparency is then added to the vector "when is an object behind an occluder hidden or visible?" From then on, infants include information about the transparency of the occluder when representing occlusion events (e.g., Wilcox & Chapa, 2002; Luo & Baillargeon, 2008).

Why Décalages?

The EBL process described above makes clear why infants learn separately about each event category; if learning is triggered by exposure to situations where similar physical representations lead to contrastive outcomes, then a new variable can be identified only within the context of a specific event category. Events from different categories will yield different physical representations, and contrastive outcomes associated with these different representations will not elicit learning, even if they are in fact contrastive from an abstract or adult point of view (e.g., "object placed inside container—object does not protrude above container" versus "object placed inside tube—object protrudes above tube"). The reason why the learning process is so rapid (or indeed, possible) is thus that it is highly constrained. Infants do not compare arbitrary groups of events and look for invariants or critical variables that might explain similarities or differences between them. The only situation that can trigger variable learning is one where events with similar physical representations yield outcomes that differ along a specific vector.

The preceding discussion helps make clear why infants would learn separately about each event category—but it does not explain why several months sometimes separate the acquisition of the same variable in different event categories. For example, why do infants identify the variable height at about 3.5 months in occlusion events, but only at about 7.5 months in containment events, 12 months in covering events, and 14 months in tube events (e.g., Baillargeon & DeVos, 1991; Hespos & Baillargeon, 2001a; Gertner et al., 2005; Li & Baillargeon, 2005; Wang et al., 2005; Hespos & Baillargeon, 2006; Wang & Baillargeon, 2006)?

The EBL account suggests two possible reasons for such décalages. One has to do with the first step in the EBL process; because exposure to appropriate contrastive outcomes is necessary to trigger learning, it follows that variables will be learned later when exposure is less frequent. Thus, infants may identify height as a containment variable long before they identify it as a covering variable simply because, in everyday life, infants have more opportunities to notice that objects inside containers sometimes protrude above them and sometimes do not than to notice that objects placed under covers sometimes extend beneath them and sometimes do not.

A second reason why infants may identify a variable sooner in one event category than in another has to do with the second step in the EBL process. After noticing the contrastive outcomes for a variable, infants must discover what conditions map onto these outcomes; this discovery may be more difficult in some categories than in others. To illustrate, consider once again the finding that infants identify height as an occlusion variable several months before they identify it as a containment variable. Prior research (e.g., Baillargeon 1994, 1995) indicates that when infants begin to reason about a continuous variable in an event category, they can reason about the variable qualitatively but not quantitatively; they are not able at first to encode and reason about absolute amounts. In order to encode the heights of objects and occluders or containers qualitatively, infants must compare them as they stand side by side. It may be that infants have more opportunities to perform such qualitative comparisons with occlusion than with containment events. In the case of occlusion events, infants will often see objects move behind the side edges of occluders, making it easy to compare their heights as they stand next to each other (e.g., when a bowl is pushed behind a cereal box). In the case of containment events, however, there may be relatively few instances in which objects are placed first next to and then inside containers; caretakers will more often lower objects directly into containers, giving infants no opportunity to compare their heights (e.g., Hespos & Baillargeon, 2001a; Wang et al., 2004).

The preceding analysis predicts that infants who are exposed in the laboratory (or at home) to appropriate observations for a variable should identify it earlier than they otherwise would. Wang and Baillargeon (2008a) recently tested this prediction: They attempted to "teach" 9-month-old infants the variable height in covering events (recall that this variable is typically not identified until about 12 months of age) (Wang et al., 2005; Wang & Baillargeon, 2006). The results of these teaching experiments were positive and as such support both the EBL account and the speculation above that the décalage in infants' identification of the variable height in containment and covering events stems from the fact that infants are typically exposed to appropriate observations for this variable at different ages in the two categories.

Detecting Variable Violations Through Core Knowledge

So far, we have considered two different processes by which infants reason about physical events. First (see Fig. 4–1), we saw that infants—even very young infants—represent basic information about events and interpret this information in accordance with their core knowledge. Events whose outcomes are inconsistent with the core knowledge are flagged as violations.

Second (see Fig. 4–7), we saw that, with experience, infants come to include additional information, or variable information, in their physical representations of events. For each event category, infants identify vectors and variables relevant for predicting outcomes in the category. When watching an event, infants first categorize it, access their knowledge of the variables that have been identified as relevant for the category, and include information about each of these variables in their physical representation of the event. This information is then interpreted in accordance with the variable rules. Events inconsistent with the rules are flagged as violations. When infants' knowledge is still limited—because they have acquired no variable, or have acquired only the initial variable(s), in a vector—they typically err in their responses to events; they fail to flag as violations impossible events consistent with their faulty knowledge (e.g., a tall object that fails to remain visible above a short occluder), and they flag as violations ordinary and even commonplace events that happen to be inconsistent with their faulty knowledge (e.g., a tall object that remains visible above a short occluder).

In this section, we examine a third process by which infants reason about physical events. We suggested at the start of this chapter that all of the information infants include in their physical representation of an event is interpreted in terms of their core knowledge. If this is correct, and the information infants represent about a variable is interpreted not only in terms of the variable rule but also in terms of their core knowledge, then infants might be able to detect additional violations involving the variable. Here we focus on change violations.

Change Violations

Consider the variable height in containment events, which is identified at about 7.5 months of age; infants now recognize that a tall object should protrude above a short but not a tall container (Hespos & Baillargeon, 2001a, 2006). Let us assume that infants this age are shown an event in which a tall object is lowered inside a very tall container. Infants will represent the basic information about the event, categorize it as a containment event, and access their knowledge of this event category, which will specify height as a relevant variable. Infants will then include information about the relative heights of the object and container in their physical representation of the event and will interpret this information in accordance with the variable rule; because the object is shorter than the container, it will not protrude above it. The object in fact does not protrude above the rim of the container, and the event is not flagged as a violation. However, what if the object is then removed from the container and is revealed to be much shorter than before? If infants can use the height information only to predict whether the object should be visible above the rim of the container, then they will fail to detect this violation. On the other hand, if the height information, once represented, becomes subject to the core knowledge, then infants should have no difficulty detecting this change violation. According to the persistence principle, objects exist continuously in time and space, retaining their physical properties as they do so. Thus, a tall object cannot spontaneously change into a shorter object, and the event should be flagged as a violation.

This line of reasoning suggests that infants who have identified height or width as a relevant variable in an event category should be able to detect both interaction and change violations involving the variable. Interaction violations refer to events in which two or more objects interact in a manner inconsistent with their respective individual properties (e.g., a tall object that becomes fully hidden inside a short container). Change violations, in contrast, refer to events in which the individual properties of objects are not maintained over time (e.g., a tall object that becomes much shorter while briefly hidden inside a tall container).

Several experiments provide evidence for the preceding analysis (see Fig. 4–12). First, consider the variable width in occlusion events. Results show that (1) 4-month-olds are surprised when a wide object becomes fully hidden behind a narrow occluder (Wang et al., 2004) and (2) 4.5-month-olds are surprised when a large ball changes into a small ball when passing behind a narrow occluder (too narrow to hide both balls simultaneously) (Wilcox, 1999). Infants can thus use width information in occlusion events to judge whether an object can become fully hidden behind an occluder and to detect a change to the object's width as it emerges from behind the occluder.[9]

Next, consider the variable height in containment events. Results indicate that (1) 7.5-month-olds are surprised when a tall object is lowered into a short container until it becomes almost fully hidden (Hespos & Baillargeon, 2001a) and (2) 8-month-olds are surprised when a tall object lowered into a tall container is much shorter when removed from the container (Li & Baillargeon, 2005). Infants can thus use height information in containment events to predict whether an object will protrude above the rim of a container and also to detect a change to the object's height as it emerges from the container.

Finally, consider the variable height in covering events. Results have shown that (1) 12-month-olds (but not 11-month-olds) are surprised when a short cover is lowered over a tall object until the object becomes fully hidden (Wang et al., 2005) and (2) 12.5-month-olds (but not 11-month-olds) are surprised when a tall cover is lowered over a tall object and then removed to reveal a much shorter object (Wang & Baillargeon, 2006). Infants can thus use height information in covering

Width in Occlusion Events
Interaction violation

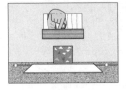  

Change violation

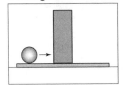  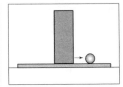

Height in Containment Events
Interaction violation

 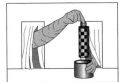 

Change violation

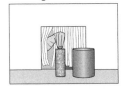  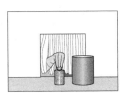

Height in Covering Events
Interaction violation

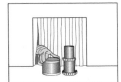  

Change violation

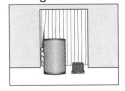  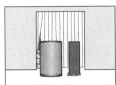

events to predict whether an object will extend beneath the rim of a cover and also to detect a change to the object's height when uncovered.

Additional research is needed to more fully explore the relation between infants' ability to detect interaction and change violations involving height or width information. The present analysis suggests, for example, that infants who were "taught" (through exposure to appropriate condition–outcome observations in the home or laboratory) that a tall object will protrude above a short but not a tall container should ipso facto (1) be able to detect surreptitious changes to the height of an object that is briefly lowered into a container and also (2) be able to use height information to determine whether an object that is retrieved from a large container is the same object that was placed inside it or a different object. Thus, if a short object is placed inside a large bucket, and a tall object is next retrieved from inside it, infants should be surprised if the bucket is then shown to be empty. Furthermore, the reverse should also be true: Infants who are "taught" that height information is useful for determining whether the object that is retrieved from a container is the same object that was placed inside it should ipso facto be able to detect violations in which tall objects fail to protrude above short containers.

Core Knowledge and Variable Rules

Implicit in the preceding discussion is a fundamental claim about the development of infants' physical reasoning: With experience, infants learn *what* variable information to include in their physical representations of events, not *how* to interpret this information. Infants' core knowledge provides a causal framework that enables them to immediately interpret variable information once represented.

Of course, the causal framework provided by infants' core knowledge is sharply limited; it will not help them understand the day–night cycle or the workings of refrigerators, telephones, televisions, light bulbs, and space shuttles. But it is sufficient to help infants understand the implications of simple variables for objects' displacements and interactions: for example, to help them understand that tall objects cannot become fully hidden behind short occluders, that wide objects cannot be lowered inside narrow containers, that small frog-like objects cannot spontaneously change into tall prince-like objects, and that an object that disappears at one end of a wide occluder cannot instantaneously reappear at the other end of the occluder.

One question that might be raised at this juncture is the following: If infants' core knowledge enables them to reason about any variable information once represented, then why are variable rules necessary? Why not assume that infants (1) learn what variable information to include in their physical representations of events and (2) simply interpret this information in terms of their core knowledge? The answer, we believe, is that variable rules facilitate the process of variable

---

Figure 4–12. Examples of interaction and change violations infants detect that involve: (a) width in occlusion events (Wilcox, 1999; Wang et al., 2004), (b) height in containment events (Hespos & Baillargeon, 2001a; Li & Baillargeon, 2005), and (c) height in covering events (Wang et al., 2005; Wang & Baillargeon, 2006).

identification in everyday life by leading infants to form specific expectations about events' outcomes and—most importantly—to adjust these expectations when different outcomes arise.

Infants' core knowledge is used to interpret an event as it *actually* unfolds; whatever basic and variable information is included in the event's physical representation is interpreted in terms of the core knowledge, and the event is flagged as a violation if and only if it unfolds in a manner inconsistent with this knowledge. Outside of the laboratory, infants will of course rarely encounter such core violations. Infants' variable rules, in contrast, represent hypotheses about how an event is *likely* to unfold; they specify the conditions under which each outcome in a vector will occur. As infants identify more variables, their hypotheses about these conditions become more accurate—or more finely tuned, one might say. In the initial stages, however, when infants' hypotheses are still coarse, they will often be confronted—as they observe events in daily life—with events inconsistent with their rules (thus producing what we called errors of commission). These violations provide infants with negative feedback; they signal to infants that their current physical knowledge is flawed and that additional variables are needed to specify the conditions under which the contrastive outcomes in the vector are likely to occur. As Leslie (2004) put it, "Paying more attention is what you do if you are an active learner who has identified a learning opportunity. A violation of expectation happens when you detect that the world does not conform to your representation of it. Bringing representation and world back into kilter requires representation change, and computing the right change is a fair definition of learning" (p. 418).

INDUCING INFANTS TO SUCCEED AT DETECTING VARIABLE VIOLATIONS: PRIMING MANIPULATIONS

The account of infants' physical reasoning presented in the previous section rests on two central claims. The first is that infants' physical representations of events initially include only basic information and become increasingly richer and more detailed as infants gradually identify relevant variables. Event category by event category, vector by vector, variable by variable, infants identify the variables that are useful for predicting outcomes, and begin to include information about these variables in their physical representations. The second central claim of our account is that infants primarily learn what information to include in their physical representations of events, not how to interpret this information once represented. Infants' core knowledge provides a causal framework for interpreting both the basic and the variable information infants include in their physical representations of events.

If these two claims are correct, then the following prediction should hold: If infants could be induced, through some contextual manipulation, to include information about a variable they have not yet identified in their physical representation of an event, then this information should become subject to their core knowledge, allowing them to immediately detect violations involving the variable (see Fig. 4–13).

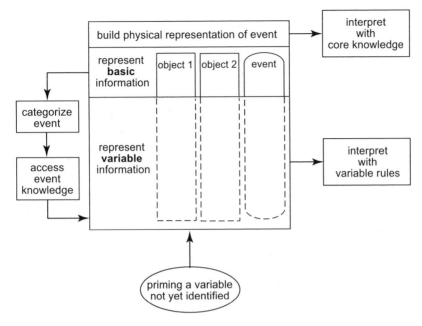

Figure 4–13. An account of infants' physical reasoning: How priming helps infants represent information about a variable they have not yet identified.

Several recent lines of experimentation support this prediction; it turns out that there are many different ways of temporarily inducing infants who have not yet identified a variable to include information about it in their physical representation of an event (e.g., Wilcox & Chapa, 2004; Gertner et al., 2005; Li & Baillargeon, 2005; Yuan & Baillargeon, 2005; Li & Baillargeon, 2006; Ng & Baillargeon, 2006; Wilcox, this volume). From this perspective, infants' physical-reasoning system thus appears extremely porous—a highly desirable characteristic in a system that must primarily learn to attend to more and more information over time.

In this section, we focus on priming manipulations, which are typically designed to make a particular variable (or particular values of a variable) salient to infants. Highlighting the variable renders infants more likely to include information about it when watching a subsequent physical event; this information then becomes subject to infants' core knowledge, allowing them to detect violations they would not have detected otherwise.

Priming Infants to Attend to Color Information in an Occlusion Event

We saw earlier that young infants are not surprised when a green ball disappears behind a narrow screen and a red ball then reappears from behind it (Wilcox, 1999). Although width is identified as an occlusion variable by 4 months of age (e.g., Wang et al., 2004), color is not identified until much later, at about 11.5

months of age (e.g., Wilcox, 1999; Ng & Baillargeon, 2006). As a result, young infants typically include no color information in their physical representation of the narrow-screen event, and assume that the same ball is moving back and forth behind the screen. In a seminal series of experiments, Wilcox and Chapa (2004) asked whether 9.5-month-old infants could be primed to attend to the color information in this event.

The infants first received two pairs of priming trials. Each pair consisted of a pound event, in which a green cup was used to pound a peg, and a pour event, in which a red cup was used to pour salt. Different green and red cups were used in the two pairs of trials. Next, the infants saw a test event in which a green and a red ball appeared successively from behind a narrow (narrow-screen event) or a wide (wide-screen event) screen. Results indicated that, following the priming trials, the infants who saw the narrow-screen event looked reliably longer than did those who saw the wide-screen event. Additional results revealed that 7.5-month-old infants could also be primed to detect the violation in the narrow-screen event but required three pairs of priming trials (with three different pairs of green and red cups) to do so. Together, these results suggested that the infants perceived the association in the priming trials between the color and function of the cups (green–pound, red–pour). This association made the colors green and red more salient for the infants. As a result, the infants were more likely to include information about the colors of the green and red balls in their physical representations of the test events. This information, once represented, became subject to the persistence principle, and the infants realized, when watching the narrow screen, that the green ball (1) filled most of the space behind the narrow screen and (2) could not spontaneously change from a green to a red ball.

In subsequent experiments, Wilcox and her colleagues (this volume) replicated their initial findings with 9-month-old infants using new color–function pairings. The infants now saw priming events in which long-handled spoons of different colors were used to stir salt in a bowl or to lift a bowl by its hook. Results indicated that the infants looked reliably longer at the narrow- than at the wide-screen event when the spoons used in the priming trials were the same colors as the balls (green and red)—but not when they were different (yellow and blue). These results suggest that the effect of the priming manipulation was quite specific; because the colors green and red were paired with different object functions in the situation, the infants were more likely to attend to these same colors when they next encountered them in another, very different event. However, watching priming events involving yellow and blue spoons did not serve to make infants more likely to include information about the colors of the balls in the narrow- and wide-screen events. The priming manipulation thus served to highlight the colors green and red for the infants—not color information generally.

In another series of experiments, Wilcox and Chapa (2004) primed 5.5-month-old infants to attend to pattern information in an occlusion event. These experiments built on the finding that infants younger than 7.5 months of age are not surprised when a dotted ball disappears behind a narrow screen and a striped ball reappears from behind it (Wilcox, 1999). Using a pound-pour manipulation similar to that described above, Wilcox and Chapa found that, after receiving three pairs of priming trials involving three different dotted and striped green cups, infants looked reliably longer at the narrow- than at the wide-screen event. Finally, 4.5-month-old infants could also be primed to include pattern information in their physical representation of the narrow-screen event, but both cups had to be present in each priming trial to allow simultaneous comparison of their patterns.

The priming results obtained by Wilcox and her colleagues (Wilcox & Chapa, 2004; this volume) provide strong support for the central claim of our account of infants' physical reasoning: Infants learn *what* information to include in their physical representations of events, not *how* to interpret this information once represented. Infants aged 4.5 to 9.5 months who could be induced to represent information about the colors (green and red) or patterns (dotted and striped) of the balls in a narrow-screen event immediately detected the persistence violation in the event.

Priming Infants to Attend to Color Information in a Containment Event

We saw earlier that 12.5-month-old infants are not surprised when a toy is lowered into a narrow container (slightly larger than the toy) and another toy, identical except for color, is then removed from the container (Ng & Baillargeon, 2006). Although width is identified as a containment variable at about 4 months of age (e.g., Wang et al., 2004), color is not identified until some (as yet unspecified) time after 12.5 months of age (Ng & Baillargeon, 2006). As a result, 12.5-month-old infants typically include no color information in their physical representation of the narrow-container event and assume that the same toy is being lowered into and retrieved from the container. In a recent experiment, we attempted to prime 12.5-month-olds to include color information in their physical representations of containment events (Ng & Baillargeon, 2006). This experiment also examined whether it might be possible to highlight a variable for infants through a simple perceptual contrast, by showing them objects that exhibit different values of the variable but are otherwise identical.

The infants were assigned to a baseline or a priming condition. The infants in the baseline condition received two pairs of test trials (see Fig. 4–14). Each pair consisted of a change and a no-change event, and order of presentation was counterbalanced across infants. At the start of each event, the infants saw a "Boohbah" toy resting on an apparatus floor to the right of a small container. The container was only large enough to hide a single Boohbah; the infants were shown the container in a brief orientation procedure before the test session. An experimenter's gloved hand grasped the toy, lifted it, and lowered it into the container. The hand then paused briefly above the container. Next, the hand retrieved the toy from inside the container and returned it to its original position on the apparatus floor. For one quarter of the infants (purple-orange condition), a purple Boohbah was placed inside the container, and an orange (change event) or a purple (no-change event) Boohbah was removed from it. The other infants were assigned to an orange-purple, a pink-yellow, or a yellow-pink condition. The infants in the priming condition received a single priming trial before the test trials, in which they saw all

No-change Event

Change Event

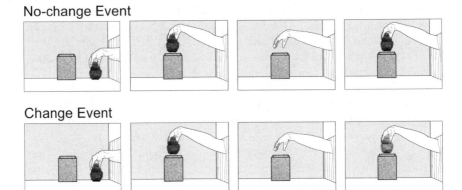

Figure 4–14. Test events used in Ng and Baillargeon (2006).

four Boohbahs resting side by side on the apparatus floor in front of the container (see Fig. 4–15). From left to right, the Boohbahs were purple, yellow, pink, and orange and were identical except for color.

We reasoned that if the priming trial highlighted the fact that Boohbahs came in a variety of colors, then the infants might be more likely to include information about the color of the Boohbah shown at the start of each test event (e.g., to determine which specific Boohbah was being used in the event). This color information would then become subject to the persistence principle, allowing the infants to detect the violation in the change event; a purple toy cannot spontaneously turn into an orange toy, or a pink toy into a yellow one.

The infants in the priming condition looked reliably longer at the change than at the no-change event, whereas those in the baseline condition tended to look equally at the two events. These results suggest that the priming trial was sufficient to induce the infants in the priming condition to include information about the color of the Boohbah in the test events. Thus, the infants in the purple-orange priming condition, for example, presumably reasoned that the purple Boohbah (1) filled most of the narrow container and (2) could not spontaneously change into an orange Boohbah. Like the results of Wilcox and Chapa (2004; Wilcox, this volume), the present results support the claim that, with experience, infants learn *what* information to attend to in events, not *how* to interpret this information. The single, static priming trial the infants received could not teach them that objects retain their colors when lowered into containers—it could only induce them to represent the color of the toy in the events.

In future research, we hope to modify the priming trial to determine what does and does not constitute an adequate priming experience for infants in this situation. For example, we suspect that showing four Boohbahs of one color (e.g., all purple), or showing four balls of the same colors as the different Boohbahs, would not constitute an adequate priming trial. Conversely, we suspect that showing four different Boohbahs whose colors do not match those in the test events (e.g., green, blue, white, and gray), would constitute an adequate priming trial. Investigating

Figure 4–15. Priming trial used in Ng and Baillargeon (2006).

these various possibilities should help us better understand the mechanism that makes possible successful priming. Regardless of the outcomes of these experiments, however, the main thrust of the present research is the demonstration that infants who are induced to include information about a variable they have not yet identified in their physical representation of an event can then detect a change violation involving this variable.

Priming Infants to Attend to Height Information in a Tube Event

At 8 months of age, infants detect a surreptitious change to the height of an object in a containment but not a tube event; they are surprised when a tall cylindrical object lowered into a tall container is much smaller when removed from the container—but they are not surprised when the container is replaced with a tube (Li & Baillargeon, 2005). By this age, infants have identified height as a containment but not a tube variable; recall that height is identified at about 7.5 months in containment events but only at about 14 months in tube events (e.g., Hespos & Baillargeon, 2001a; Gertner et al., 2005; Hespos & Baillargeon, 2006; Wang & Baillargeon, 2006). In a recent experiment, we asked whether 8-month-old infants could be primed to attend to height information in a tube event (Li & Baillargeon, 2005).

The infants were assigned to a baseline or a priming condition. The infants in the baseline condition first received a familiarization trial in which they saw an

Familiarization Event

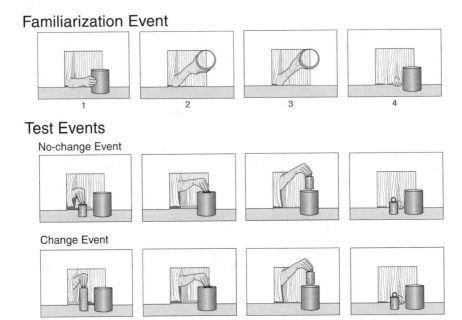

Test Events

No-change Event

Change Event

Figure 4–16. Familiarization and test events used in Li and Baillargeon (2005).

experimenter's gloved hand rotate a tall tube forward and backward (to show it was open at both top and bottom) and then place it upright on the apparatus floor (see Fig. 4–16). Next, the infants received a single test trial in which they saw either a change or a no-change test event. At the start of the change event, a tall cylindrical object with a red knob attached to its top stood to the left of the tube; the cylindrical portion of the object was the same height as the tube. The hand grasped the knob at the top of the object, lifted the object, and lowered it into the tube until only the knob and the very top of the object remained visible above the rim. The hand gently twisted the object back and forth for a few seconds and then returned it to its original position on the apparatus floor. When removed from the tube, the cylindrical portion of the object was only half as tall as previously. The no-change event was identical to the change event, except that the short object was used throughout the event. The infants in the priming condition were tested using the same procedure, with one exception: They received two static priming trials following the familiarization trial and prior to the test trial (see Fig. 4–17). In one trial, three cylindrical objects stood side by side on the apparatus floor: At one end was the tall object used at the start of the change event, at the other end was the short object used in the change and no-change events, and between them was a medium-sized object. The three objects were identical except for their heights; the cylindrical portion of the tall, medium, and short objects was 15, 11.3, and 7.5 centimeters, respectively. In the first priming trial, the objects were ordered from tall to short, from left to right; in the second trial, the objects were ordered from short to tall.

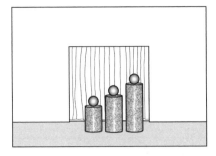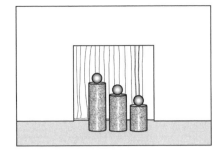

Figure 4–17. Priming trials used in Li and Baillargeon (2005).

In the priming condition, the infants who saw the change event looked reliably longer than those who saw the no-change event; in the baseline condition, in contrast, the infants looked about equally at the two events. These results suggested that the priming trials served to highlight height information for the infants in the priming condition; as a result, the infants were more likely to include height information in their physical representations of the test events. This height information then became subject to the infants' core knowledge, and the change event was flagged as a persistence violation; the infants realized that the tall object could not spontaneously change into a short object. The simple priming trials used here thus allowed infants to detect a height violation in a tube event 6 months before they typically do so. Such results provide strong evidence that the development of infants' physical reasoning involves primarily learning *what* information to attend to in each event category, and not learning *how* to interpret this information. The priming trials could not teach the infants that objects typically retain their heights when lowered into tubes—they could only make height information salient for the infants.

In future research, we hope once again to modify our priming trials to determine what constitutes an adequate height-priming experience for 8-month-old infants in this situation. For example, would infants be equally successful if shown only two cylindrical objects, the short and tall objects used in the change event? Or if shown short, medium, and tall cylindrical objects that differ in pattern and color from those used in the test events? Answers to these and related questions will help us gain a clearer understanding of the mechanisms that underlie successful priming.

INDUCING INFANTS TO SUCCEED OR FAIL AT DETECTING VARIABLE VIOLATIONS: CARRYOVER MANIPULATIONS

According to our account of infants' physical reasoning, infants who are induced, through some contextual manipulation, to include information about a variable they have not yet identified in their physical representation of an event should then be able to detect change and interaction violations involving the variable. In the

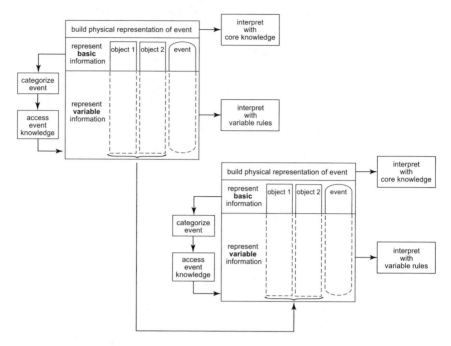

Figure 4–18. An account of infants' physical reasoning: How infants carry over variable information from one event representation to the next.

previous section, we discussed priming manipulations, which are designed to simply highlight a variable (or particular values of a variable). In this section, we discuss a very different sort of manipulation: carryover manipulations.

The point of departure for this research was the following question: What happens when infants see the same objects in two successive events from different event categories? Do they represent each event separately? Or do they carry over whatever variable information they included in their representation of the first event to their representation of the second event? The second alternative seemed to us more efficient, and hence more plausible (see Fig. 4–18). After all, why would infants represent the same information about the same objects over and over again as the objects move from one event to another? This would seem a waste of time and effort, and we already know from analyses of infants' perseverative errors in various tasks that infants attempt to be as efficient as possible (for reviews, see Aguiar & Baillargeon, 2000, 2003).

We reasoned that if infants carry over variable information from one event representation to the next, then infants who see an event in which a variable has been identified, followed by an event in which this same variable has not been identified, should show a *positive* carryover effect; the variable information included in the first event representation should be carried over to the second event representation, allowing infants to detect persistence violations involving the variable earlier than they otherwise would. Exposure to a single initial event would thus be sufficient to induce infants to detect a variable persistence violation in a subsequent event. As long as infants spontaneously include the appropriate variable information in their representation of the first event, this information should be—fortuitously—available to them when reasoning about the second event (e.g., Wang & Baillargeon, 2005).

At the same time, we realized that the converse should also be true: If variable information is carried over from one event representation to the next, then infants who see an event in which a variable has not been identified, followed by an event in which this same variable has been identified, should show a *negative* carryover effect; information about the variable should be absent from the first and hence from the second event representation, causing infants to fail to detect persistence violations they would have been able to detect otherwise.

Do infants show negative as well as positive carryover effects when they see the same objects involved in two successive events from different categories? A recent experiment (Li & Baillargeon, 2006) addressed this question. This experiment examined 8.5-month-old infants' ability to detect a surreptitious change to the height of an object in an event sequence comprising an occlusion and a covering event.

The infants were assigned to an occlusion-covering or a covering-occlusion condition. The infants in the occlusion-covering condition received either a change or a no-change test trial (see Fig. 4–19). At the beginning of the change trial, a short cylinder stood next to a tall rectangular cover with a knob attached to its top; the cylinder was half as tall as the rectangular portion of the cover. To start, an experimenter's gloved hand grasped the knob at the top of the cover, rotated the cover forward to show its hollow interior, and then replaced the cover next to the cylinder (orientation). Next, the hand slid the cover in front of the cylinder, fully hiding it, and then returned the cover to its original position on the apparatus floor (occlusion event). Finally, the hand lowered the cover over the cylinder, again fully hiding it, and then returned the cover to its initial position next to the cylinder (covering event). When the cover was removed from over the cylinder in the covering event, the cylinder was now as tall as the rectangular portion of the cover. In the no-change trial, the tall cylinder was used throughout the trial. The infants in the covering-occlusion condition (see Fig. 4–20) received similar change and no-change trials, except that the occlusion and covering events were performed in the reverse order: The cover was placed first over and then in front of the cylinder. The surreptitious change to the height of the cylinder in the change trial thus occurred in the occlusion rather than in the covering event.

Because the variable height is identified at about 3.5 months in occlusion events (Baillargeon & DeVos, 1991) but not until about 12 months in covering events (McCall, 2001; Wang et al., 2005; Wang & Baillargeon, 2006), we expected the 8.5-month-old infants in the occlusion-covering condition to show a positive carryover effect. When watching the occlusion event, the infants would categorize the event, access their knowledge of occlusion events, and include information about the relative heights of the cover and cylinder in their physical representation of the event. When the infants next saw the covering event, this height information would be carried over into this new physical representation;

No-change Trial
Orientation

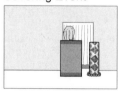 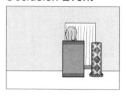 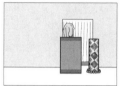

Occlusion Event

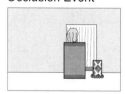  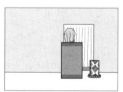

Covering Event

 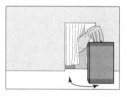 

Change Trial
Orientation

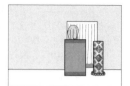  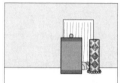

Occlusion Event

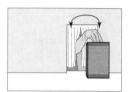 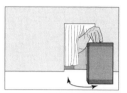 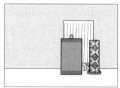

Covering Event

Figure 4–19. Test events used in the occlusion-covering condition of Li and Baillargeon (2006).

No-change Trial
Orientation

Covering Event

Occlusion Event
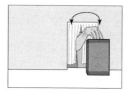

Change Trial
Orientation

Covering Event
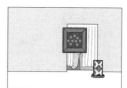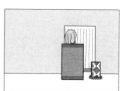

Occlusion Event

Figure 4–20. Test events used in the covering-occlusion condition of Li and Baillargeon (2006).

the information would then be interpreted in terms of the persistence principle, allowing the infants to detect the violation in the change event: A short cylinder cannot spontaneously change into a taller cylinder.

In contrast, we expected the infants in the covering-occlusion condition to show a negative carryover effect. When watching the covering event, the infants would include no height information in their physical representation of the event. As a result, no height information would be carried over when the infants next represented the occlusion event. The infants would thus fail to detect the persistence violation in the change event.

Results supported our predictions. In the occlusion-covering condition, the infants who saw the change trial looked reliably longer than those who saw the no-change trial; in the covering-occlusion condition, in contrast, the infants looked about equally during the two trials. Thus, whereas the 8.5-month-olds in the occlusion-covering condition *succeeded* in detecting a violation that infants typically cannot detect until about 12 months of age, the 8.5-month-olds in the covering-occlusion condition *failed* to detect a violation that infants typically can detect at 3.5 months of age. Seeing a particular event first thus helped infants detect a surreptitious change violation, or prevented them from detecting the same violation.

These results are interesting for several reasons. First, they provide strong support for the notion that infants detect variable persistence violations when they include information about the relevant variables in their physical representations of the events. The infants in the occlusion-covering condition carried over the height information from their physical representation of the first event to their physical representation of the second event. This information, once represented, became subject to the persistence principle, allowing the infants to detect the violation in the change event 3.5 months before they would otherwise have done.

Second, future research will need to address the discrepancy between the present results and those in the object-individuation literature (e.g., Xu & Carey, 1996; Wilcox & Baillargeon, 1998a; Wilcox & Chapa, 2002; Xu, 2002, 2003). In a seminal task designed by Xu and Carey (1996), two distinct objects (e.g., a ball and a toy duck) emerge successively from behind a wide screen. First, one object emerges to one side of the screen and then returns behind it; next, the other object emerges to the other side of the screen and then returns behind it. After several repetitions, the screen is removed to reveal either one of the objects (one-object outcome) or both objects (two-object outcome). In this task, 10-month-olds typically give no evidence that they expect two objects to be present when the screen is removed. But if infants carry over object representations from one event to another, why would they fail at this task? Why would infants fail to carry over the object representations they formed during the occlusion event to the post-occlusion event?

Our tentative answer to this question rests on two broad assumptions. The first is that infants carry over object representations from one event to another only when the available spatiotemporal information makes it possible to unambiguously *track* the objects from the first to the second event (e.g., Baillargeon, 2008; Wang & Baillargeon, 2008). In our carryover task, infants can establish continuous traces for the cover and cylinder from the first to the second event; at all times, infants know where each object is located, even when the cylinder is hidden (e.g., Leslie, Xu, Tremoulet, & Scholl, 1998; Scholl & Leslie, 1999). In the task of Xu and Carey (1996), in contrast, the available spatiotemporal information is not sufficient to determine that two objects are present behind the screen in the first event, or (a fortiori) to track the objects across the two events.

Our second assumption is that, when objects cannot unambiguously be tracked from one event to another, as in the task of Xu and Carey (1996), infants use a different strategy to determine how many objects should be present in the second event. Specifically, infants (1) retrieve their physical representation of the first event, (2) examine the basic spatiotemporal and identity information included in the representation to determine how many distinct objects emerged on either side of the screen, and (3) expect at least the same number of objects to be present in the second event (because the screen is wide, additional objects could also be present). We have referred to this strategy as involving the *mapping* of object representations from event to event (e.g., Wilcox & Baillargeon, 1998a, 1998b).

To see why a mapping strategy would lead infants to fail at the task of Xu and Carey (1996), consider what basic spatiotemporal and identity information infants represent when watching a ball and a toy duck emerge successively from behind a screen. The basic spatiotemporal information specifies the visible path that the ball and the duck follow on either side of the screen but is insufficient to establish whether they are the same object or different objects. The basic identity information for the ball and the duck is actually the same information, because both objects are closed and self-propelled. In terms of the basic information represented, there is thus nothing to suggest that there is more than one closed, self-propelled object emerging alternately on either side of the screen (recall that size, shape, pattern, and color information is variable information and is not included at the basic level). As a result, when the screen is removed and infants examine the basic information in their physical representation of the occlusion event, this information specifies that one closed, self-propelled object emerged from behind the screen. Infants thus form an expectation that at least one closed, self-propelled object should be present in the new, post-occlusion event. Because both the one- and the two-object outcomes are consistent with this expectation, neither outcome appears unexpected.

The preceding analysis makes a number of interesting predictions. For example, it suggests that infants should succeed at the task of Xu and Carey (1996) if the occlusion event involves two objects that receive different identity descriptions at the basic level: not two closed, self-propelled objects, as above, but instead a closed and an open object, or an inert and a self-propelled-object. Experiments are under way in different laboratories to test these predictions, with promising results. Meanwhile, possible support for the present analysis comes from recent experiments (e.g., Bonatti, Frot, Zangl, & Mehler, 2002; Wu & Baillargeon, 2008) showing that 10-month-old infants succeed at the task of Xu and Carey if the two objects that emerge successively from behind the screen are a human-like object (e.g., a self-propelled human doll) and a non-human-like object (e.g., a self-propelled toy animal), but not two human-like objects (e.g., two distinct self-propelled human dolls) or two non-human-like objects (e.g., two distinct self-propelled toy animals).

These results suggest that by 10 months of age, if not before, the basic identity information infants represent about objects includes whether they are human-like or not. Additional experiments are testing these speculations.

CONCLUSIONS

The account of infants' physical reasoning presented in this chapter rests on two central claims. One is that infants' physical representations of events initially include only basic information and become increasingly richer and more detailed as infants gradually identify relevant variables. The other claim is that infants primarily learn *what* information to include in their physical representations, not *how* to interpret this information once represented. Infants' core knowledge provides a causal framework for interpreting both the basic and the variable information infants include in their physical representations.

According to our account, the primary task of development, with respect to infants' physical reasoning, thus consists in the gradual identification of variables. Over the course of the first year or so, infants identify dozens and dozens of variables; event category by event category, vector by vector, variable by variable, infants learn what information to pay attention to when watching events. One analogy for this developmental process might be the following: Infants' physical-reasoning system can at first draw no more than rough blueprints of events, containing only a few key pieces of information; over time, these blueprints become increasingly detailed as infants learn what additional pieces of information should be included to better predict events' outcomes.

The Persistence Principle Revisited

As was mentioned earlier, Spelke and her colleagues (e.g., Spelke et al., 1992; Carey & Spelke, 1994; Spelke, 1994; Spelke et al., 1995b) have suggested that principles of continuity (objects exist and move continuously in time and space) and cohesion (objects are connected and bounded entities) guide infants' interpretation of physical events from birth. According to these principles, infants should be surprised if an object disappears into thin air or breaks apart—but they should not be surprised if an object surreptitiously changes size, shape, pattern, or color. And, indeed, we have seen that infants often fail to detect such violations.

However, we have offered an alternative interpretation for these failures. This interpretation rests on three main points. First, we have proposed that, instead of the separate principles of continuity and cohesion, infants possess a single, stronger principle of persistence, which states that objects exist and move continuously in time and space, retaining their physical properties as they do so (Baillargeon, 2008). From this perspective, a cohesion violation is only an extreme shape or size violation.

Second, the persistence principle can be applied only to the information infants include in their physical representations of events. Because infants initially include relatively little information in these representations, they often fail to detect persistence violations. Infants cannot be surprised when a tall object becomes shorter when briefly lowered into a tall tube, or when a purple toy becomes orange when briefly lowered into a container, if they did not include height and color information in their representations of the events.

Third, infants who are induced, through priming, carryover, or other contextual manipulations (e.g., Wilcox & Chapa, 2004; Gertner et al., 2005; Li & Baillargeon, 2005, 2006; Ng & Baillargeon, 2006; Wilcox, this volume), to include information about a variable they have not yet identified in their physical representation of an event can immediately detect persistence violations involving the variable.

The persistence principle states, in essence, that objects persist as they are in time and space. Why would such a constraint be helpful to infants? In this chapter, we have discussed several answers to this question. One is that the persistence principle helps young infants interpret the limited, basic information they represent about events (e.g., "object continues to exist under cover") and thus gets the task of learning about physical events off to a rapid start. Another is that the persistence principle helps infants identify relevant variables by supplying causal explanations for these variables. But a simpler way to think about the persistence principle might be to consider how infants would fare when watching, say, a ball roll along a surface toward a box some distance away if they had to check back and forth every second that the ball and box had not morphed into different objects or disappeared altogether. A notion of persistence means that the objects that are included in an event representation are expected to persist as they are within the representation, giving infants the opportunity to reason and learn about their interactions.

Future Directions

There are several directions in which our account of infants' physical reasoning needs to be extended. Three are mentioned briefly here.

A first direction concerns the links between infants' object-representation and physical-reasoning systems. We assume that, when shown two objects standing side by side at the start of an event, infants store information about the objects in their object-representation system; how detailed these representations are depends in part on how long the objects are available for examination (e.g., Hunter, Ross, & Ames, 1982; Rose, Gottfried, Melloy-Carminar, & Bridger, 1982; Hunter, Ames, & Koopman, 1983; Wagner & Sakovits, 1986; Hunter & Ames, 1988; Roder, Bushnell, & Sasseville, 2000). As the event unfolds, infants' physical-reasoning system may need to query the object-representation system for variable information. For example, if (1) infants realize they must include information about a variable in their physical representation of an event and (2) this information is no longer perceptually available (e.g., the object is now hidden), they may then access their object-representation system to retrieve the necessary information. In this view, infants who have not yet identified a variable as relevant to an event category might have encoded information about it in their object-representation system but might fail to retrieve this information to include it in their physical-reasoning system. These speculations suggest that infants who have not yet identified a variable as relevant to an event category might still demonstrate knowledge of the variable if tested in a task that taps their object-representation rather than their physical-reasoning system. Experiments are under way to investigate these and related possibilities (Li et al., 2006b).

A second direction concerns what might be called quantitative extensions of our account. Throughout this chapter, we have considered simple events involving two or three objects; for example, events in which an object is lowered into and then retrieved from a container. What would happen if infants were shown events involving multiple objects? Consider infants who have identified size, shape, and pattern as containment variables. If these infants saw containment events in which two, three, or four objects were lowered into a container, rather than only one, would they still encode the same variable information about each object? Similarly, what if infants were shown multiple events simultaneously; for example, if they saw two or more events in which one object was lowered into a container? Would infants include as much variable information about each event as if they saw a single event, or would they include less? Given infants' limited information-processing resources, we might expect them to encode less variable information with either multiple objects or multiple events, and recent evidence suggests that this is indeed the case (e.g., Mareschal & Johnson, 2003; Káldy & Leslie, 2005).

A final research direction, which we have been pursuing for some time (e.g., Baillargeon, Needham, & DeVos 1992; Needham & Baillargeon, 1993; Kotovsky & Baillargeon, 1994, 1998; Wang, Kaufman, & Baillargeon, 2003; Yuan & Baillargeon, 2005; Li, Baillargeon, & Needham, 2006a; Hespos & Baillargeon, 2008; Yuan & Baillargeon, 2008), involves extending our account to events other than those discussed in the present chapter; namely, support and collision events. So far, our results suggest that the account presented here applies equally well to these events. In all cases, infants begin with limited representations, which become richer as they identify relevant variables; core knowledge guides from birth the interpretation of the basic and variable information infants include in their event representations; and priming manipulations that highlight particular variables help infants detect violations earlier than they would otherwise have done.

Is the present account a nativist account? Yes, certainly; core knowledge is assumed to play a key role in infants' interpretation of physical events. Does the present account also emphasize learning? Here again, our answer is a resounding yes; much of what happens in the development of infants' physical reasoning is the gradual identification of variables, event category by event category, vector by vector, and variable by variable, as a result of infants' daily experiences. Core knowledge and experience are thus both necessary to explain the complex and protracted history of infants' acquisition of their physical knowledge.

Acknowledgments   This research was supported by a grant from NICHD (HD-021104) to the first author. We thank Jerry DeJong and Cindy Fisher for helpful suggestions, the staff of the University of Illinois Infant Cognition Laboratory for their help with the data collection, and the parents and infants who generously participated in the research.

Notes

1. Of course, the principle of persistence will apply somewhat differently to inert and self-propelled objects. For example, a cat can spontaneously alter its shape to some extent but a spoon cannot. Recent evidence suggests that, by 2.5 to 6 months of age, infants already recognize that some physical events may be possible for self-propelled but not inert objects (e.g., Wu & Baillargeon, 2006; Wu, Luo, & Baillargeon, 2006; Yuan & Baillargeon, 2008; Luo, Kaufman, & Baillargeon, in press).

2. One interesting question for future research is whether all rules begin as discrete functions, and then become continuous functions as needed. For example, do infants initially learn simply that objects protrude above containers when taller, but not shorter, than the containers? With such a rule, infants would be able to predict that a tall object should protrude above a short container—but not how much it should protrude.

3. We are not entirely certain which variable(s) infants attend to before 3 months of age and, thus, which variable(s) might precede lower-edge-discontinuity in the decision tree in Figure 4–5. Our working hypothesis is that there is at least one such variable, having to do with the presence of internal openings. We suspect that, by 2.5 months, infants expect an object to remain partly visible when behind an occluder with an internal opening—for example, an O-shaped screen, with a large central window. At this stage, infants would still expect an object to be hidden behind a screen shaped like an inverted U because such a screen does not present an internal opening; rather, an external opening is created when the screen is placed upright on a surface. In this manner, infants would attend first to internal and later to external openings in predicting when objects behind occluders should be visible or hidden. Experiments are planned to test these possibilities.

4. Because 3.5-month-old infants have been tested with height violations (Baillargeon & DeVos, 1991) but not yet width violations, it is unknown whether 3.5-month-old infants can in fact detect both height and width violations. If they can, then it is possible that infants represent height and width in terms of a more general size variable. In addition, to return to the issue raised in footnote 2, there is evidence that 5.5-month-olds not only can predict that a tall object should appear above a short occluder, but also can judge by how much it should protrude (Luo, Baillargeon, & Lécuyer, 2008). By 5.5 months of age, infants' rule for height in occlusion events thus appears to be a continuous rather than a discrete function.

5. Readers may wonder why variable transparency is such a late acquisition. Work by Johnson and Aslin (2000) suggests that infants do not begin to detect clear, transparent surfaces until about 7 months of age, as a result of developments in their contrast sensitivity, which might in turn be tied to the maturation of the magnocellular system.

6. Experiments with infants younger than 4.5 months are necessary to determine precisely when size and shape are identified as relevant variables and whether one variable is in fact typically identified before the other. We saw earlier that by 3.5 months, infants can reason about height and perhaps width in occlusion events (Baillargeon & DeVos, 1991; Wang et al., 2004). By 4 months, infants attend to shape information to organize static, partly occluded displays (e.g., Needham, 1998), so it may be that this variable is present by 4 months.

7. We are not claiming that all infants will show the same décalages; for example, not all infants will identify the variable height first as a containment and only later as a covering variable. Some infants may well identify the two variables at about the same time, or in the reverse order. When we say that infants identify height as a containment variable at about 7.5 months of age, what we are really saying is that 7.5-month-old infants as a group look reliably longer at a containment event that presents a height violation than at an event that presents no such violation; as a rule, about 75% of the infants show the effect. It is likely

that a few infants identify the variable earlier and that others do so later. As we make clear in the next section, the ages at which infants identify variables depend to a large extent on the ages at which they are exposed to appropriate observations from which to extract the variables. Thus, although most infants with similar day-to-day experiences may identify a variable at a certain age, infants with different experiences may identify it earlier or later.

8. Readers may wonder why we are describing this vector as "when does an object inside a container protrude above it?" as opposed to "when is an object inside a container hidden?" as with the occlusion vector in Figure 4–5. Our reason is empirical and comes from experiments on infants' responses to events involving transparent containers. In containment events, height is identified at about 7.5 months (e.g., Hespos & Baillargeon, 2001a; Li & Baillargeon, 2005; Hespos & Baillargeon, 2006) and transparency at about 9.5 months (Luo & Baillargeon, 2008). If these variables belonged to a single vector specifying when objects inside containers should be hidden, then we would expect 8.5-month-old infants to be surprised when a short object placed inside a tall, transparent container remains visible through the container; because the object is shorter than the container, infants should expect the object to be hidden, and they should be surprised when it is not (an error of commission). However, 8.5-month-old infants, in fact, are not surprised when an object placed inside a transparent container is either visible or not visible through the container (an error of omission) (Luo & Baillargeon 2008). These results suggest that, in containment events, height and transparency belong to separate vectors; whereas height belongs to a vector specifying when an object inside a container should protrude above it, transparency belongs to a vector having to do with when an object inside a container should be hidden. Thus, when a short object is lowered inside a tall transparent container, 8.5-month-old infants bring to bear their knowledge of height to predict that no portion of the object will be visible above the container. However, they cannot make a prediction as to whether the portion of the object inside the container should be hidden or visible. Apparently, it is not until infants are about 9.5 months that they form a vector specifying when objects inside containers should be hidden. This analysis leads to striking predictions concerning 7.5- and 8.5-month-old infants' responses to events involving transparent containers. When a tall object is lowered inside a short transparent container, infants should look reliably longer at the event if the top of the object is not visible above the container. However, as long as the top of the object protrudes above the container, infants should look about equally whether or not the bottom of the object is visible through the container. Experiments are planned to test these predictions.

9. We are suggesting that 4.5-month-old infants detect a change violation when a large ball disappears behind a narrow screen and a small ball reappears from behind it—but it could be argued that infants view this event as an interaction violation instead, or alternate between these two interpretations. Do infants reason that (1) because the large ball fills most of the space behind the narrow screen, it must be the only object present, and (2) the large ball cannot spontaneously become smaller (change violation)? Or do infants reason that (1) the large and small balls must be different objects and (2) the two cannot hide simultaneously behind the narrow screen (interaction violation)? We adopt the first interpretation in this chapter but recognize that further research is needed to establish which is in fact correct.

References

Aguiar, A., & Baillargeon, R. (1998). Eight-and-a-half-month-old infants' reasoning about containment events. *Child Development, 69,* 636–653.

Aguiar, A., & Baillargeon, R. (1999). 2.5-month-old infants' reasoning about when objects should and should not be occluded. *Cognitive Psychology, 39,* 116–157.

Aguiar, A., & Baillargeon, R. (2000). Perseveration and problem solving in infancy. In H. W. Reese (Ed.), *Advances in child development and behavior* (Vol. 27, pp. 135–180). San Diego: Academic Press.

Aguiar, A., & Baillargeon, R. (2002). Developments in young infants' reasoning about occluded objects. *Cognitive Psychology, 45,* 267–336.

Aguiar, A., & Baillargeon, R. (2003). Perseverative responding in a violation-of-expectation task in 6.5-month-old infants. *Cognition, 88,* 277–316.

Baillargeon, R. (1994). How do infants learn about the physical world? *Current Directions in Psychological Science, 3,* 133–140.

Baillargeon, R. (1995). A model of physical reasoning in infancy. In C. Rovee-Collier & L. P. Lipsitt (Eds.), *Advances in infancy research* (Vol. 9, pp. 305–371). Norwood, NJ: Ablex.

Baillargeon, R. (2002). The acquisition of physical knowledge in infancy: A summary in eight lessons. In U. Goswami (Ed.), *Blackwell handbook of childhood cognitive development* (pp. 47–83). Oxford: Blackwell.

Baillargeon, R. (2004). Infants' reasoning about hidden objects: Evidence for event-general and event-specific expectations. *Developmental Science, 7,* 391–424.

Baillargeon, R. (2008). Innate ideas revisited: For a principle of persistence in infants' physical reasoning. *Perspectives on Psychological Science, 3,* 2–13.

Baillargeon, R., & DeVos, J. (1991). Object permanence in young infants: Further evidence. *Child Development, 62,* 1227–1246.

Baillargeon, R., & Graber, M. (1987). Where's the rabbit? 5.5-month-old infants' representation of the height of a hidden object. *Cognitive Development, 2,* 375–392.

Baillargeon, R., Li, J., Luo, Y., & Wang, S. (2006). Under what conditions do infants detect continuity violations? In Y. Munakata & M. H. Johnson (Eds.), *Processes of change in brain and cognitive development* (Attention and Performance XXI, pp. 163–188). New York: Oxford University Press.

Baillargeon, R., Needham, A., & DeVos, J. (1992). The development of young infants' intuitions about support. *Early development and parenting, 1,* 69–78.

Baillargeon, R., Spelke, E. S., & Wasserman, S. (1985). Object permanence in 5-month-old infants. *Cognition, 20,* 191–208.

Berthier, N. E., Bertenthal, B. I., Seaks, J. D., Sylvia, M. R., Johnson, R. L., & Clifton, R. K. (2001). Using object knowledge in visual tracking and reaching. *Infancy, 2,* 257–284.

Bonatti, L., Frot, E., Zangl, R., & Mehler, J. (2002). The human first hypothesis: Identification of conspecifics and individuation of objects in the young infant. *Cognitive Psychology, 44,* 388–426.

Boudreau, J. P., & Bushnell, E. W. (2000). Spilling thoughts: Configuring attentional resources in infants' goal-directed actions. *Infant Behavior & Development, 23,* 543–566.

Bower, T. G. R. (1974). *Development in infancy.* San Francisco: W. H. Freeman.

Caramazza, A., McCloskey, M., & Green, B. (1981). Naive beliefs in "sophisticated" subjects: Misconceptions about trajectories of objects. *Cognition, 9,* 117–123.

Carey, S. (1985). *Conceptual change in childhood.* Cambridge, MA: MIT Press.

Carey, S., & Spelke, E. S. (1994). Domain-specific knowledge and conceptual change. In L. A. Hirschfeld & S. A. Gelman (Eds.), *Mapping the mind: Domain specificity in cognition and culture* (pp. 169–200). New York: Cambridge University Press.

Casasola, M., Cohen, L., & Chiarello, E. (2003). Six-month-old infants' categorization of containment spatial relations. *Child Development, 74,* 679–693.

DeJong, G. F. (1993). *Investigating explanation-based learning*. Boston, MA: Kluwer Academic Press.

Gertner, Y., Baillargeon, R., & Fisher, C. (2005, April). *Language facilitates infants' physical reasoning*. Paper presented at the biennial meeting of the Society for Research in Child Development, Atlanta, GA.

Hespos, S. J., & Baillargeon, R. (2001a). Infants' knowledge about occlusion and containment events: A surprising discrepancy. *Psychological Science, 12,* 140–147.

Hespos, S. J., & Baillargeon, R. (2001b). Knowledge about containment events in very young infants. *Cognition, 78,* 204–245.

Hespos, S. J., & Baillargeon, R. (2006). Décalage in infants' knowledge about occlusion and containment events: Converging evidence from action tasks. *Cognition, 99,* B31–B41.

Hespos, S. J., & Baillargeon, R. (2008). Young infants' actions reveal their developing knowledge of support variables: Converging evidence for violation-of-expectation findings. *Cognition, 107,* 304–316.

Hunter, M. A., & Ames, E. W. (1988). A multifactor model of infant preferences for novel and familiar stimuli. In C. Rovee-Collier & L. P. Lipsitt (Eds.), *Advances in infancy research* (Vol. 5, pp. 69–95). Norwood, NJ: Ablex.

Hunter, M. A., Ames, E. W., & Koopman, R. (1983). Effects of stimulus complexity and familiarization time on infant preferences for novel or familiar stimuli. *Developmental Psychology, 19,* 338–352.

Hunter, M. A., Ross, H. S., & Ames, E. W. (1982). Preferences for familiar or novel toys: Effects of familiarization time in 1-year-olds. *Developmental Psychology, 18,* 519–529.

Johnson, S. P., & Aslin, R. N. (2000). Infants' perception of transparency. *Developmental Psychology, 36,* 808–816.

Káldy, Z., & Leslie, A. M. (2005). A memory span of one? Object identification in 6.5-month-old infants. *Cognition, 97,* 153–177.

Karmiloff-Smith, A., & Inhelder, B. (1975). If you want to get ahead, get a theory. *Cognition, 3,* 195–212.

Kaufman, J., Csibra, G., & Johnson, M. H. (2004). Oscillatory activity in the infant brain reflects object maintenance. *Proceedings of the National Academy of Sciences, USA, 102,* 15271–15274.

Keen, R. E., & Berthier, N. E. (2004). Continuities and discontinuities in infants' representation of objects and events. In R. V. Kail (Ed.). *Advances in child development and behavior* (Vol. 32, pp. 243–279). New York: Academic Press.

Keil, F. C. (1991). The emergence of theoretical beliefs as constraints on concepts. In S. Carey & R. Gelman (Eds.), *The epigenesis of mind: Essays on biology and cognition* (pp. 237–256). Hillsdale, NJ: Erlbaum.

Keil, F. C. (1995). The growth of causal understandings of natural kinds. In D. Sperber, D. Premack, & A. J. Premack (Eds.), *Causal cognition: A multidisciplinary debate* (pp. 234–262). Oxford: Clarendon Press.

Kestenbaum, R., Termine, N., & Spelke, E. S. (1987). Perception of objects and object boundaries by 3-month-old infants. *British Journal of Developmental Psychology, 5,* 367–383.

Kochukhova, O., & Gredeback, G. (2007). Learning about occlusion: Initial assumptions and rapid adjustments. *Cognition, 105,* 26–46.

Kotovsky, L., & Baillargeon, R. (1994). Calibration-based reasoning about collision events in 11-month-old infants. *Cognition, 51,* 107–129.

Kotovsky, L., & Baillargeon, R. (1998). The development of calibration-based reasoning about collision events in young infants. *Cognition, 67,* 311–351.

Lécuyer, R., & Durand, K. (1998). Bi-dimensional representations of the third dimension and their perception by infants. *Perception, 27,* 465–472.

Leslie, A. M. (1994). ToMM, ToBY, and agency: Core architecture and domain specificity. In L. A. Hirschfeld & S. A. Gelman (Eds.), *Mapping the mind: Domain specificity in cognition and culture* (pp. 119–148). New York: Cambridge University Press.

Leslie, A. M. (1995). A theory of agency. In D. Sperber, D. Premack, & A. J. Premack (Eds.), *Causal cognition: A multidisciplinary debate* (pp. 121–149). Oxford: Clarendon Press.

Leslie, A. M. (2004). Who's for learning? *Developmental Science, 7,* 417–419.

Leslie, A. M., & Keeble, S. (1987). Do six-month-old infants perceive causality? *Cognition, 25,* 265–288.

Leslie, A. M., Xu, F., Tremoulet, P. D., & Scholl, B. J. (1998). Indexing and the object concept: Developing 'what' and 'where' system. *Trends in Cognitive Sciences, 2,* 10–18.

Li, J., & Baillargeon, R. (2005, April). *Change blindness in infancy: When do infants detect a change in an object's height?* Paper presented at the biennial meeting of the Society for Research in Child Development, Atlanta, GA.

Li, J., & Baillargeon, R. (2006, April). *Inducing 8.5-month-old infants succeed or fail at detecting height changes: Positive and negative mapping effects.* Paper presented at the Human Development Conference, Louisville, KY.

Li, J., Baillargeon, R., & Needham, A. (2006a, June). *When is an object that is released in contact with another object stable? Learning about support events in young infants.* Paper presented at the biennial International Conference on Infant Studies, Kyoto, Japan.

Li, J., Baillargeon, R., & Simons, J. D. (2006b, June). *How do infants represent physical variables? Connections between the object-recognition and physical-reasoning systems.* Paper presented at the biennial International Conference on Infant Studies, Kyoto, Japan.

Luo, Y., & Baillargeon, R. (2005). When the ordinary seems unexpected: Evidence for rule-based physical reasoning in young infants. *Cognition, 95,* 297–328.

Luo, Y., & Baillargeon, R. (2008). Infants' reasoning about transparent occluders and containers. Manuscript under review.

Luo, R., Baillargeon, R., Brueckner, L., & Munakata, Y. (2003). Reasoning about a hidden object after a delay: Evidence from robust representations in 5-month-old infants. *Cognition, 88,* B23–B32.

Luo, Y., Baillargeon, R., & Lécuyer, R. (2008). Young infants' reasoning about height in occlusion events. Manuscript under review.

Luo, Y., Kaufman, L., & Baillargeon, R. (in press). Young infants' reasoning about events involving inert and self-propelled objects. *Cognitive Psychology.*

Mareschal, D., & Johnson, M. H. (2003). The "what" and "where" of object representations in infancy. *Cognition, 88,* 259–276.

McCall, D. (2001, April). *Perseveration and infants' sensitivity to cues for containment.* Paper presented at the biennial meeting of the Society for Research in Child Development, Minneapolis, MN.

McCloskey, M. (1983). Naive theories of motion. In D. Gentner & A. L. Stevens (Eds.), *Mental models* (pp. 299–324). Hillsdale, NJ: Erlbaum.

McDonough, L., Choi, S., & Mandler, J. M. (2003). Understanding spatial relations: Flexible infants, lexical adults. *Cognitive Psychology, 46,* 229–259.

Mitchell, T. M. (1997). *Machine learning.* New York: McGraw-Hill.

Needham, A. (1998). Infants' use of featural information in the segregation of stationary objects. *Infant Behavior and Development, 21,* 47–76.

Needham, A. (2000). Improvements in object exploration skills may facilitate the development of object segregation in early infancy. *Journal of Cognition and Development, 1,* 131–156.

Needham, A., & Baillargeon, R. (1993). Intuitions about support in 4.5-month-old infants. *Cognition, 47,* 121–148.

Newcombe, N., Huttenlocher, J., & Learmonth, A. (1999). Infants' coding of location in continuous space. *Infant Behavior and Development, 22,* 483–510.

Ng, W., & Baillargeon, R. (2006, June). *Décalage in infants' reasoning about color information in occlusion and containment events.* Paper presented at the biennial International Conference on Infant Studies, Kyoto, Japan.

Ng, W., Baillargeon, R., & Wilcox, T. (2007, March). *8.5-month-olds use pattern but not color information to individuate objects in occlusion events.* Paper presented at the biennial meeting of the Society for Research in Child Development, Boston, MA.

Piaget, J. (1952). *The origins of intelligence in children.* New York: International Universities Press.

Piaget, J. (1954). *The construction of reality in the child.* New York: Basic Books.

Proffitt, D. R., Kaiser, M. K., & Whelan, S. M. (1990). Understanding wheel dynamics. *Cognitive Psychology, 22,* 342–373.

Quinlan, J. R. (1993). *C4.5: Programs for machine learning.* San Mateo: Morgan Kaufmann.

Quinn, P. (2007). On the infant's prelinguistic conception of spatial relations: Three developmental trends and their implications for spatial language learning. In J. M. Plumert & J. P. Spencer (Eds.), *The emerging spatial mind* (pp. 117–141). New York: Oxford University Press.

Roder, B. J., Bushnell, E. W., & Sasseville, A. M. (2000). Infants' preferences for familiarity and novelty during the course of visual processing. *Infancy, 1,* 491–507.

Rose, S. A., Gottfried, A. W., Melloy-Carminar, P., & Bridger, W. H. (1982). Familiarity and novelty preferences in infant recognition memory: Implications for information processing. *Developmental Psychology, 18,* 704–713.

Scholl, B. J., & Leslie, A. M. (1999). Explaining the infant's object concept: Beyond the perception/cognition dichotomy. In E. Lepore & Z. Pylyshyn (Eds.), *What is cognitive science?* (pp. 26-73). Oxford: Blackwell.

Siegler, R. S. (1978). The origins of scientific reasoning. In R. S. Siegler (Ed.), *Children's thinking: What develops?* (pp. 109–149). Hillsdale, NJ: Erlbaum.

Sitskoorn, S. M., & Smitsman, A. W. (1995). Infants' perception of dynamic relations between objects: Passing through or support? *Developmental Psychology, 31,* 437–447.

Slater, A. (1995). Visual perception and memory at birth. In C. Rovee-Collier & L. P. Lipsitt (Eds.), *Advances in infancy research* (Vol. 9, pp. 107–162). Norwood, NJ: Ablex.

Spelke, E. S. (1982). Perceptual knowledge of objects in infancy. In J. Mehler, E. Walker, & M. Garrett (Eds.), *Perspectives on mental representation* (pp. 409–430). Hillsdale, NJ: Erlbaum.

Spelke, E. S. (1994). Initial knowledge: Six suggestions. *Cognition, 50,* 431–445.

Spelke, E. S., Breinlinger, K., Macomber, J., & Jacobson, K. (1992). Origins of knowledge. *Psychological Review, 99,* 605–632.

Spelke, E. S., Kestenbaum, R., Simons, D. J., & Wein, D. (1995a). Spatiotemporal continuity, smoothness of motion, and object identity in infancy. *British Journal of Developmental Psychology, 13,* 1–30.

Spelke, E. S., Phillips, A., & Woodward, A. L. (1995b). Infants' knowledge of object motion and human action. In D. Sperber, D. Premack, & A. J. Premack (Eds.), *Causal cognition: A multidisciplinary debate* (pp. 44–78). Oxford: Clarendon Press.

von Hofsten, C., Kochukhova, O., & Rosander, K. (2007). Predictive tracking over occlusions by 4-month-old infants. *Developmental Science, 10,* 625–640.

Vosniadou, S., & Brewer, W. F. (1992). Mental models of the earth: A study of conceptual change in childhood. *Cognitive Psychology, 24,* 535–585.

Wagner, S. H., & Sakovits, L. J. (1986). A process analysis of infant visual and cross-modal recognition memory: Implications for an amodal code. In L. P. Lipsitt & C. Rovee-Collier (Eds.), *Advances in infancy research* (Vol. 4, pp. 195–217). Norwood, NJ: Ablex.

Wang, S., & Baillargeon, R. (2005). Inducing infants to detect a physical violation in a single trial. *Psychological Science, 16,* 542–549.

Wang, S., & Baillargeon, R. (2006). Infants' physical knowledge affects their change detection. *Developmental Science, 9,* 173–181.

Wang, S., & Baillargeon, R. (2008a). Can infants be "taught" to attend to a new physical variable in an event category? The case of height in covering events. *Cognitive Psychology, 56,* 284–326.

Wang, S., & Baillargeon, R. (2008b). Detecting impossible changes in infancy: A three-system account. *Trends in Cognitive Sciences, 12,* 17–23.

Wang, S., Baillargeon, R., & Brueckner, L. (2004). Young infants' reasoning about hidden objects: Evidence from violation-of-expectation tasks with test trials only. *Cognition, 93,* 167–198.

Wang, S., Baillargeon, R., Paterson, S. (2005). Detecting continuity and solidity violations in infancy: A new account and new evidence from covering events. *Cognition, 95,* 129–173.

Wang, S., Kaufman, L., & Baillargeon, R. (2003). Should all stationary objects move when hit? Developments in infants' causal and statistical expectations about collision events. *Infant Behavior and Development, 26,* 529–568.

Wilcox, T. (1999). Object individuation: Infants' use of shape, size, pattern, and color. *Cognition, 72,* 125–166.

Wilcox, T., & Baillargeon, R. (1998a). Object individuation in infancy: The use of featural information in reasoning about occlusion events. *Cognitive Psychology, 17,* 97–155.

Wilcox, T., & Baillargeon, R. (1998b). Object individuation in young infants: Further evidence with an event-monitoring task. *Developmental Science, 1,* 127–142.

Wilcox, T., & Chapa, C. (2002). Infants' reasoning about opaque and transparent occluders in an object individuation task. *Cognition, 85,* B1–B10.

Wilcox, T., & Chapa, C. (2004). Priming infants to attend to color and pattern information in an individuation task. *Cognition, 90,* 265–302.

Wilcox, T., Nadel, L., & Rosser, R. (1996). Location memory in healthy preterm and full-term infants. *Infant Behavior & Development, 19,* 309–323.

Wilcox, T., & Schweinle, A. (2003). Infants' use of speed information to individuate objects in occlusion events. *Infant Behavior and Development, 26,* 253–282.

Wilson, R. A., & Keil, F. C. (2000). The shadows and shallows of explanation. In F. C. Keil & R. A. Wilson (Eds.), *Explanation and cognition* (pp. 87–114). Cambridge: MIT Press.

Wu, D., & Baillargeon, R. (2006, June). *Can a self-propelled object rearrange its parts? 6-month-old infants' reasoning about possible object transformations.* Paper presented at the biennial International Conference on Infant Studies, Kyoto, Japan.

Wu, D., Baillargeon, R. (2008, March). *One or two humans? 10-month-olds' use of ontological and featural information to individuate objects.* Paper presented at the biennial International Conference on Infant Studies, Vancouver, Canada.

Wu, D., Luo, Y., & Baillargeon, R. (2006, June). *What object should appear in the window? 4-month-old infants' reasoning about inert and self-moving objects.* Paper presented at the biennial International Conference on Infant Studies, Kyoto, Japan.

Xu, F. (2002). The role of language in the acquiring object kind concepts in infancy. *Cognition, 85,* 223–250.

Xu, F. (2003). The development of object individuation in infancy. In F. Fagan and H. Hayne (Eds.), *Progress in infancy research* (Vol. 3, pp. 159–192). Mahwah, NJ: Erlbaum.

Xu, F., & Carey, S. (1996). Infants' metaphysics: The case of numerical identity. *Cognitive Psychology, 30,* 111–153.

Yonas, A., & Granrud, C. E. (1984). The development of sensitivity to kinetic, binocular, and pictorial depth information in human infants. In D. Engle, D. Lee, & M. Jeannerod (Eds.), *Brain mechanisms and spatial vision* (pp. 113–145). Dordrecht: Martinus Nijhoff.

Yuan, S., & Baillargeon, R. (2005, April). *Priming infants to attend to weight information in support events.* Paper presented at the biennial meeting of the Society for Research in Child Development, Atlanta, GA.

Yuan, S., & Baillargeon, R. (2008, March). *2.5-month-olds hold different expectations about the support of inert and self-propelled objects.* Paper presented at the biennial International Conference on Infant Studies, Vancouver, Canada.

5

Experience Primes Infants to Individuate Objects
Illuminating Learning Mechanisms

TERESA WILCOX AND REBECCA WOODS,
TEXAS A&M UNIVERSITY

The visual world provides infants with a wealth of information about objects and their physical properties. At the same time, as infants and objects move about in the world, visual contact is frequently lost and then, later, regained. For example, a toy train passes through a tunnel and emerges at the other side, or a favorite blanket slides behind the car seat and later moves back into view. The dynamic nature of the visual world presents infants with the challenge of determining whether an object currently in view is the same object or a different object than seen before. The outcome of this process determines how infants perceive, think about, and act on objects. Given the importance of object individuation to human cognition, researchers have invested a great deal of energy to identify the origins and development of this capacity.

Initial studies focused on the type of information infants use to individuate objects and how this changes during the first year of life. The collective outcomes of this research can be summarized in the following way. First, spatiotemporal information is fundamental to the individuation process. For example, by 3.5 months, infants use discontinuities in speed or path of motion to signal the presence of distinct objects (Baillargeon & Graber, 1987; Spelke, Kestenbaum, Simons, & Wein, 1995; Aguiar & Baillargeon, 2002; Wilcox & Schweinle, 2002, 2003). Second, young infants can also use featural information to individuate objects, but this capacity is not as well developed. For example, by 4.5 months infants use form features (e.g., shape, size), but it is not until much later that infants use surface features (e.g., color, pattern, luminance) as the basis for individuating objects (Wilcox, 1999; Tremoulet, Leslie, & Hall, 2001; Woods & Wilcox, in press). Third, and perhaps most important, studies have revealed that infants' capacity to individuate objects is not "all-or-none" but is supported in some conditions and not in others (Xu & Carey, 1996; Wilcox & Baillargeon, 1998a; Tremoulet et al., 2001; Wilcox & Chapa, 2002; Wilcox & Schweinle, 2002, 2003; Wilcox & Chapa, 2004; Wilcox, Woods, Chapa, & McCurry, 2007).

More recently, attention has shifted toward understanding the reasons that infants are more sensitive to some types of information than to others and how infants come to identify new sources of information as relevant to the individuation problem. One approach we have taken is to identify experiences that can alter infants' sensitivity to surface features. The conditions under which these experiences are most effective can reveal important information about the nature and content of infants' object representations, how infants' use these representations, and the cognitive and/or learning mechanisms that govern changes in infants' individuation capacities. This chapter focuses on this body of research.

ASSESSING OBJECT INDIVIDUATION IN INFANCY

Before we review this research, however, a discussion of the methods that we use to assess object individuation in infancy is warranted. A number of violation-of-expectation tasks have been developed to assess object individuation. One task that is particularly sensitive to developmental changes in this capacity is the narrow-screen task (Wilcox & Baillargeon, 1998a, 1998b; Wilcox, 1999; Woods & Wilcox, 2006). In the narrow-screen task, infants participate in a two-phase procedure that consists of a familiarization phase and a test phase. In the familiarization phase, infants are presented with a familiarization event in which two featurally distinct objects (e.g., a ball and a box) emerge successively to opposite sides of a wide yellow screen. The two objects move in the same depth plane (i.e., along the same axis) so that it would not be possible for them to pass each other behind the screen without colliding. The yellow screen is wide enough to hide both objects, side by side, at the same time. The purpose of the familiarization trials is to acquaint the infants with the objects they will see in the test trials. In the test phase, infants are presented with a test event (Fig. 5–1) that is identical to the familiarization event except that the wide yellow familiarization screen is replaced with a blue screen that is either too narrow (narrow-screen event) or sufficiently wide (wide-screen event) to hide both objects simultaneously. If infants (a) perceive the different-features event as involving two separate and distinct objects and (b) recognize that both objects can fit behind the wide but not the narrow screen, then they should find the narrow- but not the wide-screen event unexpected. Hence, longer looking at narrow- than wide-screen events is taken as evidence for object individuation.

In some of our first studies using the narrow-screen task (Wilcox & Baillargeon, 1998a, 1998b) we found that when the objects seen to each side of the screen varied on several feature dimensions, including shape, color, and pattern, infants 4.5 to 11.5 months successively individuated the objects (i.e., looked reliably longer at the narrow- than at the wide-screen test event). In control studies, (a) the objects were made sufficiently small to fit behind either the narrow or the wide screen or (b) the same object was seen to each side of the screen.

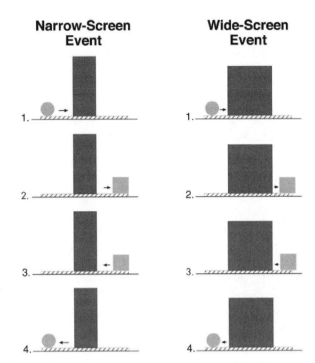

Figure 5–1. The test events of the narrow-screen task developed by Wilcox and Baillargeon (1998a, 1998b). Steps 1–4 repeat until the end of the trial.

In the control studies, infants looked equally at the narrow- and wide-screen test events, supporting Wilcox and Baillargeon's (1998a, 1998b) interpretation of the narrow-screen results. Finally, subsequent research using a different violation-of-expectation task provides converging evidence for the conclusion that young infants use featural differences to signal the presence of distinct objects (Wilcox & Baillargeon, 1998a; Wilcox & Schweinle, 2002).

Despite converging evidence from control studies and from other violation-of-expectation tasks, questions have been raised about the extent to which the narrow-screen task assesses object individuation in infants. For example, Xu and Carey (2001; Xu, Carey, & Quint, 2004) have offered an alternative interpretation for infants' looking longer at narrow- than at wide-screen events that does not involve object individuation. The logic of this account rests on a perceptual phenomenon called the tunnel effect. Under select conditions, adults perceive different-features events as involving a single object that changes it appearance when out of view. Xu and Carey have suggested that the conditions of the narrow-screen event support the tunnel effect. In this view, infants look longer at different-features narrow-screen events because they (1) perceive the event as involving a single object and (2) find changes in the objects' appearance, as it moves back and forth behind the screen, unexpected. Wide-screen events do not support the tunnel effect; that is why infants do not demonstrate prolonged looking to different-features wide-screen events. Although a plausible hypothesis, data collected in our lab using a different methodology argue against this interpretation of the narrow-screen results.

Recently, we have designed a new task, one that depends on reaching rather than looking behavior, to assess competing interpretations of the narrow-screen results (McCurry, Wilcox, & Woods, 2008). In one experiment, infants aged five to seven months (M age = six months, seven days) saw a test event in which a box disappeared behind the left edge of a screen and a ball emerged at the right edge (Fig. 5–2). The screen was either narrow or wide and consisted of a wood frame to which multiple layers of fringe were attached. The fringe occluded the area behind the screen. Before the test trials, infants were shown that the fringe allowed hands to easily pass through, and the infants were allowed to reach for objects through the fringed screen. After the ball came to rest at the right edge of the platform, the platform was moved forward so that the screen was directly in front of the infant; the infant was then allowed to reach. The event parameters (e.g., the size of the objects and the width of the screens, the rate at which the objects moved, the length of the trajectory, the time the objects were occluded) were identical to those used in our narrow-screen violation-of-expectation experiments (Wilcox & Baillargeon, 1998a, 1998b; Wilcox, 1999). If infants use the featural differences between the box and the ball to signal the presence of distinct objects and recognize that one of the objects (i.e., the box) is hidden behind the screen at the end of the event sequence, they should spend significantly more time reaching through the fringed screen than reaching for the ball at the end of the platform. In contrast, if infants interpret the event as involving a single object, which changes its appearance when behind the screen, they should spend more time reaching for the visible ball at the end of the platform than reaching through the fringed screen. The results revealed that the infants spent significantly more time reaching through the fringed screen than reaching for the ball at the end of the platform, as if they were searching for the hidden box. In addition, 23 of the 28 infants tested (83%) demonstrated this pattern of reaching. Most importantly, the reaching behavior of the infants in the narrow- and wide-screen conditions did not differ reliably. Together, these results suggest that the infants interpreted the box–ball event as involving two objects and that this interpretation did not vary by screen width.[1]

There is an alternative interpretation of the box–ball results, however, that should be considered. It is possible that the infants reached more to the screen than to the ball because the screen was closer to them and they found it more interesting, and not because they were searching for the box behind the screen. To assess this interpretation, another group of five- to seven-month-olds (M age = 6 months, 8 days) were tested using the procedure described above with one difference: A ball was seen to both sides of the screen. If the infants who saw the box–ball event spent more time reaching to the screen than to the ball because the screen was closer and more interesting, then the infants who saw the ball–ball event should also reach more to the screen than to the ball. In contrast, if the infants who saw the ball–ball event spent more time reaching to the screen because they were attempting to retrieve the box that was hidden behind the screen, then the infants who saw the ball–ball event should direct their reaching behavior to the visible ball (since the screen does not hide a second object). The results revealed that the infants spent significantly more time reaching for the ball than for the screen. In addition, 24 of the 28 infants tested (86%) reached more often to the ball than to the screen. These results suggest two conclusions. First, the infants interpreted the ball–ball event as involving a single object, a ball that moved behind the screen and came to rest at the right edge of the platform. Second, the reaching behavior of the ball–ball infants is better explained by a directed search for the hidden box than as an interest in the fringed screen.

In summary, the outcome of these search experiments provides converging evidence for the conclusion that the narrow-screen violation-of-expectation task assesses infants' capacity to individuate objects and not lower-level perceptual processes, such as the tunnel effect. This result is important because most of the experiments described in this chapter use the narrow-screen task to assess object individuation. The outcome of these search experiments also suggests that the fringed-screen task is a sensitive and reliable measure of object individuation in infancy. Hence, we now have another method with which to investigate developmental changes in infants' individuation capacities.

INFANTS' DIFFERENTIAL SENSITIVITY TO FORM AND SURFACE FEATURES

At the same time that our investigations have indicated that young infants use featural information to individuate objects, they have also revealed that infants are not equally sensitive to all types of featural information. Notice that in the box–ball and ball–ball studies described so far, the objects seen to each side of the screen differed on many feature dimensions. Object features can be divided into two broad categories: those features that specify the three-dimensional form of an object and those that convey information about surface properties. We have systematically investigated infants' sensitivity to form and surface features during the first year of life using the narrow-screen task (Wilcox, 1999; Wilcox et al., 2007 [Experiment 1]; Woods & Wilcox, 2006). In these experiments, the objects seen to each side of the screen varied on only one feature dimension at a time (e.g., the objects differed in only shape or color). The results of these studies revealed that by 4.5 months, infants use form features, such as shape or size, as the basis for individuating objects. In contrast, it is not until later in the first year that infants use surface features, such as pattern, color, or luminance. Most relevant to this chapter is the development of infants' sensitivity to color information. We have found that it is not until 11.5 months that infants use color differences to individuate objects. These data are consistent with data obtained in studies of object segregation and identification, where an advantage for form over color information has also been observed (Needham, 1999; Tremoulet et al., 2001). This pattern of results is intriguing because by 11.5 months, infants can perceive color differences, yet they fail to draw on these differences to individuate objects.

Figure 5–2. The ball–box test events of the search task of McCurry, Wilcox, and Woods (2008).

123

EXPLAINING INFANTS' GREATER SENSITIVITY TO FORM THAN TO COLOR INFORMATION

There are probably several factors that contribute to infants' greater sensitivity to form than color information. It is likely that the developmental hierarchy favoring form features reflects, at least to some extent, the nature of the developing visual system. Because color vision is initially quite poor (Peeples & Teller, 1975; Adams, Courage, & Mercer, 1994; Adams, 1995; Adams & Courage, 1998; Teller, 1998), young infants have difficulty getting good information about color. On the other hand, infants' sensitivity to areas of high contrast (Adams & Maurer, 1984; Stephens & Banks, 1987) and to motion-related information (Kellman, 1984; Slater & Morison, 1985; Slater, Morison, Town, & Rose, 1985; Kellman & Short, 1987; Slater, Mattock, & Brown, 1990; Arterberry & Yonas, 2000) presents even young infants with many opportunities to gather information about object form. However, visual maturation cannot fully explain the developmental hierarchy favoring form features. First, infants are sensitive to color differences long before they use those differences to individuate objects. By 4.5 months, infants detect, categorize, and demonstrate memory for color information (Bornstein, 1975; Bornstein, Kessen, & Weiskopf, 1976; Moskowitz-Cook, 1979; Banks & Salapatek, 1981; Powers, Schneck, & Teller, 1981; Hayne, Rovee-Collier, & Perris, 1987; Catherwood, Crassini, & Freiberg, 1989; Brown, 1990; Banks & Shannon, 1993; Teller & Palmer, 1996; Franklin & Davies, 2004). Second, recent research indicates that the type of information a feature conveys (i.e., the extent to which it gives rise to object form) is a better predictor of whether that feature will be used to individuate objects than the age at which the feature can be perceived (Woods & Wilcox, 2006).

We have suggested that the developmental hierarchy favoring form features reflects, to a greater extent, information-processing biases (Wilcox, 1999; Wilcox, Schweinle, & Chapa, 2003). According to this hypothesis, when faced with an individuation problem, infants (who have limited information-processing resources) attend to those features that are intimately tied to objects and that are predictive and stable over time. Form features specify the physical nature of objects: the space they occupy, their substance, and how they will move and interact with other objects. Form features are also important for interpreting physical events. For example, the size and shape of an object determines whether it can fit into a container or serve as a source of support for another object. In addition, the form of an object rarely changes or becomes altered, and even young infants expect object form to remain stable across time and situations (Meltzoff & Borton, 1979; Spelke, 1979; Gibson & Walker, 1984; Slater & Morison, 1985; Bahrick, 1987; Granrud, 1987; Slater et al., 1990). In contrast, color information has little predictive value. Although color features typically co-occur with other object properties that are meaningful, color information is not unambiguously linked to objects or relevant to understanding the way in which the physical world operates (e.g., the color of an object does not predict whether it will fit into a container or support another object). In addition, color information is often perceived by infants as unstable across viewing conditions (Dannemiller & Hanko, 1987; Dannemiller,

1989). Because of these factors, infants do not view color information as particularly salient when tracking objects across space and time.

Implicit in this analysis is the idea that if infants could be led to view color as predictive and intimately linked to objects across context, they would be more likely to use color differences to individuate objects. That is, the experience of viewing color information as constant, in a world in which color is typically arbitrary, would lead infants to perceive color information as relevant to object individuation. This conceptual framework forms the foundation for the priming studies we have conducted.

We have used two different approaches to test the hypothesis that infants can be primed to attend to surface features through select experiences. One approach is to make surface features functionally relevant. In these experiments, infants view events in which the color of an object predicts the function in which it will engage. The second approach is to facilitate infants' perception of color as a stable and enduring object property. In these experiments, infants are allowed multisensory (i.e., visual and tactile) exploration of the objects before the test event. These two sets of priming studies are described in the next two sections.

PRIMING SERIES I: MAKING COLOR PREDICTIVE BY PAIRING COLOR WITH OBJECT FUNCTION

In our first set of priming studies, we examined the extent to which pairing color with object function would increase infants' sensitivity to color differences. There is evidence that infants are sensitive to the functional properties of objects and find these properties particularly salient when observing and interacting with objects (Freeman, Lloyd, & Sinha, 1980; Meltzoff, 1988a, 1988b; Pier-LeBonniec, 1995). The fact that infants attend so closely to object function led us to hypothesize that if color were predictive of function, infants would find color differences more salient. That is, priming would be most effective if color were paired with an object property to which infants are already sensitive.

Color–Function Priming

In the first experiment of this series, 9.5-month-olds saw two pairs of pretest events prior to the familiarization and test events; each pair consisted of a pound event and a pour event (Fig. 5–3) (Wilcox & Chapa, 2004). In the first pair of pretest events, a green can with a handle pounded a peg; then a red can with a handle poured salt. The two cans were identical in appearance except for their color. In the second pair of pretest events, the green and red cans were replaced with green and red cups (Fig. 5–4). That is, the first pair of pretest events was seen with Object Pair 1 of Fig. 5–4 and the second pair of pretest events was seen with Object Pair 2 of Fig. 5–4. Following the pretest events, the narrow-screen procedure was employed. In the test event, infants saw a green ball–red ball event with the narrow or the wide screen. Previous research indicates that when viewing this occlusion sequence, infants younger than 11.5 months look equally at the

Pound Event

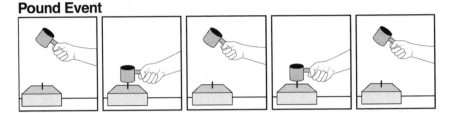

Pour Event

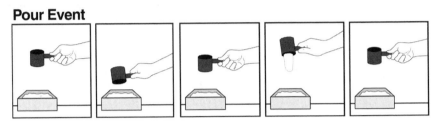

Figure 5–3. The pound–pour events of Wilcox and Chapa (2004). The cup that pounded was green, and the cup that poured was red.

narrow- and the wide-screen test event (Wilcox, 1999; Wilcox et al., 2007 [Experiment 1]). However, after viewing the pound–pour events, the 9.5-month-olds looked reliably longer at the narrow- than at the wide-screen test event, as if they had now used the color difference to individuate the balls. These results suggest that showing the infants the functional value of attending to color information (the only way the infants could distinguish between the two containers and the function they would serve was by their color) heightened infants' sensitivity to color features in the test event.

Additional research revealed two constraints on the effectiveness of this priming procedure (Wilcox & Chapa, 2004). First, the actions in which the objects engage must be functionally relevant. For example, in one experiment, 9.5-month-olds were tested using the same procedure, with one modification: In the pound event, the green containers moved up and down to the right of the peg, without ever coming in contact with the peg; and in the pour event, the red containers made scooping and pouring motions to the right of the box with the salt, without actually scooping or pouring salt. Hence, the pound–pour motion events were identical to the original pound-pour events, except that the actions the objects performed were functionally relevant. The infants in this experiment looked about equally at the two test events, as if they failed to use the color difference to individuate the objects. Simply seeing the objects perform distinct actions was not sufficient to induce infants to attend to color information. Second, infants need to see at least two pairs of pound–pour events with two different object pairs.

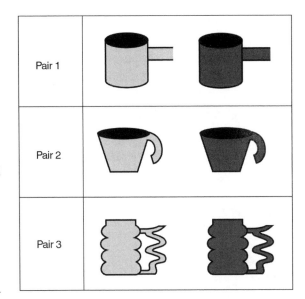

Figure 5–4. The object pairs used in the pound–pour events of Wilcox and Chapa (2004). The cups on the left were green, and the cups on the right were red. Object Pairs 1 and 2 were used with 9.5-month-olds and Object Pairs 1, 2, and 3 were used with 7.5-month-olds.

If 9.5-month-olds see two pairs of pound–pour events with the same object pair (i.e., Object Pair 1 of Fig. 5–4), they do not demonstrate color priming in the individuation task. Similar results are obtained with 7.5-month-olds, except that the younger infants need to see three pairs of pretest trials with three different object pairs (Fig. 5–4). Together, these results suggest that in order for infants to extract the rule that green objects function differently than red objects, they must see multiple pairs of red and green objects (i.e., multiple exemplars). Collectively, these data suggest that it is the formation of categorical event representations in which color is linked to object function that increases infants' sensitivity to color differences.

The Nature of the Representations That Are Formed During Color–Function Priming

In subsequent studies (Wilcox et al., in press), we examined the nature of the representations that are laid down during the priming experience. One issue we have focused on is the level of specificity (or abstraction) at which infants represent feature–function events. For example, in the pound–pour experiments, the infants could have represented the pretest events as (1) green and red objects perform different functions or (2) different-colored objects perform different functions. These make different predictions about the kind of information to which infants will be primed (i.e., green and red only or all colors). To assess these predictions, we tested 9.5-month-olds using a procedure that differed from the pound–pour procedure in two ways. First, the pound–pour events were replaced with stir–lift

Stir Event

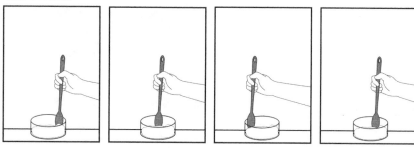

Lift Event

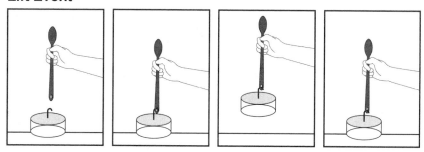

Figure 5–5. The stir–lift events of Wilcox, Woods, and Chapa (in press). The spoon that stirred was green, and the spoon that lifted was red.

events; green spoons stirred salt in a bowl, and red spoons lifted a bowl by a hook (Fig. 5–5). Two pairs of spoons were used (Fig 5–6). Second, the colors of the spoons seen in the stir–lift events were the same as (i.e., green and red) or different from (i.e., yellow and blue) the colors of the balls. If infants are primed to attend only to the color difference seen in the stir–lift event, the infants in the same-colors but not the different-colors condition should successfully individuate the green and red ball. In contrast, if infants are primed to attend to color differences more generally, the infants in both conditions should individuate the green and red balls. The results indicated that the infants in the same-colors condition looked reliably longer at the narrow-screen than at the wide-screen test event. In contrast, the infants in the different-colors condition looked about equally at both test events. The infants were primed to attend only to the color difference seen in the stir–lift events, suggesting that their representation of the events was quite specific.

It is possible, however, that, given the appropriate exemplars, infants would form event representations that were more abstract. There is evidence from the categorization research that when category exemplars are made more variable, infants' categorical representations become more inclusive (Quinn, Eimas, & Rosenkrantz,

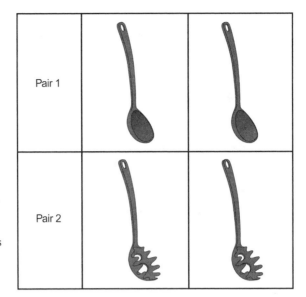

Figure 5–6. The object pairs used in the stir–lift experiments of Wilcox, Woods, and Chapa (in press). In the same-colors condition, the spoons in each pair were green and red. In the different-colors condition, the spoons in each pair were yellow and blue.

1993). Perhaps infants would be more likely to generalize to other colors in the test event if each pair of pretest events (e.g., each exemplar of the relation between color and function) were seen with a different color pair. To assess this possibility, 9.5-month-olds were tested using the stir–lift procedure described above, except the first pair of spoons was yellow and blue, and the second pair was purple and orange (Wilcox et al., in press). To our surprise, the results suggested that "old" 9.5-month-olds (9 months, 13 days to 10 months, 5 days) responded differently to this manipulation than did "young" 9.5-month-olds (8 months, 22 days to 9 months, 12 days). For ease in discussion, we will refer to these two groups as 9.5-month-olds and 9-month-olds, respectively. The 9.5-month-olds looked reliably longer at the narrow-screen than at the wide-screen test event, indicating that they individuated the green and the red ball. In contrast, the 9-month-olds looked about equally at the narrow- and the wide-screen test events, indicating that they failed to use the difference in color to individuate the balls. These results suggest two conclusions. First, after viewing events in which different-colored objects performed different functions, the 9.5-month-olds extracted from the experience that color differences, more generally, are important. Hence, they attend to other, novel colors in the test events. Second, there is an important change during the ninth month of life in infants' capacity to form event categories that are more inclusive. Whereas the 9.5-month-olds successfully formed event categories that generalized across color, the 9-month-olds failed to do so.

Finally, we investigated the extent to which we could facilitate the younger infants' formation of event categories that were more inclusive (Wilcox et al., in press). The goal of these studies was to identify the underlying basis for nine-month-olds' difficulty in forming inclusive event categories. Two different approaches were used. One approach was to show 9-month-olds the yellow and blue spoons together in the pretest events. Again, drawing from the categorization research, there is evidence that infants 3 to 18 months in age are more likely to demonstrate enhanced performance on categorization tasks when they are allowed to directly compare items than they do when they are presented with items one at a time (Quinn, 1987; Namy, Smith, & Gershkoff-Stowe, 1997; Needham, 2001, Needham, Dueker, & Lockhead, 2005; Oakes & Ribar, 2005). Gentner and Namy (1999) argued that the process of comparison facilitates the extraction of deeper and more abstract relations among category members. On the basis of these findings, we tested nine-month-olds using the stir–lift procedure with the yellow or blue and the purple or orange spoons, with one difference. During the pretest trials, both spoons were visible. When the yellow spoon stirred salt, the blue spoon sat, propped up and in full view, next to the bowl. Similarly, when the blue spoon lifted the bowl, the yellow spoon sat, propped up, next to the bowl being lifted. In this experiment, the nine-month-olds successfully individuated the objects in the green ball–red ball test event, suggesting that direct comparison of the two spoons (i.e., exemplars) in each pair of pretest events facilitated infants' capacity to form a more abstract representation of the stir–lift events.

Another approach we used to facilitate the younger infants' formation of categories that were more inclusive was to show them more exemplars. Previous studies have revealed that presenting infants with more exemplars can sometimes improve color–function priming. For example, in the pound–pour experiments of Wilcox and Chapa (2004), 9.5-month-olds were successfully primed after viewing two pairs of pound–pour events, whereas 7.5-month-olds needed to see three pairs of pound–pour events. Perhaps the nine-month-olds in the stir–lift experiments would be more likely to extract the rule that color is predictive if they were shown an additional set of colored spoons. To assess this hypothesis, another group of nine-month-olds were tested using the stir–lift procedure, except that they were presented with an additional pair of stir–lift events with an additional set of spoons; a brown spoon lifted, and a cream spoon stirred. In contrast to the direct-comparison manipulation, this manipulation did not lead to their looking at the narrow-screen test event for significantly longer than at the wide-screen test event. Seeing an additional exemplar pair did not help the nine-month-olds form a more inclusive event category.

What do these two sets of findings reveal about why 9-month-olds are more limited than 9.5-month-olds in their capacity to form inclusive event categories? One interpretation of these results is that nine-month-olds have difficulty forming event categories that link object color to object function because, as the pretest events unfolded before them, they are unable to keep track of which spoon did what. Infants may be unable to identify, for example, whether the current spoon differs in color from the previous spoon, whether the previous spoon stirred or lifted, or which exemplars "go together" to form a pair. Without a clear representation of the structure of each event, and how the events are related, infants are unable to form a categorical representation of the stir–lift events. When the relation between the exemplars is made more obvious by showing infants the exemplars together during the pretest events, infants demonstrate increased sensitivity to color differences. In contrast, when infants are shown additional exemplars but are not allowed to directly compare the exemplars in each pair, increased sensitivity to color information is not observed. For younger infants, it is not sufficient to simply see more exemplar pairs in the pretest events; the relation between the exemplars in the stir–lift events must be made transparent before infants are able to form color–function categories that support individuation by color.

Related Priming Work

The positive results obtained in the color–function experiments raise the question of whether infants can be primed to attend to other surface features. For example, it is not until 7.5 months that infants spontaneously use pattern differences to individuate objects (Wilcox, 1999). Can younger infants be primed to attend to pattern information? Using the pound–pour procedure, we have assessed the extent to which 5.5- and 4.5-month-olds can be primed to individuate objects on the basis of pattern differences (Wilcox & Chapa, 2004). In these studies, infants saw pound–pour pretest events in which dotted containers pounded the peg, and striped containers poured salt. The pound–pour pretest events were followed by a dotted ball–striped ball test event. Both the 4.5- and the 5.5-month-olds demonstrated pattern priming: After viewing the pound–pour events, they used the difference in pattern to individuate the dotted and the striped ball. However, in order for the 4.5-month-olds to successfully form a categorical representation of the pound–pour events and then attend to pattern differences in the test event, they needed to see the containers presented simultaneously in the pretest events. For example, in the pound event, while the dotted container pounded the nail, the striped container sat close by in the display. Likewise, in the pour event, while the striped container poured salt, the dotted container sat close by. These results mirror those obtained with the nine-month-olds in the different-colors experiment: In order to generalize across multiple color pairs in the stir–lift pretest events, nine-month-olds needed to see the exemplars (i.e., the spoons in each pair) together. These results also provide converging evidence for the conclusion that direct comparison of exemplars is highly effective in facilitating in infants the formation of categories that are more inclusive.

Finally, it should be noted that other researchers have also reported, in other physical domains, that infants can be led, through select experiences, to attend to information to which they typically do not attend (Wang & Baillargeon, 2005). For example, there is evidence that, by 3.5 months, infants attend to height information when interpreting occlusion events (Baillargeon & Graber, 1987; Baillargeon & DeVos, 1991). In contrast, it is not until about 12 months that infants attend to height when interpreting uncovering events (Wang, Baillargeon, & Paterson, 2005). Wang and Baillargeon (2005) examined whether infants could be led to attend to height in an uncovering event if the object involved was first seen in an occlusion event. The results revealed that viewing an event in which height has already been identified as a relevant variable (i.e., an occlusion event) can lead infants to attend to height information in an event in which they typically do not attend to height information (i.e., an uncovering event). These findings provide converging evidence for the idea that infants' object representations are flexible and can be altered by recent experiences.

Summary

The outcome of the color–function experiments reported here reveals a great deal about the structure of the infant mind and how early representations are influenced by recent experiences. First, the color–function results illustrate just how hard infants work to make sense of the world. When observing physical events, infants identify relevant relationships between different types of information and use these relationships to build object and event categories. At the same time, infants do not attend to any and all associations or regularities. The actions the objects perform must be functionally relevant in order for color priming to be supported. We suspect that color–function pairings worked—infants built categories that included this information—because infants perceive object function as a pervasive, meaningful, and salient object property. Apparently, infants use information that is already meaningful to them to identify new sources of information as relevant to the individuation problem. We also suspect that there are other object properties (e.g., the mechanical or causal properties of objects) that infants perceive as useful and meaningful that will support color priming. For example, it is possible that viewing color–mechanics pairings (i.e., objects that are green are self-propelled, and those that are red are inert) would prime infants to attend to color differences.

Second, the nature of the event categories that infants form depends on the exemplars seen. For example, when the exemplars (i.e., pairs of spoons) were all of the same color pair (i.e., yellow and blue), infants' event categories were relatively specific: Infants failed to generalize to the green and red balls in the test trials. However, when the exemplar pairs were more variable (infants saw a pair of yellow and blue spoons and a pair of orange and purple spoons), 9.5-month-olds successfully generalized to the green and red balls in the test events. Nine-month-olds were also able to generalize across color, but only when they were allowed to directly compare the exemplars during the pretest events. Although unpredicted, these results point to an important transition during the ninth month in infants' capacity to form event categories that are more inclusive.

Third, the formation of event categories, which occurs quickly and with relatively few exemplars, has unprecedented effects on object processing. The fact that infants organize objects and events into categories is a well-documented finding (for reviews, see Quinn & Eimas, 1996; Mandler, 1997; Baillargeon, 1998; Madole & Oakes, 1999). The color–function priming results are unique in demonstrating that the formation of event categories can influence how infants perceive and think about objects in subsequent and unrelated events. Infants' propensity to form categorical representations of physical events is a powerful tool. It allows infants to organize physical events as they unfold before them, aids in their interpretation of those events, and biases how they interpret future events.[2]

Finally, the present results point to a flexibility in the type of information that infants include in their object representations. Although infants may not spontaneously attend to color differences in occlusion events, they can be led to do so if color information is made functionally relevant. Hence, sensitivities are dependent, at least to some extent, on the situation and infants' recent experiences.

PRIMING SERIES II: LINKING COLOR TO OBJECTS THROUGH VISUAL AND TACTILE EXPLORATION

The second approach we have taken to color priming is quite different from that of the color–function experiments. The rationale behind this approach is that if we can lead infants to believe that color features are intimately tied to objects, and remain stable over time and situations, infants will be more likely to use color differences as the basis for individuating objects.

What kinds of experiences might lead infants to link color to objects such that they will include color information in their object representations? Once infants can sit up unsupported and begin to reach for and actively manipulate objects, around five months of age (Rochat, 1989; Streri, 1991/1993; Rochat & Goubet, 1995), simultaneous visual and tactile exploration is one of the most common mechanisms for learning about objects. Visual and tactile exploration provides infants with the opportunity to experience the same information in more than one modality (e.g., shape encoded tactilely and visually) and to link information from one modality to another (e.g., link the color of an object to its shape). In other words, the redundancy in information that multimodal experiences affords increases the likelihood that amodal features will be encoded. It also provides a structure with which to integrate modality-specific information. Together, these experiences lead to the formation of multimodal object representations that are richer and more robust than unimodal representations (Slater, Quinn, Brown, & Hayes, 1999; Hernandez-Reif & Bahrick, 2001; Bahrick & Lickliter, 2002; Bahrick, Flom, & Lickliter, 2004). Hernandez-Reif and Bahrick (2001) reported that six-month-olds were more likely to include color and pattern in their representation of an object and to later recognize that object based on its color and pattern information if they were allowed to explore the object in two modalities simultaneously.

Together, these findings led us to hypothesize that infants might be more likely to include color in their object representations and then use color to individuate objects if they were allowed multisensory exploration of the objects before test trials. To test this hypothesis, we examined the extent to which simultaneous visual and tactile exploration of objects increases infants' sensitivity to color information in a subsequent individuation task.

Color Priming Through Multisensory Exploration

In the first of a series of experiments, 10.5-month-olds were assigned to one of two conditions: multisensory exploration or unisensory exploration (Wilcox et al., 2007). In the multisensory exploration condition (Fig. 5–7), infants were presented with two pre-exposure trials before the familiarization and test events. In the first pre-exposure trial, infants were allowed to look at and touch the green ball for

Figure 5–7. An infant being handed a ball and engaging in multisensory exploration. Infants were presented with a green ball on the first pre-exposure trial and a red ball on the second pre-exposure trial.

60 seconds. In the second pre-exposure trial, the same procedure was used with the red ball. The balls were presented successively, never together, and the pre-exposure trials were conducted in a room different from that of the test trials. Following the pre-exposure trials, infants were escorted to the testing room where the narrow-screen procedure was employed. In the test trials, they saw the green ball–red ball event with the narrow or the wide screen. In the unisensory exploration condition, infants were tested using the same procedure, with one important difference: Infants were allowed to look at but not touch the balls during the pre-exposure trials. The results indicated that the infants in the multisensory exploration condition looked reliably longer at the narrow- than at the wide-screen test event, whereas the infants in the visual exploration condition looked about equally at the two test events. Combined visual and tactile exploration of the objects, but not visual exploration alone, increased infants' sensitivity to color information in the test trials.

One interpretation of these results, and the one we would like to offer, is that simultaneous visual and tactile exploration led the infants to form multimodal representations of the balls, which included color information. Once color information was integrated into their object representations, infants drew on this information to individuate the balls. However, there is an alternative, weaker interpretation of the data. It is possible that two manual presentations of the ball led the infants to conclude that two physically distinct balls were present. That is, the experience of tactilely encountering the balls on two separate occasions (i.e., two trials) was sufficient to signal the presence of two objects. According to this interpretation, it was the number of times the balls were manually presented to the infants, and not color information, that led the infants to individuate the balls.

To assess this interpretation, another group of 10.5-month-olds was tested using the multisensory exploration procedure described above, with one important difference: The infants were presented with the same ball on both pre-exposure trials. Half of the infants were presented with the green ball twice, and the other half were presented with the red ball twice. Following the multisensory exploration control procedure, infants saw the narrow-screen green ball–red ball test event.

The data obtained with the infants in the multisensory exploration control condition, who saw only the narrow-screen event, were compared to the data obtained with the infants in the multisensory exploration condition (narrow-screen event), who individuated the balls, and the infants in the unisensory exploration condition (narrow-screen event), who failed to individuate the balls. The results revealed that the looking times of the infants in the multisensory exploration control condition differed reliably from those of the infants in the multisensory exploration condition but not from those of the infants in the unisensory exploration condition. The infants in the multisensory exploration control condition, like the infants in the unisensory exploration condition, failed to individuate the green and the red ball. These results suggest that the multisensory exploration procedure facilitates infants' performance on the individuation task because it increases their sensitivity to color information and not because two manual presentations signal two distinct objects.

Additional Multisensory Priming Results

In a subsequent experiment, we assessed whether visual exploration would be sufficient to support color priming, (i.e., lead to increased sensitivity to color information) under more supportive conditions. Perhaps if infants, on each pre-exposure trial, were simultaneously shown the green ball and the red ball, they would be more likely to use color information as the basis for individuating objects. That is, if the task of establishing distinct object representations was made easier for the infants, by giving them clear spatiotemporal information about the number of balls present in the pre-exposure trials, infants would find it easier to integrate color into their object representations.

To assess this hypothesis, 10.5-month-olds were tested in one of two conditions that were similar to the multisensory exploration and unisensory exploration conditions described above, with one important difference: In the pre-exposure trials, the green ball and the red ball were presented together, side by side. Hence, infants were given clear spatiotemporal information that two objects—a green ball and a red ball—were present in the pre-exposure trials.

The results indicated that the infants in the multisensory, but not the unisensory, exploration condition looked reliably longer at the narrow- than at the wide-screen test event. That is, only the infants in the multisensory exploration condition individuated the balls in the test event. These results have two important implications. First, they suggest that infants do not simply transfer information about number of objects seen in the pre-exposure trials to the test trials. In both conditions, infants saw two spatiotemporally distinct objects in the pre-exposure trials. Yet the infants in the unisensory exploration condition did not interpret the test event as involving two objects. Second, these data provide converging evidence for the conclusion that combined visual and tactile exploration is critical to color priming in this situation. Even when spatiotemporal information signals the presence of two distinct objects—a green ball and a red ball—infants do not integrate color information into their object representations unless they are allowed simultaneous tactile and visual exploration of the balls.

At first glance, these results may appear in conflict with other data that suggest that spatiotemporal information is fundamental to the individuation process. For example, if infants are given clear spatiotemporal information, in the apparatus and immediately before the test event, about the number of objects present (e.g., infants are shown two objects simultaneously), they use that information as the basis for individuating objects (Spelke, et al., 1995; Xu & Carey, 1996; Aguiar & Baillargeon, 2002; Wilcox & Schweinle, 2003). Why does spatiotemporal information presented during the pre-exposure trials fail to facilitate performance in the test trials? We would argue that during the pre-exposure experience infants form representations of the objects that either include, or do not include, information about the color of those objects. Infants include color information when they are allowed multisensory exploration of the objects but not when they are allowed unisensory exploration. When infants' representations of the balls do not include color information, so that there is no way to determine whether the balls seen to each side of the screen in the test trials are distinct, infants are unable to complete the individuation process. Hence, infants do not simply assume that because two objects were seen in the pre-exposure trials that two objects are involved in the test event. Interpretation of the test event depends on infants' capacity to integrate color information into their object representations in the pre-exposure trials.

The Development of Multisensory Priming

The positive results obtained in the multisensory conditions led us to question whether multisensory priming could be obtained in younger infants. To address this question, 9.5-month-olds were tested using the multisensory exploration, different-context procedure. To our surprise, the results were negative: The 9.5-month-olds looked about equally at the narrow- and the wide-screen test event. Unlike the 10.5-month-olds, who benefited from multisensory exploration, the 9.5-month-olds' sensitivity to color information was not altered by combined visual and tactile exploration of the balls. Why does multisensory exploration facilitate color priming in 10.5-month-olds but not in 9.5-month-olds? There are at least two possible explanations for this pattern of results. One possibility is that 9.5- and 10.5-month-olds engage in different types of behaviors during the pre-exposure trials, some of which are more likely to support multisensory priming than are others. For example, perhaps 10.5-month-olds spend more time interacting with the objects or being in combined visual and tactile contact with the objects than 9.5-month-olds do. Alternatively, the exploration behaviors of 9.5- and 10.5-month-olds during the pre-exposure trials do not differ reliably, but 9.5-month-olds process and use the information acquired through multisensory experiences in a different way, a way that does not support color priming.

As a first step toward assessing these two possible interpretations, we have investigated the extent to which 9.5- and 10.5-month-olds engage in different types of exploratory behaviors during the pre-exposure trials. In an initial experiment, we coded the visual and tactile behaviors of 9.5- and 10.5-month-old infants during multisensory exploration of the objects (Wilcox et al., 2005). The behaviors we assessed included the amount of time infants spent acting on the object (e.g., tapping, scratching, rubbing, grasping, mouthing, banging, rolling), the amount of time infants spent in combined visual and tactile exploration of the ball (i.e., were touching and looking at the object simultaneously), and the amount of time infants spent in contact with the ball with one hand or both hands together. The results suggested that although the age groups varied in their tendency to use one or two hands in their exploration of the balls (the 9.5-month-olds were more likely than the 10.5-month-olds to engage in two-handed exploration), they did not vary reliably in the overall amount of time they spent tactilely exploring the ball or in the amount of time they spent in combined visual and tactile exploration. We believe, however, that these negative findings need to be interpreted with caution. For example, it is possible that there are subtle age differences in exploratory behaviors that were not captured in this initial study. Perhaps analysis of more specific behaviors (e.g., rolling or tapping the ball) with larger sample sizes would bring these subtle differences to light. In addition, the fact that the age groups did not differ significantly in the type of exploratory behaviors in which they engaged does not necessarily mean that exploratory behaviors are not correlated with individuation performance. It is possible that individual differences in the way in which infants interact with objects better predict individuation performance than does age group.

Of course, it is possible that subsequent research will fail to identify a direct relationship between exploratory behaviors and individuation performance. If we find that 9.5- and 10.5-month-olds do not differ in the type of exploratory behaviors in which they engage, and that exploratory behaviors do not predict individuation performance, then we must consider the alternative hypothesis: 9.5- and 10.5-month-olds do not acquire and use information gained through similar behavioral interactions in the same way. This is a more complicated problem that will require creative methods of study.

Summary

The outcomes of the multisensory priming experiments indicate that combined visual and tactile exploration of objects prior to an individuation task can lead to increased sensitivity to color information in 10.5-month-olds. Unisensory exploration does not have the same effect: Visual exploration alone does not prime infants to attend to color differences in the individuation task. We have proposed that combined visual and tactile exploration of objects leads to the formation of object representations that are richer and more robust and more likely to include color information. That is, multisensory exploration provides infants with the opportunity to form representational structures with which color information can be integrated.

Perhaps the most striking aspect of these results is that a very simple manipulation—allowing infants to look at and touch the balls at the same time—can lead infants to attend to color differences. This everyday experience in which infants frequently engage can have profound effects on the type of information infants include in their object representations. At the same time, we have much to learn about the relation between infants' exploratory behaviors and the kind of information to which they attend and that they represent. For example, we have yet to identify whether it is the type of behaviors in which infants engage or the way in which they process and use the information they glean that predicts performance on an individuation task. This area is ripe for investigation, and the outcomes of future studies have the potential to enhance our understanding of the mechanisms that underlie developmental changes in infants' representational capacities.

Finally, the multisensory priming experiments revealed an intriguing developmental progression in the extent to which infants benefit from visual and tactile exploration of objects. In contrast to the positive results obtained with the 10.5-month-olds, the results of studies with the 9.5-month-olds showed that the younger group did not demonstrate increased sensitivity to color differences after multisensory exploration of the objects. The charge of future research will be to identify the underlying basis for this age-related difference in color priming.

CONCLUSIONS

In our priming studies, we have identified two different mechanisms by which we can increase infants' sensitivity to color information in an individuation task: color–function priming and multisensory priming. The outcome of these studies has shed light on the development of object individuation by showing how select experiences can influence the kind of information infants include in their object representations and by revealing the ways that infants begin to identify new sources of information as important to the individuation problem.

The findings obtained in the color–function priming experiments suggest that one way to increase infants' sensitivity to color information is to make color differences predictive of object properties that infants already find salient (e.g., function). By attending to the relation between color and an already salient object property, infants come to recognize that color, a property they typically find of little value, may in fact be relevant. They then bring this information to bear in a subsequent individuation task. However, there are some interesting limitations to the extent to which this priming mechanism is effective. First, some object properties are more meaningful and salient than others and hence are more effective as a prime. Second, the capacity to form event categories that link one object property to another constrains the priming processes.

The findings obtained in the multisensory priming experiments reveal a very different way that infants can be led to attend to color information: through simultaneous visual and tactile exploration of the objects. Combined visual and tactile exploration, prior to the individuation task, provides infants with the opportunity to form multimodal representations of the objects. These multimodal representations are more likely than unimodal representations to include color information and, hence, are more likely to support individuation by color. At the same time, there is much to learn about multisensory priming. For example, compared to what we know about color–function priming, we know little about the nature of the representations that are laid down during the multisensory priming experience. Are the representations formed during multisensory experiences specific or abstract? If infants were shown different objects (e.g., a green truck and a red truck) or different color pairs (e.g., yellow and blue balls, and purple and orange balls) during the pre-exposure trials, would they still demonstrate sensitivity to the color difference in the green ball–red ball test event? Investigations of this sort would allow us to identify similarities between the kinds of representations (e.g., specific or abstract) laid down during color–function and multisensory priming.

Finally, we have yet to determine whether the priming effects we have identified with either procedure are transient or long-term. Do these experiences "teach" infants that color is important to object individuation, leading infants to attend to color differences on a regular basis? Or is infants' sensitivity to color differences increased in the short term only? The charge of future research will be to identify the impact that color–function and multisensory experiences have on infants' sensitivity to color (and pattern) information across time and other situations.

In conclusion, the priming studies offer insight into the development of infants' use of features to individuate objects. Of primary importance is that infants can be led to attend to new object properties through select experiences with objects. Future research will address the constraints and limitations of the priming mechanisms we have identified and seek to identify other experiences that will enhance infants' ability to individuate objects. We are confident that further investigation using these and similar procedures will continue to reveal important information about the structure of early object knowledge, the types of experience that can alter this knowledge, and the mechanisms by which this occurs.

Acknowledgments The research described in this chapter was supported by grants from the National Institute of Child Health and Human Development (HD-36741 and HD-46532) and the Advanced Research Program of the Texas Higher Education Coordinating Board (SBS-3656) to the first author. We are grateful to the infants and parents who so graciously agreed to participate in the research.

Notes

1. In the narrow-screen violation-of-expectation task, the objects typically move back and forth behind the screen, rather than follow a single trajectory across the platform. To assess whether multiple emergences of the objects are more likely to give rise to the perception of a single object, particularly when a narrow screen is employed, an additional group of infants (*M* age = 6 months, 4 days) were tested using the narrow-screen ball–ball procedure with one difference: The objects reversed direction twice, to travel three lengths of the platform. Again, the infants spent significantly more time reaching to the screen than to the ball; 11 of the 13 infants tested (85%) demonstrated this pattern of reaching. Infants interpret the ball–ball event as involving two objects regardless of whether the objects follow a single trajectory or emerge multiple times from behind the screen.

2. It is important to clarify the distinction between the categorical event representations we have been discussing and the kind of event categorization that Baillargeon and her colleagues have proposed (e.g., Baillargeon, 1998; Baillargeon & Wang, 2002). The former includes local categories that are created "on the fly," that are used in select situations, and that are probably transient. The latter refers to global categories (e.g., occlusion, containment, support) that are deeply embedded in infants' physical knowledge, are used continuously, and remain stable over time.

References

Adams, R. J. (1995). Further exploration of human neonatal chromatic-achromatic discrimination. *Journal of Experimental Child Psychology, 60,* 344–360.

Adams, R. J., & Courage, M. L. (1998). Human newborn color vision: Measurement with chromatic stimuli varying in excitation purity. *Journal of Experimental Child Psychology, 68,* 22–34.

Adams, R. J., Courage, M. L., & Mercer, M. E. (1994). Systematic measurement of human neonatal color vision. *Vision Research, 34,* 1691–1701.

Adams, R. J., & Maurer, D. (1984). Detection of contrast by the newborn and 2-month-old infant. *Infant Behavior and Development, 7,* 415–422,

Aguiar, A., & Baillargeon, R. (2002). Developments in young infants' reasoning about occluded objects. *Cognitive Psychology, 45,* 267–336.

Arterberry, M. E., & Yonas, A. (2000). Perception of structure from motion by 8-week-old infants. *Perception and Psychophysics, 62,* 550–556.

Bahrick, L. (1987). Infants' intermodal perception of two levels of temporal structure in natural events. *Infant Behavior and Development, 10,* 387–416.

Bahrick, L., & Lickliter, R. (2002). Intersensory redundancy guides early perceptual and cognitive development. In R. Kail (Ed.), *Advances in child development and behavior* (Vol. 30, pp. 153–187). New York: Academic Press.

Bahrick, L., Lickliter, R., & Flom, R. (2004). Intersensory redundancy guides the development of selective attention, perception, and cognition in infancy. *Current Directions in Psychological Science, 13,* 99–102.

Baillargeon, R. (1998). Infants' understanding of the physical world. In M. Sabourin, F. I. M. Craik, & M. Robert (Eds.), *Advances in psychological science: Vol. 1 Cognitive and biological aspects* (pp. 503–529). London: Psychology Press.

Baillargeon, R., & DeVos, J. (1991). Object permanence in 3.5- and 4.5-month-old infants: Further evidence. *Child Development, 62,* 1227–1246.

Baillargeon, R., & Graber, M. (1987). Where's the rabbit? 5.5-month-old infants' representation of the height of a hidden object. *Cognitive Development, 2,* 375–392.

Baillargeon, R., & Wang, S. (2002). Event categorization in infancy. *Trends in Cognitive Sciences, 6*, 85–93.

Banks, M. S., & Salapatek, P. (1981). Infant pattern vision: A new approach based on the contrast sensitivity function. *Journal of Experimental Child Psychology, 31*, 1–45.

Banks, M. S., & Shannon, E. (1993). Spatial and chromatic visual efficiency in human neonates. In C. E. Granrud (Ed.), *Visual perception and cognition in infancy* (pp. 1–46). Hillsdale, NJ: Erlbaum.

Bornstein, M. H. (1975). Qualities of color vision in infancy. *Journal of Experimental Child Psychology, 19*, 401–419.

Bornstein, M. H., Kessen, W., & Weiskopf, S. (1976). Color vision and hue categorization in young human infants. *Journal of Experimental Psychology: Human Perception and Performance, 2*, 115–129.

Brown, A. M. (1990). Development of visual sensitivity to light and color vision in human infants: A critical review. *Vision Research, 30*, 1159–1188.

Catherwood, D., Crassini, B., & Freiberg, K. (1989). Infant response to stimuli of similar hue and dissimilar shape: Tracing the origins of the categorization of objects by hue. *Child Development, 60*, 752–762.

Dannemiller, J. L. (1989). A test of color constancy in 9- and 20-week-old human infants: Following simulated illuminant changes. *Developmental Psychology, 25*, 171–184.

Dannemiller, J. L., & Hanko, S. A. (1987). A test of color constancy in 4-month-old human infants. *Journal of Experimental Child Psychology, 44*, 255–267.

Franklin, A. & Davies, I.R.L. (2004). New evidence for infant colour categories. *British Journal of Developmental Psychology, 22*, 349–377.

Freeman, N. H., Lloyd, S., & Sinha, C. G. (1980). Infant search tasks reveal early concepts of containment and canonical usage of objects. *Cognition, 8*, 243–262.

Gentner, D., & Namy, L. (1999). Comparison in the development of categories. *Cognitive Development, 14*, 487–513.

Gibson, E. J., & Walker, A. S. (1984). Development of knowledge of visual-tactual affordances of substance. *Child Development, 55*, 453–460.

Granrud, C. E. (1987). Size constancy in newborn infants. *Investigative Ophthalmology and Visual Science, 28*(Suppl.), 5.

Hayne, H., Rovee-Collier, C., & Perris, E. E. (1987). Categorization and memory retrieval by three-month-old infants. *Child Development, 58*, 750–767.

Hernandez-Reif, M., & Bahrick, L. (2001). The development of visual-tactual perception of objects: Amodal relations provide the basis for learning arbitrary relations. *Infancy, 2*, 51–72.

Kellman, P. J. (1984). Perception of three-dimensional form by human infants. *Perception & Psychophysics, 36*, 353–358.

Kellman, P. J., & Short, K. R. (1987). Development of three-dimensional form perception. *Journal of Experimental Psychology: Human Perception and Performance, 13*, 545–557.

Madole, K. L., & Oakes, L. M. (1999). Making sense of infant categorization: Stable processes and changing representations. *Developmental Review, 19*, 263–296.

Mandler, J. M. (1997). Development of categorization: Perceptual and conceptual categories. In G. Bremner, A. Slater, & G. Butterworth (Eds.), *Infant development: Recent advances*. Hove, England: Erlbaum.

McCurry, S., Wilcox, T., & Woods, R. (2008). Beyond the search barrier: New evidence for object individuation in young infants. Manuscript under review.

Meltzoff, A. N. (1988a). Infant imitation after a 1-week delay: Long-term memory for novel acts and multiple stimuli. *Developmental Psychology, 24*, 470–476.

Meltzoff, A. N. (1988b). Infant imitation and memory: Nine-month-olds in immediate and deferred tests. *Child Development, 59,* 217–225.

Meltzoff, A. N., & Borton, R. W. (1979). Intermodal matching by human neonates. *Nature, 282,* 403–404.

Moskowitz-Cook, A. (1979). The development of photopic spectral sensitivity in human infants. *Vision Research, 19,* 1133–1142.

Namy, L. L., Smith, L. B., & Gershkoff-Stowe, L. (1997). Young children's discovery of spatial classification. *Cognitive Development, 12,* 163–185.

Needham, A. (1999). The role of shape in 4-month-old infants' segregation of adjacent objects. *Infant Behavior and Development, 22,* 161–178.

Needham, A. (2001). Object recognition and object segregation in 4.5-month-old infants. *Journal of Experimental Child Psychology, 78,* 3–24.

Needham, A., Dueker, G. & Lockhead, G. (2005). Infants' formation and use of categories to segregate objects. *Cognition, 94,* 215–240.

Oakes, L. M., & Ribar, R. J. (2005). A comparison of infants' categorization in paired and successive presentation familiarization tasks. *Infancy, 7,* 85–98.

Peeples, D. R., & Teller, D. Y. (1975). Color vision and brightness discrimination in two-month-old infants. *Science, 189,* 1102–1103.

Pieraut-LeBonniec, G. (1985). From visual-motor anticipation to conceptualization: Reaction to solid and hollow objects and knowledge of the function of containment. *Infant Behavior and Development, 8,* 413–424.

Powers, M. K., Schneck, M., & Teller, D. Y. (1981). Spectral sensitivity in human infants at absolute visual threshold. *Vision Research, 21,* 1005–1016.

Quinn, P. C. (1987). The categorical representation of visual pattern information in young infants. *Cognition, 27,* 145–179.

Quinn, P. C., & Eimas, P. D. (1996). Perceptual organization and categorization in young infants. In C. Rovee-Collier & L. P. Lipsitt (Eds.), *Advances in Infancy Research* (Vol. 10, pp. 1–36). Norwood, NJ: Ablex.

Quinn, P. C., Eimas, P. D., & Rosenkrantz, S. L. (1993). Evidence for representations of perceptually similar natural categories by 3-month-old and 4-month-olds infants. *Perception, 22,* 463–475.

Rochat, P. (1989). Object manipulation and exploration in 2- and 5-month-old infants. *Developmental Psychology, 25,* 871–884.

Rochat, P., & Goubet, N. (1995). Development of sitting and reaching in 5- and 6-month-old infants. *Infant Behavior and Development, 18,* 53–68.

Slater, A., Mattock, A., & Brown, E. (1990). Size constancy at birth: Newborn infants' responses to retinal and real size. *Journal of Experimental Child Psychology, 49,* 314–322.

Slater, A., & Morison, V. (1985). Shape constancy and slant perception at birth. *Perception, 14,* 337–344.

Slater, A., Morison, V., Town, C., & Rose, D. (1985). Movement perception and identity constancy in the new-born baby. *British Journal of Developmental Psychology, 3,* 211–220.

Slater, A., Quinn, P. C., Brown, E., & Hayes, R. (1999). Intermodal perception at birth: Intersensory redundancy guides newborn infants' learning of arbitrary auditory-visual pairings. *Developmental Science, 2,* 333–338.

Spelke, E. S. (1979). Perceiving bimodally specified events in infants. *Developmental Psychology, 15,* 626–636.

Spelke, E. S., Kestenbaum, R., Simons, D. J., & Wein, D. (1995). Spatiotemporal continuity, smoothness of motion and object identity in infancy. *British Journal of Developmental Psychology, 13,* 113–143.

Stephens, B. R., & Banks, M. S. (1987). Contrast discrimination in human infants. *Journal of Experimental Psychology: Human Perception and Performance, 13,* 558–565.

Streri, A. (1993). *Seeing, reaching, touching: The relations between vision and touch in infancy.* Cambridge, MA: MIT Press. (Originally published 1991)

Teller, D. Y. (1998). Spatial and temporal aspects of infant color vision. *Vision Research, 38,* 3275–3282.

Teller, D. Y., & Palmer, J. (1996). Infant color vision: Motion nulls for red/green vs. luminance-modulated stimuli in infants and adults. *Vision Research, 36,* 955–974.

Tremoulet, P. D., Leslie, A. M., & Hall, G. D. (2001). Infant individuation and identification of objects. *Cognitive Development, 15,* 499–522.

Wang, S., & Baillargeon, R. (2005). Inducing infants to detect a physical violation in a single trial. *Psychological Science,* 542–549.

Wang, S., Baillargeon, R., & Paterson, S. (2005). Detecting continuity violations in infancy: A new account and new evidence from covering and tube events. *Cognition, 95,* 129–173.

Wilcox, T. (1999). Object individuation: Infants' use of shape, size, pattern, and color. *Cognition, 72,* 125–166.

Wilcox, T., & Baillargeon, R. (1998a). Object individuation in infancy: The use of featural information in reasoning about occlusion events. *Cognitive Psychology, 37,* 97–155.

Wilcox, T., & Baillargeon, R. (1998b). Object individuation in young infants: Further evidence with an event monitoring task. *Developmental Science, 1,* 127–142.

Wilcox, T., & Chapa, C. (2002). Infants' reasoning about opaque and transparent occluders in an individuation task. *Cognition, 85,* B1–B10.

Wilcox, T., & Chapa, C. (2004). Priming infants to attend to color and pattern information in an individuation task. *Cognition, 90,* 265–302.

Wilcox, T., & Schweinle, A. (2002). Object individuation and event mapping: Infants' use of featural information. *Developmental Science, 5,* 132–150.

Wilcox, T., & Schweinle, A. (2003). Infants' use of speed information to individuate objects in occlusion events. *Infant Behavior and Development, 26,* 253–282.

Wilcox, T., Schweinle, A., & Chapa, C. (2003). Object individuation in infancy. In F. Fagan & H. Hayne (Eds.). *Progress in Infancy Research* (Vol. 3, pp. 193–243). Mahwah, NJ: Lawrence Erlbaum Associates.

Wilcox, T., Woods, R., & Chapa, C. (in press). Color–function categories that prime infants to use color information in an individuation task. *Cognitive Psychology.*

Wilcox, T., Woods, R., Chapa, C., & McCurry, S. (2007). Multisensory exploration and object individuation in infants. *Developmental Psychology, 43,* 479–495.

Woods, R., & Wilcox, T. (2006). Infants' use of luminance to individuate objects. *Cognition 99,* B43–B52.

Xu, F., & Carey, S. (1996). Infants' metaphysics: The case of numerical identity. *Cognitive Psychology, 30,* 111–153.

Xu, F., & Carey, S. (2001). The emergence of kind concepts: A rejoinder to Needham & Baillargeon (2000). *Cognition, 74,* 285–301.

Xu, F., Carey, S., & Quint, N. (2004). The emergence of kind-based object individuation in infancy. *Cognitive Psychology, 49,* 155–190.

6

How Infants Learn Categories

LISA M. OAKES, JESSICA S. HORST, KRISTINE A.
KOVACK-LESH, AND SAMMY PERONE,
UNIVERSITY OF IOWA

This chapter is about how infants learn categories. Clearly, infants are exceptionally good at learning categories. There is a large literature showing that from a very young age infants respond to adult-defined categorical contrasts ranging from animal categories such as dog, cat, and land animal, to categories such as food, furniture, and vehicle (e.g., Ross, 1980; Mandler & McDonough, 1993; Quinn, Eimas, & Rosenkrantz, 1993; Oakes, Coppage, & Dingel, 1997). Moreover, many studies suggest that the basic processes of categorization are similar from infancy to adulthood—like adults, infants detect correlations among attributes and use those correlations to categorize stimuli (Younger & Cohen, 1986), extract prototypes of stimulus sets (Bomba & Siqueland, 1983; Younger, 1985), and make use of differences in perceptual variability to establish category boundaries (Quinn et al., 1993; Oakes et al., 1997). In this chapter we answer the question, How do infants learn categories? Our focus will be on how infants learn categories in familiarization and habituation tasks, a context that we believe both provides deep understanding into the processes of categorization and mimics many of infants' real-life encounters with objects in important ways. Thus, understanding how infants learn categories in these laboratory tasks will provide an understanding of how infants learn categories in "the world."

We have been charged with answering five specific questions about how infants learn (in our case) categories. The five questions are: (1) Is innate/previously acquired structure required to explain learning? (2) Which aspects of the environment support learning? (3) What kinds of learning processes are evident? Are these specific to a domain, or more general? Do they change with development? (4) What is the nature of the representations derived from learning? (5) How does previous learning generalize to new instances? These questions provide an excellent framework for understanding the development of infants' ability to learn and acquire categories, and addressing these questions will be important for a complete understanding of the development of category learning during infancy. In the following sections, we address each of these questions in the context of the results of our work on how infants learn categories in familiarization tasks.

DEFINING CATEGORIZATION

Before we embark on this endeavor, however, it is important to be explicit about what we mean by categorization. The term *categorization* is widely used and yet rarely defined. We focus on the process of categorization, emphasizing how infants learn new categories rather than on the nature of the underlying representation for those categories. We believe that the process of categorization involves the on-line formation of groups based on the detected similarities and differences among objects. At various ages and in various contexts, individuals may detect various similarities and differences among items. Similarities and differences are detected as people attend to and perceive items and compare those items to each other and to previously encountered items. At any given moment, therefore, infants need not already "possess" a particular category relevant to a set of items. Rather, infants may have some knowledge relevant to the categorization task at hand, but they create and revise categories online as they encounter new information.

Categories, therefore, need not be stable, previously acquired representations (although some categories are formed frequently and therefore become relatively stable). Instead, we conceive of categories as emergent products of infants' detection of regularities and commonalities in the environment around them in both real time and over developmental time. These ideas have much in common with other views. Rogers and McClelland (2004), for example, have recently demonstrated the emergence of categorical structure within a connectionist model as that model learned about a collection of loosely related items (e.g., several different trees and animals). Jones and Smith (1993) argued that categories are emergent, dynamic products of multiple sources of information and are continuously created in context. Similarly, Smith (2000) and Samuelson and Smith (2000) maintained that knowing and the real-time processes of attention, perception, and memory cannot be separated. To assume that stable representations are the primary means of determining category membership in the absence of the learners' goals and intentions or psychological processes such as attention, perception, and memory undermines the flexibility of human cognition (Thelen & Smith, 1994). Indeed, Barsalou (1983) has shown that adults flexibly form ad hoc categories, such as "things you take from your house in a fire." The importance of such ad hoc categories for the present discussion is that items are regrouped in the moment in response to a particular goal or context, and we, like others (e.g., Jones & Smith, 1993), suggest that the basic psychological processes involved in creating such ad hoc categories are fundamentally the same as those involved in forming more stable categories such as dog, shoe, and fruit.

Figure 6–1. Example of instances that can be categorized.

Consider the collection of objects depicted in Figure 6–1. There are many types of similarities among these objects. For example, you might create a group that includes the robin, the rooster, and the duck (birds)—they share some similarities in features; they have two legs, feathers, similarly shaped bodies, and so on. Alternatively (or on a different occasion), you might create a group that includes the cow, the rooster, and the lamb—they also share some similar features; they are found on farms and they are domesticated. Importantly, the rooster was included in both groups. When attending to similarities based on overall shape, the rooster is grouped with other birds. When attending to similarities based on where the objects typically are found, the rooster is grouped with other farm animals.

Which one of these is the "real" category? You might argue that the bird category is more real than the farm-animal category. After all, birds share similar genetic structure not shared with other farm animals, and birds have similar behaviors (such as flying and eating worms); therefore the category bird might be construed as having a more "real" core or essence than the category farm animal. In our research, we have not asked whether infants know the "real" categories, or whether "real" categories are more easily learned than other categories, or even whether infants are sensitive to the same categories that adults are; rather we have asked under what conditions infants form one legitimate category versus a different legitimate category. As adults, we flexibly include objects in particular categories depending on our goal, the task, and the kinds of similarities that the goals, task, and our knowledge make salient. That is why categorization is the online formation of groups—we compare instances on line, note the commonalities among those instances, relate those instances to previous items we have encountered or groups we have formed, and form new groups (or change existing groups) as a result. This is how we can form the kinds of ad hoc categories described by Barsalou (1983). We also form relatively stable categories that we bring with us to new situations. The fact that we all know what is meant when someone says "bird" suggests that we do create stable categories. However, stable categories may simply be those categories that are created most frequently, making them no more or less real than categories created less frequently. And even relatively stable categories change as we encounter new information—when we first learn that a penguin is a bird, for example, our bird category changes somewhat.

It is important to point out that many categories that are created frequently may be those that have some objective perceptual similarity—such as shape or the presence of a feature such as wings, or functional similarity—such as "is sit-on-able" or "flies" or "lays eggs." Stable categories that are agreed upon by virtually all the adults of a given culture may not be random. It is also becoming clear, however, that even very stable categories that are highly agreed upon are somewhat arbitrary. For example, whales can be legitimately categorized with fish on the basis of their behavior and habitat (and indeed fish and whales are categorized together when creating an aquarium), or whales can be legitimately categorized as mammals on the basis of biological properties. When forming categories of trees, individuals with different types of expertise—based on education and work in forestry, landscaping, or maintenance—have different stable, agreed-upon categories of trees based on different weighting of real similarities among them (Medin, Lynch, Coley, & Atran, 1997). Similarly, Lopez et al. (1997) observed that American and Itzaj participants sorted a collection of mammals differently; for example, American participants relied more on size than did the Itzaj participants, and Itzaji participants differentiated smaller mammals based on behavior more than did American participants.

We must include one additional qualifier about what we mean by categorization before we begin to address the questions outlined earlier. In our work and thinking we are specifically focused on object categories. It may be that the same or similar processes are involved in categories that are more abstract, such as peace or justice. At this point, our main focus is on infants' categorization of the objects and people in their environment (we believe this is one of infants' main foci at this point in development). Future work may reveal the relation between the categorization we observe in infancy and other forms of categorization.

GENERAL LEARNING MECHANISMS

Whether or not infants require innate structures to learn categories obviously depends on what one means by *innate structures*. The problem is that different theorists define or interpret innate structures differently. For example, innate structures may be domain-specific modules (see, for example, Leslie, Friedman, & German, 2004, in the context of theory of mind). Such modules may be necessary for infants' to learn categories. In this case, one might posit modules for handling input of a particular type and developmental change in learning categories in a particular domain depends on those modules and their output. In the domain of conceptual development, infants may have some innate core knowledge of what an object is that may guide the development of further conceptual knowledge about objects and object categories. Certainly this is the type of innate structure advocated by Elizabeth Spelke and her colleagues (e.g., Spelke, Breinlinger, Macomber, & Jacobson, 1992) and convincingly argued against by Nora Newcombe (2002).

A less radical conception is that innate structures are biases or constraints that induce the system to selectively attend to some types of features (such as faces or movement trajectories) of input for further processing and to selectively ignore other types of features (such as body shapes or the presence of particular parts). Jean Mandler (2004) has suggested that this type of innate structure may cause infants to selectively learn about movement properties (and ignore detailed information such as ear shape or head length that might differentiate dogs from cats, for example) and thus become able to differentiate animates from inanimates. Importantly, this type of innate structure differs from the type described earlier because the system does not possess any innate knowledge; rather, the system is biased to attend to some types of information and will therefore learn more about some features of the world than about others.

Finally, we view innate structures as extremely general features of the cognitive system; to learn categories infants need only domain-general mechanisms for learning, remembering, and perceiving (a view that has much in common with that of Rakison, 2005). Importantly, these general systems themselves are both products of development and continue to develop; they thus place ever-changing constraints on how infants can learn categories. For example, at birth, infants have extremely poor visual acuity and their sensitivity to contrast is quite different from that of adults (Slater & Johnson, 1998). French, Mermillod, Quinn, Chauvin, and Mareschal (2002) recently developed a connectionist model that mimics the acuity- and contrast-sensitivity of young infants and have shown that, with reduced acuity, the model most easily detected exactly the same category boundaries that young infants detect. The development of these extremely general structures, and not some predetermined category-specific structures, determines what infants learn. As these general mechanisms and systems develop, new constraints are placed on what information is available for processing. For example, young infants are able to represent only a single item in their visual short-term memory (Ross-Sheehy, Oakes, & Luck, 2003), which severely constrains what information they can learn about the visual world. There are rapid changes in visual short-term memory abilities in the first year of life (Ross-Sheehy et al., 2003; Oakes, Ross-Sheehy, & Luck, 2006), resulting in different constraints on learning.

PROCESSES THAT SUPPORT CATEGORY LEARNING

Before we can address the remaining questions, we need to establish what is actually required for infants to learn categories. In the last section, we argued that to learn categories infants use domain-general systems for learning, remembering, and perceiving. Consider a habituation or familiarization procedure in which infants are presented with a series of items all from the same adult-defined category (e.g., dog), and then their interest in a novel item from that category and a novel item from a contrasting category (e.g., cat) are tested (see Fig. 6–2). In this context, to learn the adult-defined category presented during familiarization, infants must attend to the individual items, perceive and remember at least some of their features, compare the items, and detect commonalities and differences among the items. We assume that if infants recognize the commonalities inherent in the adult-defined category presented during familiarization (in this case, the exclusive category of dogs), then they should look longer at the new out-of-category item than at the new within-category item. Exactly this pattern of responding has been found in many studies. For example, Oakes and Ribar (2005) found that six-month-old infants familiarized with pictures of dogs or cats failed to increase their looking at a picture of a novel within-category item, suggesting that they perceived it as similar to the familiar item, but they did significantly increase their looking at a picture of a novel out-of-category item (e.g., a novel cat, if familiarized with dogs), suggesting that they perceived those items as different from the familiar

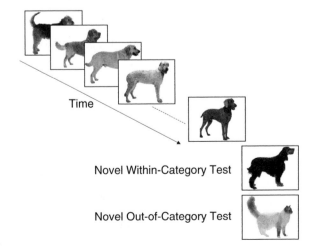

Figure 6–2. Example of sequence of trials when using habituation or familiarization to assess infants' categorization.

Time

Novel Within-Category Test

Novel Out-of-Category Test

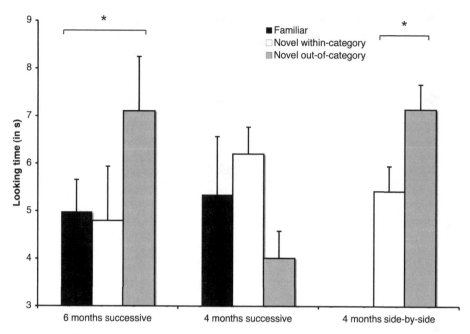

Figure 6–3. Results reported by Oakes and Ribar (2005) for infants' responding to novel within-category and novel out-of-category items following familiarization with items from one category (i.e., cats or dogs). Duration of looking (in s) to a familiar item, a novel within-category item and a novel out-of-category item by six-month-old and four-month-old infants (error bars represent +1 *SE*) following familiarization with cats or dogs presented one at a time on successive trials, and duration of looking (in s) to a novel within-category item and a novel out-of-category item by four-month-old infants (error bars represent +1 *SE*) following familiarization with cats or dogs presented in pairs on successive trials. Based on data from Oakes, L. M., & Ribar, R. J. (2005). *A comparison of infants' categorization in paried and successive presentation familiarization tasks. Infancy, 7*, 85–89.

item (see the left-most portion of Fig. 6–3). In the language of categorization, therefore, we conclude that the category that infants formed (or that was tapped or reminded) during familiarization included the novel within-category item and excluded the novel out-of-category item.

In fact, this is a somewhat odd category-learning task—at least in comparison to how categorization is often assessed in older children or adults. In those studies, participants are often explicitly told that the items will be from different categories and the goal is to name or to sort the items (e.g., Samuelson & Smith, 1999; Johansen & Palmeri, 2002). Infants, in contrast, are not given the explicit goal of forming categories. Infants do not know that the goal of the experiment is to categorize the stimuli; indeed, when they see the first picture of a dog, they are not aware that they will be shown a series of pictures, that the experimenter hopes to discover something about their categorization, or that they should remember this picture because at some point in the near future their memory for the picture or for items like it will be tested. In this way, the task is like implicit memory tasks used with adults; infants may learn the categories implicitly (at least initially) as they attend to, perceive, and remember the individual items. In fact, we do know that adults extract categorical structure even when they are not explicitly engaged in the task of categorizing the stimuli (e.g., Reed, Squire, Patalano, Smith, & Jonides, 1999). Moreover, this is likely the way young infants in the "real world" learn categories. Indeed, even adults extract categories in this way on a daily basis by discovering them as they use objects and encounter them in different contexts (this point was elegantly made by Markman & Ross, 2003). Assessing infants' categorization in this way, therefore, will reveal the real processes that infants use every day in learning categories.

Learning categories in a habituation or familiarization context, as in real-world contexts, requires attention, perception, and memory. Thus, understanding category learning in these contexts requires us to understand how these processes are used together. Note, however, that it is impossible to know from data like those presented by Oakes and Ribar (2005) whether we have documented a category that infants *possessed,* or shown how quickly infants can learn a category of dogs that excludes cats, or whether we have documented a category that is some combination of information infants already possessed and new information learned in the task. We do know that infants can learn artificial categories (e.g., Younger, 1985; Horst, Oakes, & Madole, 2005) and that infants' responding to categorical distinctions is highly dependent on the context (e.g., Oakes et al., 1997; Ribar, Oakes, & Spalding, 2004). Thus, even if infants are bringing knowledge to the task (for example, a representation of dogs that includes information such as that it has four legs, a particular-shaped nose, and a tail), they readily adapt it to the immediate context.

Mandler (2004) has made a distinction between familiarization tasks in which infants are provided with objects to explore and manipulate and familiarization tasks in which infants are shown pictures of objects. She argues that tasks in which infants can actually manipulate objects involve a higher level of active engagement on the part of the infants and as a result tap their previously acquired conceptual knowledge. Tasks in which infants are presented with pictures of objects, in contrast, involve a passive, online process of perceptual categorization. These assumptions have been questioned (Younger & Fearing, 1998; Oakes & Madole, 2003; Younger & Furrer, 2003), however, and researchers have shown that the same processes appear to operate both when infants are shown pictures and when they are given objects to manipulate (e.g., Younger & Furrer, 2003). In our framework, therefore, the process of learning categories in a familiarization context involves active and passive processes regardless of whether the task involves handling objects or just viewing them. Differences are not in the processes tapped by each task but in the information to which infants have access in each task (e.g., texture, taste, and weight are available in object-handling tasks but not in tasks in which infants can only look at the stimuli). Therefore, we argue that, regardless of whether they are presented with objects to manipulate or pictures to view, infants learn about the categorical relations, at least in part, during the familiarization phase of the experiment.

ASPECTS OF THE ENVIRONMENT THAT SUPPORT INFANTS' CATEGORY LEARNING

Because infants do not have the explicit goal of categorizing in familiarization contexts, they are not likely actively engaged in the process of forming categories in those contexts (at least when they encounter the first few stimuli). Much like amnesiac patients who do not have the explicit goal of categorization (Knowlton & Squire, 1993; Reed et al., 1999), infants are likely actively engaged in the processes of perceiving, remembering, and comparing items, and categories *emerge* as infants engage these processes. Therefore, the learning of categories is supported in environments, contexts, or tasks that support infants' ability to perceive, remember, and compare items. In fact, infants' learning of categories in the world is also likely influenced by the context in exactly the same way. As described earlier, infants' category learning in everyday contexts is similar to implicit learning tasks—infants extract category commonalities as they perceive the features of the individual items, remember those items, recall from memory previously encountered items, and compare items. Therefore, identifying the aspects of the context that influence infants' categorization in the laboratory will help us understand how aspects of the context influence infants' categorization in their everyday lives. We have found that at least two aspects of the context influence infants' categorical responding: how the stimuli are presented and the level of variability among the to-be-categorized items.

One of the most fundamental processes of categorization is comparison. Comparison involves the active alignment of two representational structures in order to detect commonalities or differences between them (Markman & Gentner, 2000). Therefore, it is not surprising that the method of stimulus presentation and the level of variability among to-be-categorized items both affect how easily comparisons can be made and influence infants' category learning. Attending, perceiving, and remembering clearly are essential for categorization, but alone they will not allow the formation of groups of similar items. Comparison is the key process that allows categories to be formed (Gentner & Namy, 1999). Comparison, and not categorization, is likely the active process, and categorization derives from the process of comparison. As memories of new items are formed, infants (and adults) compare those items to previously encountered items—from previous trials or from a previous point in the infants' (or adults') life, or both. This act of comparing items is central to human cognition and allows us to form analogies, detect statistical regularities, and create categorical groups (Markman & Gentner, 2000). Therefore, aspects of the context that influence infants' comparison of items will also influence the boundaries that define the categories they learn—infants will form different categorical groups in contexts that make it easier for them to detect the similarities and differences among the items as compared to contexts that make it more difficult to detect those similarities and differences.

In the next two subsections, we will describe our research that has examined how experimental contexts influence the categories infants learn, presumably by influencing the ease with which they could compare individual items. This research is fundamental to understanding the development and process of categorization in the habituation or familiarization context. Moreover, this research provides insight into the factors that likely influence infants' categorization outside the laboratory.

Presenting Items Singly or in Pairs

One aspect of the context that should influence infants' comparison of items is whether those items are presented singly or in pairs. When items are presented in pairs, infants should more easily be able to align them (no memory is required), and it may be more obvious to infants that they should engage in comparison.

Infants do respond differently when items are presented one or two at a time (Reznick & Kagan, 1983; Younger & Furrer, 2003; Oakes & Ribar, 2005). For example, Oakes and Ribar (2005) found that four-month-old infants responded to the categorical distinction between dogs and cats only when items were presented in pairs. When items were presented one at a time, four-month-old infants, unlike the six-month-old infants described earlier, failed to look longer at the novel out-of-category item relative to the novel within-category item (see middle portion of Fig. 6–3). This failure was particularly striking because Quinn and his colleagues (e.g., Quinn et al., 1993) have shown that three- to four-month-old infants are sensitive to the distinction between cats and dogs. However, in Quinn's studies the stimuli were presented in pairs. When Oakes and Ribar presented four-month-old infants with exactly the same set of stimuli using paired presentation, infants did respond to the distinction between cats and dogs (see rightmost portion of Fig. 6–3). Apparently, in this version of the task—despite the fact that infants viewed the exact same set of items, and for even less time—four-month-old infants could more easily extract the commonalities that defined the exclusive category of *cat* or *dog*. Kovack-Lesh and Oakes (2007) replicated this effect in 10-month-old infants' attention to the adult-defined categories of *dog and horse* in an *object-examining task.*

Why does presenting items in pairs induce infants to respond to narrower or more exclusive categorical contrasts? There are at least three ways that presenting items in pairs may facilitate comparison and as a result facilitate the detection of subtler similarities among items. First, comparing items presented in two different trials requires that infants keep active their memory of the first object encountered during the inter-trial interval. However, the memory of the first item likely fades over the course of the inter-trial interval, thus limiting the comparisons infants can make. Comparing items presented in the same trial, in contrast, requires infants to remember an item only over an extremely brief inter-glance interval (because infants simply need to move their eyes from one screen to the next, which they frequently do). Thus, the difference observed for infants' categorization in the two tasks might reflect differences in the time required for infants to maintain a memory of the to-be-compared item. The successive presentation task used by

Oakes and Ribar (2005) was an infant-controlled procedure in which the stimulus remained on the screen until the infant looked away; the next trial began when the infant oriented to an attention-getting stimulus. In this task, 6-month-old infants, who did attend to the distinction between dogs and cats, had much shorter inter-trial intervals than did the four-month-old infants (approximately 3 s as compared to almost 5 s), who failed to attend to the distinction between dogs and cats. Schöner and Thelen (2006) have recently proposed a dynamic-field theory of infant habituation as a time-dependent process, and consequently the inter-stimulus interval should make an important contribution to the behavior of the infant in looking tasks. Although we do not know at this point why this difference in inter-trial interval exists in the study by Oakes and Ribar (2005) (e.g., whether it reflects differences in attention, motor control, or some aspects of processing the stimuli), it does correspond to the significantly different memory demands placed upon the infants at the two ages.

Second, the paired-presentation task may facilitate comparison by allowing infants to update their memory of the items to be compared during the comparison process. When items are presented one at a time, infants may fail to encode some detail important for comparing earlier items with subsequently encountered items (e.g., the shape of the ears). Because the item is no longer available, it is impossible to retrieve that information, and the opportunity for comparing along that dimension is lost. When items are presented in pairs, in contrast, infants can glance back-and-forth between the two items and can therefore update or change their representations of each item (e.g., encoding information about the shape of the ears) and thus make more detailed comparisons. Indeed, for this reason, Cohen and Gelber (1975) argued that the paired-comparison procedure may be a more sensitive test of infant memory than the single-presentation habituation task. Obviously, infants do compare even when items are presented one at a time, or else they would not detect any commonalities among the items. But they may extract different kinds of commonalities in the paired presentation task because they are able to repeatedly update their representation of the to-be-compared items.

Finally, the paired-presentation format may facilitate comparison because seeing different items simultaneously—even briefly—may induce infants to attend to commonalities and differences among items (as opposed to the details of individual items), or to attend to *different* details of the individual items (i.e., those that are important for categorization). That is, presenting items in pairs may make it more explicit to infants that the goal of the task is to compare those items. Over trials, infants may even learn to attend to different commonalities and differences among items when items are presented in pairs than when they are presented one at a time. The differences in categorization we observed may not reflect infants' engaging in more back-and-forth comparison when different pairs are present but rather may reflect infants' engaging in different kinds of learning about the objects in the two contexts. To test this possibility, Kovack-Lesh and Oakes (2007) familiarized 10-month-old infants in an object-examining task with identical pairs of dogs or horses. Typically, the end of one trial is marked by the removal of the items, and the beginning of the next trial is marked by the presentation of new items—thus, items from the two trials are never presented at the same time. Kovack-Lesh and Oakes compared this traditional format with a condition in which one of the items from the next trial was presented *before* the current items were removed (thus, there was one new item and two old items present). Then one of the old items was removed (leaving one old item and one new item present), and finally, the second new item was presented and the second old item removed (leaving only the two new items). This modification allowed infants a brief exposure to different items presented simultaneously (approximately 6.5 s), but did not provide them an extended opportunity to glance back and forth between the two items to engage in direct comparison of those items (in fact, infants usually watched the action of the experimenter rather than scrutinizing the two different items that were now side by side). This brief transition was sufficient to induce infants to respond to the more exclusive category of dogs or horses (see Fig. 6–4). Like infants in a condition in which two different dogs or horses were presented simultaneously on each trial, these infants significantly preferred the out-of-category item. Apparently, at least for 10-month-old infants in

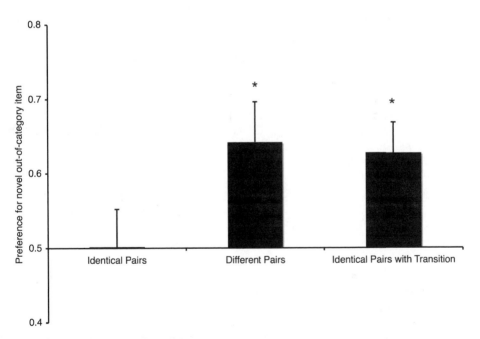

Figure 6–4. Results reported by Kovack-Lesh and Oakes (2007) for 10-month-olds infants' responding in an object-examining task to novel within-category and novel out-of-category items following familiarization with pairs of dogs or pairs of horses. Infants' duration of looking to the novel within-category and novel out-of-category (in s) is presented (error bars represent +1 *SE*) for infants familiarized with identical pairs of items, different pairs of items, and identical pairs with some overlap between trials (identical pairs with transition). Scores significantly different from chance (.50), $p < .05$, are indicated by an asterisk.

the object-examining task, exposure to different items side-by-side is an important aspect of the context that supports learning of a particular type of category—a fairly narrow or exclusive category. That is, the original differences we observed for infants familiarized with different versus identical pairs do not appear to reflect differences in infants' ability to conduct extensive direct comparisons on line during each familiarization trial. Rather, learning about an item that was initially encountered in the context of other items induced infants to engage in more comparison across trials; they apparently attended to and learned about features of the items that helped them compare those items to items presented in other trials.

Together, these studies demonstrate that aspects of the context that support infants' ability to compare instances influences the particular commonalities and differences infants learn and, as a result, the kinds of categories they form. These studies are the first steps in understanding these processes. We suspect that all three of the differences between paired- and successive-presentation tasks just described (keeping the memory active during the inter-trial interval, being able to update memory for individual items, and attending to similarities and differences) influence infants' learning of categories. The findings presented here set the stage for future research uncovering how these factors combine to influence infant categorization.

The Level of Within-Category Variability During Familiarization

Gentner and her colleagues have shown that children and adults engage in deeper levels of comparison when the to-be-compared items are easily alignable (Loewenstein & Gentner, 2001) and when more commonalities and differences are recognized among alignable instances (Gentner & Gunn, 2001). Thus, one way to facilitate or attenuate infants' comparison of items presented in different trials is to manipulate the similarity among the items encountered across trials. Gentner and her colleagues (Kotovsky & Gentner, 1996; Loewenstein & Gentner, 2001) have observed that when, in successive trials, children are first presented with items that are easily aligned, they are more successful at comparing items that are difficult to align on later trials (the notion of progressive alignment). Therefore, infants may more readily compare items across trials if those items are easily aligned but may have more difficulty comparing those items when they are less alignable.

In three separate investigations, we found that reducing the variability among items presented during familiarization induces infants to learn categories that are more exclusive than they learn when familiarized with a set of highly variable items—presumably because they are more effective at comparing items presented on adjacent trials when the items are more similar. For example, Ribar, Oakes, and Spalding (2004) found that 6- to 13-month-old infants who were familiarized in an object-examining task with a set of land animals that were all black and white in coloring (e.g., a panda, a black-and-white cow, a black-and-white tiger) learned the arbitrary category of black-and-white animals, whereas infants who were familiarized with land animals that were of various colors learned a broader category—one that included both land and sea animals (see Table 6–1). Specifically, during the test phase, infants who had been familiarized with black-and-white land animals increased their looking at any new land or sea animal that was not black-and-white, whereas infants familiarized with the variable set of land animals failed to significantly increase their looking at any new animals—even a new sea animal. Familiarizing infants with items that share many commonalities appears to facilitate their comparison of those items across trials, and as a result they learn narrower categories. Of course, in this experiment, the black-and-white animals shared features that the variable animals did not (specifically, black-and-white coloring). It is noteworthy that some infants in each condition were shown a black-and-white killer whale, and others were shown a blue dolphin. Infants did not respond differently to these two tests, indicating that infants did not simply respond to black-and-white coloring.

We observed the same pattern of results when 10-month-old infants were familiarized in an object-examining task with land animals or sea animals that had been judged by adults to be more or less similar to one another (Oakes et al., 1997). Infants familiarized with a similar set of items learned a relatively exclusive category—land *or* sea animals—and infants familiarized with a variable set of items learned a relatively broad category—one that included both land *and* sea animals (see Table 6–1). These results confirm that the previous pattern does not simply reflect how infants respond when the familiarization items are similar along a single, salient dimension, but rather that similarity among the items more broadly influences infants' ability to compare items presented in different trials.

Finally, Oakes and Spalding (1997) found that the exclusivity of the category learned by 10-month-old infants tested in an object-examining task depends on how the items are distributed during familiarization. In the studies just described, infants were familiarized with different sets of items, and thus the sets

Table 6–1 Pattern of Results Obtained in Three Studies Manipulating the Amount of Variability During Familiarization

	Familiarization Condition	
Study	*Similar*	*Variable*
Black-and-White Animals (Ribar et al., 2004)	Narrow	Broad
Range of Variability (Oakes et al., 1997)	Narrow	Broad
Exemplar Distribution (Oakes & Spalding, 1997)	Narrow	Broad

Note: "Narrow" indicates that a relatively exclusive category was formed (e.g., black-and-white land animals, sea animals). "Broad" indicates that a relatively inclusive category was formed (e.g., animal).

were characterized by *different* commonalities. Oakes and Spalding familiarized all infants with exactly the same six land or sea animals but varied the frequency of particular items during familiarization. In a similar–frequent condition, infants were presented with three "similar" items (e.g., horse, cow, and zebra) frequently and three "dissimilar" items (e.g., ram, rabbit, and bear) infrequently. In a dissimilar–frequent condition, infants were presented with the three dissimilar items frequently and the three similar items infrequently (an example of a sequence of familiarization trials in each condition is provided in Fig. 6–5). This manipulation is mimics the differences in experience between two infants who are exposed to the same range of dogs, with one infant frequently seeing a German shepherd and the other infant frequently sees a Chihuahua. Importantly, not only did the infants see the same conceptual category, but they were familiarized with exactly the same exemplars. Thus, the infants experienced the same range of variability, but the variability was distributed quite differently in their experience. This way of manipulating variability has been shown to have a

Similar Frequent	Dissimilar Frequent
Horse	Horse
Zebra	Ram
Ram	Rabbit
Cow	Bear
Zebra	Rabbit
Rabbit	Cow
Cow	Ram
Horse	Bear
Cow	Bear
Bear	Rabbit
Zebra	Ram
Horse	Zebra

Figure 6–5. Examples of sequences of trials in the similar–frequent and dissimilar–frequent familiarization conditions used by Oakes and Spalding (1997). See text for details.

powerful influence on how adults form categories of novel items (Homa, Dunbar, & Nohre, 1991), and on the emergence of expertise in connectionist models (Rogers & McClelland, 2004).

Once again, the variability presented during familiarization influenced which category infants learned. When infants were exposed to less variability (in this case by seeing similar items frequently), they responded to the narrower, more exclusive category (see Table 6–1). As we observed in both of the previous studies, infants in the dissimilar–frequent condition, who experienced more variability, responded to a global category of animal—one that included both land and sea animals. Infants in the similar–frequent condition, on the other hand, responded to the narrower category of "land animal" or "sea animal." It is important to remember that these differences were observed despite the fact that all infants saw exactly the same items during familiarization.

Together, these studies provide converging evidence that infants' categorization is context dependent. Our results demonstrate that aspects of context that influence how easily infants can compare instances dramatically change the particular category that they learn. The main point, therefore, is that infants' learning of categories depends on how the context supports their ability to attend to and perceive the to-be-remembered items, and to remember previously encountered similar items and to compare different items.

KINDS OF LEARNING PROCESSES THAT ARE EVIDENT AS INFANTS LEARN CATEGORIES

When learning, creating, and generating categorical groups, infants must detect regularities in the input—for example, that all the animals are black-and-white in coloring, or that they all have eyes and a mouth—and they need to learn details of the individual items. Infants need not only learn the commonalities that specify groups and help them define category boundaries, but they must also learn and encode those features that differentiate or individuate items. It is not enough to learn the category dog—one must also learn to recognize grandma's basset hound Betty as a particular instance of the category dog. Moreover, when encountering a new dog, people can recognize a few moments later that they have seen that particular dog and can recognize in which categories that dog can be included. Therefore, when infants are faced with a collection of items from the same category, processes must be at work to allow them to learn about regularities, generalize across instances, and encode the individual items. The question is this: What kinds of processes are involved in learning (remembering, encoding) those commonalities and differences?

There is a large literature on the mechanisms of category learning in adults, and debates rage about whether a single process or multiple processes are required (see Ashby & Maddox, 2005, for a review). Moreover, neuropsychological evidence suggests that each type of learning is subserved by a different neural structure (Ashby & Ell, 2001; Squire, 2004). Patients with medial temporal lobe damage have difficulty remembering individual items even though they can extract the commonalities among a collection of items (Knowlton & Squire, 1993). Parkinson's patients with basal ganglia damage but intact medial temporal lobes have difficulty with rule-based classification tasks (Ashby, Noble, Filoteo, Waldron, & Ell, 2003; Moody, Bookheimer, Vanek, & Knowlton, 2004). It is not clear, however, how these differences in the role of neuroanatomical structures in adult memory and classification-task performance map onto the differences in infants' performance observed in familiarization tasks. When infants learn particular items in a task, is this evidence that they have intact, engaged medial temporal structures? For example, Quinn and colleagues have shown that three- to four-month-old infants remember individual instances of female faces and humans (Quinn & Eimas, 1998; Quinn, Yahr, Kuhn, Slater, & Pascalis, 2002). It is unlikely, however, that they have the same type of accessible, explicit memory representations for those individual items as an adult would. This debate is beyond the scope of the present chapter, and understanding of the development of the relevant neural structures in human infancy is far too incomplete to allow strong conclusions. But these issues are important for developmentalists to consider and should inform future research.

For the present purposes, however, it is clear that infants can engage in processes that allow them to learn both commonalities among items and individual instances (whether by a single system or by separate explicit and implicit memory systems). The results of statistical learning studies (e.g., Saffran, Aslin, & Newport, 1996; Kirkham, Slemmer, & Johnson, 2002; Fiser & Aslin, 2002) show that infants have the ability to extract regularities over many encounters with items. Moreover, a number of studies have shown that infants are sensitive to the statistically regular associations among features of items (e.g., that animals with a particular type of tail also tend to have a particular type of legs) and can use these associations to divide items into categorical groups (Rakison, 2004; Younger, 1985). Infants can also rapidly learn the features of individual items. For example, Fagan (1974) found that four- to five-month-old infants learned the features of an individual face after only 20 seconds of exposure and the features of a complex visual pattern after less than 5 seconds of exposure. Thus, from an early age, infants are capable of both extracting commonalities over time and rapidly learning detailed information about individuals.

It now appears that infants are capable of both types of learning even when familiarized with a *collection* of items from within a category. Clearly, the many studies showing that infants will learn artificial categories in the laboratory over the course of familiarization demonstrates that they can learn regularities over several presentations of items, each lasting several seconds (e.g., Younger, 1985; Horst et al., 2005). Even more impressive is that infants appear to rapidly learn about the individual instances when they are presented with a collection of new items from a category. Quinn and his colleagues (2002) showed that infants reared by a female caregiver remembered the 12 individual female faces presented in a category task. We recently observed that four-month-old infants who have pets at home can remember 12 individual instances of cats presented during familiarization (Kovack-Lesh, Horst, & Oakes, in press).

In general, therefore, the literature suggests that infants possess the neural structures necessary both for learning individual items and for extracting commonalities in an implicit memory task. But when do infants engage in each type of learning? Smith (2005) has suggested an additional mechanism that may contribute to differences in when infants learn individual items versus when they learn to extract the commonalities among items in the category. Specifically, she notes that the kinds of categories for which infants have been shown to remember individual exemplars in the laboratory (e.g., faces, pets) are categories for which infants have extensive experience with a few individuals in a large number of contexts. For other kinds of categories, infants experience a large number of individual exemplars, each in a few contexts (e.g., sippy cups, coffee cups, paper cups). Smith argues that these contextual differences may induce infants' learning of individual instances in one case and their learning of the commonalities in the other case. Thus, whether infants learn individual instances, commonalities, or both must be a function of both the developmental status of the underlying neural mechanisms and the context in which infants encounter the exemplars.

Horst, Oakes, and Madole (2005) found that the nature of the category to which infants are exposed determines, in part, whether they learn individual items or the commonalities among those items. In this study, we familiarized 10-month-old infants with a category that was either organized around a common function (e.g., squeezing caused the objects to squeak) or a common appearance (e.g., purple, rounded objects). We observed that infants learned individual instances when presented with the category defined by a common appearance presumably because they had to ignore variations in the more difficult-to-process, highly salient functions of the objects. In contrast, infants learned the commonalities when presented with categories defined by a common function, presumably because the unvarying feature was the more difficult-to-process, highly salient feature. This pattern is consistent with that described by Smith and Minda (1998) in their study of adults' learning of novel categories. Therefore, it appears that for both infants and adults whether the learning processes result in learning individuals or commonalties depends, in part, on the structure of the category.

It is clear that the processes involved in learning categories allow infants both to learn regularities or commonalities and to learn individual instances. The kinds of learning we have identified are characteristics of learning about and forming memories of items in general, and not specific to the tasks of actively forming categorical groups of similar objects. When encountering new items, infants learn about individuals, compare these individuals over time, and extract commonalities among individuals. These are general processes of memory.

Infants do engage in both kinds of learning across a broad set of domains. As described earlier, infants learn the statistical regularities in speech and language input (Saffran et al., 1996; Gomez & Gerken, 1999) and visual events (Kirkham et al., 2002), and they can form correlations both among features of visually presented stimuli (Younger, 1985) and between words and visual images of objects (Werker, Cohen, Lloyd, Cassasola, & Stager, 1998). Therefore, extracting regularities—an important aspect of learning commonalities among items within a category—is a domain-general ability. In addition, infants learn the details of new auditory and visual stimuli—including speech tokens, abstract shapes, and faces—from early in infancy (see Kellman & Arterberry, 1998, for a review). Thus, remembering the features of individuals is also domain general.

These basic learning mechanisms are present from an early age. Developmental changes related to the basic abilities to encode information about individuals or commonalities among individuals are probably related to development of the neuroanatomical structures involved in perceptual and memory abilities. Infants may become able to detect more features, encode them more quickly, remember information longer, and so on. For categorization, the important developmental change may be in infants' ability to use the two kinds of learning together—determining when, for example, one should ignore new information about the instances and focus on the regularities among those instances. Developmental changes may be more evident when looking at how the two processes work together and how contextual effects engage one process more or less than the other. We are only beginning to understand how these mechanisms work to allow infants to discover categorical contrasts in familiarization tasks, but we expect that future research will reveal developmental changes in how infants use these two mechanisms together to create and re-create categorical groups. This future work will inform us about how infants attend to and learn these two types of information in the "real world."

The Nature of the Representations Formed During Category Learning

The aim of our work has been to explicitly examine the process of learning categories and not to examine the nature of the representation formed. It is impossible to truly separate these two aspects of learning categories, however, so our work does have implications for the nature of the representation that is formed during the learning of categories. There are two different ways of approaching this question: (1) What information is contained in the representation? and (2) What are the characteristics of the representation—is it accessible or inaccessible? Static or dynamic? Procedural or declarative? Modifiable or rigid?

Our work clearly has implications for understanding the content of infants' categorical representations. Specifically, one of our main findings has been that such content is dynamic and changing. As described earlier, the content of the representation (e.g., whether infants represent a category as including black-and-white coloring or features that are characteristic of cats but not dogs) is complexly determined by the task and stimulus context and by the infants' past experience with the to-be-learned category. The demonstrations described in the preceding sections show that the content of infants' representations changes as we manipulate how the items are presented (e.g., singly or two at a time), the level of within-category variability, and the age at which we test infants. What is the mechanism by which the task and stimulus context and the infants' experience influence the representation? One possibility is selective attention. The task and stimulus context and infants' experience may guide infants' attention to some features, dimensions, or properties, which in turn determines exactly what information is represented about objects and the category. For example, Quinn and Eimas (1996) have shown that infants selectively attend to the head and facial region of animals when categorizing. Rakison (2004) has argued that infants' attention system is biased to orient toward movement, although whether or not infants use that information to form categories depends on the developmental state of their information-processing abilities more generally. This way of thinking about selective attention ultimately has its roots in the writings of William James (1890), who wrote that experience is shaped by what one attends to, and that in fact the only items that can shape the mind are those that are attended to.

Selective attention, therefore, is an important determinant of the content of infants' categorical representations. At various points in development, in various contexts, and with various levels of familiarity (among other factors) infants will selectively attend to different features. For example, as infants become more sophisticated in their manipulation of objects, they may become more aware of commonalities among objects in texture, rigidity, and function (Bushnell & Boudreau, 1993; Oakes & Madole, 2003; Needham, this volume). Similarly, infants who have extensive experience with dogs or cats may focus more attention to the head and face area of the stimuli than might infants who have little experience with dogs or cats. The point is that the content of the representation will be influenced by how infants attend to the to-be-categorized items. The work described here provides an important foundation for understanding how this process works. An important next step is to conduct additional research directly evaluating how manipulating selective attention results in differences in the content of infants' representations.

Our work also has implications for some of the characteristics of the representation (e.g., whether it is static or dynamic, modifiable or rigid). Specifically, the studies discussed here demonstrate that the categorical representations learned in familiarization tasks are dynamic and modifiable, rather than static or rigid. Representations change over the course of familiarization. Even whether or not infants exhibit a preference for a novel or a familiar stimulus depends on when during familiarization they are probed, presumably because their representation of the familiar item changes over time (e.g., Hunter, Ross, & Ames, 1982; Roder, Bushnell, & Sasseville, 2000). Horst et al. (2005) explicitly probed the content of infants' representations of a category at various points during familiarization and found that their representations changed as the items and category became more familiar. For example, infants familiarized with a category defined by a common function represented the common features early in learning and the individuals later in learning. Familiarization with a particular set of items did not induce a single representation of the category; rather the representation changed as infants became more familiar with the collection of items.

It is likely that representations formed in the "real world" are also dynamic in this way. Infants (and children and adults) accumulate knowledge about familiar objects every day, and that new information *must* change the representations previously formed for those objects. It does not matter when one learns that a penguin is a bird, for example; learning this fact changes one's category bird regardless of whether this fact is learned at age 3 or age 83. Therefore, we argue that representations are dynamic and flexible, changing with additional knowledge and experience.

This does not mean that representations do not become relatively stable. In the language of dynamic systems theory (Thelen & Smith, 1994), categorical groups likely are attractor states that become more stable over time. The more experience one has with birds, for example, the more stable one's category bird becomes—it becomes more difficult to alter that representation, or the representation can be changed only in minor ways. The fact that speakers of English understand what the words bird, cat, house, and school mean is good evidence that at least some categorical groups become reasonably stable. However, it is also clear that categorization is flexible and dynamic.

How flexibility changes with development, however, is a complex issue. Ellis and Oakes (2006) found that more cognitively advanced 14-month-old infants (at least with respect to vocabulary and attention to superordinate categorical distinctions) were more flexible in their categorization of a set of items in a sequential-touching task. When presented with a collection of eight objects—four balls and four blocks, two of each type being compressible—all infants initially categorized the items by shape. The overwhelming majority of infants touched all the balls then all the blocks, or vice versa. After a demonstration that some of the balls and blocks were compressible (i.e., an experimenter "squished" each object one at a time in a can crusher), the more advanced infants shifted to categorizing the objects by compressibility. The less developed infants rigidly continued to categorize items using the initial dimension they had discovered. Thus, categorization is not flexible only at specific points in development; rather flexibility in categorization changes depending on the context, and infants' knowledge about the kinds of items being categorized, among other things.

Our studies have shown that the categorical representations infants form in experiments (and probably in real life) are dynamic and flexible. Our data have less to say about whether the representations infants form in the laboratory are accessible or inaccessible, or procedural or declarative. As described earlier, amnesiac patients perform similarly to the infants in our studies (Knowlton & Squire, 1993; Reed et al., 1999), suggesting that accessible representations are not necessary for our tasks. Of course, this evidence does not tell us whether infants' representations are accessible, although some have used this evidence to draw such conclusions (see Rose, Feldman, & Jankowski, 2004; Snyder, 2007). Moreover, as described above, the tasks used to assess categorization in infancy are similar to *implicit* memory tasks used with adults. The similarity to implicit memory tasks, however, does not preclude infants' forming explicit, declarative, or accessible memories in those tasks. At this point, we do not believe that our data speak to this issue. A number of other theorists have dealt with this issue in detail (e.g., Karmiloff-Smith, 1992; Mandler, 2004), and research into this area may someday provide deeper insight into this aspect of infants' representations.

Generalization of Learning to New Instances

As it is clear by now, in our view, category learning does not stop. Infants (and adults) do not acquire information about a variety of instances, form a group of those instances, and then fail to change or update that group in the face of new information. Rather, categorical groups shift as people detect commonalities among items and new information. Importantly, infants participating in a categorization experiment using a familiarization-test procedure do not know when the learning phase (or familiarization phase) ends and the testing phase begins. Infants know only that they are presented with objects or pictures, and they study and explore those items as they are encountered. Infants' responding to the test items in a familiarization task, therefore, reflects learning on several different timescales; learning during the previous trial, even if that previous trial (from the experimenter's perspective) is a test trial; learning over the course of familiarization; and learning over their own developmental history and experience with similar items in the "real world" outside the laboratory.

By definition, learning involves the accumulation of information over time. Detecting regularities involves the gradual process of noting commonalities among instances (by comparing those instances). Therefore, representations of previously encountered items influence how infants learn about and represent newly encountered items. This is true regardless of when these items were encountered. Obviously, because infants' memories change over time and with repeated exposure to items (e.g., Hunter et al., 1982; Roder et al., 2000; Bauer, this volume), the kind of influence previous learning will have on infants' performance in a particular experiment or to a particular set of stimuli will be a function, in part, of the strength and nature of that representation. Pauen (2002) has argued that "single process" views of categorization—like the one described here in which infants' performance reflects significant online learning of the items—do not allow for the effect of previously acquired knowledge on infants' categorical responding in familiarization tasks. It should be clear from the present discussion that nothing is further from the truth—infants' learning is always on line, and that learning occurs over many timescales. As a result, we predict that infants' learning of a collection of items in a categorization task in a laboratory will be influenced by their history with similar items—their immediate history in the laboratory, and their long-term history in the "real world." Moreover, learning in the laboratory is not excluded from infants' history, and thus learning in the laboratory likely influences what infants learn outside of the laboratory, as was elegantly illustrated by Samuelson (2002).

Our view is similar to the model developed by Quinn (2002). Based on his observations that infants' learning of items from familiar categories differs from their learning of items from less familiar categories, Quinn has developed a model of how infants' representations of categories change with increasing familiarity with exemplars from those categories. Specifically, categorical representations during early infancy consist of incoherently clustered exemplars. As infants acquire experience with exemplars and the ability to learn and remember the commonalities and differences among exemplars, representations at the level of summary representations emerge. If infants acquire extensive experience with exemplars from a category, the summary representation may be enriched by information about individuals. These representations then influence how infants learn about items.

Consistent with Quinn's model, we found that when familiarized with a collection of 12 pictures of cats, only four-month-old infants with pets at home learned the individual cats (Kovack-Lesh et al., in press). Thus, infants' learning outside the laboratory influences their learning in the laboratory. Category learning does not have a starting point and a stopping point. Each time infants encounter objects—whether during a trial of a familiarization study, at the park, while playing at home, and so on—they learn about and form representations of those objects. Sometimes they may engage in actively processing the information about the objects and form explicit, accessible memory representations. Other times they may engage in more passive learning processes and form implicit memory representations that are not accessible. But, when infants encounter items in a familiarization task in a laboratory, they do not know that they should learn about those items without reference to their previously acquired knowledge. Thus, how infants respond in familiarization tasks reflects not only their learning during the several minutes of the laboratory procedure but also their learning over months of interaction with objects in their daily lives. That is, infants' responses in the laboratory reflect the convergence of processes in real time and over developmental time.

This discussion, and this chapter, has focused on infants' learning of categories in the context of familiarization tasks. However, infants' categorization abilities have also been assessed using other laboratory tasks, and responding in those other tasks may be even more influenced by infants' previous knowledge. In the sequential-touching task (Mandler, Fivush, & Reznick, 1987), for example, infants are presented with a collection of items from two adult-defined categories (e.g., animals and vehicles), and their spontaneous touching and manipulation of those items is recorded (an example of this procedure was described earlier in the context of Ellis and Oakes, 2006). Although infants may learn about the commonalities among the items as they investigate them, their touching in this task may also reflect their recognition of previously formed categorical contrasts. In the generalized-imitation task (Mandler & McDonough, 1996), an event is modeled to the infant using a set of props (e.g., a dog is given a drink from a cup), and then the infant is given a different set of props to reproduce the event. Infants are more likely to reproduce events from the same adult-defined category (e.g., a cat) than from a different adult-defined category (e.g., a car). Although the role of online learning has not been adequately addressed in these two tasks (and from our perspective some online learning should occur even in these contexts), it would not be surprising if infants' previously acquired knowledge had a strong influence on their responding in these tasks.

Clearly, we are only beginning to understand how to answer to this last question, but there is a lesson here for researchers. When we present infants with potentially familiar stimuli, we need to be extremely cautious about the conclusions we draw. Regardless of whether or not one believes that infants' responding to a particular set of stimuli primarily reflects their existing knowledge, it is important to keep in mind that (1) not all infants have the same experience, and, therefore, differences in learning history may introduce new sources of variability into your experiment, and (2) infants' performance certainly reflects not only their previous history but also what they have learned in the laboratory during the experiment.

CONCLUSIONS

In this chapter, we have discussed how infants learn categories. By systematically examining how differences in the familiarization context influences the categories infants learn, we gain deep insight into *how* infants learn categories. Infants are constantly learning categories—in their everyday lives as they interact with objects and observe events and in laboratory experiments as we present them with collections of items from within an adult-defined category. Thus, it is critically important for us to think about infants' performance in familiarization tasks not as a means of simply tapping the knowledge infants have acquired outside the laboratory but also as a means of tapping how infants learn information *given* that existing knowledge. Moreover, if we think about categories as emerging in the context of infants' attention to and perception of features of items, their ability to recall encounters with exemplars, and their comparison of such representations, we gain understanding into the nature of categorization and how infants' developing cognitive abilities influence the categories they learn.

Acknowledgments   Preparation of this manuscript and the research described here were made possible by National Institutes of Health grants HD-36060, HD-49840, HD-49143, and MH-64020. Lisa M. Oakes is now at the University of California, Davis, Jessica S. Horst is now at University of Sussex, and Kristine A. Kovack-Lesh is now at Ripon College. We express our appreciation to David Rakison for comments on an earlier draft of this chapter.

References

Ashby, F., & Ell, S. W. (2001). The neurobiology of human category learning. *Trends in Cognitive Sciences, 5,* 204–210.

Ashby, F., & Maddox, W. (2005). Human category learning. *Annual Review of Psychology, 56,* 149–178.

Ashby, F., Noble, S., Filoteo, J., Waldron, E. M., & Ell, S. W. (2003). Category learning deficits in Parkinson's disease. *Neuropsychology, 17,* 115–124.

Barsalou, L. W. (1983). Ad hoc categories. *Memory and Cognition, 11,* 221–227.

Bomba, P. C., & Siqueland, E. R. (1983). The nature and structure of infant form categories. *Journal of Experimental Child Psychology, 35,* 294–328.

Bushnell, E. W., & Boudreau, J. P. (1993). Motor development and the mind: The potential role of motor abilities as a determinant of aspects of perceptual development. *Child Development, 64,* 1005–1021.

Cohen, L. B., & Gelber, E. R. (1975). Infant visual memory. In L. B. Cohen & P. Salapatek (Eds.), *Infant perception: From sensation to cognition. Volume I: Basic visual processes* (pp. 347–404). New York: Academic Press.

Ellis, A. E., & Oakes, L. M. (2006). Infants' flexibly use different dimensions to categorize objects. *Developmental Psychology, 42,* 1000–1011.

Fagan, J. F. (1974). Infant recognition memory: The effects of length of familiarization and type of discrimination task. *Child Development, 45,* 351–356.

Fiser, J., & Aslin, R. N. (2002). Statistical learning of new visual feature combinations by infants. *Proceedings of the National Academy of Science, 99,* 15,822–15,826.

French, R. M., Mermillod, M., Quinn, P. C., Chauvin, A., & Mareschal, D. (2002). *The importance of starting blurry: Simulating improved basic-level category learning in infants due to weak visual acuity*. Proceedings of the 24th Annual Conference of the Cognitive Science Society London: LEA.

Gentner, D., & Gunn, V. (2001). Structural alignment facilitates the noticing of differences. *Memory & Cognition, 29,* 565–577.

Gentner, D., & Namy, L. L. (1999). Comparison in the development of categories. *Cognitive Development, 14,* 487–513.

Gomez, R. L., & Gerken, L. (1999). Artificial grammar learning by 1-year-olds leads to specific and abstract knowledge. *Cognition, 70,* 109–135.

Homa, D., Dunbar, S., & Nohre, L. (1991). Instance frequency, categorization, and the modulating effect of experience. *Journal of Experimental Psychology: Learning, Memory, & Cognition, 17,* 444–458.

Horst, J. S., Oakes, L. M., & Madole, K. L. (2005). What does it look like and what can it do? Category structure influences how infants categorize. *Child Development, 76,* 614–631.

Hunter, M. A., Ross, H. S., & Ames, E. W. (1982). Preferences for familiar or novel toys: Effects of familiarization time in 1-year-olds. *Developmental Psychology, 18,* 519–529.

James, W. (1890). *The principles of psychology*. New York: Holt.

Johansen, M. K., & Palmeri, T. J. (2002). Are there representational shifts during category learning? *Cognitive Psychology, 45,* 482–553.

Jones, S. S., & Smith, L. B. (1993). The place of perception in children's concepts. *Cognitive Development, 8,* 113–139.

Karmiloff-Smith, A. (1992). *Beyond modularity: A developmental perspective on cognitive science*. Cambridge, MA: MIT Press.

Kellman, P. J., & Arterberry, M. E. (1998). *The cradle of knowledge: Development of perception in infancy*. Cambridge, MA: MIT Press.

Kirkham, N. Z., Slemmer, J. A., & Johnson, S. P. (2002). Visual statistical learning in infancy: Evidence for a domain general learning mechanism. *Cognition, 83,* B35–B42.

Knowlton, B. J., & Squire, L. R. (1993). The learning of categories: Parallel brain systems for item memory and category knowledge. *Science, 262,* 1747–1749.

Kotovsky, L., & Gentner, D. (1996). Comparison and categorization in the development of relational similarity. *Child Development, 67,* 2797–2822.

Kovack-Lesh, K. A., Horst, J. H., & Oakes, L. M. (in press). The cat is out of the bag: The joint influence of previous experience and looking behavior on infant categorization. *Infancy*.

Kovack-Lesh, K. A., & Oakes, L. M. (2007). Hold your horses: How exposure to different items influences infant categorization. *Journal of Experimental Child Psychology, 98,* 69–93.

Leslie, A. M., Friedman, O., & German, T. P. (2004). Core mechanisms in "theory of mind." *Trends in Cognitive Sciences, 8,* 529–533.

Loewenstein, J., & Gentner, D. (2001). Spatial mapping in preschoolers: Close comparisons facilitate far mappings. *Journal of Cognition & Development, 2,* 189–219.

Lopez, A., Atran, S., Coley, J. D., Medin, D. L., & Smith, E. E. (1997). The tree of life: Universal and cultural features of folkbiological taxonomies and inductions. *Cognitive Psychology, 32,* 251–295.

Mandler, J. M. (2004). *The foundations of mind: Origins of conceptual thought*. New York: Oxford University Press.

Mandler, J. M., Fivush, R., & Reznick, J. S. (1987). The development of contextual categories. *Cognitive Development, 2,* 339–354.

Mandler, J. M., & McDonough, L. (1993). Concept formation in infancy. *Cognitive Development, 8,* 281–318.

Mandler, J. M., & McDonough, L. (1996). Drinking and driving don't mix: Inductive generalization in infancy. *Cognition, 59,* 307–335.

Markman, A. B., & Gentner, D. (2000). Structure mapping in the comparison process. *American Journal of Psychology, 113,* 501–538.

Markman, A. B., & Ross, B. H. (2003). Category use and category learning. *Psychological Bulletin, 129,* 592–613.

Medin, D. L., Lynch, E. B., Coley, J. D., & Atran, S. (1997). Categorization and reasoning among tree experts: Do all roads lead to Rome? *Cognitive Psychology, 32,* 49–96.

Moody, T. D., Bookheimer, S. Y., Vanek, Z., & Knowlton, B. J. (2004). An implicit learning task activates medial temporal lobe in patients with Parkinson's disease. *Behavioral Neuroscience, 118,* 438–442.

Newcombe, N. S. (2002). The nativist-empiricist controversy in the context of recent research on spatial and quantitative development. *Psychological Science, 13,* 395–401.

Oakes, L. M., Coppage, D. J., & Dingel, A. (1997). By land or by sea: The role of perceptual similarity in infants' categorization of animals. *Developmental Psychology, 33,* 396–407.

Oakes, L. M., & Madole, K. L. (2003). Principles of developmental change in infants' category formation. In D. H. Rakison & L. M. Oakes (Eds.), *Early category and concept development: Making sense of the blooming, buzzing confusion* (pp. 132–158). New York: Oxford University Press.

Oakes, L. M., & Ribar, R. J. (2005). A comparison of infants' categorization in paried and successive presentation familiarization tasks. *Infancy, 7,* 85–98.

Oakes, L. M., Ross-Sheehy, S., & Luck, S. J. (in press). Rapid development of binding in visual short-term memory. *Psychological Science.*

Oakes, L. M., & Spalding, T. L. (1997). The role of exemplar distribution in infants' differentiation of categories. *Infant Behavior and Development, 20,* 457–475.

Pauen, S. (2002). Evidence for knowledge-based category discrimination in infancy. *Child Development, 73,* 1016–1033.

Quinn, P. C. (2002). Beyond prototypes: Asymmetries in infant categorization and what they teach us about the mechanisms guiding early knowledge acquisition. *Advances in Child Development and Behavior, 29,* 161–193.

Quinn, P. C., & Eimas, P. D. (1996). Perceptual cues that permit categorical differentiation of animal species by infants. *Journal of Experimental Child Psychology, 63,* 189–211.

Quinn, P. C., & Eimas, P. D. (1998). Evidence for a global categorical representation of humans by young infants. *Journal of Experimental Child Psychology, 69,* 151–174.

Quinn, P. C., Eimas, P. D., & Rosenkrantz, S. L. (1993). Evidence for representations of perceptually similar categories by 3-month-old and 4-month-old infants. *Perception, 22,* 463–475.

Quinn, P. C., Yahr, J., Kuhn, A., Slater, A. M., & Pascalis, O. (2002). Representation of the gender of human faces by infants: A preference for female. *Perception, 31,* 1109–1121.

Rakison, D. H. (2004). Infants' sensitivity to correlations between static and dynamic features in a category context. *Journal of Experimental Child Psychology, 89,* 1–30.

Rakison, D. H. (2005). Infant perception and cognition: An evolutionary perspective on early learning. In B. J. Ellis (Ed.), *Origins of the social mind: Evolutionary psychology and child development* (pp. 317–353). New York: Guilford Press.

Reed, J. M., Squire, L. R., Patalano, A. L., Smith, E. E., & Jonides, J. (1999). Learning about categories that are defined by object-like stimuli despite impaired declarative memory. *Behavioral Neuroscience, 113,* 411–419.

Reznick, J. S., & Kagan, J. (1983). Category detection in infancy. In L. P. Lipsitt & C. K. Rovee-Collier (Eds.), *Advances in infancy research* (Vol. 2, pp. 78–111) Norwood, NJ: Ablex.

Ribar, R. J., Oakes, L. M., & Spalding, T. L. (2004). Infants can rapidly form new categorical representations. *Psychonomic Bulletin & Review, 11,* 536–541.

Roder, B. J., Bushnell, E. W., & Sasseville, A. M. (2000). Infants' preferences for familiarity and novelty during the course of visual processing. *Infancy, 1,* 491–507.

Rogers, T. T., & McClelland, J. L. (2004). *Semantic cognition: A parallel distributed processing approach.* Cambridge, MA: MIT Press.

Rose, S. A., Feldman, J. F., & Jankowski, J. J. (2004). Infant visual recognition memory. *Developmental Review, 24,* 74–100.

Ross, G. S. (1980). Categorization in 1- to 2-year-olds. *Developmental Psychology, 16,* 391–396.

Ross-Sheehy, S., Oakes, L. M., & Luck, S. J. (2003). The development of visual short-term memory capacity in infants. *Child Development, 74,* 1807–1822.

Saffran, J. R., Aslin, R. N., & Newport, E. L. (1996). Statistical learning by 8-month-old infants. *Science, 274,* 1926–1928.

Samuelson, L. K. (2002). Statistical regularities in vocabulary guide language acquisition in connectionist models and 15–20-month-olds. *Developmental Psychology, 38,* 1016–1037.

Samuelson, L. K., & Smith, L. B. (1999). Early noun vocabularies: Do ontology, category structure and syntax correspond? *Cognition, 73,* 1–33.

Samuelson, L. K., & Smith, L. B. (2000). Grounding development in cognitive processes. *Child Development, 71,* 98–106.

Schöner, G., & Thelen, E. (2006). Using dynamic field theory to rethink infant habituation. *Psychological Review, 113,* 273–299.

Slater, A., & Johnson, S. P. (1998). Visual sensory and perceptual abilities of the newborn: Beyond the blooming, buzzing confusion. In F. Simion & G. Butterworth (Eds.), *The development of sensory, motor and cognitive capacities in early infancy: From perception to cognition.* East Sussex: Psychology Press.

Smith, J., & Minda, J. P. (1998). Prototypes in the mist: The early epochs of category learning. *Journal of Experimental Psychology: Learning, Memory, & Cognition, 24,* 1411–1436.

Smith, L. B. (2000). From knowledge to knowing: Real progress in the study of infant categorization. *Infancy, 1,* 91–97.

Smith, L. B. (2005). Emerging ideas about categories. In L. Gershkoff-Stowe and D. H. Rakison (Eds.), *Building object categories in developmental time. Carnegie Mellon Symposia on cognition.* (pp. 159–173). Mahwah, US: Lawrence Erlbaum Associates, Publishers.

Snyder, K. A. (in press). Neural mechanisms of attention and memory in preferential-looking tasks. In L. M. Oakes & P. J. Bauer (Eds.), *Short- and long-term memory in infancy and early childhood: Taking the first steps toward remembering.* New York: Oxford University Press.

Spelke, E. S., Breinlinger, K., Macomber, J., & Jacobson, K. (1992). Origins of knowledge. *Psychological Review, 99,* 605–632.

Squire, L. R. (2004). Memory systems of the brain: A brief history and current perspective. *Neurobiology of Learning & Memory, 82,* 171–177.

Thelen, E., & Smith, L. B. (1994). *A dynamic systems approach to the development of cognition and action*. Cambridge, MA: MIT Press.

Werker, J. F., Cohen, L. B., Lloyd, V. L., Cassasola, M., & Stager, C. L. (1998). Acquisition of word-object associations by 14-month-old infants. *Developmental Psychology, 34,* 1289–1309.

Younger, B. A. (1985). The segregation of items into categories by 10-month-old infants. *Child Development, 56,* 1574–1583.

Younger, B. A., & Cohen, L. B. (1986). Developmental changes in infants' perception of correlations among attributes. *Child Development, 57,* 803–815.

Younger, B. A., & Fearing, D. D. (1998). Detecting correlations among form attributes: An object-examining test with infants. *Infant Behavior & Development, 21,* 289–297.

Younger, B. A., & Furrer, S. (2003). A comparison of visual familiarization and object-examining measures of categorization in 9-month-old infants. *Infancy, 4,* 327–348.

7

Multiple Learning Mechanisms in the Development of Action

KAREN E. ADOLPH, NEW YORK UNIVERSITY,
AND AMY S. JOH, DUKE UNIVERSITY

Everybody says that infants *learn* to walk, but what do they mean by "learn?" Does learning refer to experience-related changes, or is it only a convenient euphemism for innate abilities that mature according to a predetermined biological timetable? The aim of this chapter is to show that, indeed, infants do learn to sit, crawl, walk, and so forth, and to offer some suggestions as to how experience leads to learning.

In infant development research, the pendulum is shifting from a focus on innate competencies to the role of learning in performance. Clearly, multiple learning mechanisms are available to infants. Many modern procedures commonly used to infer innate competencies rely on venerable forms of association learning, such as habituation, discrimination learning, and classical and operant conditioning. In addition, recent research has highlighted infants' ability to benefit from priming and visual expectancies (Baillargeon, 2004; Johnson, Slemmer, & Amso, 2004; Wang, Baillargeon, & Brueckner, 2004). Infants demonstrate statistical learning, such as conditional and transitional probabilities (Saffran, Aslin, & Newport, 1996; Saffran, 2003; Smith & Yoshida, 2005), and symbolic rule learning based on simple patterns of input (Marcus, Vijayan, Bandi Rao, & Vishton, 1999). Given sufficient experience, infants acquire learning sets (Adolph, 2002, 2005). This chapter illustrates how the study of goal-directed motor actions—the rich array of exploratory and performatory behaviors displayed in everyday locomotion—may provide new insights into the processes and mechanisms of infant learning.

We argue that two separate learning mechanisms are important for the development of balance and locomotion. One learning mechanism, learning sets, is especially well suited for coping with the variability and novelty that characterize everyday actions. Learning sets are optimal for promoting transfer of learning to a broad range of new problems. A second mechanism, association learning, links particular cues with consequences. Unlike learning sets, association learning is not optimal for dealing with novelty and variability because transfer of learning is limited to a narrow range of problems that shares similar cues and contexts. Given its limitations, association learning may serve as a fallback mechanism when learning sets are not viable.

Our argument is not that learning sets and association learning are the only mechanisms for controlling balance and locomotion—other learning mechanisms may also play a role. Rather, we suggest that relying on these two learning mechanisms is necessitated by the nature of the available perceptual information for controlling motor actions. We garner evidence for learning from the four postural milestones in infant development: sitting, crawling, cruising, and walking. We focus on balance and locomotion because postural control is the foundation for all motor actions involving the torso and extremities (Reed, 1982, 1989; Bertenthal & Clifton, 1998; Adolph & Berger, 2005, 2006).

In the first part of the chapter, we set the stage for our argument by describing different sources of perceptual information that specify variations in surface layout (the shape and the dimensions of the path) versus variations in friction and rigidity (the resistance of the ground surface against the body). Different types of exploration are required to generate the necessary visual and tactile information for surface layout and for friction and rigidity. In the second section, we describe the signature characteristics of learning sets and association learning. We argue that learning sets are an optimal mechanism for responding adaptively to variations in surface layout but not to variations in friction and rigidity and that the converse is true for association learning. Our account leads to different predictions regarding the time course of learning and the breadth of transfer of learning to new problems for surface layout and for friction and rigidity. In the subsequent sections, we outline the evidence for the separate learning mechanisms: learning sets for surface layout and association learning for friction and rigidity. Finally, we conclude the chapter by revisiting the two learning mechanisms and placing them in relation to broader issues of learning and development.

EXPLORATION OF SURFACE LAYOUT VERSUS FRICTION AND RIGIDITY

A central issue for postural control is the problem of selecting the appropriate actions for moving through a variable environment. Two types of environmental changes are particularly relevant for controlling balance and locomotion. One type of change, variations in surface layout, affects possibilities for stance and locomotion by changing the shape of the path in three dimensions: the narrow and winding path between the piles of laundry littering the floor, the steep stairs leading down to the garage, the low gate on which visitors bang their heads, and the sloping road before the intersection. A second type of change, variations in the material properties of each ground surface-footwear pairing, affects friction and rigidity by changing the size of the necessary, resistive forces for friction and rigidity conditions: the smooth bathroom tiles and the wet feet that slide over them, the deformable piles of laundry and the surprisingly firm mattress on the bed, and the slippery stairs leading down to the dusty street.

Novelty and Variability in Postural Development

For infants, the problem of coping with variability and novelty is heightened because learning is nested in the context of developmental change. Infants' bodies and skills change dramatically over the first two years of life (for review, see Adolph & Berger, 2005). They experience rapid fluctuations in muscle mass and fat. Their overall body dimensions become leaner and less top-heavy. Their height and weight increase in large and sudden spurts; for example, infants can grow 0.5 to 1.5 centimeters in a single day (Lampl, Veldhuis, & Johnson, 1992). Their proficiency at balance and locomotion shows rapid improvements and decrements as they discover new strategies for moving their bodies from place to place and for transitioning between postures. Typically, improvements are most striking in the first few months after the onset of a new locomotor skill (for review, see Adolph & Berger, 2006). All of these developmental changes alter the biomechanical constraints on movement, creating novel and variable situations for maintaining balance and locomoting through the environment.

Moreover, infants' bodies and skills change in a unique way during the first years of life. Infants acquire new postural-control systems in the course of development (Adolph, 2002, 2005). Figure 7–1 illustrates four major postural-control systems in infant development: sitting (unsupported with the legs outstretched), crawling (on belly and on hands and knees or feet), cruising (moving sideways in an upright posture, holding onto furniture or a railing for support), and walking (with the hands free, while facing forward). These four postures typically appear between 6 and 16 months of age, in the illustrated order. However, the sequence can vary among infants and cultures (e.g., some infants skip crawling altogether), and the age range at skill onset is extremely wide (Frankenburg & Dodds, 1967; Hopkins & Westra, 1988, 1989, 1990). The important point with

Sitting   Crawling   Cruising   Walking

Figure 7–1. The four postural control systems in their typical order of development. Each posture denotes a distinct problem space that requires unique strategies for obtaining relevant perceptual information, keeping balance, and locomoting through the environment.

regard to novelty is that no infant acquires all four postures simultaneously. The postures appear staggered over several months so that at each point in development, infants are experts in an earlier developing posture and novices in a later developing one.

Each postural-control system represents a different problem space defined by a unique set of parameters for maintaining balance. Each posture has a different key pivot around which the body rotates (the hips for sitting, the wrists for crawling, the shoulders for cruising, and the ankles for walking) and a different region of permissible postural sway within which the body can rotate before falling (Fig. 7–1). There are different muscle groups for keeping the body upright and for propelling it forward, different vantage points for viewing the ground ahead, different correlations between visual and vestibular information, different access to mechanical information from touching the ground, and so on (Adolph, 2002, 2005). In short, each posture requires moving different body parts and is controlled by different sources of perceptual information.

Developmental changes in infants' bodies and skills bring about corresponding changes in the environment. New postures and vantage points and new and improved forms of mobility open up a new world of opportunities for learning. As infants gain access to new places and surfaces, they experience aspects of the environment for the first time. Stairs, slopes, furniture, corners, and doorways present new variations in surface layout. Carpet, wood, tile, grass, sand, ice, and water present new friction and rigidity conditions. As E. J. Gibson (1992) put it, watching a child discover a playground for the first time is a revelation in attention to new affordances for action. For a crawling infant, the playground slide may be a shelter to sneak beneath. For a cruiser, the same apparatus provides poles, stairs, and edges to support pulling to a stand and practicing upright skills. For a toddler, the sliding surface offers opportunities for climbing upward and multiple means for descent.

Exploration

In the face of so much variability and novelty, how might infants keep balance during stance and locomotion? Perceptual exploration is the key to adapting to changing constraints on action (J. J. Gibson, 1979; E. J. Gibson, 1988; E. J. Gibson & Pick, 2000; von Hofsten, 2003, 2004). Exploration provides feedback about the consequences of the last movement and informs infants' decisions about what to do next. Movements of the eyes, head, torso, arms, and legs generate perceptual information about the status of the body, the features of the environment, and the relationship between the two. Optic flow, for example, generated by whole-body movement during locomotion specifies the speed and direction of movement and the time to contact a distant obstacle (Lee, 1993). Turning the head to peer over the edge of a precipice or around a corner generates motion parallax providing depth cues for perceiving the surface layout. Rubbing the foot along the ground provides tactile information about friction and rigidity. Note that exploration is not sufficient for adaptive responding—infants might see or feel an obstacle and plunge forward nonetheless—but exploratory movements are necessary for generating the requisite perception information to guide appropriate motor decisions.

Exploratory movements can be deliberate, such as when infants poke out their feet to test an obstacle in the path. However, more frequently, exploration is incidental, such as when crawlers' hands touch a new surface in the course of crawling or when walking movements generate information for friction underfoot (Adolph, Joh, & Eppler, 2008; Joh, Adolph, Narayanan, & Dietz, 2007). Because the eyes are "parked" in front of the face, incidental visual exploration typically provides the first source of information about an upcoming obstacle (Patla, 1998). If a happenstance glance indicates that something may be amiss, focused and deliberate exploratory movements will follow (Adolph, Eppler, Marin, Weise, & Clearfield, 2000). The velocity and amplitude of forward movements decrease, body sway increases, head and eyes point directly at the potential obstacle, and various means may be employed for engaging in tactile exploration with the hands or feet (e.g., positioning the body to probe the surface with a foot, grabbing a handhold to augment balance during the probe).

Locomotor movements involve large displacements of the body. Walkers require a relatively long response period and multiple walking steps to modify gait appropriately in preparation for an upcoming obstacle, whether they dampen forces to brace themselves for contact with the obstacle, increase forces to leap over the obstacle, or redirect forces to veer around it (Patla, 1989; Patla, Robinson, Samways, & Armstrong, 1989; Patla, Prentice, Robinson, & Neufeld, 1991). Thus, prospective control of locomotion depends on reliable visual cues from a distance to instigate the sequence of more focused exploration (Adolph et al., 2000; Adolph et al., 2006). There is no reason to modify current gait patterns, stop to engage in tactile exploration, or search for alternative routes or methods of locomotion if incidental visual exploration does not alert walkers to a potential threat to balance. Without advance warning, prospective control is impossible. Walkers might plant an unsuspecting foot on the obstacle, and the only recourse is reactive adjustments (e.g., waving the arms and quickly bending the torso to try to avoid or mitigate a fall).

Information for Surface Layout Versus Friction and Rigidity

The sequential process of exploration is well suited for coping with variations in surface layout, but not for variations in friction and rigidity. The difference stems from the nature of the perceptual information. Changes in the shape and dimensions of the path are specified by reliable visual cues, whereas changes in friction and rigidity are not (Adolph et al., 2000; Joh, Adolph, Campbell, & Eppler, 2006). Friction and rigidity are resistive forces that emerge only when two surfaces come into contact, such as when the foot presses against the ground during walking. In addition, the manner of contact between the surfaces (e.g., the velocity and angle of the foot as it touches the ground) determines the size of the resistive forces. Because friction and rigidity result from the interaction between two surfaces, the appearance of a single surface cannot serve as a cue for friction and rigidity conditions. The same shiny wooden floor may be slippery or resistive, depending on the walker's footwear and walking patterns.

Moreover, visual cues for friction and rigidity are variable and context-dependent. Slippery surfaces can be shiny or matte, dark or light. Deformable surfaces can be bumpy or smooth, patterned or plain. Even shine, which adult walkers use most frequently as a visual cue for slip, is not reliable for specifying friction conditions because there is no such phenomenon as "shine constancy." Shine perception is strongly affected by the color of the ground surface, overhead lighting conditions, and viewing distance and angle—factors that do not affect the actual friction condition (Joh, Adolph, Campbell et al., 2006). Adults rate dark surfaces as looking shinier and more slippery compared with white surfaces, even when gloss levels are equal across displays. They rarely judge white surfaces as looking shiny or slippery unless they view the surface from directly above—too late to modify walking patterns in preparation for stepping onto the surface. In other words, for detecting *novel* variations in friction and rigidity, there are no reliable visual cues.

TWO LEARNING MECHANISMS IN THE DEVELOPMENT OF ACTION

Differential availability of visual information from a distance leads to a reliance on two different learning mechanisms—learning sets for surface layout and association learning for friction and rigidity. In a perfect world, where all obstacles are reliably specified by visual cues from a distance, presumably, infants would rely solely on learning sets—the mechanism that promotes the broadest transfer to novel challenges for postural control. However, in our imperfect world, where novel variations in friction and rigidity cannot be specified reliably with visual cues, infants must also rely on association learning. The price of relying on a learning mechanism with narrow transfer is increased errors in prospective control in novel situations.

Learning Sets

An optimal learning mechanism for coping with variability and novelty is the learning set. Our notion of learning sets is based on Harlow's (1949, 1959; Harlow & Kuenne, 1949) idea that acquiring the ability to solve problems is more effective for a broader range of situations than learning particular solutions for particular problems. Like the adage, "Give a man a fish and you feed him for a day; teach a man to fish and you feed him for a lifetime," learning sets provide a means rather than a quick fix. With learning sets, learners acquire a set of information-generating behaviors and heuristic strategies for figuring out solutions to novel problems rather than for learning simple cue-consequence associations or facts (Stevenson, 1972). As Harlow put it, they are "learning to learn." With learning sets, transfer is limited only by the boundaries of the particular problem space. Accordingly, acquiring a learning set entails recognizing the problem space, identifying the relevant parameters for operating within it, acquiring the exploratory procedures and strategies for generating the appropriate information, and knowing how to use the resulting information to solve the problem at hand.

For example, in Harlow's (1949; Harlow & Kuenne, 1949; Harlow, 1959) original studies, adult monkeys acquired learning sets to solve discrimination problems. Monkeys were required to choose a target object from a pair of objects that differed on multiple characteristics (e.g., small green triangle and large yellow cylinder) and shifted in their left–right positions. The target object yielded a food reward. After a block of 10 trials, the experimenter introduced a new pair of objects (e.g., striped rectangle and polka-dot star). At first, the monkeys searched haphazardly or learned associations between cues and the food reward (e.g., polka-dot stars hide raisins). The process continued over hundreds of trial blocks until monkeys could find the food reward with new pairs of objects after only one presentation of a new pair of objects. Instead of using trial and error or cue-consequence associations, they had acquired a learning set: They learned to explore one object by lifting it and to track the one in the pair that covered the reward, a sort of win–stay/lose–shift rule, for the remaining trials in the block. Altogether, learning to learn for discrimination problems meant that the monkeys recognized the pairs of objects as the problem space, identified the perceptual qualities of the objects as the relevant parameters (color or shape rather than their spatial position), possessed the necessary exploratory procedures to visually differentiate the two objects and search the wells beneath them, abstracted the win–stay/lose–shift strategy, and used the information to track the food reward.

Learning sets have three important characteristics. First, within the particular problem space, learning sets allow a broad transfer of learning to novel problems. For example, after acquiring a learning set for discrimination problems, Harlow's monkeys demonstrated perfect performance with pairs of completely novel shapes. Thus, learning sets are a far cry from mere stimulus generalization. With learning sets, monkeys had acquired a means for coping with novelty. Note, however, that in Harlow's simple model system, the problem space was extremely small: Monkeys with expertise solving discrimination problems showed no ability to solve oddity problems and vice versa. The learning set was limited to the type of problem that defined that problem space.

In the immensely more complex task of infants' balance and locomotion, each postural-control system operates like a distinct problem space. Within a posture, the range of problems is enormous. Every movement on every surface constitutes a different problem for postural control. Every change in infants' body growth and skill level creates different biomechanical constraints on balance and locomotion. For each postural-control system in development, learning to learn would mean that infants must recognize the new posture as a new problem space, identify the relevant parameters for keeping balance, acquire the appropriate exploratory procedures to determine the current constraints on balance, and learn to use the resulting information to calibrate the settings of the parameters on line (Adolph, 2002; Adolph & Eppler, 2002; Adolph, 2005). After acquiring a learning set for walking, for example, infants should be able to maintain balance during stance and locomotion when faced with variations in the layout of the terrain, while carrying loads and wearing different clothes and shoes, after developmental changes in body growth and skill levels, and in different goal contexts. The scope of transfer should be limited only to the boundaries of the upright postural-control system.

Just as learning sets do not transfer between discrimination problems and other types of problems (e.g., oddity), learning sets should not transfer between postural-control systems. Infants must acquire separate learning sets for sitting, crawling, cruising, and walking. Because the parameters, exploratory movements, and relations between perceptual information and the various parameters differ among postural systems, learning sets for earlier developing postures should not transfer to later developing ones. The ability to respond adaptively to variations in surface layout while crawling, for example, should not help infants after they begin walking.

The second distinguishing characteristic of learning sets is that acquisition is extremely slow. In general, the larger the problem space, the slower the acquisition. Harlow's adult monkeys required dozens of blocks of trials with different pairs of objects—several thousand trials—distributed over multiple sessions to acquire learning sets for discrimination problems (Harlow, 1949; Harlow & Kuenne, 1949; Harlow, 1959). And this was with a relatively simple task. Exploratory procedures for searching under the objects were simple, few, and already existed in monkey's repertoires. Monkeys could solve the discrimination problems by applying a fixed exploratory strategy and a win–stay/lose–shift rule.

Learning to learn in discrimination problems is easy compared to acquiring learning sets for postural-control systems, which requires enormous amounts of experience. Because balance and locomotion occupy an immense problem space for each posture, human infants might require massive amounts of experience—hundreds of thousands of "trials" of balance shifts and steps—over weeks or months to acquire a learning set to cope with the exigencies of postural control in everyday life. Indeed, recent research suggests that infants' everyday locomotor experience is a mini marathon. The quantity of experience is sufficiently massive to facilitate the acquisition of learning sets (Adolph & Berger, 2006). Fourteen-month-old toddlers, for example, typically take more than 2,000 steps in the course of an hour; strung together, end to end, infants walk the length of more than 40 football fields in the course of a day (Garciaguirre & Adolph, 2006) in a variety of contexts, differing in location, goal, and social interaction.

Compared to the discrimination problems in Harlow's model system, the problem space for postural control is extremely broad. Infants must work to keep their bodies in balance during all of their waking hours. Crawlers are engaged in balance and locomotion for approximately 5 hours per day, and walkers for approximately 6 hours (Adolph, 2002). Infants travel through all of the open rooms in their homes, averaging exposure to 12 different ground surfaces per day (Chan, Biancaniello, Adolph, & Marin, 2000). Exploration in the service of balance and locomotion is complex and varied. Many—perhaps an infinite number—of exploratory movements of eyes, head, and body yield information in visual, tactile, and proprioceptive modalities.

Moreover, for each postural-control system, infants must discover and hone the exploratory swaying, looking, and touching movements that are required to generate perceptual information for balance and locomotion. Rather than learning fixed strategies or rules, learning to gauge the current constraints on balance requires infants to detect dynamic and probabilistic functions. In fact, everyday experience with balance and locomotion may impede learning about fixed rules and thereby facilitate the acquisition of learning sets. On average, 14-month-old walking infants lose their balance and fall 15 times per hour, which suggests that they may fall more than 90 times per day (Garciaguirre & Adolph, 2006). Falls are not related to the appearance of the ground surface because they are not pre-cipitated by variations in surface layout or in friction and rigidity. Most falls are simply a byproduct of the variability in infants' own motor systems.

The third critical characteristic of learning sets is a reliance on adequate per-ceptual information to elicit the appropriate exploratory procedures and strategies in the learning set. In Harlow's discrimination task, monkeys relied on visual in-formation about object properties to guide their manual search. Similarly, learn-ing sets for postural-control systems require visual information from a distance to prompt more focused exploratory movements to gauge upcoming threats to balance. Learning sets are an optimal solution for coping with novel changes in surface layout because infants can see changes in surface layout from a distance. Visual depth cues (e.g., motion parallax, convergence, texture gradients) can reli-ably specify stairs, slopes, narrowing of the path, and so on. These visual cues are sufficient to prompt infants to modify their ongoing locomotion, slow down, direct their attention to the obstacle, and, if necessary, begin searching for an alternative solution.

Unlike variations in surface layout, novel changes in friction and rigidity are not specified by reliable visual cues. Thus, infants who have laboriously acquired learning sets for postural control—and adults who have had learning sets for up-right posture for dozens of years—are not likely to execute the full range of ex-ploratory movements in their repertoires based only on visual information about friction and rigidity. Accordingly, variations in friction are a leading cause of ac-cidental injury from falling in people across all ages and stages of learning and development (National Safety Council, 2003). Rather than controlling balance prospectively, people are most likely to be surprised by novel changes in friction and rigidity and forced to respond reactively after stepping haphazardly onto the offending surface.

Association Learning

Association learning is a fallback mechanism for coping with variations in fric-tion and rigidity because fixed associations are not well suited for controlling bal-ance and locomotion under novel and variable conditions. By association learning, we mean pairings between cues and consequences. When two events co-occur, they can become associated (e.g., stepping onto a white, shiny patch of ground on a cold, winter day results in slipping); with repeated pairings, the association between the cue and the consequence becomes stronger. In principle, associated pairings could lead to a stereotyped motor response (e.g., see ice patch, walk around it) or to a variety of appropriate responses (leap over it, step carefully onto it, coast over it, etc.). Moreover, the exploratory behaviors in a learning set could mediate between the learned association and the motor decision, and vice versa. That is, associations between particular cues and consequences can instigate the exploratory procedures and strategies in a learning set by shifting attention to the relevant cues in similar situations (e.g., after slipping on an ice patch, becoming vigilant about potential ice patches during the remainder of the walk). Conversely, initiating the exploratory procedures in a learning set can lead to forming a learned association (e.g., tactile exploration of a steep stair can reveal the potential for slipping and lead to the formation of an association between the sight of the stair and the aversive consequence).

Given their reliance on particular cues or a class of cues, association learning and learning sets share an important similarity: Prior experiences with irrelevant cues can impede learning when the cues subsequently become relevant. For example, after initially experiencing a particular cue—a clicker sound—without any consequences, rats exhibit learned irrelevance. Later, they take longer to associate the clicker sound with a shock. They require more pairings of the clicker and shock to display a freezing response compared with rats that had not previously experienced the uncorrelated click (Baker & Mackintosh, 1979). With learning sets, animals learn to ignore a class of cues. Harlow's monkeys learned to ignore the spatial location of the target shapes while acquiring learning sets for discrimination problems. If this previously irrelevant type of cue were to become relevant, monkeys would find it more difficult to incorporate it into the learning set.

In the more complex case of balance and locomotion, infants may learn to ignore cues such as the color, texture, and shine of the ground surface because this class of cues (i.e., visual appearance of the ground surface) is not typically relevant for balance and locomotion. Although variations in the ground may cause infants to fall, infants' falls are not usually caused by variations in the ground surface; most falls occur on a flat, rigid, high-traction surface (Garciaguirre & Adolph, 2006). Moreover, information that was previously irrelevant for one postural-control system (e.g., tactile, underfoot information for crawling) may impede acquisition of a learning set for a later developing posture in which the information becomes relevant (e.g., cruising and walking). Learned irrelevance changes motivation and attention. After learning that a cue is not correlated with the consequence, animals stop looking for the correlation and stop attending to the cue.

Association learning differs from learning sets in three important ways. First, association learning requires an initial encounter with the particular cue–consequence pairing. In novel situations, it is impossible to respond adaptively on the first trial. Walkers must experience wet feet from stepping into a puddle and a slip from stepping onto a patch of ice in order to avoid these consequences in the future. In contrast, learning sets can function in novel situations without a history of prior errors. Monkeys solved new discrimination problems on the first trial (Harlow, 1949; Harlow & Kuenne, 1949; Harlow, 1959), and experienced infants can determine whether a new configuration of the surface layout is safe or risky on their first encounter (e.g., Adolph, 1997).

Second, with association learning, transfer of learning is relatively narrow. Transfer is limited to the particular cues in the learned pairing and the context in which the pairing was formed. Rats, for example, freeze with fear in a corner of their cage after learning to associate a tone with a shock. But, they ignore a different tone that results in the same consequence, and they ignore the same tone when placed into a different cage. However, when exposed to the original tone in the original cage, the rats freeze once again (Bouton & Bolles, 1979). Likewise, in the case of balance and locomotion, cue–consequence associations can guide adaptive motor decisions only when new cues and contexts are sufficiently similar to the learned ones (e.g., on a cloudy, cold day, the patch of ice may not appear shiny; on a sunny, warmer day, walkers may ignore shiny regions of sidewalk) and when the current status of the body does not change the consequences (ice is not slippery if walkers are wearing crampons).

A third important difference between association learning and learning sets is that associated pairings are relatively easy to form. Infants and many species of animals can learn multiple, complex, hierarchical associations that elicit adaptive responses in the presence of the appropriate cues and contexts. Moreover, under optimal training conditions, association learning can be fast, requiring only a fraction of the trials needed for learning sets. For example, in a classic task (Lashley, 1930), rats stood on a raised jumping stand facing two cues varying in size, shape, color, or pattern. One cue marked a door that opened when the rats jumped head-first into it; the other marked a solid wall into which the animals crashed, falling into a safety net below. Given the salience of the consequence, rats learned to identify the relevant cue at 100% correct performance after only 20 to 30 trials. Under optimal conditions, with a single, high-contrast stimulus to mark the door (e.g., a white square versus a black one), rats showed 100% correct performance after only 4 trials.

Similarly, under the appropriate circumstances, human infants show fast association learning. Three-month-olds learn to associate their foot kicks with the jiggling of an overhead mobile after only a few minutes of practice (Rovee & Rovee, 1969; Lewis, Alessandri, & Sullivan, 1990). In the typical set-up, infants lie supine with a ribbon tied from one ankle to the mobile. Spontaneous leg movements cause the colorful mobile elements to move and to jingle and clack together. Distinctly colored and patterned bumpers lining the walls of the crib optimize the speed of learning by making the context more salient and distinct.

Summary of Dissociations Between Learning Sets and Association Learning

Experience-related improvements in infants' motor decisions are crucial to both learning sets and association learning, and both mechanisms rely on the appropriate cues to instigate an adaptive response. However, the two learning mechanisms lead to different predictions about patterns of learning for surface layout and for friction and rigidity.

For surface layout, a learning-set mechanism would predict a long, slow acquisition period before infants could respond adaptively. Acquiring a learning set should require weeks or months of practice for each postural-control system in development. Infants should be indifferent to feedback from errors in a single test session. Improvements in the accuracy of infants' motor decisions should be gradual, as new exploratory behaviors and strategies enter infants' repertoires and become more finely honed. However, once a learning set is acquired, experienced infants should make adaptive motor decisions on their first encounter with a novel obstacle (e.g., a steep slope or narrow bridge) in their experienced posture. Visual depth cues from a distance should elicit an array of focused, exploratory behaviors. Infants should be able to update their assessment of their own abilities in accordance with changes in functional body dimensions and level of locomotor skill. For example, they should correctly treat the same slope or bridge differently depending on the current biomechanical constraints. However, learning sets predict no transfer of learning between postures. Infants should display more adaptive responding in their more experienced posture, even when tested in both postures on the identical slope or narrow bridge.

An association-learning mechanism would make very different predictions about coping with variability and novelty in the surface layout. Learning should be relatively fast, possibly occurring in a single test session under optimal conditions with salient cues and consequences. Even for the most experienced infants, learning should require errors, at least on the first encounter with a novel obstacle, and errors should decrease with repeated encounters. Improvements in the accuracy of infants' motor decisions should be all or none, depending on whether infants have formed the appropriate association. However, learning should be restricted to the particular cues and context of the training situation. Learning may not transfer, for example, from shallow to steep slopes, or from slopes to drop-offs and bridges, even within the same posture. When cues or contexts change, infants should again show a lack of adaptive responding. Given similar visual cues about the status of the surface layout, association learning would predict that infants treat the same slope or bridge similarly, regardless of the current biomechanical constraints on action. They should not update their motor decisions in accordance with changes in their bodies and skill levels; they should show no decrement over developmental transition in postural milestones. Thus, in an experienced posture, infants' responses to changes in body dimensions and skill levels should be less accurate if they are relying on learned associations than on learning sets. But over the transition from experienced postures to later developing ones, responses should be more accurate.

An association-learning mechanism makes identical predictions for how infants should cope with variations in friction and rigidity as for variations in surface layout: Infants should show fast, all-or-none learning of particular cues and consequences following an initial encounter. Predictions of learning sets, however, differ between these two types of environmental changes. According to a learning-set account, infants should frequently fail to respond adaptively to novel changes in material substance because friction and rigidity are not specified reliably by visual cues from a distance. Without a visual prompt, infants are not likely to use all of the exploratory procedures and compensatory strategies in their learning set. In addition, learning sets and association learning share a common prediction for friction and rigidity: Infants may err in multiple encounters with an obstacle because they have learned to ignore visual cues such as color, texture, and shine in the formation of a learning set. The fact that falling is typically unrelated to the appearance of the ground surface may lead to learned irrelevance.

EVIDENCE FOR LEARNING SETS: COPING
WITH CHANGES IN SURFACE LAYOUT

In dozens of studies, researchers have observed how infants respond to changes in the surface layout that pose a challenge for balance and locomotion (reviewed in Bertenthal & Clifton, 1998; Adolph & Berger, 2005; Adolph & Berger, 2006). Here, we describe a subset of these studies that were designed to test the predictions of learning sets (reviewed in Adolph, 2002; Adolph & Eppler, 2002; Adolph, 2005). The studies shared a common logic and procedure: Infants were observed as they encountered novel challenges to balance and locomotion at the edge of an adjustable slope or gap in the surface of support (Fig. 7–2, panels A-E). The slant of the slope (0° to 90°) or width of the gap (0 cm to 90 cm) varied in continuous gradations from trial to trial. A motorized mechanism varied the degree of slope by moving a landing platform up and down; a platform varied gap width by sliding back and forth along a calibrated track. Caregivers stood at the bottom of the incline or the far side of the gap and encouraged their infants to traverse the obstacle. A highly trained experimenter followed alongside infants to ensure their safety if they began to fall.

In the first part of each test session, we used a psychophysical staircase procedure to determine the limit of each infant's ability—a motor threshold (e.g., Adolph, 1995, 1997, 2000). Increments of greater difficulty were presented after successful trials (infants safely traversed the obstacle) and easier increments were presented after unsuccessful trials (infants fell or refused to cross) in an up-and-down pattern (hence, the "staircase") until we identified the steepest slope or widest gap that infants could navigate successfully on the majority of trials. The estimates of individualized motor thresholds allowed us to assess the adaptiveness of infants' motor decisions relative to their current physical abilities. This normalization process was crucial because at the same age, infants show large individual differences in abilities, and their abilities change dramatically from week to week. A slope or gap that is safe for a more skilled infant might be risky for a poorly skilled one; what might be a risky slope one week might be easily navigated the following week when infants' abilities improve.

In the second part of the session, the experimenter presented probe trials at safe and risky increments (i.e., within and beyond infants' ability, respectively). Adaptive decisions for action require infants to detect the current limits of their own bodies and skills relative to incremental changes in the degree of slant or the width of the gap. That is, infants should attempt safe increments within their ability and select alternative strategies or avoid risky increments beyond their ability. Thus, the role of everyday experience with each posture in adaptive motor decisions was of central interest for evaluating the learning-set account. To determine the informational basis of infants' motor decisions, we examined their exploratory activity before selecting a motor response—their latency to initiate traversal and their exploratory looking and touching behaviors. To assess behavioral flexibility in infants' responses, we observed the type and number of strategies infants used for coping with risky obstacles—whether they simply avoided the obstacle or generated alternative methods of traversal.

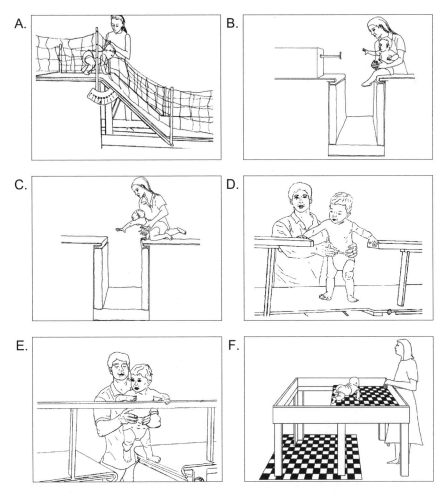

Figure 7–2. Tasks and apparatuses used in studies of learning sets. (A) Crawling and walking infants descending a slope. (B) Sitting infants leaning forward to reach for toys at the edge of a gap in the floor. (C) Crawling infants leaning forward to cross over a gap in the floor. (D) Cruising infants spanning a gap in the handrail. (E) Cruising infants crossing over a gap in the floor. (F) Crawling and walking infants on the visual cliff. All apparatuses, except for the visual cliff, were adjustable in continuous increments.

Slopes

One way to test the learning-set account is to observe infants longitudinally, as they transition from one postural-control system to another. Accordingly, infants were observed every three weeks, from their first week of crawling until thirteen weeks after they began walking, on the adjustable sloping apparatus (Fig. 7–2A) (Adolph, 1997). To ensure that improvements in infants' motor decisions were not due to repeated practice with slopes, a control group of infants was tested only

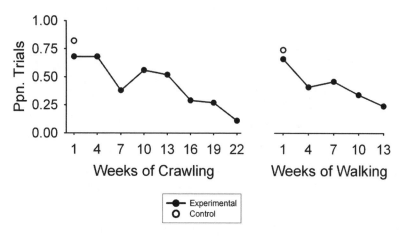

Figure 7–3. Proportion of trials on which infants attempted to descend risky slopes and fell. Risky slopes were defined as slopes steeper than infants' individualized motor thresholds. The infants in the experimental group were tested every 3 weeks, from their first week of crawling until 13 weeks after they began walking. The infants in the control group were tested only 3 times, in their first week of crawling, tenth week of crawling, and first week of walking.

three times: in their first and tenth weeks of crawling and in their first week of walking.

The findings present strong evidence for the acquisition of learning sets for coping with variations in surface layout. As shown in Figure 7–3, in their first weeks of crawling and walking, infants attempted impossibly steep slopes and fell on trial after trial, requiring rescue by the experimenter. The average error rate was 75% on risky slopes. Over weeks of everyday crawling and walking experience, motor decisions steadily improved. Infants' decisions became more closely aligned to the limits of their own abilities, and their error rates decreased. That is, infants scaled their decisions to the relative amount of risk, an impressive feat-given the dramatic changes in their bodies and skills over the weeks of testing. As in Harlow's (Harlow, 1949; Harlow & Kuenne, 1949; Harlow, 1959) studies with monkeys, infants learned extremely slowly. Typically, infants required 10 weeks of crawling and walking experience before errors decreased to 50%, and 22 weeks before errors decreased below 10%.

Learning was not the result of repeated practice on slopes. Infants in the control group displayed the same error rates at each of the three matched session times as the infants tested repeatedly, and none of the infants had experience descending playground slides or other slopes outside the laboratory. As further evidence that learning was not dependent on practice descending slopes, crawling infants in several cross-sectional studies showed similar motor decisions and exploratory activity at 8.5, 11, and 12 months of age when age-matched to the infants observed longitudinally; walking infants in cross-sectional research showed similar responses at 12, 14, and 18 months of age (Adolph, Eppler, & Gibson,

1993; Adolph, 1995; Mondschein, Adolph, & Tamis-LeMonda, 2000; Adolph & Berger, 2006; Adolph, Tamis-LeMonda, Ishak, Karasik, & Lobo, 2008). At the same testing age—12 months—infants showed adaptive motor decisions if they were experienced crawlers but fell down risky slopes if they were novice walkers (Adolph et al., 2008). Learning did not involve a rigid motor-response pattern. Rather, from trial to trial within the same session, individual infants used multiple alternative strategies for coping with risky slopes: sliding down in a sitting position, sliding headfirst prone, backing down feet first, and avoiding descent entirely (Siegler, Adolph, & Lemaire, 1996; Adolph, 1997).

Moreover, as predicted by learning sets, infants showed no evidence of transfer between crawling and walking. Error rates were just as high in the first week of walking as in the first week of crawling, and learning was no faster the second time around. As shown in Figure 7–3, learning curves for crawling and walking were similar. In fact, learning was so posture-specific that infants showed no evidence of transfer, even from trial to trial. After infants began walking, six consecutive trials on an impossibly steep, 36-degree slope were added to the end of each session. On the first two trials, when infants began in their unfamiliar upright posture, they walked over the brink and fell. On the third and fourth trials, when infants were returned to their familiar crawling posture, they slid down or avoided descent. On the last two trials, when infants started in their unfamiliar walking posture, they again walked over the edge and fell.

Like their motor decisions, infants' exploratory behaviors failed to transfer from crawling to walking. When infants faced slopes from their new upright posture, new parts of their bodies were required to gather information from a new, higher vantage point. In their first weeks of crawling, infants stopped and stared down the slope with their hands over the brink, but plunged down nonetheless. Over weeks of crawling, infants' visual and tactile exploration became increasingly discriminating, fast, and efficient. By their last weeks of crawling, a quick glance and touch on risky slopes was sufficient to support an adaptive motor decision. But when infants began walking, they had to learn new ways of exploring slopes. Experienced walkers either stopped with their feet straddling the brink and rocked back and forth over their ankles or made small stepping movements. After they engaged in visual and tactile exploration, their motor decisions were more accurate. On safe slopes, infants attempted to walk, and on risky slopes they refused.

A second way to test the learning-set account is to probe the extent of transfer within an experienced postural-control system. In this case, we tested 14-month-old walking infants on the adjustable slope. Previous work showed that by 14 months of age, most infants have at least several weeks of walking experience and respond adaptively to variations in surface slant (Adolph et al., 1993; Adolph, 1995). The longitudinal data showed that infants update their assessment of their abilities across naturally occurring changes in their body dimensions and locomotor skill. Here, we experimentally manipulated infants' bodies and skills and observed whether they adapted their motor decisions to their new physical abilities during the testing session (Adolph & Avolio, 2000). Infants were loaded with lead-weight shoulder packs on some trials and no-weight packs on other trials.

The lead- and no-weight conditions were interspersed so that infants would have to gauge possibilities for walking at the start of each trial.

As expected, the lead-weight packs made infants' bodies more top-heavy and their balance more precarious. As a result, their walking skill was diminished and their motor thresholds were lower in the lead-weight condition. The critical evidence for learning sets was infants' motor decisions under the two load conditions. Infants correctly attempted to walk down steeper slopes on the no-weight pack trials compared to the lead-weight pack trials. That is, infants updated their motor decisions from trial to trial, based on the current status of the loads in their shoulder packs. They treated the same degree of slope as safe in the no-weight condition and as risky in the lead-weight condition. As in earlier studies, exploratory looking and touching increased with risk level, and infants used a variety of alternative descent strategies to navigate risky slopes.

Gaps

A third way to test the learning-set account is to compare infants' motor decisions at the same chronological age and in the same novel task in experienced versus novice postures. Accordingly, we tested 9-month-olds in an experienced sitting posture and in a less familiar crawling posture at the edge of an adjustable gap spanning a deep precipice (Adolph, 2000). On average, infants had 3 months of sitting experience but only 1 month of crawling experience. The infants' task was the same in both postures: They were encouraged to lean over the gap to retrieve an attractive toy (Fig. 7–2, panels B-C). Infants began in a sitting or crawling position on a stationary starting platform. A movable landing platform slid back and forth along a calibrated track to create the adjustable gap.

As shown in Figure 7–4, at every risky gap size, infants were more likely to display adaptive responses in their experienced sitting posture than in their less familiar crawling posture. In the experienced sitting posture, infants scaled their motor decisions to the limits of their abilities. They fell into the gap on only 19% of risky trials, and most errors were clustered at gaps slightly wider than their motor thresholds. In contrast, in the less experienced crawling posture, infants erred repeatedly. They fell into impossibly wide gaps on 61% of risky trials, and learning was not related to experiences in the laboratory. After falling, infants received the same gap increment on the next trial and fell again (90% of repeated trials). When tested in the crawling posture, nearly half of the sample in two experiments plunged headfirst into the widest (90 cm) gap. Moreover, there was no within-session learning: Infants were equally likely to err in the crawling posture and to respond adaptively in the sitting posture, regardless of whether they were tested in the crawling condition first (where the experimenter rescued them on dozens of trials) or second.

A fourth way to test the learning-set account is to compare infants' motor decisions at the same chronological age in tasks that are relevant to balance and locomotion in an experienced posture versus a later developing posture. In this case, we tested 11-month-old infants who were experienced at "cruising" but who could not yet walk (Leo, Chiu, & Adolph, 2000). Typically, infants cruise—move

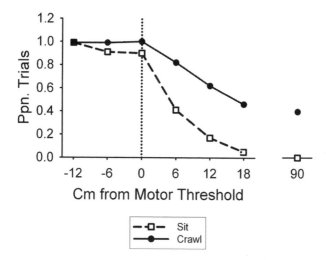

Figure 7–4. Proportion of trials on which infants attempted to cross the gap in the floor and fell. Data are normalized to each infant's motor threshold, represented by 0 on the X-axis. On the X-axis, the negative numbers represent safe gaps (increments smaller than motor thresholds); the positive numbers represent risky slopes (increments larger than motor thresholds).

sideways in an upright posture, hanging onto furniture for support—for a few months before walking. Traditionally, researchers have assumed that cruising and walking are manifestations of the same upright balance control system (McGraw, 1935; Haehl, Vardaxis, & Ulrich, 2000; Metcalfe & Clark, 2000). That is, practice cruising teaches infants how to keep balance while walking. However, while cruising, infants use their arms for balance and steering; while walking, infants use their legs. Thus, we put the traditional assumption to the test. We asked whether cruising might be a distinct balance-control system with a separate learning set for coping with potential threats to balance.

In the condition relevant for cruising, infants were encouraged to traverse a continuously solid floor with an adjustable gap in a handrail that they could hold onto for balance (Fig. 7–2D). In the condition relevant for walking, infants were presented with a continuously solid handrail and an adjustable gap in the floor (Fig. 7–2E). In both conditions, an assistant called infants' attention to the obstacle at the start of each trial. In the handrail–gap condition, infants matched their motor decisions to the probability of cruising successfully. For gaps wider than their motor thresholds, infants avoided traversal or crawled to the second handrail. However, in the floor–gap condition, infants appeared to be oblivious to the fact that they need a floor to support their bodies. Most infants attempted to cruise over the widest gaps in the floor, clinging to the handrail as their feet dangled into the precipice. Further evidence for failure to transfer between cruising and walking postures was provided by a group of newly walking infants. New walkers erred in both conditions; they attempted to span impossibly wide gaps in the handrail and stepped into impossibly wide gaps in the floor.

The Visual Cliff

A recent study with infants on a "visual cliff" posed a challenge to the learning-set account (Witherington, Campos, Anderson, Lejeune, & Seah, 2005). As first devised by E. J. Gibson and Walk (e.g., 1960), the visual cliff is a large glass table, divided in half by a narrow starting board (Fig. 7–2F). On the "shallow" side, a patterned surface is placed directly beneath the glass (3 cm), providing visual information for a solid surface. On the "deep" side, the patterned surface lies on the floor far below (90 cm), creating the illusion of an abrupt drop-off. Infants are placed on the starting board and encouraged to cross by caregivers standing at the far end.

To test transfer across developmental changes in posture, 12-month-old crawlers and walkers were tested on the visual cliff in a between-subject design (Witherington et al., 2005). Infants in the crawling group averaged 3.5 months of crawling experience, and all infants in the walking group had less than two weeks of walking experience. In contrast to the prediction of learning sets, the walkers were more likely to avoid crossing the deep side of the visual cliff than the crawlers. However, in another study, infants avoided the apparent drop-off when tested in their experienced crawling posture, but the same infants wheeled straight over the safety glass when tested in an upright posture in a mechanical baby walker (Rader, Bausano, & Richards, 1980).

Studies using the visual cliff have also yielded conflicting findings regarding the role of locomotor experience (for review, see Adolph & Berger, 2006). In the most frequently cited study, infants with 6 weeks of crawling experience were more likely to avoid crawling over the deep side of the cliff than infants with only 2 weeks of crawling experience (Bertenthal, Campos, & Barrett, 1984). The finding is especially striking because infants' age was equated across the two groups. However, other studies found the opposite effect, while controlling for infants' age: Novice crawlers were more likely to avoid the apparent drop-off than experienced crawlers (Richards & Rader, 1981, 1983).

Albeit famous, the visual cliff is not an optimal paradigm for assessing infants' responses to novel variations in surface layout. Discrepant findings may stem from methodological limitations of the apparatus (Adolph & Berger, 2006). The safety glass is particularly problematic. For example, because infants have trouble keeping their bodies on the narrow centerboard, some researchers score crossing only after infants have traveled halfway across the safety glass (Sorce, Emde, Campos, & Klinnert, 1985). As a consequence, findings may be biased toward avoidance responses, although if the safety glass were not there, infants would have tumbled to the floor as soon as their weight shifted off the centerboard. A second problem with the safety glass is that it presents infants with conflicting perceptual information about the deep side of the visual cliff. The drop-off looks risky, but feels safe to the touch. Indeed, the deep side is perfectly safe for locomotion, and infants quickly learn that they can cross it after one or two trials. When infants were tested longitudinally, avoidance responses attenuated rather than increased (Campos, Hiatt, Ramsay, Henderson, & Svejda, 1978; Eppler, Satterwhite, Wendt, & Bruce, 1997). Thus, researchers are limited to between-subject designs with only a single trial per infant on each side. In addition to problems stemming from the safety glass, the fixed dimensions of the apparatus preclude conclusions about the accuracy of infants' responses and whether responses are scaled to each infant's current abilities.

Summary: Surface Layout and Learning Sets

Evidence from several developmental designs, various experimental arrangements with slopes and gaps, and psychophysical methods to normalize the relative risk to infants' bodies and skills supports a learning-set account of infants' ability to cope with novel and variable changes in the surface layout. The evidence is consistent with learning sets and inconsistent with association learning: Learning required weeks—or months—of everyday experience with the newly acquired postural-control system. Learning did not require encounters with particular cues in particular contexts; experienced infants could show adaptive responses with a novel obstacle on their first trial. Experienced infants showed broad transfer to novel variations in the surface layout and to changes in their own bodies and skills. And, infants showed no evidence of transfer between experienced postures and later developing ones.

EVIDENCE FOR ASSOCIATION LEARNING: COPING WITH CHANGES IN FRICTION AND RIGIDITY

Studies on infants' responses to variations in the friction and rigidity conditions of support surfaces present different methodological challenges than the research involving variations in the dimensions of the surface layout. With an adjustable apparatus, researchers can easily present infants with continuous changes in dimensions of the surface layout, such as gradations in the degree of slope or width of gap. In contrast, experimental manipulations of friction and rigidity conditions are difficult: They cannot be continuously adjusted by turning a crank or pulling a lever. Instead, material substance must be altered by presenting infants with different surfaces or different apparatuses. Moreover, even an infinitely large collection of surfaces would not guarantee continuous adjustments in friction or rigidity because the size of the emergent forces depends on infants' bodies and the manner of contact. Thus, researchers must rely on categorical rather than continuous comparisons of material substance: infants' responses to wobbly foam and rigid wooden handrails (Berger, Adolph, & Lobo, 2005); deformable waterbed and rigid plywood surfaces (E. J. Gibson, Riccio, Schmuckler, Stoffregen, Rosenberg, & Taormina, 1987); watery, rigid, elastic, and net surfaces (Ruff, 1984; Palmer, 1989; Bourgeois, Khawar, Neal, & Lockman, 2005); and slippery, squishy, and sticky surfaces (Stoffregen, Adolph, Thelen, Gorday, & Sheng, 1997).

Here, we describe a new methodological approach designed to test prospective control of balance and locomotion in the context of association learning. We tested participants' motor decisions over a series of consecutive trials as they approached a single, well-marked, deformable or low-friction obstacle on a rigid, high-friction walkway. The novel changes in rigidity and friction conditions were created with large foam-filled blocks and a large Teflon insert, respectively.

To encourage learning, the obstacles were marked with various types of visual cues that differentiated them from the surrounding walkway in color, texture, pattern, and shine. In the foam-pit paradigm, the foam blocks were bumpy with rounded edges and were covered with a brown and gold flowered, stretchy material. The rest of the walkway was covered with blue, smooth, and shiny vinyl. In the Teflon-floor paradigm, the Teflon insert was white, smooth, flat, square-edged, and shiny. The remainder of the walkway was covered with blue, plush, and textured carpet. Contrast trials (in which the foam pit was replaced with rigid wooden blocks and the Teflon was replaced with high-friction carpet) in a baseline condition served to highlight the visual cues that marked the challenging friction/rigidity condition.

The obstacles ensured that participants would fall if they stepped haphazardly onto the foam or Teflon. In the foam-pit paradigm, the internal sections of the foam blocks were carved out so that the foam would suddenly depress several inches under the lightest infant's weight. In the Teflon-floor paradigm, the entire walkway was tilted gently, and infants wore nylon stockings to ensure that they would slip if they did not change their ongoing walking patterns. An experimenter followed alongside participants to ensure their safety, and caregivers stood at the far side of the obstacle and encouraged them to cross.

The benefit of this methodological approach is that we could observe participants' exploratory activity and motor decisions on their first encounter with the obstacle to determine whether visual cues such as color, texture, pattern, and shine alert walkers to novel variations in rigidity or friction. In addition, if participants fell on the first trial, we could examine association learning over subsequent encounters with the obstacle over the test session. On an association-learning account, participants should pair the visual cues for the obstacle with the consequence of falling and avoid falling on subsequent encounters.

Foam Pit

In one series of experiments, we used a cross-sectional design to test age-related changes in association learning (Joh & Adolph, 2006). We tested five groups of children (15-, 21-, 27-, 33-, and 39-month-olds) and a comparison group of adults on the walkway containing a foam pit (Fig. 7–5A). All of the participants were experienced at keeping balance in an upright postural control system and could be expected to show adaptive motor decisions to novel variations in the surface layout: Even the youngest infants (the 15-month-olds) had, on average, 3 months of walking experience. Thus, if forewarned, participants should also show adaptive responses to variations in rigidity and friction. In addition to the salient visual cues that distinguished the foam pit from the surrounding walkway,

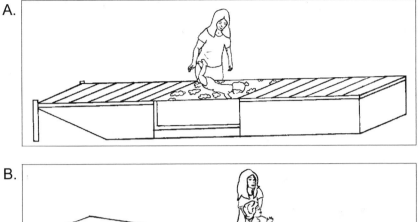

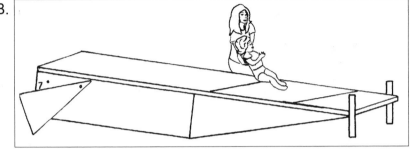

Figure 7–5. Tasks and apparatuses used in studies of association learning. (A) Crawling and walking infants, children, and adults falling on a walkway interrupted by a deformable foam pit. (B) Walking infants slipping on a walkway interrupted by a low-friction Teflon floor.

the consequences of falling were also highly salient. The foam pit was large enough that the younger children could fall headfirst into the foam without intervention by the experimenter. Experimenters caught the older children and assisted adults when they fell.

On their first trial, every participant walked straight into the foam pit and fell. In contrast to participants' performance in tasks involving novel variations in surface layout, everyday walking experience did not facilitate adaptive responses to novel variations in rigidity conditions. Visual cues for the foam pit—the bumpy surface and rounded edges of the foam blocks and the coincident change in the color, pattern, and texture of the material covering the foam pit—were not sufficient to elicit hesitation or focused exploration on the first encounter with the obstacle. In fact, across all ages, participants often gasped when they fell, indicating that the consequences were unexpected and salient.

The crucial test of learning, however, was the number of trials required to avoid falling on subsequent trials. The learning criterion was 2 consecutive no-fall trials. As shown in Figure 7–6, the 15-month-olds required 7 trials, on average, to meet the learning criterion. Only 2 out of 18 infants (11%) showed 1-trial learning (they avoided falling from their second trial) and 4 out of 18 infants (22%) showed no evidence of learning (they fell on 16 consecutive foam-pit trials without pausing,

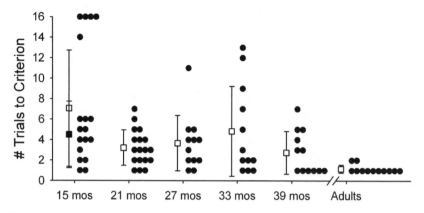

Figure 7–6. Number of trials required to meet the learning criterion (2 consecutive trials on which participants avoided falling) for walking infants, children, and adults in the foam-pit experiment. The circles represent individual data. The open squares represent group averages with all participants included. The filled square represents group average for the 15-month-old learners only.

exploring the foam pit, or testing alternative positions). With the non-learners excluded, the 15-month-olds averaged 4.5 trials to meet the learning criterion.

Older children and adults fared better on two counts. No participants in the older age groups fell on every foam-pit trial. That is, all of the older children and adults met the learning criterion eventually during the testing session. In addition, the number of participants showing 1-trial learning increased with age, from 11% at 15 months to 50% at 39 months and 83% by adulthood.

However, two findings were similar across the age groups. First, learning was all-or-none: Before stepping onto the foam pit, participants rarely showed changes in hesitation, tactile exploration at the brink, or shifts in position until the learning criterion trials. For example, on their falling trials, 15-month-olds required only 7 seconds to walk into the foam pit; and on the two no-fall learning criterion trials, infants spent 16 seconds on the platform before they embarked onto the foam pit using an alternative locomotor strategy. Within each age group, speed of learning was not predicted by duration of walking experience, the number of serious falls, gender, or weekly exposure to ground surfaces varying in material properties.

A second similarity across age groups is that learning to avoid falling did not involve a stereotyped motor response (Fig. 7–7). On trials in which they refused to walk into the foam pit, infants crossed in crawling, backing, and sitting positions, detoured off the side of the starting platform, appealed to the experimenter for help, or simply avoided traversal altogether. Older children sometimes employed a diving strategy in which they ran down the length of the walkway and dove into the foam pit. Adults leaped over the entire foam pit or stepped into it cautiously.

In addition, we used a different developmental design—a longitudinal study—to test transfer in association learning (Joh & Adolph, 2005). Infants were observed on the foam pit apparatus every three weeks, from 10.5 months until 15 months

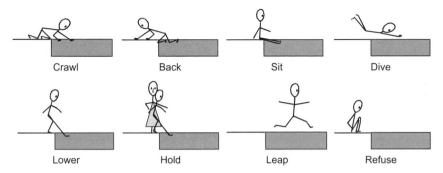

Figure 7–7. Various alternative locomotor strategies for avoiding falling into the foam pit.

of age. At the start of the study, all infants were crawlers; by the end of the study, all were walkers. This design allowed us to track the transfer of learning across 7 test sessions and across the transition from crawling to walking. To determine whether infants' responses were the result of experience with the foam pit, the 15-month-olds in the previous foam-pit experiment (Joh & Adolph, 2006) served as an age-matched control. In addition, to test transfer of learning across contexts, we moved the foam pit to a different location in the lab. At infants' first walking session (infants were different ages) and the last testing session (all infants were 15 months old), after testing them on the foam pit in its original location, we moved the brown flowered covering to a different walkway.

Three sets of findings indicate that learning to avoid falling into the foam pit depended on context-specific associations between the visual cues for the foam pit and the consequence of falling rather than on the formation of a learning set. First, the number of trials to meet the learning criterion decreased steadily over the 7 test sessions. At their first session, at 10.5 months of age, infants averaged 10 consecutive falls before learning. At their last session, at 15 months of age, infants averaged only 4 falls. Across sessions, approximately a quarter of the infants never learned from falling. When the non-learners were excluded from the analysis, on their last session, infants required only 0.2 trials to learn from falling because 10 out of 19 infants avoided falling on the first trial, providing further evidence that they had remembered the visual cues for the foam pit from previous sessions. In comparison, the infants who were tested only once in previous work averaged 7 falls (4.5, excluding the non-learners) at 15 months of age.

The second important finding was that learning transferred over the developmental transition from crawling to walking postures. Because infants began walking at different points during the study, they were different ages and had different numbers of previous sessions at their first walking session. When the sessions were normalized to infants' first walking session, we found a steady decrease in the number of trials to learning criterion over weeks of crawling, over weeks of walking, and from infants' last crawling session to their first walking session.

The third finding in support of association learning on the foam pit was that learning from falling was highly context-dependent. At infants' first walking session and last test session, we tested them on a different walkway in a different location in the laboratory, but otherwise retained the other aspects of the training context: the same visual cues for the foam-pit obstacle, the same experimenters, and the same toys and apparatuses in a cluttered laboratory. Moreover, the new walkway was less than 5 feet away from the location of the original walkway. Despite the minor change in the context, infants behaved as if they had not seen the foam pit previously on multiple occasions. Although the learners had avoided walking onto the foam pit a few minutes earlier, they stepped into it in the altered context without hesitation or tactile exploration.

Slippery Teflon

We replicated the foam-pit results with another group of 15-month-olds on a slippery Teflon obstacle (Joh, Adolph, & DeWind, 2005). In this case, the cues for the obstacle resembled ice (white, shiny, smooth, flat surface) but may have been less salient than the cues for the foam pit because the Teflon was not patterned, textured, or brightly colored (Fig. 7–5B). The consequences of falling were aversive but may have been less salient than those of falling face first into the foam pit. Because infants slipped backward as soon as they stepped onto the Teflon insert, an experimenter caught them for safety as they began to fall.

As in the foam-pit experiments, visual cues to differentiate the novel surface from the surrounding walkway did not elicit focused exploration at the brink of the obstacle. And despite adults' reported reliance on shine to predict slip (Joh, Adolph, Campbell et al., 2006), every infant walked straight onto the Teflon surface and fell. Moreover, the lower salience of the Teflon experiment appeared to affect the speed of learning from falling. As a group, infants required 9.5 trials to learn to avoid falling (compared to 7 trials shown by the 15-month-olds in the foam-pit experiment). However, when the non-learners were excluded, infants required 5 trials (equivalent to 4.5 trials in the foam-pit experiment), and the same percentage of infants learned after 1 trial (11%), suggesting that salience did not affect the learners. Instead, salience seemed to affect the number of non-learners: Twice the number of infants failed to learn during the test session in the Teflon paradigm (44%) compared to those in the foam-pit paradigm (22%). As in the foam-pit experiment, hesitation, tactile exploration, and exploratory shifts in position increased only on the learning-criterion trials in the Teflon experiment, when infants had learned to link the visual cues for the Teflon with the consequence of falling.

Summary: Friction and Rigidity and Association Learning

The evidence from cross-sectional and longitudinal designs with the foam pit and slippery Teflon floor supports an association-learning account of prospective control of locomotion over changes in the rigidity and friction of the ground surface: Speed of learning was related to the salience of cues and consequences and the number of previous encounters with the particular cues and context. Learning was not related to the duration of everyday locomotor experience. Infants showed narrow transfer of learning to changes in the environmental context but no decrement in learning over the developmental transition from crawling to walking. Across age groups, learning was relatively fast and occurred within the course of a single test session. However, 1-trial learning increased with age, and the number of non-learners decreased with age, indicating that infants take longer than older children and adults to associate the visible appearance of the ground with the consequence of falling.

COPING WITH COVARIATIONS IN SURFACE LAYOUT AND FRICTION/RIGIDITY

Frequently, changes in surface layout occur simultaneously with changes in friction and rigidity conditions. The slope in the road might be shallow or steep; the surface of the road might be dry or wet concrete. The snowdrift in the path might be large or small; the obstacle might be composed of tightly or loosely packed snow. In such cases, learning sets and association-learning mechanisms should operate in concert. The visual-depth cues for surface layout should elicit focused exploration of the obstacle and thereby generate perceptual information for rigidity and friction. Associated links between visual cues for material substance and consequences for balance should facilitate more adaptive responding with repeated encounters with the obstacle.

Crossing Bridges with Wooden and Wobbly Handrails

We used a bridge and handrail apparatus to examine infants' responses to covariations in surface layout and rigidity. Previous work showed that 16-month-olds can take two aspects of the surface layout into account when deciding whether to walk over a potential obstacle: the width of a bridge spanning a large crevice, and the presence of a solid handrail to augment balance on narrow bridges (Fig. 7–8A) (Berger & Adolph, 2003). Infants' decisions to walk or not depended on both bridge width and handrail presence. On the wide bridges, infants walked straight across the bridge without hesitation, regardless of whether the handrail was available. However, on narrow bridges, motor decisions depended on handrail presence. When the handrail was absent, infants refused to leave the starting platform. When the handrail was available, infants used it to augment their balance. They turned sideways and walked slowly and carefully across the bridge, gripping the rail tightly with both arms.

Here, we introduced material substance as a factor by varying the rigidity of the handrail (Berger et al., 2005). The bridges were designed to pose a challenging problem in terms of surface layout: Narrow (10- and 20-cm) bridges were too difficult to walk across without a handrail to augment balance; on the wider (40-cm) bridge, a handrail was unnecessary. The handrails were designed to provide a viable solution for crossing the narrow bridges, but only when the handrails were

A.    B.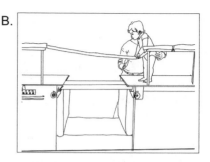

Figure 7–8. Task and apparatus used for studies of covariations in bridge width and handrail rigidity. (A) Infants walking across a bridge using a wooden handrail for support. (B) Infants walking across a bridge using wobbly rubber or foam handrails. The bridges varied in width (12–72 cm for the wooden handrail task, 10–40 cm for the wobbly handrail task), changing infants' need to use handrails. All bridges were 74 cm long, and spanned a 76-cm deep crevice.

sufficiently rigid. On some trials, the handrail was made of sturdy wood, as in the earlier work, and it could support infants' weight. On other trials, the handrail was made of pliable rubber or foam and depressed to infants' knees when they leaned on it (Fig. 7–8B). Visually, the three handrails were distinct: The wooden handrail was tan and had a wood-grain appearance, the rubber handrail was shiny yellow, and the foam handrail was matte blue. In addition, they were shaped differently: The wooden handrail had square edges whereas the wobbly ones had rounded edges. However, the rigidity of the handrail could be determined only by direct contact: The wobbly aspect of the rubber and foam rails could be revealed only by touch.

Infants took the rigidity of the handrail into account when deciding whether to walk. They crossed the narrow bridges more frequently on trials with the wooden handrail than on trials with the wobbly handrails. As predicted by learning sets, on trials with the narrow bridges, infants paused at the edge of the bridge and explored possible solutions for crossing the precipice by probing the bridge with their feet, exploring the handrail manually, and testing various ways of using the handrail to cross the bridge. They hesitated longer and spent more time engaged in tactile exploration (pushing, tapping, squeezing, rubbing, and even mouthing the handrail) on trials with the wobbly handrails. However, as predicted by association learning, infants showed evidence of learning over trials. On their second encounter with the wobbly handrails, infants showed less tactile exploration and their motor decisions were more discriminating, suggesting that they had linked the visual appearance of the handrail with the consequences for augmenting balance.

Two additional findings were unexpected. Although the wobbly handrails were designed to be functionally equivalent to having no handrail available for augmenting balance, infants attempted the narrow bridges at surprisingly high frequencies on trials with the wobbly handrails. A related surprise was that their attempts were largely successful. Infants managed to use the deformable rails

Figure 7–9. Strategies infants invented to use the wobbly rubber and foam handrails to help them walk over the narrower bridges.

adaptively by employing inventive strategies shown in Figure 7–9. For example, with a "hunchback" strategy, they walked sideways, stooped over, pressing down on the handrail so that it depressed to their knees; with a "mountain climbing" strategy, they faced forward, learned backward, and pulled up on the handrail like a rope, dragging themselves along hand over hand. Thus, even when association learning played a role in guiding infants' subsequent exploration and motor decisions, as in our previous work, their responses were flexible and varied, rather than rigid and stereotyped.

Using Friction Underfoot to Guide Locomotion Over Slopes

To examine infants' responses to covariations in surface layout and friction condition, we covered the adjustable sloping apparatus with high- and low-friction surfaces. The benefit of this method was that we could retain the precision of the psychophysical procedures used in earlier studies of surface layout. Specifically, we examined whether walkers extrapolate from incidental tactile information about friction that they feel beneath their feet on flat ground to visual information about upcoming changes in surface slant. Infants were tested on the same adjustable sloping walkway used in previous studies of learning sets (e.g., Adolph, 1997), and adults were tested on a sturdier version that had the same dimensions.

In the high-friction condition, the entire walkway was covered with a novel rubber surface; in the low-friction condition, it was covered with a novel vinyl surface. Both surfaces were visually similar (shiny blue) to minimize the likelihood that participants could associate the appearance of the surface coverings with the consequences for maintaining balance. Participants wore nylon tights to exaggerate the effects of the rubber and vinyl and to keep footwear constant across participants. We used the psychophysical staircase procedure to estimate motor thresholds for each participant in each friction condition and presented additional probe trials on safe and risky increments to assess the adaptiveness of their motor decisions.

As in the lead-weighted shoulder pack study (Adolph & Avolio, 2000), we examined the extent of transfer within an experienced postural-control system. In two experiments, we tested 14-month-old walking infants on the adjustable slope under high- and low-friction conditions (Lo, Avolio, Massop, & Adolph, 1999; Adolph et al., 2008). In the first experiment, high- and low-friction trials were interspersed, and in the second experiment, friction conditions were blocked. In both experiments, infants could feel their feet slip or grip the ground as they walked across the flat starting platform toward the slope. The critical questions were whether underfoot information about friction prompted focused visual and tactile exploration at the brink of the slope and whether infants' motor decisions were based on perceptual information about friction, slope, or both.

The results of both experiments were similar, regardless of whether friction conditions were interspersed or blocked. Infants' ability to walk down slopes was severely compromised in the low-friction condition: They could manage only 0- to 6-degree slopes without slipping and falling. Every infant could walk down steeper slopes in the high-friction condition: Motor thresholds ranged from 6 to 26 degrees. Most important, infants' motor decisions were based primarily on the degree of slope, not on friction. Despite feeling their feet slip on the flat starting platform, infants showed depressed levels of exploration in the low-friction condition. Without sufficient perceptual information, infants walked over the brink of risky low-friction slopes and fell.

In contrast to their dismal performance in the low-friction condition, infants' behavior in the high-friction condition replicated findings from previous studies with 14-month-olds on slopes (Adolph et al., 1993; Adolph, 1995, 1997; Adolph & Avolio, 2000). Infants paused to explore slopes steeper than their motor thresholds by looking and touching before initiating descent. Consequently, they generated sufficient information to support an adaptive avoidance response. Normalized data showed that infants attempted risky low-friction slopes far beyond their abilities, but they scaled their attempts on high-friction trials to the conditional probability of success. When analyzed by absolute degree of slope, high- and low-friction curves were superimposed, meaning that infants' motor decisions were based on surface slant, not friction.

Several follow-up experiments showed that adults, like infants, do not incorporate underfoot information about friction into their decisions for walking down upcoming slopes (Joh, Adolph, Narayanan et al., 2007). Adults stood on a flat starting platform feeling the low-friction vinyl or high-friction rubber beneath their feet and looked at an adjustable slope a few steps ahead. They grossly overestimated their ability to cope with the low-friction surface and underestimated their abilities on the high-friction surface. But, when adults were instructed to generate the appropriate tactile information by placing part of their foot over the brink—so that they could obtain information about slant and friction simultaneously—their motor decisions matched their abilities.

To summarize, without distinct visual cues to differentiate friction conditions, walkers cannot form associations between the appearance of the ground surface and the consequences for locomotion. Both infant and adult walkers were aware that the slippery vinyl surface was more difficult; as in earlier work, their reactive adjustments were appropriately geared to the friction conditions (Stoffregen et al., 1997). In low-friction trials, they walked more slowly and stiffly upright toward the brink of the slope. However, neither infants nor adults appeared to realize that the feeling of slip on flat ground presaged dire consequences on a small, upcoming slope. In both high- and low-friction trials, when infants stopped at the brink to engage in tactile exploration, their motor decisions reflected the actual possibilities for walking successfully. The problem was that only the visual cues for surface slant prompted walkers to engage in tactile exploration at the brink. If the surface of the slope had been visually distinct from the rest of the walkway (e.g., a different color), as the wobbly handrails had been, infants may have eventually associated the visual cues with slipping and increased the frequency of exploratory touching on shallow slopes in the low-friction condition.

CONCLUSIONS

When people speak of an infant "learning" to walk, what they probably have in mind is an infant taking wobbly steps across the room. However, learning to walk is no more about producing stepping movements than learning to talk is about producing vocal sounds. Walking—like talking—involves producing the appropriate behaviors to fit the requirements of the current situation. Thus, infants have truly learned to walk when they can steer through a cluttered room, accommodate their movements to the requirements of different surface properties, modify their actions in accordance with the continual variations in their own bodies and skill levels, and select the appropriate responses from their repertoire. To be functionally useful, walking must be adapted to the constraints of the environment and the body. In short, learning to walk means perceiving and using affordances for locomotion adaptively.

Exploration for Action

Sitting, crawling, cruising, and walking are not just motor skills—they are perceptual–motor skills. Infants need relevant perceptual information to guide their motor actions adaptively. Exploratory movements of the eyes, head, and body generate the necessary perceptual information. Visual information from a distance is especially important because gross motor skills involve large displacements of the body and errors can have serious consequences for maintaining balance. Visual depth cues are a reliable source of information about novel variations in the surface layout. With visual depth cues, infants have sufficient time to explore upcoming obstacles and to plan a reasonable course of action. In contrast, novel variations in friction and rigidity are not reliably specified by visual cues from a distance because they are emergent forces. The relevant perceptual information is created only during an event involving both contact surfaces (e.g., rubbing the foot against the brink of a slope). Without contact between the foot and the obstacle, only associations formed during prior encounters can link arbitrary visual cues with the consequences for balance and locomotion.

We suggest that differences in the availability of visual information from a distance create a reliance on different learning mechanisms: learning sets for surface layout and association learning for friction and rigidity. In principle, learning sets alone could be sufficient for coping with both surface layout and friction and rigidity if infants were willing to employ all of the exploratory procedures in their repertoires in response to arbitrary visual cues such as color, texture, and shine. However, in practice, infants and adults dispense their exploratory behaviors more efficiently. They continue on a current course of action unless visual depth cues alert them to a potential obstacle, or prior encounters with a similar surface in a similar situation were linked with a loss of balance. Thus, infants and adults must rely on association learning as a fallback mechanism for guiding prospective control under variable conditions of friction and rigidity. The cost of economy, however, is that they also must incur a high frequency of falls on their first encounter with a slippery or squishy surface.

Learning in Development

We also suggest that studies of infants maintaining balance in stance and locomotion under challenging and novel conditions provide a useful model system for investigating general principles of learning and development. In terms of learning, our studies of infants walking down slopes, leaning over gaps, and so on indicate that psychological functions with a high demand for adaptability and flexibility are best served by a learning mechanism that facilitates broad transfer of learning. Adaptability and flexibility are critical for maintaining balance in stance and locomotion because the constraints on balance are continually changing. Learning sets, albeit slow and difficult to acquire, are an optimal learning mechanism for ensuring broad transfer.

In terms of development, these studies provide a dramatic example of psychological functions that are ontogenetic adaptations, that is, functions specific to particular periods of development. For years, research from developmental systems theory has stressed the view that infants are not miniature adults (Oppenheim, 1981, 1984). Many of infants' behaviors are adaptations to their particular developmental niche. The studies described in this chapter suggest that crawlers are not little walkers. Earlier appearing postural-control systems involve qualitatively different psychological functions from later developing ones. Learning to maintain balance in a sitting posture does not teach infants to maintain balance while crawling; crawling does not ensure adaptive responding while walking; and even cruising, which shares the similarity of upright posture with walking, does not teach infants to respond adaptively to novel changes in the ground surface. Sitting, crawling, cruising, and walking show four separate learning curves after the onset of each postural milestone.

Finally, the studies described in this chapter provide insights into the ontogeny of learning. That is, learning occurs *in* development. Infants acquire learning sets and paired associations in the larger context of ongoing developmental changes. The two processes are linked in the sense that learning and development are concurrent, but developmental changes need not be specific to the type of learning mechanism employed or to the nature of what is being learned. Developments in one domain can serendipitously constrain and/or facilitate learning in a different domain.

We have suggested that the ongoing developmental changes in infants' bodies, skills, and environments may facilitate the acquisition of learning sets by providing infants with immense amounts of practice with continually varying and novel stimuli. Reciprocally, infants' episodic physical growth, fluctuating motor skills, and shifting landscapes may constrain them from forming associations between particular facts about their bodies or environments and the consequences for postural control. Yesterday's body size may be different from the size of the body today. Poor crawling skill last week may be replaced by proficient crawling this week. The high frequency of infants' falls and near falls may lead them to ignore the particular appearance of the ground surface. Our studies of balance and locomotion in infants suggest that the nested structure of learning in development may be responsible for selecting the optimal learning mechanisms for each psychological function.

Acknowledgments   We thank Mark Blumberg for his helpful suggestions and comments. We also thank Lana Karasik, Jessie Garciaguirre, and Michael Smith for their assistance with the figures. Work on this chapter was supported by National Institute of Health grants HD-33486 and HD-42697 to Karen Adolph.

References

Adolph, K. E. (1995). A psychophysical assessment of toddlers' ability to cope with slopes. *Journal of Experimental Psychology: Human Perception and Performance, 21,* 734–750.

Adolph, K. E. (1997). Learning in the development of infant locomotion. *Monographs of the Society for Research in Child Development, 62*(3, Serial No. 251).

Adolph, K. E. (2000). Specificity of learning: Why infants fall over a veritable cliff. *Psychological Science, 11,* 290–295.

Adolph, K. E. (2002). Learning to keep balance. In R. Kail (Ed.), *Advances in child development and behavior* (Vol. 30, pp. 1–30). Amsterdam: Elsevier Science.

Adolph, K. E. (2005). Learning to learn in the development of action. In J. Lockman & J. Reiser (Eds.), *Action as an organizer of learning and development: The 32nd Minnesota Symposium on Child Development* (pp. 91–122). Hillsdale, NJ: Lawrence Erlbaum.

Adolph, K. E., & Avolio, A. M. (2000). Walking infants adapt locomotion to changing body dimensions. *Journal of Experimental Psychology: Human Perception and Performance, 26,* 1148–1166.

Adolph, K. E., & Berger, S. E. (2005). Physical and motor development. In M. H. Bornstein & M. E. Lamb (Eds.), *Developmental science: An advanced textbook* (5th ed., pp. 223–281). Mahwah, NJ: Lawrence Erlbaum.

Adolph, K. E., & Berger, S. E. (2006). Motor development. In D. Kuhn & R. S. Siegler (Eds.), *Handbook of child psychology: Vol. 2: Cognition, perception, and language* (6th ed., pp. 161–213). New York: John Wiley.

Adolph, K. E., & Eppler, M. A. (2002). Flexibility and specificity in infant motor skill acquisition. In J. W. Fagen & H. Hayne (Eds.), *Progress in infancy research* (Vol. 2, pp. 121–167). Mahwah, NJ: Lawrence Erlbaum.

Adolph, K. E., Eppler, M. A., & Gibson, E. J. (1993). Crawling versus walking infants' perception of affordances for locomotion over sloping surfaces. *Child Development, 64,* 1158–1174.

Adolph, K. E., Eppler, M. A., Marin, L., Weise, I. B., & Clearfield, M. W. (2000). Exploration in the service of prospective control. *Infant Behavior and Development, 23,* 441–460.

Adolph, K. E., Joh, A. S., & Eppler, M. A. (2008). *Infants' perception of affordances of slopes under high and low friction conditions.* Manuscript submitted for publication.

Adolph, K. E., Tamis-LeMonda, C. S., Ishak, S., Karasik, L. B., & Lobo, S. A. (2008). *Locomotor experience and use of social information are posture specific.* Manuscript submitted for publication.

Baillargeon, R. (2004). Infants' reasoning about hidden objects: Evidence for event-general and event-specific expectations. *Developmental Science, 7,* 391–424.

Baker, A. G., & Mackintosh, N. J. (1979). Preexposure to the CS alone, US alone, or CS and US uncorrelated: Latent inhibition, blocking by context or learned irrelevance? *Learning and Motivation, 10,* 278–294.

Berger, S. E., & Adolph, K. E. (2003). Infants use handrails as tools in a locomotor task. *Developmental Psychology, 39,* 594–605.

Berger, S. E., Adolph, K. E., & Lobo, S. A. (2005). Out of the toolbox: Toddlers differentiate wobbly and wooden handrails. *Child Development, 76,* 1294–1307.

Bertenthal, B. I., Campos, J. J., & Barrett, K. C. (1984). Self-produced locomotion: An organizer of emotional, cognitive, and social development in infancy. In R. N. Emde & R. J. Harmon (Eds.), *Continuities and discontinuities in development* (pp. 175–210). New York: Plenum Press.

Bertenthal, B. I., & Clifton, R. K. (1998). Perception and action. In D. Kuhn & R. S. Siegler (Eds.), *Handbook of child psychology: Vol. 2: Cognition, perception, and language* (5th ed., pp. 51–102). New York: John Wiley.

Bourgeois, K. S., Khawar, A. W., Neal, S. A., & Lockman, J. J. (2005). Infant manual exploration of objects, surfaces, and their interrelations. *Infancy, 8,* 233–252.

Bouton, M. E., & Bolles, R. C. (1979). Contextual control of the extinction of conditioned fear. *Learning and Motivation, 10,* 445–466.

Campos, J. J., Hiatt, S., Ramsay, D., Henderson, C., & Svejda, M. (1978). The emergence of fear on the visual cliff. In M. Lewis & L. Rosenblum (Eds.), *The development of affect* (pp. 149–182). New York: Plenum.

Chan, M. Y., Biancaniello, R., Adolph, K. E., & Marin, L. (2000, July). *Tracking infants' locomotor experience: The telephone diary.* Poster presented to the International Conference on Infant Studies, Brighton, UK.

Eppler, M. A., Satterwhite, T., Wendt, J., & Bruce, K. (1997). Infants' responses to a visual cliff and other ground surfaces. In M. A. Schmuckler & J. M. Kennedy (Eds.), *Studies in perception and action IV* (pp. 219–222). Mahway, NJ: Lawrence Erlbaum.

Frankenburg, W. K., & Dodds, J. B. (1967). The Denver Developmental Screening Test. *Journal of Pediatrics, 71,* 181–191.

Garciaguirre, J. S., & Adolph, K. E. (2006, June). *Infants' everyday locomotor experience: A walking and falling marathon.* Paper presented to the International Society for Infant Studies, Kyoto, Japan.

Gibson, E. J. (1988). Exploratory behavior in the development of perceiving, acting and the acquiring of knowledge. *Annual Review of Psychology, 39,* 1–41.

Gibson, E. J. (1992, April). *Perceptual learning and development.* Presentation to the Indiana University Psychology Department Colloquium, Bloomington, IN.

Gibson, E. J., & Pick, A. D. (2000). *An ecological approach to perceptual learning and development.* New York: Oxford University Press.

Gibson, E. J., Riccio, G., Schmuckler, M. A., Stoffregen, T. A., Rosenberg, D., & Taormina, J. (1987). Detection of the traversability of surfaces by crawling and walking infants. *Journal of Experimental Psychology: Human Perception and Performance, 13,* 533–544.

Gibson, E. J., & Walk, R. D. (1960). The "visual cliff." *Scientific American, 202,* 64–71.

Gibson, J. J. (1979). *The ecological approach to visual perception.* Boston: Houghton-Mifflin.

Haehl, V., Vardaxis, V., & Ulrich, B. D. (2000). Learning to cruise: Bernstein's theory applied to skill acquisition during infancy. *Human Movement Science, 19,* 685–715.

Harlow, H. F. (1949). The formation of learning sets. *Psychological Review, 56,* 51–65.

Harlow, H. F. (1959). Learning set and error factor theory. In S. Koch (Ed.), *Psychology: A study of a science* (pp. 492–533). New York: McGraw-Hill.

Harlow, H. F., & Kuenne, M. (1949). Learning to think. *Scientific American,* 3–6.

Hopkins, B., & Westra, T. (1988). Maternal handling and motor development: An intracultural study. *Genetic, Social and General Psychology Monographs, 114,* 379–408.

Hopkins, B., & Westra, T. (1989). Maternal expectations of their infants' development: Some cultural differences. *Developmental Medicine and Child Neurology, 31,* 384–390.

Hopkins, B., & Westra, T. (1990). Motor development, maternal expectations, and the role of handling. *Infant Behavior and Development, 13,* 117–122.

Joh, A. S., & Adolph, K. E. (2005, April). *Crawling, walking, and learning about falling.* Poster presented at the meeting of the Society for Research in Child Development, Atlanta, GA.

Joh, A. S., & Adolph, K. E. (2006). Learning from falling. *Child Development, 77,* 89–102.

Joh, A. S., Adolph, K. E., Campbell, M. R., & Eppler, M. A. (2006). Why walkers slip: Shine is not a reliable cue for slippery ground. *Perception & Psychophysics, 68,* 339–352.

Joh, A. S., Adolph, K. E., & DeWind, N. K. (2005, November). *Learning from slipping and falling.* Poster presented at the meeting of the International Society for Developmental Psychobiology, Washington, DC.

Joh, A. S., Adolph, K. E., Narayanan, P. J., & Dietz, V. A. (2007). Gauging possibilities for action based on friction underfoot. *Journal of Experimental Psychology: Human Perception and Performance, 33,* 1145–1157.

Johnson, S. P., Slemmer, J. A., & Amso, D. (2004). Where infants look determines how they see: Eye movements and object perception performance in 3-month-olds. *Infancy, 6,* 185–201.

Lampl, M., Veldhuis, J. D., & Johnson, M. L. (1992). Saltation and stasis: A model of human growth. *Science, 258,* 801–803.

Lashley, K. S. (1930). The mechanism of vision. I. A method for rapid analysis of pattern-vision in the rat. *Journal of Genetic Psychology, 37,* 453–360.

Lee, D. N. (1993). Body-environment coupling. In U. Neisser (Ed.), *The perceived self: Ecological and interpersonal sources of self-knowledge* (pp. 43–67). Cambridge: Cambridge University Press.

Leo, A. J., Chiu, J., & Adolph, K. E. (2000, July). *Temporal and functional relationships of crawling, cruising, and walking.* Poster presented at the International Conference on Infant Studies, Brighton, UK.

Lewis, M., Alessandri, S. M., & Sullivan, M. W. (1990). Violation of expectancy, loss of control, and anger expressions in young infants. *Developmental Psychology, 26,* 745–751.

Lo, T., Avolio, A. M., Massop, S. A., & Adolph, K. E. (1999). Why toddlers don't perceive risky ground based on surface friction. In M. A. Grealy & J. A. Thompson (Eds.), *Studies in perception and action V* (pp. 231–235). Mahwah, NJ: Lawrence Erlbaum.

Marcus, G. F., Vijayan, S., Bandi Rao, S., & Vishton, P. M. (1999). Rule learning by seven-month-olds infants. *Science, 283,* 77–80.

McGraw, M. B. (1935). *Growth: A study of Johnny and Jimmy.* New York: Appleton-Century.

Metcalfe, J. S., & Clark, J. E. (2000). Sensory information affords exploration of posture in newly walking infants and toddlers. *Infant Behavior and Development, 23,* 391–405.

Mondschein, E. R., Adolph, K. E., & Tamis-LeMonda, C. S. (2000). Gender bias in mothers' expectations about infant crawling. *Journal of Experimental Child Psychology, 77,* 304–316.

National Safety Council. (2003). *Injury facts®.* Itasca, IL: National Safety Council.

Oppenheim, R. W. (1981). Ontogenetic adaptations and retrogressive processes in the development of the nervous system and behavior: A neuroembryological perspective. In K. J. Connolly & H.F.R. Prechtl (Eds.), *Maturation and development: Biological and psychological perspectives* (pp. 73–109). Philadelphia: J. P. Lippincott.

Oppenheim, R. W. (1984). Ontogenetic adaptations in neural and behavioral development: Toward a more "ecological" developmental psychology. In H.F.R. Prechtl (Ed.), *Continuity of neural functions from prenatal to postnatal life* (pp. 16–30). Oxford: Blackwell Scientific Publications.

Palmer, C. F. (1989). The discriminating nature of infants' exploratory actions. *Developmental Psychology, 25,* 885–893.

Patla, A. E. (1989). In search of laws for the visual control of locomotion. *Journal of Experimental Psychology: Human Perception and Performance, 15,* 624–628.

Patla, A. E. (1998). How is human gait controlled by vision? *Ecological Psychology, 10,* 287–302.

Patla, A. E., Prentice, S. D., Robinson, C., & Neufeld, J. (1991). Visual control of locomotion: Strategies for changing direction and for going over obstacles. *Journal of Experimental Psychology, 17,* 603–634.

Patla, A. E., Robinson, C., Samways, M., & Armstrong, C. J. (1989). Visual control of step length during overground locomotion: Task-specific modulation of the locomotor synergy. *Journal of Experimental Psychology, 15,* 603–617.

Rader, N., Bausano, M., & Richards, J. E. (1980). On the nature of the visual-cliff-avoidance response in human infants. *Child Development, 51,* 61–68.

Reed, E. S. (1982). An outline of a theory of action systems. *Journal of Motor Behavior, 14,* 98–134.

Reed, E. S. (1989). Changing theories of postural development. In M. H. Woollacott & A. Shumway-Cook (Eds.), *Development of posture and gait across the lifespan* (pp. 3–24). Columbia, SC: University of South Carolina Press.

Richards, J. E., & Rader, N. (1981). Crawling-onset age predicts visual cliff avoidance in infants. *Journal of Experimental Psychology: Human Perception and Performance, 7*, 382–387.

Richards, J. E., & Rader, N. (1983). Affective, behavioral, and avoidance responses on the visual cliff: Effects of crawling onset age, crawling experience, and testing age. *Psychophysiology, 20*, 633–642.

Rovee, C. K., & Rovee, D. T. (1969). Conjugate reinforcement of infant exploratory behavior. *Journal of Experimental Child Psychology, 8*, 33–39.

Ruff, H. A. (1984). Infants' manipulative exploration of objects: Effects of age and object characteristics. *Developmental Psychology, 20*, 9–20.

Saffran, J. R. (2003). Statistical language learning: Mechanisms and constraints. *Current Directions in Psychological Science, 12*, 110–114.

Saffran, J. R., Aslin, R. N., & Newport, E. L. (1996). Statistical learning by 8-month-olds infants. *Science, 274*, 1926–1928.

Siegler, R. S., Adolph, K. E., & Lemaire, P. (1996). Strategy choice across the life span. In L. M. Reder (Ed.), *Implicit memory and metacognition* (pp. 79–121). Mahwah, NJ: Erlbaum.

Smith, L. B., & Yoshida, H. (2005). Linguistic cues enhance the learning of perceptual cues. *Psychological Science, 16*, 90–95.

Sorce, J. F., Emde, R. N., Campos, J. J., & Klinnert, M. D. (1985). Maternal emotional signaling: Its effects on the visual cliff behavior of 1-year-olds. *Developmental Psychology, 21*, 195–200.

Stevenson, H. W. (1972). *Children's learning.* New York: Appleton-Century-Crofts.

Stoffregen, T. A., Adolph, K. E., Thelen, E., Gorday, K. M., & Sheng, Y. Y. (1997). Toddlers' postural adaptations to different support surfaces. *Motor Control, 1*, 119–137.

von Hofsten, C. (2003). On the development of perception and action. In K. J. Connolly & J. Valsiner (Eds.), *Handbook of developmental psychology* (pp. 114–140). London: Sage.

von Hofsten, C. (2004). An action perspective on motor development. *Trends in Cognitive Sciences, 8*, 266–272.

Wang, S., Baillargeon, R., & Brueckner, L. (2004). Young infants' reasoning about hidden objects: Evidence from violation-of-expectation tasks with test trials. *Cognition, 93*, 167–198.

Witherington, D. C., Campos, J. J., Anderson, D. I., Lejeune, L., & Seah, E. (2005). Avoidance of heights on the visual cliff in newly walking infants. *Infancy, 7*, 285–298.

8

Learning in Infants' Object Perception, Object-Directed Action, and Tool Use

AMY NEEDHAM, DUKE UNIVERSITY

During the first year of life, infants experience objects through multiple modalities of exploration, including visual, oral, and manual. This exploratory activity is one of the richest sources of information about objects that infants generate (Ruff, 1984; Gibson, 1988; Rochat, 1989). Even so, we know relatively little about the specific ways in which this activity promotes learning and how infants' subsequent encounters with an object are affected by their prior exploration of it. What do infants learn when exploring objects via one or more of these modalities that can be brought to bear during later encounters? How prior experiences influence subsequent perceptual, cognitive, and motor processing is the focus of this chapter.

Many researchers have investigated connections among perception, action, and cognition in early development (Bushnell & Boudreau, 1993; Bertenthal, 1996; Hofstadter & Reznick, 1996; Adolph 1997; Diamond, 2000; von Hofsten, 2000; Bell, 2001; Keen, 2003). These questions have taken on new significance over the past several years, as the neural bases of various perceptual, motor, and cognitive skills are being established. For example, there has been increasing interest in the interplay between processes that are thought to have purely visual–cognitive relevance (potentially subserved by the ventral pathway of visual processing) and those that are thought to have relevance for action (potentially subserved by the dorsal pathway of visual processing). The relations between the "what" and the "where" or "how" pathways have been of interest in the adult literature, and researchers have begun to investigate the developmental origins of the interactions between these pathways.

One question that is often raised about the relations among perception, action, and cognition is the extent to which we are aware of various aspects of our perceptual and motor processing. Certainly some aspects of perceptual and motor skill are outside our awareness. The Müller-Lyer illusion, in which observers see two lines of equal length as being of different lengths because there are arrowhead- (angles in) or arrow-tail (angles out) lines attached to each end, is one example. This illusion persists even when the observer measures both lines and can confirm that the lines are equal in length. Similarly, we tend to be unaware of the motor processes that we employ to ride a bike or catch a ball. However, many perceptual and motor processes are affected by learning or knowledge. One example in the visual domain is that learning new concepts affects perceptual judgments (Gold-stone, 1994; Gauthier, Williams, Tarr, & Tanaka, 1998). In the motor domain, our actions on objects anticipate the expected weight of the object (Gordon, Westling, Cole, & Johansson, 1993; Flanagan, King, Wolpert, & Johansson, 2001) and our future actions with the object (Claxton, Keen, & McCarty, 2003). These phenomena suggest that there are relations among these processes. I give examples in this chapter of how learning is a key contributor to all three.

ORIGINS OF PERCEPTUAL, MOTOR, AND COGNITIVE PROCESSES

One of the more comprehensive accounts of infants' developing skill in interpreting and interacting with the physical world was advanced by Gibson and Pick (2000). According to their approach, perception and action provide critical inputs for each other—perception allows for action, and action allows for perception. Taken together, perceptual-motor activity provides the critical input needed by children's cognitive systems to help them develop expectations about the world around them.

According to this view, infants show evidence of at least four hallmarks of human behavior during the first year of life: seeking and using order, exercising agency, demonstrating prospectivity, and exhibiting flexibility. These behaviors are present in all humans, and evidence can be found for them early in development. Still, relatively little is known about the specific ways in which each of these abilities develops. In this chapter, I will focus on the development of infants' knowledge in two domains: seeking and using order and exercising agency. In both of these domains, I will also present evidence for flexibility, making an argument for the role of learning in producing flexibility in each of these domains.

Humans (Palmer, 1999) and other animals (Cook, Goto, & Brooks, 2005) identify the orderly way in which the world is organized and use this to their benefit. This "order" could be the orderly way the world looks and sounds (e.g., gestalt principles of perceptual organization; statistical properties of speech sounds) or the orderly ways in which events transpire (e.g., when a moving ball hits a stationary ball, the stationary ball starts moving). Agency refers to an understanding of the self as an intentional actor, in control of at least some aspects of the environment. Studies by Rovee-Collier, Sullivan, Enright, Lucas, and Fagen (1980) and Rochat and Striano (1999), among others, provide evidence that infants take note of the effects they have on their environment. Flexibility is a general property of cognition, perception, and action that is not typically thought of as one of infants' strengths. In fact, infants' cognition and behavior are often thought of as rigid. This is due, at least in part, to infant cognition being tied to the learning context. What is learned in one context is often not extended to other contexts, leading to the conclusion that infants' knowledge or behavior is not under their own control but rather is rigidly tied to the context (Boller & Rovee-Collier, 1994). To the extent that we see evidence for flexibility in perception and action, then, we have evidence that these processes are not directly given by the context or by modular, immutable processes but rather are influenced by the infant's experience. One goal of this chapter is to provide evidence for flexibility in infants' perception of and action upon objects.

Seeking and Using Order

It has long been known that humans search for order in the world around them—many cues for recovering depth from two dimensions demonstrate how the visual system can exploit regularities in the environment. What is the developmental trajectory of this tendency? Over the past 25 years, much has been learned about the developmental origins of the ordering of the perceptual world in both space and time (e.g., van Giffen & Haith, 1983; Slater, Mattock, & Brown, 1990; Canfield & Haith, 1991; Slater, Mattock, Brown, & Bremner, 1991; Quinn & Bhatt, 2005). These findings show that even young infants are unlikely to experience the "great blooming, buzzing confusion," that James imagined young infants were stuck within. The developmental trajectory for this tendency appears to be one of early competence rather than a protracted period of development. This is not to say that learning is not a critically important component of these skills. We will return to this topic after describing some of the work on infants' use of generic parsing principles to determine object boundary locations.

Object Segregation Using Generic Parsing Principles

Our early work on object perception focused on infants' ability to segregate objects or see two stationary, adjacent objects as separate from each other (Needham & Baillargeon, 1997; Needham & Kaufman, 1997; Needham, 1998, Needham & Baillargeon, 1998; Needham, 1999b, 2000). When we began this work, there was evidence that infants could use spatial separations and common motion to segregate objects, but there was no evidence that other cues (e.g., featural cues such as shape, color, or pattern) were used for this purpose by infants in the first year of life (Kellman & Spelke, 1983; Kestenbaum, Termine, & Spelke, 1987; Spelke, 1990; Spelke et al., 1993). Because at the time there was no evidence that infants could use object features to define object boundaries during the first year, we wanted to first revisit the question of whether or not there were conditions under which infants would use object features to identify boundaries between stationary, adjacent objects.

Our first investigations into this issue asked whether infants would use a collection of cues, all leading to the same interpretation of the display. In one study, 8.5-month-old infants were shown two objects that differed in many attributes: shape,

Figure 8–1. Curved cylinder and box display used in studies of infants' use of object attributes and prior experience in object segregation. Reprinted from Infant Behavior and Development, 21, Needham, A., & Baillargeon, R., Effects of prior experience in 4.5-month-old infants' object segregation, 1–24, Copyright (1998), with permission from Elsevier.

color, pattern, texture (see Fig. 8–1). The two objects sat side by side on a supporting surface. If the infants were unable to use the differences in object attributes to parse the display, they should see the two objects as connected to each other. In contrast, if the infants were able to parse the objects' surfaces into separate units on the basis of differences in shape, color, pattern, and/or texture, they should see the display as clearly composed of two separate objects.

We tested the infants' perception of the display by giving the infants a brief exposure to the stationary display and then moving the display in a way that was consistent with the composition being either a single object or two separate objects. This was done by pulling one object to the side and the other object of the pair moved along with it or remained stationary. The infants' time spent looking at each event was measured and their averages were compared statistically. These analyses revealed that the infants saw the surfaces that comprised the cylinder and those that comprised the box as belonging to separate objects. These studies were the first evidence in the literature that infants in the first year of life could parse stationary, adjacent objects into two separate units. Additional studies supported this conclusion (Needham & Baillargeon, 1997; Needham & Kaufman, 1997). These findings raised many interesting questions for further study, and the one we focused on initially was investigating the developmental trajectory of infants' skill in segregating objects.

This line of questions is important because knowing when these skills actually develop could help identify the mechanisms underlying their development. To study the development of infants' object segregation, we used a display that had been useful in our initial work on this question—4.5- and 6.5-month-old infants were tested using the curved cylinder and box display and the move-apart and move-together test events as described above.

Unlike the 8.5-month-old infants, who looked reliably longer at the move-together than at the move-apart event, the younger infants looked about equally at the two events, suggesting that they did not perceive this display as being clearly composed of two separate objects. Instead, they had an indeterminate percept of the display—looking about equally at the move-together and move-apart test events.

Before embracing the conclusion that infants become capable of using objects' attributes to determine object boundaries between 6.5 and 8.5 months of age, we sought to determine whether small changes in the display that would simplify the display's spatial layout would facilitate younger infants' segregation of it. We created the straight cylinder and box display, which was the same as the curved cylinder and box display, but with a straightened cylinder and box that was turned slightly so that a flat side instead of a corner faced the baby. These changes produced objects that were more geometrically shaped and a boundary between the objects that may have been more easily interpreted. The infants were tested using the same method as before (using move-apart and move-together test events). The results showed that the infants at both ages looked reliably longer at the move-together than at the move-apart event, indicating that they parsed the display as two separate objects that they did not expect to move as a whole. Thus, infants showed us their tendency to perceive order in their environment when we used this simpler version of the cylinder and box display. These findings pushed the relevant age range of the origins of this tendency to impose order on the visual world back to the early part of the first year of life, a conclusion that was replicated in Needham (2000). These findings marked an important advance in understanding the mechanisms underlying this development; we will return to this issue later in the chapter.

However, we were still left with a rather large set of cues and types of information that infants could have used to parse this display (we set up our initial studies purposefully to "stack the deck" with multiple cues the infants could use). Our first question was whether we could identify the critical differences between these two displays that led to infants' different interpretations of the displays. Recall that it was not until infants were eight months of age that they parsed the curved cylinder and box display into two units; but infants as young as four months of age parsed the straight cylinder and box display into two units. One of the most prominent differences between these two displays was the boundary where the two objects came together. In the curved cylinder display, this boundary was oblique, relative to the infant's line of sight; in the straight cylinder display, the boundary was more or less aligned with the infant's line of sight. It was possible that this difference in the appearance of the boundary between the two objects was primarily responsible for the change in infants' percept. We took a straightforward approach to this question: We placed a screen in front of the boundary. If infants' perception of the displays were altered by this manipulation, we would know that the boundary was a critical piece of information for the segregation of the test display. However, if infants' perception of the displays was unaffected, we would know that the specific components of the boundary were not a key component in infants' parsing. Our results showed (somewhat surprisingly, from our perspective) that infants' segregation of these displays was unaffected by the occlusion of the boundary. These results indicated that the boundary was not the key piece of information about the display composition, and served as confirmation of our initial findings.

We went on to investigate infants' use of other features of the display, such as the form features (e.g., object shape) and the surface features (e.g., color and pattern) (Needham, 1999). Developmental differences in infants' use of these two classes of features have been found by others (Wilcox, 1999), with infants using form features before using surface features. Our results were in line with these findings—specifically, infants parsed the displays according to the shape information that was provided within the display, but seemed to ignore the color and pattern information. These findings should be followed up with additional studies, but seem to suggest a consistent approach that infants have to perceptual/cognitive tasks—considering shape as more reliable or more important information that surface features such as color and pattern.

Flexibility in Object Perception

The previous section provided ample evidence that infants learn about the visual regularities of objects and apply heuristics to determine the locations of object boundaries in novel scenes, which they probably encounter quite often.

Our investigation into flexibility in infants' object perception began with one of the findings from the previous section—that 4.5-month-old infants do not detect a boundary between the curved yellow cylinder and the tall blue box (see Fig. 8–1). Rather than perceiving this display as composed of two separate objects (as older infants do), they regard it as ambiguous. We embarked upon a set of studies that provided infants with a brief prior exposure to one or more objects that might alter their interpretation of the this test display (Needham & Baillargeon, 1998; Needham, 2001; Dueker, Modi, & Needham, 2003; Needham, Dueker, & Lockhead, 2005).

In the first study, infants saw either the test box or the test cylinder for 5 or 15 seconds immediately before testing (Needham & Baillargeon, 1998). In the test (as in the initial study), the infants saw either the move-apart or the move-together test event. If infants applied their prior experience to the parsing of the test display, they should have looked reliably longer at the move-together than at the move-apart event, suggesting that they parsed the display into two separate objects. Facilitation in parsing the test display was found after 5-seconds exposure to the box or 15-seconds exposure to the more complex cylinder, suggesting that more complex objects might require more time to encode and represent than simpler objects. These results demonstrate that 4.5-month-old infants represent and recognize objects, and that recognition facilitates segregation. These findings were robust enough to be maintained after a 24-hour delay and a change in context (in these memory studies, the initial exposure time to the object was in the infant's home and lasted for 2 min instead of 5–15 s).

In subsequent research, my colleagues and I asked what kinds of changes between the initial and subsequent views of the test box would be noticed by infants. That is, which small changes in the box (e.g., in the blue background color or in the color or shape of the white square texture elements covering the box) introduced between infants' initial and subsequent views of it would they notice, and which would they not notice? It stands to reason that feature changes that are noticed must be part of infants' initial representation of the object. Changes not noticed may be absent from infants' representation of the object, or the features of the object representation and those of the test object may not be adequately compared. Because we know that infants apply their prior exposure with the exact test box or test cylinder to parse the test display (discussed in the previous section), we conclude that infants would not apply their prior experience to the parsing of the objects in the test display if they detected the change in the object. Thus, we take a lack of "success" in the segregation task as evidence for discrimination between the initial and subsequent views of the object. More importantly, these findings help us determine how substantial a change between initial and subsequent views infants will tolerate before failing to detect the connection between them.

We have now tested many feature changes using this paradigm, and our findings indicate that even changes in small details of the test box prevented the use of prior experience by 4.5-month-old infants (Needham, 2001). Changes in the background color (alone) and the texture element color (alone) are detected by 4.5-month-old infants. Indeed, the only changes we have introduced that did not interfere with the facilitation typically provided by prior experience were texture element shape (when they were white circles during their first encounter and white squares in test) and the spatial orientation of the box (horizontal box to vertical box).

These results support two general conclusions. First, because even a minor change in object features interfered with the facilitation provided by prior experience, but a substantial change in spatial orientation does not, infants may share adults' tendency to look to object features when determining the identity of an object and deciding whether or not they have seen it before. Second, 4.5-month-old infants' representations of objects are surprisingly detailed and elaborate. They encode and represent objects' prominent features, such as background color, in addition to subtler features, such as the color of the small texture elements covering the box's surfaces.

It is surprising that young infants use object features in this object recognition–based task that they do not use in similar tasks. Many studies have asked why color is detected reasonably well by 3 to 4 months of age but is not used in object-individuation tasks until 11 months of age or so (e.g., see Wilcox & Woods, this volume). Also, our own work shows that infants' segregation of objects is not as affected by color and pattern as it is by object shape (Needham, 1999b). But in the current task, a change in either the color of the background of the box or in the color of the small square texture elements on the box was enough to prevent 4.5-month-old infants' transfer of experience with one box to the segregation of another. Why do infants use color in this task but not in the others? This is a puzzling question. One possibility is that the subtleties of the experimental contexts (the way the events unfold over the course of the experimental session) lead infants to attend to and represent different aspects of the objects in these different procedures. How infants' attention is drawn to different aspects of an object or event is an intriguing topic for future research.

Although infants do use color to recognize a previously seen object in this paradigm, we are left with the conclusion that infants this age are unlikely to apply what they had learned about one object to another object, even though it shared nearly all of that object's features (e.g., size, shape, most of its color and pattern, etc.). Could we identify conditions that would encourage infants to generalize? Certainly, generalization is an important skill for learning about the world and for extending one's knowledge appropriately. Perhaps in this case simultaneous prior exposure to *multiple* similar objects would encourage generalization to a novel object that could be considered part of the category.

In the next set of experiments, infants received simultaneous prior exposure to a set of three boxes, no one of which was an effective cue to the composition of the test display (Needham et al., 2005). As in the last set of studies, we expected that evidence for infants' generalization of prior experience would come from their successful parsing of the test display into two separate objects. Our results suggested that sets of boxes that had some variability but were not too dissimilar from the test box allowed infants to form representations that were effective in helping them parse the test display. Exposure to three *different* boxes seemed to be necessary—three identical boxes were ineffective and any two members of an effective set of three were not effective. Sets of three boxes that were somewhat more variable (in terms of features such as background color, texture element shape, etc.) were not effective facilitators of infants' subsequent parsing of the test display (Needham et al., 2005). Thus, infants create representations during these brief prior exposures that are different, depending both on the number of objects in the set and on the features of the objects in the set. We have shown one way in which these representations can be used.

How robust is this process of infants' use of prior experience in object segregation? As reported here, there is no reason to believe that these effects last beyond the immediate lab situation. However, we have investigated the effects of introducing a substantial delay (1–3 days) between the initial and subsequent encounters with the box. These studies have revealed that 24 hours after a 2-minute exposure to the box or the cylinder, infants use the prior exposure to segregate the test display. By 72 hours after the 2-minute exposure, there is no longer any evidence of infants' having received the prior exposure (Dueker et al., 2003).

One question raised by these findings is how complete or accurate infants' representations of the previously seen object are after 24 hours. This question has been investigated by Rovee-Collier and her colleagues (e.g., Bhatt & Rovee-Collier, 1994), who have found that the details of infants' representations tend to be inaccessible after some delay. If this fading of details were to happen in the current paradigm as well, prior experiences that did not facilitate segregation at immediate testing might become more effective after a delay, as the discrepant details are no longer present to prevent facilitation. This prediction was supported in a study in which infants were given a 2-minute exposure to the blue box with red squares before they saw the test display (featuring the box with white squares on it). Although prior exposure to this red-squares box was ineffective at immediate test, it was effective at facilitating segregation of the test display after a 24-hour delay. Thus, as predicted by our hypothesis and Rovee-Collier's prior results, infants' relative inability to retain the details of their memory representations may facilitate their extension of prior experience. Although one would not want to call this a generalization per se, the outcomes of these two processes are indistinguishable. This result demonstrates another way in which "less is more" (Newport, 1990). Remembering fewer of an object's details makes the representation relevant to more situations.

Another way that infants' generalization could be facilitated is by using representations that are based on multiple exemplars rather than representations of individual objects. In adults it has been found that representations of a category are useful for a longer period than are representations of an individual (Posner & Keele, 1968). To investigate this phenomenon in infants, we introduced a 72-hour delay (long enough to render a prior exposure to the test box itself ineffective) between the brief exposure to a group of similar boxes and testing with the cylinder and box display. These findings revealed that infants' representation of a category of boxes remained useful for generalization purposes for a longer period of time than did the representation of the single box that would itself appear in the test display.

The extent to which these contrived lab procedures reflect what might happen in the real world may be a concern for the reader. How ecologically valid is this process as we have tested it? To address this potential concern, we have adapted this procedure to be less artificial. Specifically, in our next study, the prior exposure occurred as a result of infants' everyday experiences outside the lab. The object of interest was an object often seen by infants—a key ring (see Fig. 8–2) (Needham, Cantlon, & Ormsbee Holley, 2006). According to a strict application of organizational principles using object features, the display should be seen as composed of (at least) two separate objects—the keys on one side of the screen, and the separate ring on the other side. However, to the extent that infants recognize the display as a member of a familiar category—key rings—they should group the keys and ring into a single unit that should move as a whole.

Our findings indicate that by 8.5 months of age, infants parse the display into a single unit, expecting the keys and ring to move together. Younger infants do

Figure 8–2. Key ring display. Reprinted from Cognitive Psychology, 53, Needham, A., Cantlon, J. F., & Ormsbee Holley, S. M., Infants' use of category knowledge and object attributes when segregating objects at 8.5 months of age, 345–360, Copyright (2006), with permission from Elsevier.

not see the display as a single unit and instead parse the keys and ring into separate units. Infants of both ages parsed an altered display in which the identifiable portions of the key ring were hidden by patterned covers, as being composed of two separate units. Together, these findings provide evidence that the studies of controlled prior exposure described in the previous section are consistent with the process as it occurs under natural circumstances. Infants' ordinary experiences present them with multiple similar exemplars of key rings, and presumably their representations of these objects allow infants to apply their prior experiences to novel (and yet similar) instances of the key-ring category. This application of representations from prior experiences results in infants' interpretation of the novel key-ring display as a single unit rather than as two separate units, as would be expected from feature-based principles alone. It is worth mentioning that key rings are tools, and therefore infants could be learning about their function in addition to their appearance. Future studies in which we test whether infants have expectations about key-ring function or just about the composition of a key ring, and what experiences would lead the seven-month-old infants to develop expectations about the composition of a key ring will help determine the extent to which concepts have been formed and on what basis.

Agency

The development of agency is a topic that reaches far back into the history of developmental psychology, with luminaries in the field such as James Mark Baldwin, Jean Piaget, and Lev Vygotsky discussing its importance. Changes resulting from this achievement could be observed in infants' motor skills, their cognitive skills, and possibly other skills as well. But of course new motor skills bring with them new opportunities for learning. How could infants' agentive experiences contribute to their perceptual-motor repertoire?

It is possible that infants begin to experience the feeling of agency as they successfully bring an object in their hand up to their mouth for further exploration. We know that visual and oral exploration of objects becomes much more prevalent between two and five months of age (Rochat, 1989), and one possibility is that the agentive experiences that accompany this kind of exploration serve to fuel their motivation to start reaching for objects. Others have indicated ways in which different motor skills (e.g., reaching and crawling) are related (Goldfield, 1995). It may also be true that these increases in object exploration allow infants to learn about the visual regularities of the objects that populate their world. So, perhaps infants who explore objects more actively have had more of a chance to learn that object boundaries are often located at points of discontinuity in shape, color, size, and so on. That is, they may learn through their exploration of objects that individual objects tend to be uniform on these dimensions.

To seek out evidence to begin to evaluate these ideas, my colleagues and I have undertaken a series of studies investigating the role of infants' actions in their perception and exploration of objects. In one study, four-month-old infants' performance in an object-exploration task was compared with their performance in an object-segregation task (Needham, 2000). Two standard tasks were used. In the object-exploration task, infants were handed a series of red teethers one at a time and were allowed to freely explore these objects. Infants' behavior was videotaped and later coded. In the object-segregation task, infants were shown a display consisting of two different-looking objects, and the amount of time they spent looking at either the move-together or the move-apart test event was measured. First, we separated the infants based on their performance in the exploration task into more-active and less-active explorers. The more-active explorers spend at least two thirds of the time holding each object in active visual or oral exploration of it; the less-active explorers spent less than two-thirds of the holding time engaged in visual or oral exploration. We then compared the more-active and less-active explorers' responses to the move-apart and move-together events of the segregation task. The more-active explorers showed a significant difference between the amount of time spent looking at the move-together and move-apart events, suggesting that they had parsed this display into two separate objects. In contrast, the less-active explorers spent about the same amount of time looking at the two events, indicating that they were unsure of whether the test display consisted of a single object or two separate objects. These results support the idea that by actively exploring objects infants can learn about objects—in this case, they can learn about how attributes like object shape can be used to predict the locations of object boundaries.

These findings led us to take seriously the possibility that specific aspects of infants' actions on objects were promoting learning about objects. To further investigate other relations between action and learning, my colleagues and I designed a study in which infants' action capabilities were manipulated and their potential for learning measured (Needham, Barrett, & Peterman, 2002). In this study, pre-reaching infants were given simulated reaching experience using "sticky mittens," mittens with Velcro "loop" material covering the palms, which allowed them to reach out and "grasp" objects with the Velcro "hook" material covering the object's edges. The infants' parents trained them on the use of these mittens once a day for about 10 minutes a day over a period of about two weeks at home. After this experience, the infants were brought to the lab for two object-exploration tasks; a group of inexperienced infants was also tested, to permit a comparison. In the prehension task, infants (held by a parent) sat at a table and were allowed to look at and swat at objects on the table. In the object-exploration task, infants were handed a set of red rubber teethers, one at a time, for free exploration.

Our results revealed superior performance by the experienced infants on almost every measure. In the prehension task, the experienced infants looked at the objects more and they swatted at them more while looking at them (suggesting that they were contacting the objects intentionally). In the object-exploration task, the infants engaged in more visual and manual exploration of the objects, and they showed more switching between visual and oral modalities during exploration than did the infants who had not received the simulated reaching experience. Thus, introducing a novel perceptual-motor experience over two weeks promotes attention to and exploration of objects.

Does this kind of learning also occur as a result of a brief experience with simulated reaching? Our initial findings indicate that it does. We have created a testing procedure in which infants learn about the utility of the mittens and then practice with them all in one lab session. In this procedure, infants receive pre- and posttests with an object-exploration task. Between these trials was one of two kinds of trial—sticky-mittens trials or object-dance trials. In the sticky-mittens trials, infants were fitted with sticky mittens, shown that the objects would stick to the mittens, and then allowed to swat at one object at a time for about 10 minutes. In the object-dance trials, infants were fitted with non-sticky mittens and watched as the experimenter took one object at a time through a precise "dance," with motions roughly corresponding to the motions seen during the sticky-mittens trials, also for 10 minutes. Our results showed that, although there were no differences among the measures during pretest, the infants with sticky mittens experience were more engaged in the teether during the posttest trial, based on a number of measures, compared to the infants who watched the object dance. Thus, a protracted period of practice was not necessary to produce the increase in object exploration, providing additional evidence for flexibility in early perceptual-motor behavior.

One might argue that we see evidence of flexibility in young infants' actions on objects because these processes are still very malleable at this early stage in development. Perhaps later in the first year of life, after actions on objects are much more smoothly practiced, we would not find such flexibility. To investigate this possibility, we studied 9- and 12-month-old infants' reaching for a block display that was designed to look like a single piece (alternating blue and white stripes covered its surfaces) (Needham, 1999a). To assess the effects of prior exposure, we compared two groups of infants—those who saw that the blocks were connected as a single rigid unit, and those who saw that the blocks were separate. Infants received this information about the composition of the display immediately before the display was deposited on the table within the infant's reach. Our question was whether infants who saw that the display was composed of separate objects would reach for the display differently than would infants who saw that the display was one connected piece.

The results showed that the 9.5-month-old infants did not reach differently for the block based on the number of blocks that they saw prior to testing, but the 12.5-month-old infants did. These older infants were more likely to reach with one hand when the display had been shown as a single unit, but with two hands when the display had been shown as two separate units. Also, the older infants tended to avoid the center separation point when placing their grasps after seeing it as two separate objects, but not after seeing it as a single object. Here we have shown that infants' prior experiences with objects affect their subsequent actions on those objects late in the first year of life, even when the prior experiences are brief and only visual in nature. Subsequent work by Vishton and his colleagues (Vishton, Ware, & Badger, 2005) has shown that even six-month-old infants show differences in reaching for otherwise identical 1-object and 2-object displays. Future research would identify how these subtle differences in reaching behavior might be influenced by factors such as postural changes and locomotor changes (e.g., Corbetta & Bojczyk, 2002).

Flexibility and Rigidity in Infants' Tool Use

Looking past the actual grasp of the object, researchers have begun to study the development of tool use in infancy (e.g., McCarty, Clifton, & Collard, 1999, 2001). The use of tools to accomplish certain goals can identify dependencies between perception and action (Creem & Proffitt, 2001). Indeed, infants' perception of a key ring already signals their developing knowledge of tools, with older infants succeeding in the perception task but younger infants failing (Needham et al., 2006). Studying the early development of tool use provides important information about the early interactions between object knowledge and object-directed actions. Our first study of tool use investigated infants' use of a familiar tool to accomplish a goal not typically associated with that particular tool (Barrett, Davis, & Needham, 2007). Specifically, we showed 12- to 15-month-old infants how to use a spoon to automatically activate lights inside a box by simply inserting the handle into the hole. Because of the size of the hole in the box, it was necessary to grasp the bowl of the spoon and insert the handle through the hole to turn on the lights. We compared infants' performance on this task using the spoon to their performance using a novel tool that shared some of the spoon's characteristics (see Fig. 8–3).

Even though the experimenter modeled this action, and even though the infants succeeded in the task at high levels when the opening for the tool was large enough to accommodate either end of the tool, their performance fell to low levels when they were required to grasp the spoon by its bowl and use its handle to perform the action. Using the novel tool in this way did not produce such a decrement in infants' performance. Thus, by 12 to 15 months of age, infants seem to be able to identify a novel spoon, recall the appropriate location at which to grasp

Figure 8–3. Novel tool activating the lightbox. Photo taken from infant's perspective on the lightbox, with the experimenter activating the lights (as was done in the familiarization portion of the study).

the spoon, and appropriately apply the spoon to the task (using the bowl, not the grasping end or handle). In this case, one can see evidence of both flexibility and rigidity in infants' behavior. Flexibility can be seen in infants' willingness to apply a familiar tool to a novel object to accomplish a novel task. Rigidity can be seen in infants' unwillingness to grasp and use the tool in a novel way (i.e., to grasp the bowl and use the handle as the action end).

To follow up on these findings, we sought to understand how this behavioral rigidity was created—is this something that required days and weeks and months of exposure, or did it develop relatively quickly? To answer this question, we trained infants to use the novel tool in a certain way to see whether we could produce both flexibility and rigidity to resemble something like what we observed with infants' use of the spoon.

In this study, infants were trained with one or another use of the novel tool over the course of one week (Barrett et al., 2007). All of the infants were trained to use the tool to push pom-poms out of a clear plastic tube; half were trained to grasp the straight end, and half were trained to grasp the round end. In the test, all of the infants were given two new tasks to do with the novel tool; infants' performance on these tasks would help us understand what they learned during training. One task involved inserting the tool into a box (the lightbox task described above), and another involved encircling a post with the round end of the tool. If infants' performance on the lightbox task was superior to their performance on the encircling task, we would conclude that what infants learned during training was more about how the tool functioned (as an insertion tool) than about which end was to be grasped. However, another possibility is that infants' performance in the test tasks might be predicted by which end of the novel tool they learned to grasp during training. Because one of the test tasks required a round-end grasp for success (the lightbox task), and the other required a straight-end grasp for success (the encircling task), which end infants regarded as the tool's handle might play an important role in their success in each task.

Our findings supported the latter explanation above: Infants' training transferred to the test task that required the same grasp for success as had their training task, not to the test task that required that the tool function as it had in training. At least early in infants' learning about how to use a new tool, they learn more about how to grasp the tool than about how the tool functions. How the representations of grasp location interact with knowledge of object function for infants, older children, and adults is an important topic for future research (Creem & Proffitt, 2001; Creem-Regehr & Lee, 2005; Handy, Borg, Turk, Tipper, Grafton, & Gazzaniga, 2005).

INTEGRATION

Infant Learning and Flexibility in Perceptual-Motor Domains

In this chapter, I have reviewed evidence for flexibility in infants' perception of, actions on, and use of objects during the first year of life. Having seen a box before, infants know on a subsequent encounter that a boundary should be present between that box and an adjacent novel object. Having seen a block before, infants know that it should be separate from an adjacent identical object and should separate from it when they pick it up. Seeing just one demonstration of how a novel tool works (e.g., that sticky mittens pick objects up when one swipes close to them) allows young infants to use the mittens to pick objects up. Having practice using a particular tool (or even just watching it being used by someone else), infants know where the tool should be grasped and how it should be used. Infants' perception and action are not rigidly defined by the stimulus itself or by the testing context but rather are flexible and influenced by the infant's history of perceiving and acting.

What do these findings reveal to us about infant perception, action, and cognition (specifically, learning)? There are multiple answers to this question, depending on the theoretical perspective one adopts to interpret the findings. For years, perceptual development has been conceptualized from one of two perspectives: the cognitive–enrichment view and the ecological–differentiation view. The cognitive–enrichment view assumes that the visual image is incomplete and must be augmented or enriched by knowledge about the world in order to form an accurate interpretation. This view is often espoused by those who consider perception to be a cognitive activity and by computer-vision researchers (e.g., Marr, 1982). The ecological–differentiation view holds that the visual image is quite rich all by itself and needs no augmentation or enrichment. However, there are differences in how a given image is interpreted by various observers; these differences are due to observers having different affordances or understandings about how the person fits within the environment. Differences in affordances that have been learned by various people can be a result of differences in their ages, experiences, or even motivational states. From the cognitive–enrichment view, the interpretation of the findings would be that cognitive factors (e.g., memory) are mediators of perceptual skills, motor skills, and their combination, even in infancy. Perhaps infants form a template during prior experience that they can then use to match up with subsequent views of similar objects. Like adults' perceptions, infants' perceptions of objects and events and their actions on objects are imbued with their intentions and their knowledge about what they see and do. From the ecological perspective, we would extract a different meaning from these studies. Infants' perception and action are inextricably connected to each other and are guided by affordances. As infants are exposed to and learn more about the world around them, these affordances change, resulting in a change in the resulting percept. No matter which view one takes, these findings demonstrate how prior experiences influence subsequent perception and action.

Learning Object Categories

Rather than being uncertain about the composition and function of objects well into early childhood, infants, according to our evidence, actively observe and process the objects being used around and by them. They learn about individual objects and extend their experience to subsequent encounters with those objects and to some highly similar objects they have not yet seen. Although generalization is somewhat limited at the point in development that we studied (4.5 months), normal cognitive processes such as categorization, memory, and forgetting help infants apply the knowledge gained through prior experience more broadly than they otherwise would.

Initially, infants may learn general heuristics or generic parsing principles that help them parse objects based on similarity. These skills can be thought of as quite general, but the decisions are always being made at a specific or concrete level. So, it is difficult to say how abstract or general these principles are. Also, our results identify various ways in which infants' cognitive activity can take on the appearance of generalization. First, there is actual generalization, in which infants apply something they have learned about one object or set of objects to a discriminably different object. But then there is the forgetting of the details of an object's appearance, which is not true generalization but can result in the same outcome as generalization would. Presumably, "true" generalization becomes more prevalent under appropriate conditions as infants are remembering more object details for a longer period of time, but these relations have not been established.

After accumulating more experience, infants learn categories that represent exceptions to these rules. Objects such as key rings will be parsed incorrectly quite consistently, using the similarity heuristics. Overriding the output of these principles may be difficult, but it provides a more accurate interpretation of the world. Of course, there is nothing special about key rings—infants must create these categories for many kinds of objects they encounter.

This chapter contains many examples of infants seeking order in the world around them. Together with prior research, the evidence is quite striking, and one simply cannot question the idea that infants' perception of the world around them is orderly rather than chaotic and impossible to parse. We have also provided evidence that infants have an early capacity for agency—that, when given the opportunity, infants have no trouble producing actions on objects earlier than they normally would. They quickly abandon the idea that they are incapable of accessing objects in their immediate surroundings (Needham et al., 2002). We have presented evidence for flexibility in infants' perception of objects, their actions on objects, and their use of objects. Infants are remarkably flexible creatures—their perceptions and actions do not proceed according to generic rules but instead are influenced by their varied experiences.

CONCLUSIONS

In summary, this chapter has brought together issues in perception, action, and cognition to investigate how infants' prior experiences with objects influence their subsequent perceptual and motor activity involving those objects (or similar objects). In general, it must be true that these prior experiences help infants form more accurate parsings of and plans of actions on single objects and groups of objects. Forming accurate interpretations of objects in scenes is important for understanding the stream of action going on around you (e.g., Baldwin, Baird, Saylor, & Clark, 2001) and for acting on the objects in that stream (Woodward, 1998). Our research suggests that infants have flexibility in the way they perceive and act on objects that reflects a dynamic, online processing of the objects and events around them. Thus, something about infants' prior experience (whether it is more knowledge or different affordances) leads them to perceive and act differently than they would without this prior experience. That we do tend to agree on how objects look and how best to act on objects may have more to do with the consistency in the structure of the world around us than with any consistency in our neural structures. Despite these advances in our understanding of infants' perceptual and motor skills, the intriguing puzzles presented to us by infants as they explore and learn about objects remain mysterious and entice us to discover more.

References

Adolph, K. E. (1997). Learning in the development of infant locomotion. *Monographs of the Society for Research in Child Development, 56* (3, Serial No. 251).

Baldwin, D. A., Baird, J. A., Saylor, M. M., & Clark, M. A. (2001). Infants parse dynamic action. *Child Development, 72,* 708–717.

Barrett, T. M., Davis, E. F., & Needham, A. (2007). Learning to use a tool in infancy. *Developmental Psychology, 43,* 352–368.

Bell, M. A. (2001). Brain electrical activity associated with cognitive processing during a looking version of the A-not-B task. *Infancy, 2,* 311–330.

Bertenthal, B. I. (1996). Origins and early development of perception, action, and representation. *Annual Review of Psychology, 47,* 431–459.

Bhatt, R. S., & Rovee-Collier, C. (1994). Perception and 24-hour retention of feature relations in infancy. *Developmental Psychology, 30,* 142–150.

Boller, K., & Rovee-Collier, C. (1994). Contextual updating of infants' reactivated memories. *Developmental Psychobiology, 27,* 241–256.

Bushnell, E. W., and Boudreau, J. P. (1993) Motor development and the mind: The potential role of motor abilities as a determinant of aspects of perceptual development. *Child Development, 64,* 1005–1021.

Canfield, R. L., & Haith, M. M. (1991). Young infants visual expectations for symmetric and asymmetric stimulus sequences. *Developmental Psychology, 27,* 198–208.

Claxton, L., Keen, R., & McCarty, M. (2003). Evidence of motor planning in infant reaching behavior. *Psychological Science, 14,* 354–356.

Cook, R. G., Goto, K., & Brooks, D. I. (2005). Avian detection and identification of perceptual organization in random noise. *Behavioural Processes, 69,* 79–95.

Corbetta, D., & Bojczyk, K. E. (2002). Infants return to two-handed reaching when they are learning to walk. *Journal of Motor Behavior, 34,* 83–95.

Creem, S. H., & Proffitt, D. R. (2001). Grasping objects by their handles: A necessary interaction between cognition and action. *Journal of Experimental Psychology: Human Perception and Performance, 27,* 218–228.

Creem-Regehr, S. H., & Lee, J. N. (2005). Neural representations of graspable objects: Are tools special? *Cognitive Brain Research, 22,* 457–469.

Diamond, A. (2000). Close interrelation of motor development and cognitive development and of the cerebellum and prefrontal cortex [Special issue: New directions for child development in the 21st century]. *Child Development, 71,* 44–56.

Dueker, G., Modi, A., & Needham, A. (2003). 4.5-month-old infants' learning, retention, and use of object boundary information. *Infant Behavior and Development, 26,* 588–605.

Flanagan, J. R., King, S., Wolpert, D. M., & Johansson, R. S. (2001). Sensorimotor prediction and memory in object manipulation. *Canadian Journal of Experimental Psychology, 55*, 89–97.

Gauthier, I., Williams, P., Tarr, M. J., & Tanaka, J. (1998). Training "greeble" experts: A framework for studying expert object recognition processes, *Vision Research, 38*, 2401–2428.

Gibson, E. J. (1988). Exploratory behavior in the development of perceiving, acting, and the acquiring of knowledge. *Annual Review of Psychology, 39*, 1–41.

Gibson, E. J., & Pick, A. D. (2000). *An ecological approach to perceptual learning and development.* New York: Oxford University Press.

Goldfield, E. C. (1995). *Emergent forms: Origins and early development of human action and perception.* New York: Oxford University Press.

Goldstone, R. L. (1994). Influences of categorization on perceptual discrimination. *Journal of Experimental Psychology: General, 123*, 178–200.

Gordon, A. M., Westling, G., Cole, K. J., & Johansson, R. S. (1993). Memory representations underlying motor commands used during manipulation of common and novel objects. *Journal of Neurophysiology, 69*, 1789–1796.

Handy, T. C., Borg, J. S., Turk, D. J. Tipper, C. M., Grafton, S. T., & Gazzaniga, M. S. (2005). Placeing a tool in the spotlight: spatial attention modulates visuomotor responses in cortex. *Neuroimage, 26*, 266–276.

Hofstadter, M., & Reznick, J. S. (1996). Response modality affects human infant delayed-response performance. *Child Development, 67*, 646–658.

Keen, R. (2003). Representation of objects and events: Why do infants look so smart and toddlers look so dumb? *Current Directions in Psychological Science, 12*, 79–83.

Kellman, P. J., & Spelke, E. S. (1983). Perception of partly occluded objects in infancy. *Cognitive Psychology, 15*, 483–524.

Kestenbaum, R., Termine, N., & Spelke, E. S. (1987). Perception of objects and object boundaries by three-month-old infants. *British Journal of Developmental Psychology, 5*, 367–383.

Marr, D. (1982). *Vision: A computational investigation into the human representation and processing of visual information.* San Francisco: Freeman.

McCarty, M. E., Clifton, R. K., & Collard, R. R. (1999). Problem solving in infancy: The emergence of an action plan. *Developmental Psychology, 35*, 1091–1101.

McCarty, M. E., Clifton, R. K., & Collard, R. R. (2001). The beginnings of tool use by infants and toddlers. *Infancy, 2*, 233–256.

Needham, A. (1998). Infants' use of featural information in the segregation of stationary objects. *Infant Behavior and Development, 21*, 47–76.

Needham, A. (1999a). How infants grasp two adjacent objects: Effects of perceived display composition on infants' actions. *Developmental Science, 2*, 219–233.

Needham, A. (1999b) The role of shape in 4-month-old infants' segregation of adjacent objects. *Infant Behavior and Development, 22*, 161–178.

Needham, A. (2000). Improvements in object exploration skills may facilitate the development of object segregation in early infancy. *Journal of Cognition and Development, 1*, 131–156.

Needham, A. (2001). Object recognition and object segregation in 4.5-month-old infants. *Journal of Experimental Child Psychology, 78*, 3–24.

Needham, A., & Baillargeon, R. (1997). Object segregation in 8-month-old infants. *Cognition, 62*, 121–149.

Needham, A., & Baillargeon, R. (1998). Effects of prior experience in 4.5-month-old infants' object segregation. *Infant Behavior and Development, 21*, 1–24.

Needham, A., Barrett, T., & Peterman, K. (2002). A pick-me-up for infants' exploratory skills: Early simulated experiences reaching for objects using "sticky mittens" enhances young infants' object exploration skills. *Infant Behavior and Development, 25,* 279–295.

Needham, A., Cantlon, J. F., & Ormsbee Holley, S. M. (2006). Infants' use of category knowledge and object attributes when segregating objects at 8.5 months of age. *Cognitive Psychology, 53,* 345–360.

Needham, A., Dueker, G., & Lockhead, G. (2005). Infants' formation and use of categories to segregate objects. *Cognition, 94,* 215–240.

Needham, A., & Kaufman, J. (1997). Infants' integration of information from different sources in object segregation [Special Issue: Perceptual Development]. *Early Development and Parenting, 6,* 137–147.

Newport, E. L. (1990). Maturational constraints on language learning. *Cognitive Science, 14,* 11–28.

Palmer, S. E. (1999). *Vision science: From photons to phenomenology.* Cambridge, MA: Bradford Books/MIT Press.

Posner, M. I., & Keele, S. W. (1968). On the genesis of abstract ideas. *Journal of Experimental Psychology, 77,* 353–63.

Quinn, P. C., & Bhatt, R. S. (2005). Learning perceptual organization in infancy. *Psychological Science, 16,* 511–515.

Rochat, P. (1989). Object manipulation and exploration in 2- to 5-month-old infants. *Developmental Psychology, 25,* 871–884.

Rochat, P., & Striano, T. (1999) Emerging self-exploration by 2-month-old infants. *Developmental Science, 2,* 206–218

Rovee-Collier, C. K., Sullivan, M. W., Enright, M., Lucas, D., & Fagen, J. W. (1980). Reactivation of infant memory. *Science, 208,* 1159–1161.

Ruff, H. A. (1984). Infants' manipulative exploration of objects: Effects of age and object characteristics. *Developmental Psychology,* 9–20.

Slater, A., Mattock, A., & Brown, E. (1990). Size constancy at birth: Newborn infants' responses to retinal and real size. *Journal of Experimental Child Psychology, 49,* 314–322.

Slater, A., Mattock, A., Brown, E., & Bremner, J. G., (1991). Form perception at birth: Cohen and Younger (1984) revisited. *Journal of Experimental Child Psychology, 51,* 395–406.

Spelke, E. S., (1990). Principles of object perception. *Cognitive Science, 14,* 29–56.

Spelke, E. S., Breinlinger, K., Jacobson, K., & Phillips, A. (1993). Gestalt relations and object perception: A developmental study. *Perception, 22,* 1483–1501.

van Giffen, K., & Haith, M. M. (1984). Infant visual response to Gestalt geometric forms. *Infant Behavior and Development, 7,* 335–346.

Vishton, P. M., Ware, E. A., & Badger, A. N. (2005). Different gestalt processing for different actions?: Comparing object-directed reaching and looking time measures. *Journal of Experimental Child Psychology, 90,* 89–113.

von Hofsten, C. (2000). On the early development of perception, action and cognition. In F. Lacerda, C. von Hofsten, and M. Heimann (Eds.), *Emerging Cognitive abilities in early infancy.* Hillsdale, N.J.: Erlbaum.

Wilcox, T. (1999). Object individuation: Infants' use of shape, size, pattern, and color. *Cognition, 72,* 125–166.

Woodward, A. L. (1998). Infants selectively encode the goal object of an actor's reach. *Cognition, 69,* 1–34.

9

Infants' Learning About Intentional Action

AMANDA WOODWARD, UNIVERSITY OF MARYLAND

A complete developmental account has two parts: a description of the focal aspect of psychological structure at various points in the course of development, and identification of the experiences and processes that give rise to this structure. In the study of infant cognitive development, there has often been a disconnect between these parts. Researchers who study conceptual structure in infants frequently neglect to investigate the mechanisms and experiences that give rise to this structure. On the other hand, although there have long been fruitful investigations of learning and change in infancy, by and large, these have not been recruited for understanding conceptual development in infants. A key motivation for this volume is to encourage the field to address this gap. In this chapter, I will attempt to do this in the domain of infant social cognition.

In the past two decades, powerful techniques have been developed for assessing infants' knowledge; chief among these are visual habituation or familiarization paradigms (see, for example, the chapters by Baillargeon, S. P. Johnson, Needham, Oakes, and Wilcox in this volume). Most often, this technique is used to ask whether infants at a particular age possess some piece of conceptual knowledge. Studies using this approach provided critical insights by revealing previously hidden aspects of conceptual structure in young infants. However, this approach provides only "snapshots" of infants' knowledge at various points and therefore sheds little light on the processes and experiences that may contribute to this knowledge. Indeed, it is sometimes concluded that when conceptual representations are found in infants, these representations must not depend on experience to emerge. A stronger test of this conclusion would require a closer look at infant experience and its relation to cognitive development.

In this chapter, I will consider the potential contributions of experience to infants' intentional-action knowledge. I will begin with the snapshots, outlining what infants know at various points in the first year. Then I will consider the potential role of experience in contributing to this knowledge, using the approaches that others have taken to address this issue with older children. Finally, I will turn to the question of how experience matters.

THE SNAPSHOTS: WHAT INFANTS KNOW
ABOUT INTENTIONAL ACTION

Fundamental to human experience is the perception that we live in a world of intentional agents. To adult eyes, the actions of others are not mere motions through space but are instead structured by goals, intentions, and perceptions. Adults interpret this action structure as reflecting the agent's psychological life. As the literature on theory of mind has elaborated, by three years of age, children possess detailed folk psychological concepts (Wellman, 1992). It is not yet clear how early in life folk psychological concepts can be traced (for varying perspectives on this issue, see Leslie, 1993; S. C. Johnson, 2000; Gergely & Csibra, 2003; Onishi & Baillargeon, 2005; Woodward, 2005). Nevertheless, it is clear that even in the first year of life, infants represent actions as structured with respect to external goals and objects of attention. Evidence for this ability comes from infants' looking times in familiarization and habituation experiments (Gergely, Nadasdy, Csibra, & Biro, 1995; Shimizu & S. C. Johnson, 2004; Luo & Baillargeon, 2005; Sommerville & Woodward, 2005; Woodward, 1998, 2005), their responses to social partners in controlled experimental settings (Behne, Carpenter, Call, & Tomasello, 2005; Carpenter, Nagell, & Tomasello, 1998; S. C. Johnson, Slaughter, & Carey, 1998), and their imitation of others' actions (Meltzoff, 1995; Hamlin, Hallinan, & Woodward, in press).

INSTRUMENTAL ACTIONS AS GOAL-DIRECTED

Consider the action depicted in Figure 9–1—a woman reaches for and grasps a ball. To adult eyes, this event is not just a series of physical movements and arrangements of body parts but rather an action that is structured with respect to a goal. For this reason, we describe, remember, and reproduce this event in terms of the relation between agent and goal ("She grasped the ball.") (Barresi & Moore, 1996; Bekkering, Wohlschlaeger, & Gattis, 2000; Zacks & Tversky, 2001). Like adults, infants represent instrumental actions like this one in terms of the relation between the agent and the goal object, rather than in terms of the sheer physical movements involved. To illustrate, in several experiments we showed infants events in which an actor reached toward and grasped one of two toys, as in Figure 9–1. Once infants had habituated to this event, we then reversed the positions of the toys and presented test events that varied either the goal of the reach

Figure 9–1. Goal-directed reaching.

(while preserving the physical movements of the arm) or the physical movements involved in the reach (while preserving the goal). By five to seven months of age, infants show a stronger novelty response (i.e., longer looking) in response goal changes than to changes in the physical movements of the reach (Woodward, 1998, 1999, 2003a; Guajardo & Woodward, 2004).

Critically, subsequent analyses revealed that infants' responses in the habituation procedure were not a byproduct of the way that hands entrain infants' attention. Across experiments, infants respond to a broad range of events involving both humans and inanimate objects by directing their attention to the object that is contacted. However, infants only encoded the event in terms of the actor–goal relation when the events could be identified as involving intentional agents and well-formed goal-directed actions (Kiraly, Jovanovic, Prinz, Aschersleben, & Gergely, 2003; Heineman-Pieper, 2005; Hofer, Hauf, & Aschersleben, 2005; Biro & Leslie, 2006).

These patterns in infants' looking times are paralleled by their responses in paradigms that recruit overt social behaviors. In one of these studies, Hamlin, Hallinan, and I (in press), asked whether seven-month-old infants would preferentially imitate the goal-relevant aspects of others' actions. Older children show a preference for reproducing the goals of actions rather than the physical details (Meltzoff, 1995; Bekkering et al., 2000; Carpenter, Call, & Tomasello, 2005; Schwier, Van Maanen, & Carpenter, 2006). Therefore, we reasoned that if younger infants can represent others' actions as goal-directed, they might also show this preference. We modeled object-directed reaches for infants—an adult reached for and grasped one of two small toys—and then gave infants the opportunity to act on the toys themselves. Infants systematically selected the toy that had been the adult's goal, but only when the action they viewed was one they understood as goal-directed. When infants saw the adult touch the object with the back of her hand (a gesture infants did not readily interpret as goal-directed in prior habituation experiments), they followed this gesture to look at the toy, but they chose randomly when presented with the toys. Thus, like older children, seven-month-old infants selectively reproduce the goal-relevant aspects of others' actions.

Behne and colleagues (2005) report further evidence that 9-, 12, and 18-month-old infants interpret others' actions as goal-directed. In these studies, infants played with an adult who handed them a series of small toys. At scripted points in the procedure, the adult failed to deliver the toy. Sometimes this was due to an apparent accident (the adult dropped the toy). In other cases, the adult pulled the toy away in a teasing manner. Even though the overall motions and outcomes were similar in these two conditions, infants responded to them differently. They showed signs of frustration in response to the teasing actions but not to the "accidents." Thus, infants seemed to code the adult's behavior not only as motions and results but also as intentional or not.

ATTENTION AS OBJECT-DIRECTED

Mature observers represent a broad range of actions as goal-directed or object-directed, including actions that do not involve immediate physical contact with the goal (Barresi & Moore, 1996). For example, the event depicted in Figure 9–2 is readily perceived as being structured by the invisible connection between the woman and the toy at which her gaze is directed (e.g., "She looks at the ball."). By the end of the first year of life, infants also represent this invisible connection (Phillips, Wellman, & Spelke, 2002; Woodward & Guajardo, 2002; Woodward, 2003b; Sodian & Thoermer, 2004; S. C. Johnson, Ok, & Luo, in press). In one study, we showed infants events in which a person turned to look at a toy, as depicted in Figure 9–2 (Woodward, 2003). Our question was whether infants would represent this event in terms of the relation between the person and the target of her gaze ("She looked at the toy.") or in terms of the person's physical movements ("She turned to the right."). Following infants' habituation to one event, the toys' positions were reversed and infants viewed new-object test trials, which disrupted the object to which the person directed gaze, and new-side test trials, which changed the person's physical motions while maintaining the same object as the target of attention. Twelve-month-old infants, but not younger infants, responded by looking reliably longer at new-object than at new-side trials, indicating that they encoded the experimental actions in terms of the invisible connection between the actor and the object of her attention. S. C. Johnson and colleagues (in press) have recently reported that infants who are even younger (nine-month-olds) show this response when the actor provides richer behavioral evidence concerning her focus of attention.

By 12 months, infants also relate perceptual access to other aspects of a person's intentional actions. Phillips, Wellman, and Spelke (2002) found that

Figure 9–2. Object-directed attention.

12-month-old infants use gaze direction to predict a person's next actions. Infants at this age expect that a person will reach toward the object at which she has just looked, and detect a violation when she reaches for an object she has not attended to (see also Sodian & Thoermer, 2004). Luo and Baillargeon (in press) found that 12-month-old infants interpret a person's predispositions to act, based on what she can see. When an actor chose between two toys with full visual access to both, infants assumed she would continue to reach for that object when given the choice again. However, when the actor at first had no visual access to the unchosen toy, infants did not assume she would choose the target again when given a choice between the two toys. Onishi and Baillargeon (2005) demonstrated that slightly older infants, 15-month-olds, can track a person's attention to an object across displacements and can use this information to predict her next actions. These looking-time results converge strongly with those of experiments that recruit infants' overt social responses (Tomasello & Haberl, 2003; Moll & Tomasello, 2007).

ACTIONS AS MEANS TO AN END

Mature observers represent not only the local relations between agents and the objects they grasp or attend to but also the higher order plans that relate strings of actions to ultimate goals. To illustrate, imagine seeing a woman grasp the lid of a container, as in the first panel in Figure 9–3. If we see her then open the container and grasp the toy within it, as in the second panel, we infer that her initial actions are directed at what's inside the container rather than the container itself.

Figure 9–3. A means–end sequence: Opening a box in order to obtain the toy inside it.

We represent her actions on the container as the means to attain this ultimate goal. By 12 months of age, infants also discern these higher order plans. In one study, Sommerville and I (2005) showed 12-month-old infants events in which an actor grasped one of two cloths, each of which supported a toy. The question of interest was whether infants interpreted the adult's grasp of the cloth as directed at the cloth itself or instead at the toy. To address this question, we showed infants habituation events featuring two differently colored cloths, each supporting a different toy. During habituation trials the actor pulled one of the cloths in order to obtain the toy. After habituation, the location of the toys was reversed, and infants saw the actor either grasp the same cloth as during habituation, which now held a new toy (new-object trials), or else grasp the other cloth, which now held the toy that had been the goal during habituation (new-cloth trials). Only the first step of the sequence played out—the actor remained still, having grasped the edge of the cloth. Thus, we asked whether infants interpreted this first step as directed at the cloth (the actual object grasped) or the toy (the object that could be attained if the cloth were pulled). Infants looked longer on new-object trials than on new-cloth trials, indicating that they interpreted the grasp of the cloth as directed at the toy, rather than the cloth itself.

A control condition showed that infants, like adults, used the causal structure of the event to determine that pulling the cloth was directed at getting the toy. When infants saw the same events, but with the toy beside rather than on the cloth, they did not interpret the grasp of the cloth as being directed toward getting the toy (see also Woodward & Sommerville, 2000). These results converge with findings from Carpenter and colleagues (2005) showing that 14-month-old infants preferentially imitate the ultimate goals rather than the means of observed sequences (see also Hallinan, Hamlin, DeNale, Luhr, & Woodward, 2007). Further, they concur with findings by Gergely and colleagues (Gergely & Csibra, 1998; Gergely, Bekkering, & Kiraly, 2002) that infants at this age evaluate the causal constraints in a situation in order to recover information about an agent's goal.

SUMMARY: THE SNAPSHOTS

The findings just reviewed show that infants possess well-structured knowledge about intentional action. Infants' action knowledge is robustly evident in research from many different laboratories and in paradigms that recruit a range of behaviors, including looking times, imitative responses, and other social behaviors. This research shows that infants view others' actions not as being mere movements through space, but rather as being organized by goals and objects of attention. Critically, the findings show that infants represent the relational structure of intentional actions. Although actions do serve to direct infants' attention, infants do more than simply follow this lead. They analyze observed events in terms of the relation between the agent and the objects at which her actions are directed. These intentional relations are the backbone of adult action perception and folk psychology (Barresi & Moore, 1996; Zacks & Tversky, 2001). The knowledge we see in infants, therefore, seems very likely to be the conceptual starting point for later-emerging folk psychology. Further, infants' knowledge about goal-directed action and attention has been shown to support a great deal of social learning in the second year of life (Tomasello, 1999; Baldwin & Moses, 2001; Woodward, 2003c).

These findings also reveal a change in infants' sensitivity to action structure over the course of the first year. Early in the first year, infants discern the goal structure of some, relatively concrete, actions, such as reaching. By the end of the first year, infants can discern the more abstract goals that organize strings of actions and the entirely abstract relation between a person and the object of his or her attention. This observation, that there is change, raises the question of what drives this change. It is to this question that I turn next.

IDENTIFYING CONTRIBUTORS TO INFANTS' ACTION KNOWLEDGE

Research on conceptual development in older children provides a model for how to move beyond the "snapshots." One method is to identify developmental correlates of the ability in question. Although correlation in itself cannot inform causal conclusions, knowing which abilities hang together in development can provide a foundation for generating testable causal hypotheses. Having identified the aspects of environmental input and the concomitant cognitive developments that correlate with the ability in question, researchers can then investigate potential causal relations among these factors. One powerful technique for doing this is to assess the consequences of variations in experience for subsequent knowledge and concepts. These two general approaches—seeking developmental correlates and then exploring variations in potential developmental causes—have yielded rich insight into developmental processes in many cognitive domains, including preschool theory of mind (e.g., Dunn, 1999; De Viilliers & Pyers, 2002; Hale & Tager-Flusberg, 2003; Lohmann & Tomasello, 2003), language (e.g., Huttenlocher, Haight, Bryk, Seltzer, & Lyons, 1990; Hoff & Naigles, 2002; Huttenlocher,

Vasilyeva, & Cymerman, 2002; Vasilyeva, Huttenlocher, & Waterfall, 2006), and number (e.g., Mix, Huttenlocher, & Levine, 2002). In our work, we have begun to employ both of these approaches to gain insight into the developmental drivers of infants' action knowledge.

DEVELOPMENTAL CORRELATES OF INFANTS' ACTION KNOWLEDGE

The action knowledge infants express in the habituation booth is just one aspect of a very busy life. Our initial findings pointed to a coincidence that motivated us to consider the possible connections of this knowledge to life outside the booth. The coincidence was that infants began to respond systematically when viewing particular actions in the habituation experiments at roughly the same ages that infants are known to be undergoing developments in the production of these same actions. Infants begin to respond systematically to grasping events at around five to six months, the age at which they themselves become skilled at reaching for objects (Bertenthal & Clifton, 1998; Clearfield & Thelen, 2001). Infants begin to demonstrate sensitivity to means–end relations in others' actions between 9 and 12 months, which is also the age at which infants begin to reliably produce means–end action sequences (Piaget, 1953; Willatts, 1999). Also between 9 and 12 months, infants begin to respond systematically to pointing and gaze events, and this is the age at which infants begin to point (Bates, Benigni, Bretherton, Camaioni, & Volterra, 1979; Schaffer, 1984). Further, during this period, infants are beginning to engage in increasingly frequent and complex bouts of shared attention with caregivers (Bakeman & Adamson, 1984).

These coincidences led us to ask whether there are developmental relations between these aspects of babies' experience and their ability to detect the goal structure of others' actions. Our first approach has been to assess correlations between infants' responses in the habituation experiments and focal aspects of their action experience. Especially during periods when new abilities are emerging, and there is therefore high individual variation in both infants' responses and their experiences, we predict correlations between action knowledge and the aspects of experience that may contribute to it.

Sommerville and I (2005) asked whether infants' propensity to detect the means–end structure of others' actions was related to their own ability to solve a means–end problem. Ten-month-old infants participated in two experimental procedures. One was the visual habituation paradigm, described earlier, that tested whether infants interpreted a person's actions on an intermediary (a cloth that supported a toy at its far end) as directed at the ultimate goal (the toy) or instead at the intermediary itself. As a group, ten-month-olds were random in their responses in this paradigm. In the other procedure, we presented infants with interesting toys that were out of reach, supported by cloths that extended to within reach, and gave infants the opportunity to pull the cloth to get the toy. Infants did this, in ways that were clearly well-organized attempts to get the toy, on an average of about half the trials.

We found that infants' habituation responses were strongly correlated with their actions in the cloth-pulling task. Infants who produced more well-organized means–end responses themselves showed a stronger effect in the habituation procedure. Further, we found that infants at the upper and lower ends of the spectrum in terms of their own actions seemed to endorse opposing analyses of the habituation events. Infants in the upper quartile in terms of their own actions represented the toy as the actor's goal, whereas those in the lower quartile apparently misrepresented the cloth itself as the actor's goal. The latter is a sensible analysis in some ways—infants interpreted the actions as directed at the object the actor was touching. It just missed the higher level goal that was also present in the scene.

In another series of studies, we investigated the developmental correlates of infants' understanding of object-directed attention. We had found similar developmental patterns in infants' responses to events in which a person looks at an object and events in which he or she points to an object: 9-month-olds as a group seem not to readily identify the object-directed structure of these events, whereas 12-month-olds do. Our first finding (Woodward & Guajardo, 2002) was that at nine months, infants' sensitivity to the goal structure of pointing events was predicted by whether or not the infant produced object-directed points. About one third of the infants we tested produced well-formed point gestures that were directed at identifiable objects. These infants responded like 12-month-olds, looking longer on test trials that disrupted the relation between actor and object. The other two-thirds of the nine-month-old infants did not yet point, and responded randomly on test trials. In order to make the events as simple as possible, we had the actor actually touch the toy with her pointing index finger. This gesture effectively recruited infants' attention. Regardless of whether infants were able to point or not, they followed the pointing hand to the toy. But only infants who could point went a step further and encoded the relation between the agent and the object of her attention.

Brune and I followed up on this finding, this time asking whether the same aspects of experience correlate with infants' understanding of pointing events and looking events (Brune & Woodward, 2007). We assessed two potential developmental correlates, pointing status and engagement in shared attention with caregivers, and tested each infant in two habituation sessions, one evaluating their understanding of pointing events, and the other evaluating their understanding of looking events. These two events were very similar. In both, an experimenter sat between two toys and directed her gaze at one of them. The events differed only in terms of whether the actor also pointed at the toy. We replicated the prior finding that infants' own pointing status predicted their responses to the pointing events. Interestingly, pointing status did not predict infants' responses to the gaze-only events, but shared attention did. Infants who engaged in more shared attention with their caretaker showed a stronger tendency to detect the object-directed structure of the gaze events. These findings indicate that different aspects of action experience correlate with different pieces of infants' action knowledge. Thus, although at some point children attain a general understanding of attentional relations that subsumes the particular actions that express them, initially infants may build relatively local pockets of knowledge about particular actions.

These correlational findings lend plausibility to the possibility that infants' experiences contribute to their knowledge about others' actions. Of course, these findings cannot directly inform the causal relations between experience and knowledge. Nevertheless, these results are important for several reasons. For one, they establish relations between knowledge expressed in the laboratory, and infants' life outside the laboratory. Establishing these linkages provides validation for laboratory measures, and it begins to set infant cognitive development in a broader ecological context. Critically, for the current purposes, the observed correlations nominate certain aspects of experience as potential contributors to infants' action knowledge. Subsequent research can then draw on these insights to probe the potential causal relations behind the correlation. I turn next to our initial attempts to do this.

A POTENTIAL CONTRIBUTOR: SELF-PRODUCED GOAL-DIRECTED ACTION

During the first year of life, infants' own actions undergo dramatic changes, and our correlational findings suggest that some of these changes may cascade to affect infants' action perception. There are several kinds of mechanisms by which this could occur. At a very general level, as infants engage in new goal-directed actions, like reaching and tool use, they provide themselves with informative observational experience. They see their hands reach for, grasp, and move objects, for example. From this experience, infants may extract information about the behavioral sequelae of various actions; for example, they may learn that reaching predicts grasping, and grasping predicts movement of the grasped object. This kind of statistical learning could provide a basis for segmenting online action streams at meaningful junctures (Baldwin & Baird, 2001) and thus support subsequent developments in infants' conceptual understanding of intentional action. This analysis could, of course, occur during infants' observation of others' actions in addition to occurring during their observations of their own actions. Thus, specific developmental relations between infants' own actions and their analysis of others' actions would have to be explained by infants' own actions providing more numerous and/or especially salient observational examples.

It is also plausible that the infants' first-person experience as agents provides information for analyzing others' actions that could not be gleaned by observation alone. It has long been hypothesized that first-person experience provides unique insight into others' intentions, and a number of current theoretical proposals are grounded in this hypothesis (Barresi & Moore, 1996; Tomasello, 1999; Gallese & Goldman, 1998; Meltzoff, 2007). This general proposal could be realized in a number of ways, varying both in terms of the kinds of information provided by first-person experience and the means by which this information is brought to bear in perceiving structure in others' actions. One possibility is that infants, like adults, have subjective awareness of their underlying mental intentions in acting and that this awareness provides information for understanding others' mental states (Barresi & Moore, 1996). For example, in their seminal analysis, Barresi and Moore (1996) hypothesized that infants draw on their awareness of their own states of attention in order to understand others' attentional actions. Alternatively, first-person experience may provide infants with a representation of action structure, without a representation of the mental correlates of the action (Sommerville, Woodward & Needham, 2005; Sommerville & Woodward, in press; Gerson & Woodward, in press). Of course, the nature of the relevant information may also vary with development. For example, Meltzoff (2007) has proposed a developmental account in which information sharing between the self and others is initially rooted in the body and its movements; with development, infants construct from these concrete beginnings more abstract representations of intentions (see also Gerson & Woodward, in press).

Information at these various levels of analysis could be extended to others via a process of analogical mapping, in which one's own actions and others' actions are aligned, and the information about one's own mental experiences is used to infer similar states in others (Barresi & Moore, 1996). Alternatively, information about the self may be extended to others more directly, via shared representations for action production and perception (Gallese & Goldman, 1998; Sommerville et al., 2005; Meltzoff, 2007). Recent findings documenting shared neural representations for the perception and production of action (mirror systems) suggest one medium by which this direct exchange of information could occur (Gerson & Woodward, in press).

Thus, there are a number of pathways by which infants' own goal-directed actions could provide them with unique information for understanding others' actions as goal-directed. The current empirical evidence is insufficient to reveal which, if any, of these possible mechanisms plays a role in infants' action perception. A first test of any of these possibilities is to determine whether first-person action experience changes infants' perception of others' actions. When infants begin to engage in a new form of object-directed action, does this experience create not only new ways of acting but also new ways of seeing others' actions? Until recently, even this most basic question did not have a clear empirical answer. To address this question, we have begun develop experimental interventions that support new object-directed actions in infants and then assess the effects of this experience on infants' action perception.

A FIRST TEST: REACHING FOR OBJECTS AND UNDERSTANDING OTHERS' REACHING BEHAVIOR

By five to six months of age, infants engage in well-structured goal-directed reaching. When confronted with an interesting object within arm's reach, infants at this age will generally reach for it using relatively smooth arm movements and then apprehend the object with a well-formed, object-appropriate, grasp (Bertenthal & Clifton, 1998; Clearfield & Thelen, 2001). Before this age, infants show visual interest in objects, and sometimes direct swiping or batting movements toward them, but seldom successfully apprehend them. Needham and her colleagues (Needham, Barrett, & Peterman, 2002) created Velcro-covered "sticky mittens" that permit young infants to successfully apprehend objects with their hands just by batting at them. Given practice with these mittens, infants become more organized in their efforts to apprehend the toys with the mittens.

Given that sticky-mittens experience alters infants' object-directed actions, we asked whether this experience would also alter their perception of others' actions. Sommerville, Needham, and I (Sommerville et al., 2005), gave one group of three-month-olds infants 3 minutes of sticky-mittens experience and then immediately tested them in a habituation paradigm that assessed their representation of mittened reaches as object-directed. This paradigm was identical to the one used in our prior research, except that the presenting experimenter wore an adult-sized mitten that looked similar to the ones the infant had worn. Infants viewed events in which an experimenter reached into the stage from the side in order to grasp one of two toys. Following the infants' habituation, the positions of the toys were reversed and infants viewed new-goal test events (in which the experimenter moved through the same path to grasp the other object), and old-goal test events (in which she moved through a new path in order to grasp the same object). As in prior studies, longer looking on new-goal compared to old-goal trials is evidence that infants have encoded the experimenter's actions as goal-directed. To maximize the likelihood that infants would relate their own actions to those observed in the habituation events, during the mittens phase infants interacted with small replicas of the toys in the habituation events. A control group of infants viewed the habituation events without having first engaged in the mittens intervention.

As expected, the sticky mittens affected infants' actions: Infants engaged in more object-directed manual contact with the toys while wearing the mittens than they did when they did not have the mittens. Critically, mittens experience also changed infants' responses to the actions they observed during the habituation events. After mittens practice, infants looked reliably longer on new-goal than old-goal events. In contrast, infants in the control condition did not differentiate between the test events. Furthermore, individual variation in infants' actions with the mittens predicted variation in their subsequent responses to the habituation events. Infants who had engaged in more object-directed manual contact during the mittens training showed stronger preferences for the new-goal event. Infants' preference for the new-goal event was not predicted by the infant's skill at reaching without mittens or by the extent to which the infant had gained visual familiarity with the toys during the mittens training. Rather, it was engaging in object-directed actions, per se, that seemed to be driving infants' responses to the observed actions.

These findings are the first to show that acting changes how young infants perceive others' goal-directed actions. Even so, they do not conclusively show whether first-person experience is critical for this effect. Perhaps the mittens experience was effective because it created salient observational examples of hands moving objects for the infants. Of course, three-month-old infants have had many opportunities to observe adults' hands moving objects, and these experiences seem not to support their understanding of bare-handed reaches as goal-directed—infants fail to show systematic responses for reaching events in our habituation experiments before to six months of age. Nevertheless, a stronger test would directly compare first-person and observational experience within the same experiment. Our next experiment did this.

Our initial goal was to assess the generality of the prior findings by testing whether mittens experience would also lead infants to view bare-handed reaches as goal-directed. To this end, we gave all infants practice using the sticky mittens and then assessed their responses to observed reaches that were either done with a mitten (as in the first experiment) or bare-handed. We replicated our findings for the mittened events: Mittens experience led infants to respond to the observed mittened reaches as goal-directed. However, mittens experience did not affect infants' responses to the bare-handed events. Thus, the answer to our initial question was that mittens experience seems to have a relatively circumscribed effect on infants' action perception. They seem to have learned something about *mittened* reaches, but do not generalize this to other kinds of reaches.

Having addressed this initial question, we realized that this experiment also provided a means for assessing the relative effects of observational and first-person experience. During the mittens intervention, infants not only saw their own mittened hands moving the objects, they also saw the experimenter's bare hands moving the objects. The experimenter grasped and moved the toys on the table in order to attract infants' attention to the toys, and she also periodically removed the toys from the mittens and placed them back on the table. Thus, every infant received both first-person experience with mittened actions and observational experience with bare-handed grasps. This fact allowed us to ask not only whether first-person mittened experience affected infants' perception of mittened reaches, but also whether observational experience with bare-handed reaches immediately before the habituation session affected infants' perception of subsequent bare-handed reaches.

To address this question, we first constructed subsets of infants in the two conditions who were matched in terms of their overall experience watching their own or the experimenter's hands move the objects. We then assessed the correlation within each condition between infants' relative preference for the new-goal event during test trials and the degree of their experience with the "matching" first-person or observational training event. That is, we assessed the correlation between infants' own mittened experience and their responses to the mittened habituation events and the correlation between infants' observation of the experimenter's bare-handed actions and their responses to the bare-handed habituation events. We found that, as in the first experiment, infants who had spent more time watching their own hands move the objects showed a stronger preference for the new-goal event. In contrast, there was no hint of a relation between infants' observation of the experimenter's bare hands and their subsequent responses to the bare-handed events. Thus, these findings indicate that first-person experience may be particularly informative for infants. Recent work by Sommerville and her colleagues (Sommerville, Hildebrand, & Crane, in press) has documented a similar pattern of results in older infants for novel tool-use actions. Infants who had learned to use the tool themselves showed a stronger understanding of observed tool-use events than did infants who had had only observational experience.

Although they provide critical initial evidence that infants' own actions provide structure for perceiving others' actions, these findings do not provide precise evidence concerning the kind of information conveyed (internal-state information versus action-structure information) or concerning the means by which this information is extended from oneself to the other (analogical extension versus shared representations). Clearly, further research is needed. However, recent findings from other parts of the field provide some guidance concerning the mechanisms that may be at work. Specifically, research over the past decade has revealed shared neural representations for the production and perception of action. These mirror systems have been documented in adult human and nonhuman primates (Rizzolatti, Fadiga, Gallese, & Fogassi, 1996; Grezes & Decety, 2001). Mirror systems code goal-directed or meaningful actions, rather than physical movements, per se, and they are shaped by motor learning. For example, professional ballet dancers show selective mirror responses when viewing ballet movements that are part of their own repertoire, but not when viewing dance movements that they do not themselves perform (Calvo-Merino, Grezes, Glaser, Passingham, & Haggard, 2006).

Thus, mirror systems have properties that could explain how infants' own actions would structure their action perception. As infants gain control over new modes of goal-directed action, mirror representations for these actions may arise, just as they seem to when adults gain expertise in new actions. These newly tuned mirror representations could then provide structure for action perception. There is currently debate in the field as to whether mature mirror systems make contact with mental-state information or instead provide action-level representations (Gallese & Goldman, 1998; Jacob & Jeannerod, 2005; Saxe, 2005; Hurley, in press). In the case of infants, it seems most likely that mirror systems would provide descriptions of action structure, without making contact with rich mental-state concepts. These action representations would specify the goal-directed structure of the action; that is, that the action is directed at some target. This representation of action in terms of goal relations would provide a critical representational kernel for subsequent conceptual development (Gerson & Woodward, in press). Further, these action representations would be sufficient to yield many of the findings reviewed earlier, showing that infants selectively attend to the relational structure of common human actions.

SUMMARY: IN SEARCH OF DEVELOPMENTAL CONTRIBUTORS

Following the general model of research on conceptual development in older children, we have begun to explore the factors that contribute to conceptual development in infants. We began with the observation that action production and action perception each undergo salient and critical developments in infancy. Our work has begun to indicate that this is not a chance coincidence—there are strong developmental connections between these two aspects of development. As infants gain command over new modes of goal-directed action, they also gain insight into the goal structure of those same actions in others. Our initial findings from intervention studies indicate that this correlation reflects (at least in part) causal effects of acting on action perception. Training infants in a novel goal-directed action leads infants to see that action as goal-directed when others perform it.

These relations appear to be action specific. Infants' production of the point gesture correlates with others' pointing gestures, but not with their understanding of visual attention. Infants' comprehension of visual attention, in contrast, correlates with other aspects of their experience. Similarly, our mittens intervention seemed to teach infants about the structure of *mittened* reaches, not reaches or hand actions in general. These findings suggest that, initially, infants may build pockets of knowledge about particular actions. Eventually, of course, children attain more general and abstract conceptions, understanding, for example, the underlying commonalities in varied acts of attention or apprehension. Further research is needed to investigate how and when these initial localized action concepts become more general.

CONCLUSIONS

The findings reviewed here provide initial steps toward uncovering the origins of infants' action knowledge. Like adults, infants perceive a world populated by intentional agents. By the middle of the first year of life, if not earlier, infants perceive others' actions not as being sheer movements through space but instead as being organized by goals and objects of attention. The ability to see actions as object-directed undergoes important developments during the first year. This emerging action knowledge is tied to aspects of infants' experience, and recent findings suggest that these aspects of experience may shape infants' understanding of intentional action.

These initial steps in uncovering infants' action knowledge raise many new questions. To start, there are open questions concerning the limits and nature of infants' action knowledge. The work described here has shown that infants are sensitive to the goal structure of several kinds of human actions, but the full range of actions that infants might understand has not been delimited. For example, we know little of infants' encoding of actions with social intent or of infants' understanding of the ways in which emotion relates to actions. Further, except for a few studies (e.g., Phillips et al., 2002; Luo & Baillargeon, in press), there has been little work published on infants' ability to integrate information from different aspects of a person's actions over time. Indeed, we have just begun to ask whether and when infants use the *person* as the unit of analysis in tracking goals over time (Buresh & Woodward, 2007).

The work reviewed here has focused on infants' recovery of goal structure from real-world events, that is, the actions of other people. In addition to this knowledge system, there may be other abilities that contribute to infants' perception of intentional action. Specifically, infants are sensitive to patterns of motion in abstract events (e.g., dots moving on a computer screen) that may serve as cues to intentional agency for adult observers. These cues include contingent movement (Rochat, Morgan, & Carpenter, 1997; Shimizu & S. C. Johnson, 2004), self-propelled movement (Luo & Baillargeon, 2005), equifinal variation in movements toward an object (Biro & Leslie, 2006), and rational movement toward an object (Gergely & Csibra, 1998). Further, in some cases, these cues may lead infants to view unusual events as goal-directed (Gergely et al., 1995; Kiraly et al., 2003; Shimizu & S. C. Johnson, 2004; Luo & Baillargeon, 2005; Biro & Leslie, 2006; but see Heineman-Pieper & Woodward, 2003, Woodward, 2005).

It is not yet clear how these abilities relate to infants' emerging knowledge about real-world agents and actions. One view holds that these perceptual sensitivities are inborn and guide infants' subsequent learning about real-world agents (Kiraly et al., 2003; Biro & Leslie, 2006). However, much of the evidence for sensitivity to abstract cues comes from older infants, with younger infants failing to respond or seeming less sensitive to the cues (see Hofer et al., 2005; Woodward, 2005; Biro & Leslie, 2006). Therefore, it is also possible that sensitivity to some of these cues derives from experience with real-world actions. Alternatively, the relation between perceptual sensitivities and real-world action knowledge may be more complex. These two may comprise initially independent systems that interact in as yet uncharted ways during development (see Woodward, 2005).

Finally, we have only begun to investigate the kinds of experiences that might contribute to infants' action knowledge. Self-produced actions are almost certainly only part of a large set of experiences that contribute to this system of knowledge. For example, the findings from the Brune and Woodward (2007) study suggest that infants' engagement in shared attention with caretakers may contribute to their understanding of others' states of attention, as is consistent with several theoretical proposals (Barresi & Moore, 1996; Carpenter, Nagell & Tomasello, 1998). Moreover, observational experience may also provide valuable information for infants (Baldwin & Baird, 2001).

Leaving aside these important open questions, I believe the evidence we have so far supports several significant conclusions to keep in mind as we move forward in this domain of infant cognition and in other domains as well.

Infants Have Structured, Domain-Specific Knowledge

This conclusion may seem like a truism given the past two decades of infant-cognition research. But it is worth pointing out that, as new results come in, this conclusion continues to gain support. Our results and those of others have shown that infants represent the actions of agents and the motions of objects in fundamentally different ways. Further, infants represent the relational structure of others' actions: the relation between an agent and his or her goal, the relation between an agent and the object of his or her attention, and the relations that organize actions in service of higher order goals. These well-structured action representations lay the foundation for subsequent conceptual development. In fact, several laboratories now report that infants' responses in visual habituation experiments of action knowledge predict their later performance on preschool verbal theory of mind measures (Wellman, Phillips, Dunphy-Lelii, & Lalonde, 2004; Ascher-sleben & Hohenberger, 2007; Kuhlmeier & Yamaguchi, 2007; Poulin-Dubois &

Olineck, 2007). Thus, the responses we see in preverbal infants appear to be continuous with subsequent explicit folk psychology.

Experience Contributes to This Knowledge

In the early days of infant-cognition research, the existence of knowledge in young infants was taken as strong evidence for inborn capacities. In current work, researchers have begun to actively consider the role of experience in shaping infants' knowledge. They have been led to do so by the discovery that infants' knowledge changes during the first year, that these changes correlate with changing experience, and that changes can be induced by laboratory interventions. The findings reviewed here illustrate these points in the realm of action knowledge. The other chapters in this volume document similar findings for other aspects of infant conceptual development (e.g., see the chapters by Baillargeon, S. P. Johnson, Needham, Oakes, and Wilcox). These findings have shifted the debate from whether experience matters to how it matters. Which inborn abilities provide the foundation for conceptual development, and how do they interact with experience?

Infants Create Their Own Learning Experiences

This observation harks back to the early days of our field (Piaget, 1953) and challenges many views of learning that take the learner to be a relatively passive recipient of information from the environment. By acting, infants set up the conditions for new acts of learning. In other parts of this volume, it has been shown that a varied set of learning abilities contributes to cognitive development in infancy. These abilities include associative learning (S. P. Johnson, Namy), cognitive comparison (Oakes, Wilcox), statistical learning (Saffran), and rule learning (Saffran). Our findings indicate that self-produced actions provide data as inputs to learning processes such as these can, and that these processes may yield new knowledge about action. They also raise another possibility, which is that systems that subserve motor learning have direct implications for conceptual development. Specifically, mirror representations may provide a medium for recruiting structure gleaned from acting to inform action perception.

Learning in One Domain Spills Over to Affect Developments in Others

If this proposal is right, then it points out the limits of considering conceptual development as a domain-specific process. Although knowledge may in many cases be organized with respect to cognitive domains, insights critical to reasoning in a domain can also originate in other domains or systems. This fact makes the study of knowledge development complex, as it requires researchers to think broadly in considering potential developmental factors. This approach has yielded important insights into other aspects of cognitive development. For example, we now know that early word learning recruits information from across conceptual domains, and this helps explain how one- and two-year-old children are able to acquire linguistic symbols (Woodward & Markman, 1998; Golinkoff et al., 2000).

The current findings indicate that similarly broad thinking will shed light on the emergence of intentional-action knowledge. In this case, thinking broadly will require us to reconsider the relations between *doing* and *thinking* in infancy. Piaget hypothesized that infants begin with only sensorimotor knowledge, and this knowledge provides the foundation for the later emergence of conceptual knowledge in early childhood. As this volume illustrates, this hypothesis has not been supported. Infants possess both conceptual and sensorimotor knowledge from early in life (e.g., see the chapters by Baillargeon, Bauer, S. P. Johnson, Needham, and Wilcox). Even so, the case of infants' action knowledge leads us to consider again the ways in which hands-on experience contributes to conceptual knowledge.

Acknowledgments   The work summarized in this chapter was supported by NSF (0446706) and NICHD (R01-HD35707). I thank Amy Needham for her comments on a previous version of the paper.

References

Aschersleben, G., & Hohenberger, A. (2007). *Does infant action interpretation predict later theory of mind abilities?* Paper presented at the meetings of the Jean Piaget Society, Amsterdam, The Netherlands.

Bakeman, R., & Adamson, L. B. (1984). Coordinating attention to people and objects in mother–infant and peer–infant interaction. *Child Development, 55*(4), 1278–1289.

Baldwin, D. A., & Baird, J. A. (2001). Discerning intentions in dynamic human action. *Trends in Cognitive Sciences, 5*(4), 171–178.

Baldwin, D. A., & Moses, J. A. (2001). Links between social understanding and early word learning: Challenges to current accounts. *Social Development, 10,* 311–329.

Barresi, J., & Moore, C. (1996). Intentional relations and social understanding. *Behavioral and Brain Sciences, 19,* 107–154.

Bates, E., Benigni, L., Bretherton, I., Camaioni, L., & Volterra, V. (1979). *The emergence of symbols: Cognition and communication in infancy.* New York: Academic Press.

Behne, T., Carpenter, M., Call, J., & Tomasello, M. (2005). Unwilling versus unable? Infants' understanding of intentional action. *Developmental Psychology, 41*(2), 328–337.

Bekkering, H., Wohlschlaeger, A., & Gattis, M. (2000). Imitation of gestures in children is goal-directed. *Quarterly Journal of Experimental Psychology, 53,* 153–164.

Bertenthal, B., & Clifton, R. K. (1998). Perception and action. In D.K.W. Damon & R. Siegler (Eds.), *Handbook of child psychology* (Vol. 2: Cognition, perception and language, pp. 51–102). New York: John Wiley and Sons.

Biro, S., & Leslie, A. M. (2006). Infants' perception of goal-directed actions: Development through cue-based bootstrapping. *Developmental Science, 10*(3), 379–398.

Brune, C. W., & Woodward, A. L. (2007). Social cognition and social responsiveness in 10-month-old infants. *Journal of Cognition and Development, 8*(2), 133–158.

Buresh, J. S., & Woodward, A. L. (2007). Infants track action goals within and across agents. *Cognition, 104(2),* 287–314.

Calvo-Merino, B., Grezes, J., Glaser, D. E., Passingham, R. E., & Haggard, P. (2006). Seeing or doing? Influence of visual and motor familiarity in action observation. *Current Biology, 16,* 1905–1910.

Carpenter, M., Call, J., & Tomasello, M. (2005). Twelve- and 18-month-olds copy actions in terms of goals. *Developmental Science, 8*(1), F13–F20.

Carpenter, M., Nagell, K., & Tomasello, M. (1998). Social cognition, joint attention and communicative competence from 9 to 15 months of age. *Monographs of the Society for Research in Child Development, 63*(4) Serial No. 255.

Clearfield, M. W., & Thelen, E. (2001). Stability and flexibility in the acquisition of skilled movement. In C. A. Nelson & M. Luciana (Eds.), *Handbook of developmental cognitive neuroscience* (pp. 253–266). Cambridge, MA: MIT Press.

De Viilliers, J., & Pyers, J. (2002). Complements to cognition: A longitudinal study of the relationship between complex syntax and false belief understanding. *Child Development, 17,* 1037–1060.

Dunn, J. (1999). Making sense of the social world: Mindreading, emotion and relationships. In P. D. Zelazo, J. W. Astington, & D. R. Olson (Eds.), *Developing theories of intention.* Mahwah, NJ: Erlbaum.

Gallese, V., & Goldman, A. (1998). Mirror neurons and the simulation theory of mindreading. *Trends in Cognitive Sciences, 2*(12), 493–501.

Gergely, G., Bekkering, H., & Kiraly, I. (2002). Rational imitation in preverbal infants. *Nature, 415,* 755.

Gergely, G., & Csibra, G. (1998). The teleological origins of mentalistic action explanations: A developmental hypothesis. *Developmental Science, 1,* 255–259.

Gergely, G., & Csibra, G. (2003). Teleological reasoning in infancy: The naive theory of rational action. *Trends in Cognitive Sciences, 7,* 287–292.

Gergely, G., Nadasdy, Z., Csibra, G., & Biro, S. (1995). Taking the intentional stance at 12 months of age. *Cognition, 56,* 165–193.

Gerson, S., & Woodward, A. L. (in press). Building intentional action knowledge with one's hands. In S. P. Johnson (Ed.), *Neo-constructivism.* Oxford University Press.

Golinkoff, R. M., Hirsh-Pasek, K., Bloom, L., Smith, L. B., Woodward, A. L., Akhtar, N., Tomasello, M., & Hollich, G. (2000). *Becoming a word learner: A debate on lexical acquisition.* Oxford, UK: Oxford University Press.

Grezes, J., & Decety, J. (2001). Functional anatomy of execution, mental simulation, observation, and verb generation of actions: A meta-analysis. *Human Brain Mapping, 12,* 1–19.

Guajardo, J. J., & Woodward, A. L. (2004). Is agency skin-deep? Surface features influence infants' sensitivity to goal-directed action. *Infancy, 6,* 361–384.

Hale, C. M., & Tager-Flusberg, H. (2003). The influence of language on theory of mind: A training study. *Developmental Science, 6*(3), 346–359.

Hallinan, E., Hamlin, J. K., DeNale, R. L., Luhr, S., & Woodward, A. L. (2007). *Infants imitate the goals of others.* Poster presented at the biennial meetings of the Society for Research in Child Development, Boston, MA.

Hamlin, J. K., Hallinan, E. V., & Woodward, A. L. (in press). Do as I do: 7-month-old infants selectively reproduce others' goals. *Developmental Science.*

Heineman-Pieper, J. (2005). *A science of persons: New foundations for human agency.* Unpublished doctoral dissertation, University of Chicago.

Heineman-Pieper, J., & Woodward, A. (2003). Understanding infants' understanding of intentions: Two problems of interpretation (A reply to Kiraly et al., 2003). *Consciousness and Cognition, 12,* 770–772.

Hofer, T., Hauf, P., & Aschersleben, G. (2005). Infant's perception of goal-directed actions performed by a mechanical device. *Infant Behavior & Development, 28*(4), 466–480.

Hoff, E., & Naigles, L. (2002). How children use input to acquire a lexicon. *Child Development, 73*(2), 418–433.

Hurley, S. (in press). The shared-circuits model: How control, mirroring and simulation can enable imitation, deliberation and mindreading. *Behavioral and Brain Sciences.*

Huttenlocher, J., Haight, W., Bryk, A., Seltzer, M., & Lyons, T. (1990). Early vocabulary growth: Relations to language input and gender. *Developmental Psychology, 27,* 236–248

Huttenlocher, J., Vasilyeva, M., & Cymerman, E. (2002). Language input and child syntax. *Cognitive Psychology, 45*(3), 337–374.

Jacob, P., & Jeannerod, M. (2005). The motor theory of social cognition: A critique. *Trends in Cognitive Science, 9,* 21–25.

Johnson, S. C., Slaughter, V., & Carey, S. (1998). Whose gaze will infants follow? The elicitation of gaze-following in 12-month-olds. *Developmental Science, 1,* 233–238.

Johnson, S. C. (2000). The recognition of mentalistic agents in infancy. *Trends in Cognitive Sciences, 4,* 22–28.

Johnson, S. C., Ok, S.-J., & Luo, Y. (in press). The attribution of attention: Nine-month-olds' interpretation of gaze as goal-directed action. *Developmental Science.*

Kiraly, I., Jovanovic, B., Prinz, W., Aschersleben, G., & Gergely, G. (2003). The early origins of goal attribution in infancy. *Consciousness and Cognition, 12*(4), 752–769.

Kuhlmeier, V., & Yamaguchi, M. (2007). *How does infants' performance on goal-attribution tasks relate to other social-cognitive skills?* Paper presented at the meetings of the Jean Piaget Society, Amsterdam, The Netherlands.

Leslie, A. M. (1993). TOMM, TOBY and agency: Core architecture and domain specificity. In L. A. Hirschfeld & S. A. Gelman (Eds.), *Mapping the mind: Domain specificity in cognition and culture.* Cambridge, UK: Cambridge University Press.

Lohmann, H., & Tomasello, M. (2003). The role of language in the development of false belief understanding: A training study. *Child Development, 74*(4), 1130–1144.

Luo, Y., & Baillargeon, R. (2005). Can a self-propelled box have a goal? Psychological reasoning in 5-month-old infants. *Psychological Science, 16*(8), 601–608.

Luo, Y., & Baillargeon, R. (in press). Do 12.5-month-old infants consider what objects others can see when interpreting their actions? *Cognition.*

Meltzoff, A. N. (1995). Understanding the intentions of others: Re-enactments of intended acts by 18-month-old children. *Developmental Psychology, 31,* 838–850.

Meltzoff, A. N. (2007). The "like me" framework for recognizing and becoming an intentional agent. *Acta Psychologica, 124,* 26–43.

Mix, K. S., Huttenlocher, J., & Levine, S. (2002). *Quantitative development in infancy and early childhood.* Oxford, UK: Oxford University Press.

Moll, H., & Tomasello, M. (2007). How 14- and 18-month-olds know what others have experienced. *Developmental Psychology, 43*(2), 309–317.

Needham, A., Barrett, T., & Peterman, K. (2002). A pick-me-up for infants' exploratory skills. *Infant Behavior and Development, 25,* 279–295.

Onishi, K. H., & Baillargeon, R. (2005). Do 15-month-old infants understand false belief? *Science, 308,* 255–258.

Phillips, A. T., Wellman, H. M., & Spelke, E. S. (2002). Infants' ability to connect gaze and emotional expression to intentional action. *Cognition, 85,* 53–78.

Piaget, J. (1953). *The origins of intelligence in the child.* London: Routledge & Kegan Paul.

Poulin-Dubois, D., & Olineck, K. M. (2007). *From intention-in-action to intention-in the mind: Infants' goal detection and intentional imitation predict later theory of mind.* Paper presented at the meetings of the Jean Piaget Society, Amsterdam, The Netherlands.

Rizzolatti, G., Fadiga, L., Gallese, V., & Fogassi, L. (1996). Premotor cortex and the recognition of motor activities. *Cognition Brain Resources, 3,* 131–141.

Rochat, P., Morgan, R., & Carpenter, M. (1997). Young infants' sensitivity to movement information specifying social causality. *Cognitive Development, 12*(4), 441–465.

Saxe, R. (2005). Against simulation: The argument from error. *Trends in Cognitive Science, 8*(4), 174–179.

Schaffer, H. R. (1984). *The child's entry into a social world.* London: Academic Press.

Schwier, C., Van Maanen, C., & Carpenter, M. (2006). Rational imitation in 12-month-old infants. *Infancy, 10*(3), 303–311.

Shimizu, Y. A., & Johnson, S. C. (2004). Infants' attribution of a goal to a morphologically unfamiliar agent. *Developmental Science, 7*(4), 425–430.

Sodian, B., & Thoermer, C. (2004). Infants' understanding of looking, pointing and reaching as cues to goal-directed action. *Journal of Cognition and Development, 53,* 289–316.

Sommerville, J. A., Hildebrand, E. A., & Crane, C. C. (in press). Experience matters: The impact of doing versus watching on infants' subsequent perception of tool use events. *Developmental Psychology.*

Sommerville, J. A., & Woodward, A. L. (2005). Pulling out the intentional structure of human action: The relation between action production and processing in infancy. *Cognition, 95,* 1–30.

Sommerville, J. A., Woodward, A. L., & Needham, A. (2005). Action experience alters 3-month-old infants' perception of others' actions. *Cognition, 96,* B1–B11.

Tomasello, M. (1999). *The cultural origins of human cognition.* Cambridge, MA: Harvard University Press.

Tomasello, M., & Haberl, K. C. (2003). Understanding attention: 12- and 18-month-olds know what's new for other persons. *Developmental Psychology, 39,* 906–912.

Vasilyeva, M., Huttenlocher, J., & Waterfall, H. (2006). Effects of language intervention on syntactic skill levels in preschoolers. *Developmental Psychobiology, 42*(1), 164–174.

Wellman, H. M., Phillips, A. T., Dunphy-Lelii, S., & Lalonde, N. (2004). Infant understanding of persons predicts preschool social cognition. *Developmental Science, 7*(3), 283–288.

Wellman, H. M. (1992). *The child's theory of mind.* Cambridge, MA: MIT Press.

Willatts, P. (1999). Development of means-end behavior in young infants: Pulling a cloth to retrieve a distant object. *Developmental Psychology, 35,* 651–667.

Woodward, A. L. (1998). Infants selectively encode the goal object of an actor's reach. *Cognition, 69,* 1–34.

Woodward, A. L. (1999). Infants' ability to distinguish between purposeful and non-purposeful behaviors. *Infant Behavior and Development, 22,* 145–160.

Woodward, A. L. (2003a). Infants' developing understanding of the link between looker and object. *Developmental Science, 6*(3), 297–311.

Woodward, A. L. (2003b). Infants' developing understanding of the link between looker and object. *Developmental Science, 6:3,* 297–311.

Woodward, A. L. (2003c). Infants' use of action knowledge to get a grasp on words. In S. R. Waxman (Ed.), *Weaving a lexicon.* Cambridge, MA: MIT Press.

Woodward, A. L. (2005). The infant origins of intentional understanding. In R. V. Kail (Ed.), *Advances in child development and behavior* (Vol. 33, pp. 229–262). Oxford, UK: Elsevier.

Woodward, A. L., & Guajardo, J. J. (2002). Infants' understanding of the point gesture as an object-directed action. *Cognitive Development, 17,* 1061–1084.

Woodward, A. L., & Markman, E. M. (1998). Early word learning. In W. Damon, D. Kuhn, & R. Siegler (Eds.), *Handbook of child psychology* (Vol. 2: Cognition, perception and language, pp. 371–420). New York: John Wiley and Sons.

Woodward, A. L., & Sommerville, J. A. (2000). Twelve-month-old infants interpret action in context, *Psychological Science, 11,* 73–76.

Zacks, J. M., & Tversky, B. (2001). Event structure in perception and conception. *Psychological Bulletin, 127,* 3–21.

10

Early Word Learning and Other Seemingly Symbolic Behaviors

LAURA L. NAMY, EMORY UNIVERSITY

> When they called some thing by name and pointed it out while they spoke, I saw it and realized that the thing they wished to indicate was called by the name they then uttered.
>
> Augustine of Hippo, (354–430 AD)
> *Augustine: Confessions, Book 1* (p. 16)

St. Augustine described his early language learning experience as one that was supported by an inherent appreciation of the intentional, symbolic nature of spoken words. He observed that a speaker drew attention to an object, perceived that the speaker produced a word while (or just prior to) doing so, noted that the word was produced in an intentionally referential manner, and stored in memory the link between word and referent. He had attained a symbolic understanding of words. And in reflecting upon his early learning experiences, he articulated with eerie precision the elements necessary for symbolic understanding to be achieved.

Of course, St. Augustine's reflection upon his own childhood experiences may or may not have been accurate. When children begin to acquire words, do they employ the complex array of cognitive processes and social insights described by Augustine? Or might children solve the symbol-to-referent mapping problem without necessarily gleaning insight into the intentional and referential nature of that mapping? The goal of this chapter is to review some of my work investigating the question of whether symbol users grasp Augustine's insight into intentionality and reference from the onset of their development.

I start by generating a working definition of symbols, one that could easily have been generated by Augustine himself. Although this is not necessarily meant to be a comprehensive definition on which everyone would agree, it is a useful starting point for my explorations into symbolic understanding.

A symbol is a signal produced by some user with the intention of representing information for a recipient that is not inherent in the signal itself. This signal must be comprehended by the recipient *as a representation*.

There are two pieces to this symbolic puzzle, one regarding the intentions of the symbol user and the other involving the recipients' comprehension of the user's intentions. It is this second piece of the definition in which I am particularly interested with respect to young children's early symbol interpretation. To what extent do young children comprehend the intentional and representational nature of the symbols they encounter?

In this chapter, I focus on children's grasp of object names. Within the context of object naming, this problem can be instantiated very much as Augustine described: An adult speaker produces a novel label for a child. The speaker's intention is to represent and refer to a particular object using that label. The child then successfully maps the label to the appropriate object and extends that label to other instances and other contexts. Of central importance for understanding the initial cognitive status of symbol users is whether the child understands that the label is produced with the intention of *representing* the referent. Alternatively, children may adopt a word or other symbol via association, linking it to its referent, without clear insight into the intentions of the user. That is, children might acquire their first words and other symbols via a low-level domain-general process capitalizing on basic learning principles rather than via domain-specific knowledge of how communication works and how behaviors relate to mental perspective and intention.

Although bottom-up domain-general cognitive accounts of language learning have received recent attention (Samuelson & Smith, 1998; Elman, 1999; Plunkett & Schafer, 1999; Samuelson & Smith, 1999; Samuelson, 2002; Smith, Jones, Landau, Gershkoff-Stowe, & Samuelson, 2002; Saffran & Wilson, 2003; Soderstrom, Seidl, Nelson, & Jusczyk, 2003; Thiessen & Saffran, 2003), many researchers are quick to challenge the notion that children learn symbols operantly due to the subtlety with which children discriminate cues to meaning. Recent studies have documented that infants display an impressive sensitivity to both syntactic and social-pragmatic features that distinguish naming events from other types of verbal communication (see, e.g., Baldwin, 1993a, 1993b; Baldwin et al., 1996; Tomasello, Strosberg, & Akhtar, 1996; Waxman & Markow, 1998; Waxman, 1999; Namy & Waxman, 2000; Waxman & Booth, 2000; Hall, Lee, & Belanger, 2001; Campbell & Namy, 2003). Although there is compelling evidence that children are adept at detecting naming events and mapping object names to their appropriate referents, the developmental process of discovery and use of these cues to naming is subject to debate. For example, Samuelson and Smith (1998) argued that a word-learning phenomenon reported by Akhtar, Carpenter and Tomasello (1996) and attributed by those authors to children's understanding of discourse pragmatics could actually be explained more parsimoniously by the ways that the dynamics of the task directed children's attention to the target referent.

To further highlight the alternative mechanism that might be at work during children's word learning, it may be useful to draw on a term employed in the animal communication literature, "functional reference." In many studies of nonhuman primates, including the much discussed predator-specific alarm calls generated by vervet monkeys (Cheney & Seyfarth, 1990), in addition to context-specific calls soliciting agonistic aid in conflict situations (Gouzoules, Gouzoules, & Marler, 1984), researchers have documented behaviors that appear compellingly referential and seemingly symbolic in nature. However, animal communication researchers are quick to point out that there may be lower-level associative or operant mechanisms at work. For example, macaques use different calls to elicit aid when being attacked by a higher ranking animal than when in conflict with a family member. Although these different calls appear to be employed in an intentional manner to communicate different types of messages, a given animal may simply learn to match particular calls with particular contexts because these calls have been most successful in eliciting the desired response in conspecifics in such contexts in the past. Although this explanation begs the question of why particular calls became more highly associated with particular contexts in the first place, I would argue that it may be constructive to draw a page from the animal researchers' book and acknowledge that seemingly symbolic behaviors may result from detection of reliable covariance between signal and goal rather than from symbolic insight.

The studies reviewed in this chapter explore the relationship between seemingly symbolic behavior and symbolic insight in young children by investigating what signals a naming event and, more importantly, by investigating the mechanisms by which children acquire expectations about how symbols relate to their referents. My specific goals in this chapter are to report research addressing three facets of early symbolic insight: (1) an exploration of the range of symbolic forms or symbol media that children reliably map to objects, (2) an exploration of the range of different contexts in which symbol mapping reliably occurs, and (3) an exploration of how the set of symbols and contexts in which symbol mapping occurs changes over development. Each of these facets sheds light on what children understand about how symbols relate to referent and the nature of the cognitive mechanisms that underlie symbol learning.

Below I review the basic word-learning paradigm that I have employed to study children's symbol-mapping abilities. I subsequently discuss the effect of manipulating symbol type and context within this prototypical paradigm and how those manipulations influence children's success at symbol mapping at various points in development. I conclude by discussing the implications of these data and argue that young children's seemingly symbolic behaviors likely precede symbolic insight.

BASIC WORD-LEARNING PARADIGM

The paradigm that I typically use to test children's ability to acquire novel words is a forced-choice task. Children are typically seated across a table from an experimenter. The experimenter presents a target object (e.g., a cup) to the child, and the child and the experimenter engage in a semi-naturalistic free-play session with the object. In the course of play, the experimenter draws the child's attention to the target object six to nine times by pointing to or holding up the object while orienting toward it. Each time that the experimenter draws attention to the object, she labels the target object with a novel word, saying for example, "Look at this blicket!" or "You have a blicket!" After labeling the object multiple times, the experimenter removes the target object and presents a distracter object (e.g., an apple). The experimenter and child engage in a free-play session with this object as they did with the target, and the experimenter draws attention to the object six to nine times. Although the experimenter engages in the same referential behavior, such as pointing to and drawing attention to the object, she never labels the distracter, instead saying, for example, "Look at what you have!" or "What's this?"

Following this introduction to the novel label, we typically test whether children have successfully mapped the label to the target object using a forced-choice procedure. The experimenter administers a set of target trials during which children are simultaneously presented with both the target and distracter object and are asked, "Can you get the blicket? Which one is the blicket?" The experimenter also administers a set of preference control trials in which children are presented with the target and the distracter and are asked, "Can you pick one? Which one do I get?" The purpose of these control trials is to ensure that the act of labeling the target has not simply heightened the salience of the target object relative to the distracter, independent of children's symbolic mapping of the label. Success on this task is operationalized as reliably selecting the target object on target trials while responding randomly on control trials.

Note that this paradigm includes many prototypical features of real-world object-naming contexts: The symbol employed is a word, and the word is embedded in a rich, familiar, ritualized naming routine that includes all of the social and syntactic cues that typically signal a naming event. In the research described here, however, my colleagues and I have manipulated the type of information provided or the manner in which the information is provided, in the service of uncovering the underlying cognitive processes and the contextual bases for a symbol-to-referent mapping. In the first set of studies, we manipulated the type of symbol used in this paradigm. In the second set of studies, we manipulated the availability of those social and syntactic cues inherent in a typical naming routine. Below I review each of these lines of research then give a general description of the implications of these findings for our understanding of the early basis for symbolic behavior.

SYMBOLIC FORM AND ITS RELATION TO SYMBOL MAPPING

One approach to discovering the cognitive processes supporting word learning is to investigate the specificity of children's knowledge about word-to-referent mappings. Comparing children's ability to acquire verbal forms of symbolic reference with their ability to acquire nonverbal forms speaks to whether children apprehend that words are part of a distinct and privileged syntactic system of communication or whether they master the naming function of words before appreciating the features of verbal communication that distinguish it from nonverbal signaling.

Studies of children's nonverbal communication indicate that, early in development, children use both words and gestures as symbols. At around the same time that children acquire their first words, they often also begin using gestures to refer to, request, and label objects, actions, and events. Acredolo and Goodwyn (1988, Goodwyn & Acredolo, 1993) have demonstrated that children appear to acquire gestures for the same types of referents, to use them in the same contexts, and to use them to accomplish the same communicative goals. Similar studies by Iverson and colleagues (Iverson, Capirci, & Caselli, 1994; Iverson, Capirci, Longobardi, & Caselli, 1999) support the notion that children's early communicative repertoire includes both verbal and gestural symbols but find that the use of gestures as symbols declines over the course of development. As children become more experienced communicators, words and gestures appear to take on different communicative functions, with words playing the primary symbolic role, while gestures take on a supporting role as a form of deixis (e.g., pointing) or emphasis (Iverson et al., 1994).

My colleagues and I have investigated experimentally whether children map nonverbal symbols to objects as readily as they map words to objects at various points in development. We have explored children's interpretation of a variety of nonverbal symbolic forms, including not only words and gestures but also non-verbal sounds and pictograms (i.e., printed visual symbols). We have tested both arbitrary symbols (e.g., a dropping action for a cup, a rising glissando sound for a hammer) and iconic ones (i.e., gestures that resemble some aspect of the object; e.g., a drinking action for a cup, a banging noise for a hammer). The majority of our studies on symbolic form have tested 18- and 26-month-olds, age groups that represent two distinct points in communicative development in terms of vocabulary size, syntactic development, and productive use of symbolic gestures.

In each study, we present a symbol within the context of a social-referential play routine such as those employed in object-naming events using verbal labels. The basic paradigm described above is employed, but a nonverbal symbol is substituted for the verbal labels employed in traditional word-learning studies. The results of these studies paint a developmental picture of how the range of symbols children expect to be used to name an object changes over development (Namy & Waxman, 1998; Namy, 2001; Campbell & Namy, 2003; Namy, Campbell & Tomasello, 2004; Namy, 2008). The data are summarized in Table 10–1.

First, as an important starting point, we find that children at each of the ages tested are successful at mapping novel words to objects when the words are embedded in the prototypical naming paradigm (e.g., Waxman & Hall, 1993; Woodward, Markman, & Fitzsimmons, 1994; Namy & Waxman, 1998). We find no apparent developmental change in children's performance on this task. This lack of development shift in children's word-learning performance is consistent with

Table 10–1 Range of Symbol Types Mapped at Each Age

Symbol Type	18 months	26 months
Words	√	√
Arbitrary Gestures	√	Ø
Iconic Gestures	√	√
Arbitrary Sounds	√	Ø
"Iconic" Sounds	√	√
Arbitrary Pictograms	√	√
Iconic Pictograms	√	√

√ denotes successful mapping, Ø denotes unsuccessful mapping.

that reported in previous literature and has often been taken as evidence that children understand the privileged nature of words in the communicative repertoire from early in development. However, a comparison of children's word learning and their acquisition of other types of symbols under the same controlled learning conditions reveals important developmental shifts in children's insights into word learning.

Examination of children's ability to map nonverbal symbols to objects in this same richly structured naming context early in development reveals that at 18 months of age, children readily map all symbol types tested to objects, including gestures, sounds, and pictograms (Namy & Waxman, 1998; Namy, 2001; Namy & Waxman, 2002; Campbell & Namy, 2003; Namy, Campbell, & Tomasello, 2004). These studies yield similar effect sizes across various symbol types, indicating that it is not the case that children reliably map all symbols, but still retain a priority for some forms over others. We also find no advantage for iconic over arbitrary symbols at this age (Namy et al., 2004). It appears that embedding the nonverbal symbol in a familiar naming context is sufficient to elicit a naming interpretation at ceiling levels, with no apparent facilitation when the symbol resembles its referent. Thus, these findings suggest that the form of the symbol is largely irrelevant to whether the symbol will be mapped. It appears that embedding any symbolic form in a naming routine is sufficient to yield symbol-to-referent mapping, regardless of the symbol employed.

At 26 months, we see a very different and more sophisticated pattern. At this age, children fail to map arbitrary gestures to objects, although they readily map words (Namy & Waxman, 1998). They also fail to map arbitrary nonverbal sounds (Namy, 2006; see also Woodward & Hoyne, 1999). This suggests that by 26 months children have developed more conservative expectations about the types of symbols that can be used to name objects. It appears that at 26 months children are monitoring the communicative conventions employed in their environment and have ascertained that gestures, although an integral part of natural discourse, do not tend to serve the same communicative symbolic function that words do. Consistent with this interpretation is the finding that, although 26-month-olds fail to map arbitrary gestures and sounds to referents, they succeed at mapping arbitrary pictorial symbols. Printed visual symbols are, of course, a type of arbitrary symbol (e.g., printed letters) that is culturally supported in a way that arbitrary gestures and sounds tend not to be. Children at 26 months appear to be sensitive to this distinction.

Although children inhibit mapping of arbitrary symbols at 26 months, they reliably map iconic gestures at this age (Namy et al., 2004; Namy, 2006). This pattern suggests that although children have developed a priority for words over other nonverbal symbols by 26 months, an evident resemblance between the gesture and object releases children from their conservative expectations with respect to nonverbal symbols. We find a similar pattern for nonverbal sounds, in which children inhibit mapping arbitrary sounds to objects but readily map sounds that resemble those made by the object (Namy, 2001, 2008). Even for pictures, where arbitrary symbols are accepted by 26-month-olds, the mapping of iconic pictures to their referents is significantly more robust.

Some follow-up studies with this age group indicate that these children can learn to map arbitrary gestures to objects; however, they require much more explicit training and feedback in order to do so (Namy & Waxman, 1998). Thus, although they are able to map arbitrary symbols to objects, they do so via a very different process than the one they use to map words. This priority for words over other arbitrary symbols suggests that children have developed deeper knowledge about societal conventions with respect to object naming. They appear to understand that, among hearing people, we tend not to use nonverbal symbols to name.

Although the systematicity with which 26-month-olds accept or reject novel symbols reveals some degree of sophistication regarding naming conventions, it is striking that embedding nonverbal symbols in a highly familiar naming routine is not sufficient to motivate children to interpret these unconventional symbolic forms as object names. This implies that by 26 months children have sufficiently strong convictions regarding the communicative functions of various symbolic forms that they are unwilling to override these convictions, even when the labeling intention of the user is apparent from context. They have acquired a strong priority for culturally supported symbols. However, the fact that this priority is not evident at 18 months reveals that this priority emerges as a function of experience, suggesting that different cognitive mechanisms are driving symbol learning at different ages.

By contrast, some studies involving prelinguistic infants have suggested that children come to the word-learning endeavor with an expectation that words serve a unique role in object naming (Balaban & Waxman, 1997; Xu, 2002). However, my colleagues and I (Sheehan, Namy, & Mills, 2007) have recently conducted a study using event-related potential (ERP) to index neural semantic processing of words and gestures at 18 and 26 months. This study demonstrates that using gestures to name objects elicits similar neural activity to that elicited by words at 18 months but that gestures do not appear to be regarded as semantic at 26 months. This evidence confirms a developmental shift in children's expectations about the relative roles that words and gestures serve in symbolic communication.

In addition to the developmental change we have observed between 18 and 26 months, we have also found that developmental change continues past 26 months. For example, by four years of age, children readily accept both arbitrary and iconic nonverbal symbols, suggesting that the rigidity we observe at 26 months characterizes an important *intermediate* stage in mastering communicative conventions (Namy et al., 2004). ERP evidence confirms that adults also process gestures semantically, using similar neural systems for words and gestures (Kelly, Kravitz, & Hopkins, 2004; Wu & Coulson, 2005; Sheehan, Namy, & Mills, 2008). Older children and adults appear to place a higher priority on cues to naming intention and are willing to accept unconventional symbolic forms when the symbols are inserted into familiar naming routines that clarify their meaning.

These studies reveal complexity and systematicity in symbol-mapping patterns at 26 months and beyond. However, younger children's symbol learning appears to involve fewer subtleties. Eighteen-month-olds appear to have few expectations regarding the type of symbolic form that can be appropriately employed.

The central issue for this chapter is how to characterize the status of this early symbol learning. Given the apparent flexibility with which children acquire various symbolic forms, do children appreciate the symbol user's intention to represent and refer when using words and nonverbal symbols? Or are children relying on the naming routine as a reliable index to signal a naming event, without making attributions about the user's knowledge state and intentions? Whether we characterize this early symbol use as implying a symbolic understanding appears to hinge on whether children are making attributions of intention on the part of the user. These younger infants appear fairly indiscriminate in their mapping of symbols to referents when the symbols are embedded in a naming routine, raising the possibility that children are simply using the routine as a reliable predictor of naming, without necessarily processing the intentional state of the symbol user or the social conventions governing symbol use. If this is true, this reduces the nature of the symbol-referent relationship to a more operant or instrumental one, not necessarily a representational one.

CONTEXTUAL CUES TO NAMING AND THEIR ROLE IN SYMBOL MAPPING

To further explore whether 18-month-olds appreciate the intentions of others in a naming event, my colleagues and I have manipulated the range of contexts in which children are introduced to object names. In particular, we have explored how children use the naming routine to interpret a symbol as a name, since this naming routine clearly contains important cues to intention. What elements of the naming routine are critical for children to achieve successful symbol mapping, and what is it that children appear to glean from these elements? Of particular interest is children's use of social-referential cues inherent in the naming routine. Social referential cues, such as pointing, holding objects up, orienting one's body, and directing one's gaze toward objects signal an intention to name (or at least refer to) the object. We know from work by Baldwin, Tomasello, Akhtar and others (see, e.g., Baldwin, 1993a, 1993b; Tomasello & Akhtar, 1995; Baldwin et al., 1996; Tomasello, Strosberg, & Akhtar, 1996; Campbell & Namy, 2003) that children use these cues from an early age to determine the meaning of a novel word, and over the second year of life children become increasingly more sophisticated in their use of subtle social cues to naming. However, it is clear that children's capacity to employ these cues is still developing at 18 months. Children certainly possess many social and social-cognitive skills by this point in development, but bringing these abilities to bear on a word-learning context is a greater challenge.

By 18 months of age, children appear to understand that eye gaze and pointing are important cues to reference. For example, Baldwin (1993b) has shown that children can use these cues to determine which of two referents an experimenter is labeling. Baldwin et al. (1996) have also demonstrated that children expect these cues to originate from the same source as the label. For example, they placed children in a word-learning context in which an experimenter seated across the table from the child provided a rich, interactive set of social-referential cues; however, the labels were produced by a second experimenter, hidden behind a screen. Although the labels were perfectly contingent on children's attention to the objects and were accompanied by social-referential cues, children failed to map the words to the objects when these cues were "de-coupled" from the naming source. In a recent extension of this study, Aimee Campbell and I (Campbell & Namy, 2003) replicated this "de-coupled" study for both words and nonverbal sounds. In this study, the names were emitted by a baby monitor positioned beside the child. We found that, for both words and sounds, children failed to map the symbols to the objects in this de-coupled context, although both were readily mapped when labels were produced by the same source that produced the social cues.

These findings provide compelling evidence that children understand that social-referencing cues signal naming events. However, I have conducted a series of studies that raises the possibility that children may be solving the symbol-to-referent mapping problem and may even develop expectations about how particular cues signal reference without making attributions about others' intentions. Each of these studies demonstrates that although children seem to understand the importance of these cues to intention, the cognitive processes involved may use rudimentary pattern detection rather than insight into intentionality. Below I outline two examples that demonstrate how flexibly and readily children come to use a novel set of cues to signal a naming event. In each case, these novel cues have no relation to conventional cues to intentionality; as a result, children's ability to learn to use them "on the fly" seems more likely to be a byproduct of pattern recognition.

The first example explores children's use of naming phrases to signal a naming event. Naming phrases are carrier phrases that are typically used to label an object, such as "This is a _____" or "Look at the _____." By 18 months, children understand that naming phrases signal naming events (Namy & Waxman, 2000). For example, children interpret novel words embedded in naming phrases (e.g., "Look at the blicket!") as object names. In contrast, children do not interpret novel words as object names when they are embedded in sentence frames that typically do not convey object naming (Namy & Waxman, 2000). For example, children do not interpret novel words as object names when they are presented in syntactic isolation (e.g., "Look! Blicket!")—a construction that does not typically indicate a naming event.

This study suggests that children understand how linguistic context can reflect and convey naming intention. However, we found that a very brief training period overrides children's expectations that object names should be presented in naming phrases. For example, after a brief play session in which an experimenter labeled familiar objects with their familiar basic-level names in syntactic isolation (e.g., "Look! Spoon!"), children subsequently interpreted novel words presented in isolation (e.g., "Look! Blicket!") as object names. Furthermore, after hearing familiar objects labeled with their basic-level names in a nonsense phrase (e.g., "Shalem bosher spoon!"), children subsequently interpreted novel words presented in this context (e.g., "Shalem bosher blicket!") as object names (Namy & Waxman, 2000). Thus, children appear to monitor the input to discover which behaviors are reliable indices of naming in that particular context and adapt their expectations in real time, to reflect these indices. This suggests that rather than constructing entrenched representations of what meanings are conveyed by syntactic constructions and why, children are simply identifying diagnostic cues to naming events based on the reliability of the associations between naming events and particular contextual cues. As a result, they readily adapt which cues they use as alternative cues emerge as reliable.

A second demonstration of children's ability to adapt their expectations on the fly comes from a study of children's use of social-referential cues. As we know from the studies reviewed above (Baldwin et al., 1996; Campbell & Namy, 2003), children fail to map words to objects if the words are produced by a naming source that is de-coupled from social cues. In Baldwin et al.'s study, the de-coupled naming source was a person out of view behind a screen. In our previous study (Campbell & Namy, 2003), the source was a clearly inanimate object, a baby monitor.

My colleagues and I have followed up on this finding to examine whether children would successfully map novel words to objects in this de-coupled context if the de-coupled naming source appeared oriented toward the task. To accomplish this sense of orientation toward the task while eliminating any conventional social-referential cues, we placed the baby monitor inside a teddy bear "seated" next to the experimenter and physically oriented toward the task, although the bear was obviously not capable of performing any nonverbal cues to reference. During the experimental session, the experimenter drew attention to the objects, but the teddy bear labeled the objects. We found that even though the teddy bear was oriented toward the task, children did not regard him as a naming source. Children failed to map his labels to the objects in this context. This suggests that children have, indeed, developed a strong expectation that labels must originate from the same source as the social cues.

However, as in the previous example, a brief training period overrides this expectation that words should be "coupled" with social cues to reference. After hearing the teddy bear label a familiar object with its basic-level name (e.g., "Spoon!"), children subsequently interpreted novel words produced by the teddy bear as object names. Thus, children readily mapped words to objects in this de-coupled context if the de-coupled naming source was independently established as one that produces object names (Namy, Robertson, Campbell, & Krueger, 2008).

Both of these sets of experiments reveal that at 18 months children readily adapt their expectations about which contextual cues signal a naming event, depending on the reliability of the association between these cues and naming events in the input. This adaptive mechanism operates independently of whether or not those predictive cues routinely or historically imply an intention to name on the part of the labeler. This suggests that at 18 months children may successfully map symbols to referents in the absence of an intentional understanding of the mental state of the user. That their expectations are so malleable and so readily reorganized suggests that infants have not yet acquired deep insights into the stable, enduring communicative conventions that convey naming intention. Instead, they seem to be looking for behavioral indices that most reliably predict a naming relation, without taking that extra step of drawing inferences about others' knowledge states or intentions.

Alternatively, the use of familiar labels in both experiments may have been a sufficient cue in and of itself to enable children to infer that the user has a naming intention, although the user is not employing those cues typically used to convey naming intent. Thus, it may be that the use of familiar object names leads to an attribution of intentionality. However, if so, we would expect that older children, who are more advanced and sophisticated in their reasoning about others' intentions, would be equally or more likely to make similar attributions in this case. We have found clear developmental change in this task which argues against this alternative conclusion. Just as we find that 26-month-olds are resistant to learning nonverbal symbols, we find that 26-month-olds are highly resistant to mapping novel words to objects when the labels originate from a de-coupled source, regardless of the source's prior history of naming (Namy et al., 2008).

The finding that 18-month-olds accept any symbolic form plugged into a familiar naming routine in conjunction with the finding that 18-month-olds readily adapt the cues they employ to infer a naming event based on the reliability of such cues in the input suggests that young children display seemingly sophisticated symbolic behaviors without a clear symbolic understanding. The finding that 26-month-olds display strong expectations regarding both which types of symbols serve which communicative functions and how reference is conveyed implies that insight into the symbolic nature of words is emerging over the course of the second year of life. The fact that children continue to display developmental change with heightened flexibility and sophistication in the preschool years and beyond implies that a mature understanding of symbolic representation has a prolonged developmental time course.

CONCLUSIONS

In this chapter, I have presented evidence consistent with the claim that there is marked developmental change in children's insights into the communicative conventions that govern symbol use. Although children appear equally adept at mapping words to objects throughout the second year and beyond, the studies presented here reveal that word learning at 18 months involves a different process than does word learning at 26 months. At 18 months, children regard words as one of a range of different symbolic forms that are equipotential with respect to object naming. By 26 months, children have a strong priority for words over other symbolic forms and for iconic over arbitrary nonverbal symbols. At 18 months, children have no strong expectations about the contextual cues that will signal object naming. Instead, they appear to monitor the commonalities across object-naming events and identify which cues seem to index naming most reliably. They adapt flexibly and readily acquire novel cues to naming. By 26 months, children have clear expectations about social and syntactic cues to naming and expect speakers to adhere to established communicative conventions.

I began this chapter by arguing that St. Augustine got it right: Insight into the intentional and representational nature of a symbol is required for symbolic understanding. The data presented here raise the possibility that children's early seemingly symbolic behavior may not imply symbolic understanding. The patterns observed are consistent with the notion that symbolic insight emerges only as a function of experience with using symbols. That is, children may begin to use and interpret symbols without understanding their inherently intentional and representational nature. However, having begun to use symbols, children become increasingly more aware of the ways in which the communicative conventions that govern symbol use and communicative intentions relate to communicative behaviors.

If it is the case that very young symbol users lack representational understanding, how does this transition from nonrepresentational to representational understanding occur? Clearly, there is empirical work to be done to address this question; however, I would propose that change is gradual and continuous. My studies indicate that young children are perpetually monitoring and adapting to the regularities observed in their environment and capitalize upon their experiences with familiar names to inform their ability to interpret novel words.

This process creates a bidirectional feedback loop between learning words and identifying reliable cues to meaning. Children's first words are acquired slowly, with effort, and, presumably, associatively. Once children have accrued a small database of known words, they can use the instances in which these words are employed to help them identify which contextual aspects reliably predict naming events. This, in turn, helps children identify subsequent naming events more readily. The learning system builds on itself over time. For example, identification of gross general cues to naming, such as particular carrier phrases, can direct children's attention to the relevance of syntactic constructions to word meaning. Once children have established that syntactic context is relevant to word meaning, they can begin to identify and use subtler syntactic distinctions. In this manner, children's appreciation of how context conveys meaning becomes increasingly subtle and sophisticated. As a result, children discover the symbolic nature of the symbolic behaviors they have employed while acquiring an increasingly stronger commitment to established communicative conventions over time.

References

Acredolo, L., & Goodwyn, S. (1988). Symbolic gesturing in normal infants. *Child Development, 59,* 450–466.
Akhtar, N., Carpenter, M., & Tomasello, M. (1996). The role of discourse novelty in early word learning. *Child Development, 67,* 635–645.
Augustine (1960). *Confessions* (A. C. Outler, Trans. and Ed.). Philadelphia: Westminster Press.
Balaban, M., & Waxman, S. R. (1997). Do words facilitate object categorization in 9-month-old infants? *Journal of Experimental Child Psychology, 64,* 3–26.
Baldwin, D. A. (1993a). Early referential understanding: Infants' ability to recognize referential acts for what they are. *Developmental Psychology, 29,* 832–843.
Baldwin, D. A. (1993b). Infant's ability to consult the speaker for clues to word reference. *Journal of Child Language, 20,* 395–418.
Baldwin, D. A., Markman, E. M., Bill, B., Desjardins, R. N., Irwin, J. M., & Tidball, G. (1996). Infants' reliance on a social criterion for establishing word-object relations. *Child Development, 67,* 3135–3153.

Campbell, A. L., & Namy, L. L. (2003). The role of social-referential context in verbal and nonverbal symbol learning. *Child Development, 74,* 549–563.

Cheney, D., & Seyfarth, R. (1990). The assessment by vervet monkeys of their own and another species' alarm calls. *Animal Behaviour, 40*(4), 754–764.

Elman, J. (1999). The emergence of language: A conspiracy theory. In B. MacWhinney (Ed.), *The emergence of language* (pp. 1–27). Mahwah, NJ: Erlbaum.

Goodwyn, S., & Acredolo, L. (1993). Symbolic gesture versus word: Is there a modality advantage for the onset of symbol use? *Child Development, 64,* 688–701.

Gouzoules, S., Gouzoules, H., & Marler, P. (1984). Rhesus monkey (*Macaca mulatta*) screams: Representational signalling in the recruitment of agonistic aid. *Animal Behaviour, 32*(1), 182–193.

Hall, D., Lee, S., & Belanger, J. (2001). Young children's use of syntactic cues to learn proper names and count nouns. *Developmental Psychology, 37,* 298–307.

Iverson, J.M., Capirci, O., Longobardi, E., & Caselli, M. C. (1999). Gesturing in mother-child interactions. *Cognitive Development, 14*(1), 57–75.

Iverson, J. M., Capirci, O., & Caselli, M. C. (1994). From communication to language in two modalities. *Cognitive Development, 9,* 23–43.

Kelly, S., Kravitz, C., & Hopkins, M. (2004). Neural correlates of bimodal speech and gesture comprehension. *Brain and Language, 89*(1), 253–260.

Namy, L. L. (2001). What's in a name when it isn't a word? 17-month-olds' mapping of non-verbal symbols to object categories. *Infancy, 2,* 73–86.

Namy, L. L. (2008). *The basis for an iconicity advantage in symbol learning at 26 months.* Manuscript under revision.

Namy, L. L., Campbell, A. L., & Tomasello, M. (2004). The changing role of iconicity in non-verbal symbol learning: A U-shaped trajectory in the acquisition of arbitrary gestures. *Journal of Cognition & Development, 5,* 37–57.

Namy, L. L., Robertson, R., Campbell, A. L., & Krueger, A. (2008). *When Teddy talks: Young children's interpretation of novel words produced without social cues to reference.* Manuscript under revision.

Namy, L. L. & Waxman, S. R. (1998). Words and gestures: Infants' interpretations of different forms of symbolic reference. *Child Development, 69,* 295–308.

Namy, L. L., & Waxman, S. R. (2000). Naming and exclaiming: Infants' sensitivity to naming contexts. *Journal of Cognition and Development, 1,* 405–428.

Plunkett, K., & Schafer, G. (1999). Early speech perception and word learning. In M. Barrett (Ed.), *The development of language: Studies in developmental psychology* (pp. 51–71). Hove, UK: Psychology Press.

Saffran, J. R., & Wilson, D. P. (2003). From syllables to syntax: Multilevel statistical learning by 12-month-old infants. *Infancy, 4,* 273–284.

Samuelson, L. K. (2002). Statistical regularities in vocabulary guide language acquisition in connectionist models and 15–20-month-olds. *Developmental Psychology, 38,* 1016–1037.

Samuelson, L. K., & Smith, L. B. (1998). Memory and attention make smart word learning: An alternative account of Akhtar, Carpenter, and Tomasello. *Child Development, 69,* 94–104.

Samuelson, L. K., & Smith, L. B. (1999). Early noun vocabularies: Do ontology, category structure and syntax correspond? *Cognition, 73,* 1–33.

Sheehan, E., Namy, L. L., & Mills, D. L. (2007). Developmental changes in neural activity to familiar words and gestures. *Brain and Language,* 101, 246–259.

Sheehan, E. A., Namy, L. L., & Mills, D. L. (2008). Semantic processing of spoken words and meaningful gestures. Manuscript in preparation.

Smith, L. B., Jones, S. S., Landau, B., Gershkoff-Stowe, L., & Samuelson, L. (2002). Object name learning provides on-the-job training for attention. *Psychological Science, 13,* 13–19.

Soderstrom, M., Seidl, A., Nelson, D. G. K., & Jusczyk, P. W. (2003). The prosodic bootstrapping of phrases: Evidence from prelinguistic infants. *Journal of Memory & Language, 49,* 249–267.

Thiessen, E. D., & Saffran, J. R. (2003). When cues collide: Use of stress and statistical cues to word boundaries by 7- to 9-month-old infants. *Developmental Psychology, 39,* 706–716.

Tomasello, M., & Akhtar, N. (1995). Two-year-olds use pragmatic cues to differentiate reference to objects and actions. *Cognitive Development, 10,* 201–224.

Tomasello, M., Strosberg, R., & Akhtar, N. (1996). Eighteen-month-old children learn words in non-ostensive contexts. *Journal of Child Language, 23,* 157–176.

Waxman, S. R. (1999). Specifying the scope of 13-month-olds' expectations for novel words. *Cognition, 70,* B35–B50.

Waxman, S. R., & Booth, A. E. (2000). Principles that are invoked in the acquisition of words, but not facts. *Cognition, 77,* B33–B43.

Waxman, S. R., & Hall, D. G. (1993). The development of a linkage between count nouns and object categories: Evidence from 15- to 21-month-old infants. *Child Development, 64,* 1224–1241.

Waxman, S. R., & Markow, D. B. (1998). Object properties and object kind: Twenty-one-month-old infants' extension of novel adjectives. *Child Development, 69,* 1313–1329.

Woodward, A. L., & Hoyne, K. L. (1999). Infants' learning about words and sounds in relation to objects. *Child Development, 70,* 65–77.

Woodward, A. L., Markman, E. M., & Fitzsimmons, C. M. (1994). Rapid word learning in 13- and 18-month-olds. *Developmental Psychology, 30,* 553–566.

Wu, Y. C., & Coulson, S. (2005). Meaningful gestures: Electrophysiological indices of iconic gesture comprehension. *Psychophysiology, 42,* 654–669.

Xu, F. (2002). The role of language in acquiring object kind concepts in infancy. *Cognition, 85*(3), 223–250.

11

Symbol-Based Learning in Infancy

JUDY S. DELOACHE, UNIVERSITY OF VIRGINIA;
AND PATRICIA A. GANEA, BOSTON UNIVERSITY

Picture a person—an infant or toddler—in the process of learning new information about the world. It seems likely that you may have generated some of the following types of images—a baby looking intently at a talking adult as if trying to
figure out what the words mean, an infant working intently to fit one object inside
another, a toddler wobbling uncertainly while attempting to walk from one piece
of furniture to another.

Now picture another person—an adult—also in the process of learning new
information about the world.

We would guess that your images this time might include an adult having a
conversation with another person, reading a newspaper, watching a documentary
on television, consulting a road map, interpreting a graph, and so on. Notice the
stark contrast in these images of how very young versus mature humans go about
the process of acquiring information about their world. Most of the infants' efforts
involve *direct*, physical interaction with the world. By interacting directly with the
environment and objects in it, infants gain valuable information about what they
are capable of doing, the properties of objects, the meaning of words, and so on.
For the adults, most routes to acquiring new information involve a variety of symbolic media that represent the environment and objects in it, in addition to ideas,
beliefs, and so on. Because of their ability to acquire information indirectly, in the
absence of direct experience, adults have vastly greater opportunities for learning
than infants do.

This difference between the learning possibilities for adults and older children
versus infants and toddlers is profound. Nothing distinguishes humans from other
species more than our use of symbols for acquiring information. Our capacity for
symbolization enables us to learn new information provided to us by other people,

whether in conversation or via symbolic artifacts. Indeed, without symbols, the cultural preservation and transmission of information from one generation to succeeding ones would be impossible. Becoming symbol-minded (DeLoache, 2002) is required for full participation in any society, so beginning to master some of the symbolic media that play a prominent role in one's society is a fundamental learning task of early childhood.

A crucial benefit of coming to understand the nature and use of various symbolic media is the possibility of then exploiting those media to learn about the world. A recurrent theme of this chapter is the relation between learning *about* various types of symbols and learning *from* them.

We review some of the growing literature on symbol-based learning in the first few years of life, focusing particularly on very recent research involving two of the most common and influential symbolic media in the lives of very young children. We begin with the most powerful and prevalent symbol system—language—and consider how infants and very young children come to acquire new information from what they hear people say, even when the entities to which the information applies are absent. Next, we consider early learning with respect to another nearly ubiquitous type of symbol—pictures.

LANGUAGE-BASED LEARNING

A vast literature documents the early steps of language development, including research on the processes involved in speech perception, word learning, and syntactic and pragmatic development in infancy. Less attention has been focused on *language as a tool*, as a means of acquiring information about the world. Parents and older siblings expose infants and toddlers to massive amounts of information simply by talking to them. They tell young children the names of people, animals, and objects, and they communicate a great deal of conceptual information about those entities. Often, the entity being discussed is physically present, but the potential of language as a source of new knowledge would be markedly restricted if one could learn only from information provided about the here and now. Because of language, we can learn new information about entities around the corner or on the moon.

The ability to use language to communicate about something not currently perceptible is made possible by the symbolic nature of language (Werner & Kaplan, 1956; Brown, 1958; Hockett, 1960). A word (or larger unit of speech) stands for something by virtue of a purely abstract relation between words and referents. Very early in development, however, the name of an object or person may be associated with the relevant entity without there being a *symbolic* relation between them.

Suppose, for example, a mother calls her very young child into the kitchen and says, "Do you want a cookie?" The child's mental representation of cookies might be activated because the sound "cookie" is associated with the jar in which they are normally kept, the room in which the jar and its contents are to be found, the period right after lunch when cookies are usually offered, his mother—the usual offerer, and so on. At this point, the word is simply an associate of but not a symbol for cookies. Later in development, however, the child could hear the same phrase while playing in the yard and be inspired to come into the house, go to the kitchen, and wait expectantly by the cookie jar. At this point, the word is functioning symbolically.

In a seminal paper, Huttenlocher and Higgins (1978) provided an extensive analysis of possible ways to distinguish between nonsymbolic (associative) links versus symbolic relations between words and concepts in the early phases of language development. They concluded that the strongest evidence that a word is understood or used symbolically comes from the child's performance of some behavior that could be based only on an active representation of an absent entity (as in the cookie jar example).

Early in the second year of life, infants begin to provide evidence of understanding references to absent entities. This momentous developmental step marks the advent of an enormous expansion in the extent to which an infant can share a focus of attention with another person. In particular, joint attention and communication can now occur about things that are not currently present. As a consequence, it becomes possible for children to acquire new information about entities they have never directly experienced; they become capable of learning simply from hearing new information attributed to non-present entities.

Understanding Displaced Speech

A large literature exists on the *production* of references to absent objects or events—also referred to as displaced speech—from early theoretical views (Werner & Kaplan, 1956; Brown, 1958; Hockett, 1960) to recent empirical investigations (e.g., Veneziano & Sinclair, 1995; Adamson & Bakeman, 2006). Infants first begin referring to absent entities at around 17 or 18 months of age.

Much less is known about the development of the ability to *comprehend* displaced speech. Early information on this topic came from naturalistic observations conducted in the homes of infants (Lewis, 1936; Huttenlocher, 1974; Sachs, 1983). When an infant's parent referred to a person or object that was not present, the researchers noted any response on the part of the infant indicating that hearing the name brought the entity to mind. For example, upon hearing a favorite toy mentioned, the infant's going to search for it in the toy box where it was usually kept was taken as evidence that the child understood the reference to the absent object. This research established that the ability to understand another person's reference to something not present in the environment is evident as early as 13 months of age, at least when infants are in their own homes (Lewis, 1936; Huttenlocher, 1974).

Home observation studies, often of the researcher's own child, have also revealed that when parents refer to non-present entities in conversation with their infants, they often provide assistance to help the child understand what they're talking about (e.g., Sachs, 1983). One form of assistance is talking about a unique, highly familiar referent (e.g., "Where's Daddy?" or "See the moon?"), leaving little room for ambiguity with respect to the topic of conversation. Another strategy to facilitate comprehension is to refer to an absent entity in conjunction with some perceptually available cue, such as the container in which the object is usually found, or an object belonging to the person mentioned (Shimpi, 2005).

Recent laboratory studies of the comprehension of displaced reference have furthered our understanding of the early development of this vital ability. One factor that has emerged from this work is the importance of contextual support: Whether a very young child responds to the mention of an absent referent depends on multiple aspects of the situation.

For example, Saylor (2004) established that children as young as 12 months of age are capable of responding to the mention of an absent entity when there is something available to remind them of its existence. In this research, the infants first saw two objects from familiar categories. The objects differed in color, and each rested in front of a panel of the same color as the object itself. The objects were then removed. When the experimenter subsequently mentioned one of the now-absent objects, the matching panel that had previously been associated with the object was available to serve as a reminder of the object. Hearing the object named, the infants looked and gestured to the panel of the matching color, indicating that hearing the name of the object had brought it (and its color) to mind.

Related evidence suggests that quite young infants may respond to the mention of a non-visible entity *only* when there is some form of contextual support. In another study by Saylor and Baldwin (2004), 12- to 31-month-old infants heard an experimenter refer to an absent familiar person—the child's own father. Hearing the experimenter talk about "Daddy," the infants from 15 months on responded in some way (e.g., looking toward the door of the laboratory playroom and even searching for their absent parent). The 12-month-olds, however, showed no discernible response. Thus, there was no evidence that hearing the name of an extremely familiar and highly valued absent person caused 12-month-olds to think about him.

Ganea and Saylor (2008) asked whether a different result might occur if there was additional contextual support for very young infants' response to hearing the name of a beloved person. In their study, the child was accompanied to the lab by two people—either both parents or one parent and a sibling. The trio spent some time together in the testing room, and then one of the child's companions left the room. Shortly afterward, the experimenter referred to the absent person. The majority (88%) of the 13-month-olds and all of the 15-month-olds responded in a meaningful way to the name of their out-of-view sibling or parent.

In combination with the previous research, this study indicates that children are more likely to comprehend and react to a reference to an absent entity in a supportive context. There were two factors that may have contributed to better performance than was seen in the Saylor and Baldwin (2004) study. First, the absent individual had been in the room in which the reference to him or her occurred; thus, the person was associated with the current context in the child's mind. Second, there was a relatively short delay (only 2 min) between when the child had last seen the person and when the reference to him or her was heard.

Systematic evidence specifically delineating the importance of contextual factors in the early comprehension of absent reference has recently been provided (Ganea, 2005). In an initial study, 13- and 14-month-old infants were first taught a proper name—Max—for a novel stuffed animal. (They were taught a name for the toy so that it could later be referred to in its absence.) The toy was then put in a basket that was placed beside a couch, and the experimenter and child sat on the floor in front of the couch to read a picture book. The toy was out of sight in the basket, but quite nearby and easily accessible. (See Fig. 11–1.)

The picture book that the experimenter read to the child had been specially designed to provide a natural way that the experimenter could repeatedly refer to "Max" without providing any other reminders of the existence of the out-of-sight toy. The toy was never depicted in the book, but the text repeatedly referred to it. ("This is the park where Max likes to play. He likes to go down the slide.") As in the other studies of comprehension of absent reference described above, the question was whether the child would do something to indicate that his or her mental representation of the toy had been activated by hearing its name.

The infants provided evidence of comprehension of absent reference. Upon hearing Max referred to, most of them (86%) did something to reestablish contact (either visual or physical) with the toy. Some simply looked to where the invisible toy was concealed in the basket beside the couch, and sometimes they also pointed

Figure 11–1. In the first study in Ganea's (2005) research on comprehension of absent reference by 13- and 14-month-old infants, a toy was out of sight but readily accessible in a basket beside the couch when the child heard it referred to. In the subsequent two studies, the toy was farther back, beside the couch, making it somewhat less readily accessible. This slight contextual change affected the children's performance. Reprinted from Ganea (2005). Contextual factors affect absent reference comprehension in 14-month-olds. *Child Development, 76,* 989–998. With permission from Blackwell.

toward it. Some children actually got up and went over to reestablish contact with the toy. Thus, by 13 months of age, hearing the newly learned name of a currently absent object in a novel environment can bring the object to mind.

Two additional studies employed the same basic approach, but contextual factors were varied. In the second study, everything was the same as in the first, but the toy was less readily accessible. It was placed farther back to the side of the couch so that it was not visible to the child unless he or she actually got up and went toward it. In the third study, the procedure was the same as in the second one, but a 15-minute delay (a walk down the hallway for a drink of water) was interposed between when the toy was placed in the basket and when it was referred to in the picture-book interaction.

The 13-month-old children less frequently reacted to the name of the absent object in these two studies than did the infants in the first one. When the toy was less readily accessible, only 50% of the children reacted to hearing it referred to by looking, pointing, or going over to reestablish contact with it. When the toy was both less accessible *and* there was a 15-minute delay from when the infant had last seen it, only 19% of the children responded to its name.

This series of studies provides direct evidence that comprehension of absent reference is context-dependent. Hearing a reference to something not immediately present may or may not prompt a very young child to respond to it, depending on various factors. When the out-of-sight toy was readily accessible (i.e., nearby and easy to get to), the infants more often responded to hearing its name than they did when it was slightly less accessible. Similarly, a delay between when the object was last seen and when the reference to it was heard led to a lower rate of responding.

Recent research by Shimpi (2005) provides evidence of a further step in the development of the comprehension of absent reference—an effect of hearing a reference to an absent object on the activation of associated information. In the crucial condition in this study, infants of 14, 18, and 22 months of age were shown pairs of video images of common objects (e.g., wheel, flower). With the two images on the screen, the infants heard a word ("car") that was not the name of either object, but that was associated with one of them. When the 18- and 22-month-olds (but not the 14-month-olds) heard the name of a familiar but absent object ("car"), they looked longer at the picture of the object commonly associated with it (the wheel). Thus, hearing the name of the familiar type of absent object not only brought it to mind but also directed the older infants' attention to something associated with that object.

To summarize, at the beginning of their second year, infants take a crucial preliminary step toward mastery of one of the core features of language—the use of words to communicate beyond the here and now. However, whether they respond overtly to hearing an absent object referred to depends on the complex interaction of multiple representational and contextual factors (Ganea, 2005).

With respect to *representational* factors, for a child to respond to hearing the name of an absent object—"doggie," for example—the child's mental representation of dogs in general or of a particular dog has to be activated. (We use "object" here, even though the absent entity could also be a person, pet, substance, etc.)

The likelihood that an object representation will be activated by mention of the object depends on the strength of the child's mental representation of both the object itself and its name. Further, activation depends on the strength of the word–object link. Thus, the more experience a child has had with an object and the more times the child has heard the name in connection with it, the more likely it is that hearing the object named when it is out of sight will activate its representation.

With respect to *contextual* factors, activation of the object representation is more likely to happen in a context with which the object has been directly associated. Similarly, activation is more likely the more recently the object was encountered. The presence of something that the child has experienced in association with the object also makes mental activation more likely.

The affective importance of the object—the child's emotional attachment to it—may also matter. We suspect that a child would be more likely to respond to hearing the name of a beloved security object (if the child could be separated from it in the first place) than to a less emotionally salient entity. Similarly, a response to the name of an absent parent or family member should occur earlier than a response to the mention of a relatively unfamiliar person that the child just met. Note that these examples of affective salience are inherently confounded with amount of experience, but these factors could be teased apart in future research.

Presumably, all these and many other representational and contextual factors interact to determine whether a young infant does anything in response to hearing an absent entity referred to. Future research on the interaction of these and other factors could markedly enhance our understanding of what brings about the beginning of the comprehension of references to absent objects. One general difficulty with this line of research is that inferences can be drawn only if the child makes an observable response to the mention of an absent object. When children fail to respond, it could be that they are incapable of understanding a reference to an absent object or that for some reason they are not at the moment motivated to do anything overt. Future research employing imaging techniques might further our understanding of this phenomenon, as it could reveal specific neural activation to the mention of an absent object when no behavioral response is observable.

Learning from Displaced Speech

The emergence early in the second year of life of the comprehension of references to absent objects sets the stage for the development of the ability to *acquire new information* about non-present entities and events. Often when someone communicates information to us about a known person (place, object, situation, etc.), the topic of the message is absent. We accommodate such information by updating our mental representation of the person with the recently received information. Thus, if we are told that our dog got into the mud hole again, we update our mental representation of the pet, regretfully incorporating his current bedraggled state.

Young children frequently hear information that provides the basis for updating: "Mommy's getting her hair cut." "The cookies are done now." When are infants capable of revising their mental representation of an object or situation based on what someone tells them has happened? What is involved in the emergence and early development of this ability?

We are not aware of any existing research on this important topic. Accordingly, we have been examining infants' ability to incorporate new information into their mental representation of a currently absent object (Ganea, Shutts, Spelke, & DeLoache, 2007). Our specific question concerns the modification of an existing mental representation of an absent object, based solely on hearing something new about it.

To examine this topic, we first taught infants a proper name for a stuffed animal. Then—with the toy out of sight in another room—we informed the infant that the toy had undergone a change in state. What we wanted to know was whether the infants' mental representation of the toy would be modified to accommodate the change that they had been told about but had not witnessed.

In this study, 19- and 22-month-old infants were initially shown three stuffed animals—for example, two identical frogs and one pig. One of the frogs was then put away, and the children learned a proper name—"Lucy"—for the remaining one. (A proper name was taught so the specific toy could later be referred to in its absence.) The child and experimenter played for a while with Lucy and the pig (which was never given a proper name). Next, the toys were left behind as the experimenter and child went to the adjoining room to read an unrelated picture book.

As they were engaged in the reading interaction, an assistant entered, carrying a bucket of water, and announced, "I'm going to go next door and wash the table." She went into the room in which the toys were located, closing the door behind her. About two minutes later, she returned and exclaimed in an agitated voice, "I'm so sorry—I spilled water on Lucy. Lucy's all wet!" Then the experimenter and child returned to the first room to "see Lucy." The question was whether the child's mental representation of Lucy had been modified on the basis of the new information.

Upon entering, the child saw the three toys on the table. One of the two frogs was sopping wet, as was the nameless pig. The child was asked to indicate which toy was Lucy. Our reasoning was that if the infants identified the thoroughly drenched frog as Lucy, it would indicate that hearing "Lucy's all wet" had (1) activated their mental representation of Lucy (a frog) *and,* of primary importance for this study, (2) led to the incorporation into that representation of what they heard had happened to Lucy. Thus, successful identification would provide evidence that the infants had updated their mental representation of the absent entity.

The majority (80%) of the 22-month-old children selected the wet frog as Lucy. Thus, this age group showed evidence of being able to incorporate new information into an existing mental representation of an absent object. The 19-month-olds, however, did not perform above chance (45% correct). They did remember the object–name relation, as shown by the fact that they almost always ignored the pig, identifying one of the two frogs as Lucy. Nevertheless, they did not use the information they had heard about the toy in its absence to identify which particular frog was Lucy.

To see if the younger children might be able to update if the task were simplified, a new group of 19-month-olds was given the same experience, but the test involved only the two identical animals—one wet and one dry. Even with this less demanding task, selection of the correct toy was not above chance.

An additional test confirmed that the poor performance of the younger children was not due to a simple failure to understand what was said to them. Everything was the same for a new group of 19-month-olds except that the two animals were in full view when they heard about the spilling accident. When the experimenter informed them that she had spilled water on Lucy ("Look what happened! I spilled water all over Lucy.), they were standing in front of the two identical animals—one wet and one dry. The children were then asked to indicate which of the toys was Lucy. This procedure eliminated the need to update a representation of an *absent* object. All that was needed to respond correctly was to understand what the experimenter said about the toys they could see and update their representation of a *present* object.

The majority of children (70%) selected the correct toy (a rate marginally above chance). This result indicates that, in the previous studies, the 19-month-olds' failure to use the information about the out-of-view toy cannot be attributed to difficulty understanding the experimenter's description of the spilling event. Rather, their poor performance seems to be primarily due to difficulty incorporating new information into their existing representation of an absent object.

The results of this series of studies suggest that the ability for updating an existing representation of an absent object may emerge quite rapidly in the second half of the second year (that is, between 19 and 22 months). However, it is also possible that 19-month-olds are capable of updating but that the manifestation of this ability depends on a complex interaction of representational and contextual factors (as is true for the comprehension of absent reference in general—Ganea, 2005). Thus, they might be capable of updating their representation of an absent object under less challenging conditions than those examined so far.

Future research will further explore this important ability. One question concerns the extent to which prior experience might affect infants' updating. For example, we suspect that updating may occur more readily for an object for which the infant already has a rich mental representation. Thus, 19-month-olds, who failed to incorporate new information about a change to a recently encountered object might succeed with a highly familiar one. Temporal factors might also matter, with updating more likely for objects, whether familiar or new, that infants have recently interacted with than ones they have not seen for some time. The type of transformation might also make a difference. For example, our intuition is that a change in the location of an object ("I moved Lucy to the couch.") should be easier to update than a change in the object itself.

PICTURE-BASED LEARNING

Infants and young children are exposed to a variety of kinds of symbols other than language, with one of the most common being pictures. Pictorial representations have substantial potential to support learning about the world, in part because young children have so much exposure to them. Pictorial media are abundant in most modern societies, and the majority of homes in the United States contain many pictures—family photographs, magazines, children's books, and so on. Thus, the possibility exists for learning from pictures early in life.

But when and how do young children actually begin to acquire information from pictures? What is required to do so? At a minimum, the abilities to perceive pictures, to remember pictorial information, and to relate pictorial representations to what they represent would seem to be necessary. However, it would presumably not be necessary to have achieved full-fledged *pictorial competence*—mastery of the myriad factors involved in perceiving, interpreting, understanding, and using pictures, in addition to knowledge of the conventions and techniques of pictorial representation (DeLoache, Pierroutsakos, & Troseth, 1996; DeLoache, 2002).

An abundance of research on a wide variety of topics testifies to the ability of infants to *perceive* a relation between a picture and its referent right from birth. For example, newborns recognize photographs of their mother's face (Pascalis, de Schonen, Morton, Deruelle, & Fabre-Grenet, 1995) and five-month-olds can relate pictures of people and objects to the real people and objects depicted (Dirks & Gibson, 1977; DeLoache, Strauss, & Maynard, 1979). In spite of these early abilities, there are limits to infants' pictorial competence that might interfere with picture-based learning.

Understanding Pictures

To use pictures as a source of information about the world, it would seem necessary to understand something about the difference between pictures and their referents and about the nature of the representational relation between depiction and depicted. Specifically, some appreciation of the symbolic nature of pictures may be necessary for the acquisition of new information via pictures.

Manual Exploration of Pictures

There is substantial evidence that a symbolic interpretation of pictures emerges only gradually. A lack of appreciation of the basic nature of the pictorial medium is reflected in how young infants interact with pictures. Rather than simply looking at depictions, as older individuals do, infants between four and nine months of age manually explore them (Murphy, 1978; DeLoache, Pierroutsakos, Uttal, Rosengren, & Gottlieb, 1998; Callaghan, Rochat, MacGillivray, & MacLellan, 2003; Pierroutsakos & DeLoache, 2003; Yonas, Chov, Alexander, & Jacques, 2003; Pierroutsakos, Lewis, Brewer, & Self, 2004). When presented with a highly realistic color photograph of an object, infants touch, rub, pat, and scratch at the depicted object, and sometimes even grasp at it as if trying to pluck it off the page. A few infants have even leaned over and applied their lips to the nipple of a depicted baby bottle!

The extent to which infants manually explore depicted objects is related to how much the depictions resemble real objects (Pierroutsakos & DeLoache, 2003). Color photographs elicit the most manual activity, and black-and-white line drawings the least. Thus, the more a depicted object looks like a real object, the more infants try to physically interact with it.

Manual exploration of depicted objects tends to occur only if infants are constrained in their interaction with pictures. In the original research (DeLoache et al., 1998), pictures were presented in a board book, and the experimenter did not permit the infant to pick up the book itself. In recent research (Callaghan, Rochat, MacGillivray, & MacLellan, 2003), infants in one condition were presented with pictures mounted on cardboard and were allowed to interact with them however they chose. In this case, infants up to nine months did not manually explore the depicted objects. Instead, they treated the cardboard-mounted pictures as objects in and of themselves, picking them up and manipulating them. In another condition, in which the experimenter prevented the infants from treating the pictures in this way by holding the pictures down on the table, the infants attended to and manually explored the depicted objects, just as in the earlier studies. Both types of behaviors exhibited by these infants—ignoring the depicted objects to act on the picture–object itself and manually exploring the depicted objects—are immature responses to pictures. Both indicate a lack of appreciation of the nature and use of pictures.

Our basic interpretation of infants' manual exploration of pictures is that it reveals confusion about the true nature of depicted objects (DeLoache et al., 1998; Pierroutsakos & DeLoache, 2003; Pierroutsakos et al., 2004). To some extent the highly realistic color photos typically used in this research do look like real objects, and they presumably activate infants' conceptual representations of the categories of the objects, in addition to motor schemes for interacting with them. At the same time, however, these depicted objects provide few of the visual cues for three-dimensionality that real objects offer. Infants thus manually explore pictures, not because they in any way misperceive them and not because they believe the depicted objects to be real objects, but because they find pictures somewhat puzzling. They touch, rub, and grasp at them out of interest and uncertainty.

This interpretation is supported by research examining infants' manual behavior toward pictures in which their exploration of the depicted objects was compared to their exploration of non-pictorial areas of high contrast in the same picture (Pierroutsakos & DeLoache, 2003). Each of the depicted objects used in the original set of studies (DeLoache et al., 1998) was centered in a cardboard square with a circular dark area completely surrounding it. Thus, the highest amount of contrast on the page was the edge of the dark area. If infants' manual exploration of pictures is elicited by the depicted object, they should focus most of their manual activity on the depiction, ignoring the high-contrast border. Otherwise, they should explore the edge of the surrounding dark area at least as much as, or more than, the depicted objects. In fact, the infants' manual exploration was overwhelmingly directed to the depicted objects in the center of the page. It was the depicted objects themselves that attracted their investigatory attention.

Manual exploration of depictions is strongly related to age; infants' physical interaction with depicted objects is an inverted U-shaped function of age. It increases from four to nine months of age (Pierroutsakos et al., 2004), probably due in part to improving motor control of arm and hand movements, making it increasingly possible for a baby to accurately contact and explore a small image. Manual exploration then decreases from 9 to 18 months, at which point it is quite rare (DeLoache et al., 1998). The decline in manual behavior toward pictures presumably reflects infants' learning about the nature of pictures and how they differ from real objects.

Simultaneous with infants' decrease in manual exploration of depicted objects between 9 and 18 months of age is an increase in their pointing to and talking about pictures. This switch indicates a growing appreciation of how people interact with pictures—they look at, point to, and talk about them. Thus, by the middle of the second year of life, children growing up in a picture-rich society have come to understand and use pictures as a vehicle for communicating with other people, whether for requesting or offering information. This new orientation to pictures sets the stage for the next major step in pictorial competence—appreciation of the symbolic nature of pictures.

Understanding the Symbolic Nature of Pictures

Evidence regarding the emergence of an understanding of the referential nature of pictures has recently come from an elegant series of studies by Preissler and Carey (2004). Specifically, they established that infants as young as 18 months of age appreciate that a word that is used to refer to a depicted object refers to the real object as well. The children were taught a label ("whisk") for a small line drawing of an object (a whisk) that was unfamiliar to them. Subsequently, they were presented with a pair of stimuli—the simple drawing for which they had learned the label and a real whisk—and asked to indicate "whisk."

The results were quite dramatic: The infants *never* selected the picture alone, in spite of the fact that they had initially learned the label for it. Instead they all indicated either the object alone or the object and its picture. Both of these choices offer evidence of extending the label learned with the picture to the real object. Thus, by 18 months of age, very young children who hear a novel word applied to a depicted object assume that the word refers to the real object that is depicted.

New research indicates that very young children's symbolic interpretation of pictures may depend on the nature of the pictures (Ganea, Preissler, Butler, Carey, & DeLoache, 2008). Children in this study were taught a novel word ("blicket") for one of two novel objects depicted in a specially constructed picture book. The pictures in the book were highly realistic color photographs of the two novel objects and several familiar objects.

To assess whether the children had learned the novel label for the depicted object during the book interaction, they were shown pictures of the novel target and the novel non-target and asked to indicate the "blicket." Only after a child had answered this question correctly on two consecutive trials, indicating that the name–object link had been learned, did we proceed with the test.

The first test, the Picture–Object Test, was the same as the symbolic test used by Preissler and Carey (2004): The children were presented with the *picture* of the target object and the *real* target object and asked to show "a blicket." Selection of the picture alone would suggest little or no appreciation of the symbolic nature of pictures. In contrast, choosing the object or both the object and picture would indicate an appreciation of the nature of the picture–referent relation.

In the next test, the Real Object Bias Test, the children were shown a *picture* of the target and the *real* non-target object and asked to show the "blicket." This test was a measure of any general tendency to choose objects over pictures, and hence provided important information to evaluate performance on the Picture–Object Test. Selection of the non-target object on this test would indicate a simple preference for objects over pictures.

On the last test, the Extension Test, the children were presented with the two real objects (target and non-target) and asked to show the "blicket." This test was a measure of children's application of the newly learned word to the real object.

Based on their responses to the first two tests—the Picture–Object Test and the Real Object Bias Test—the children were categorized in one of three groups, as shown in Figure 11–2. (1) Children who indicated the picture on the Picture–Object Test and selected the picture on the Real Object Bias Test were considered to have made an *associative response*. They associated the label with the picture with which it was learned but not with the real object. (2) Children who selected either the object alone or both the picture and the object on the Picture–Object Test *and* also chose the object on the Real Object Bias Test were considered to have a general *object bias*. (3) Children who selected the object alone or both the picture and the object on the Picture–Object Test *and* selected the picture on the Real Object Bias Test were categorized as giving a *symbolic response*. They selected the real object as an appropriate referent for the label, but not on the basis of a simple object bias.

The results showed a gradual increase in the number of children who made a symbolic response when presented with both the picture of the blicket and the real blicket. Specifically, 55% of the 15-month-olds, 69% of the 18-month-olds, and 81% of the 24-month-olds indicated the object alone or both the object and the picture when asked to show a "blicket" on the Picture–Object Test (these children also responded correctly to the Real Object Bias Test, by indicating the picture

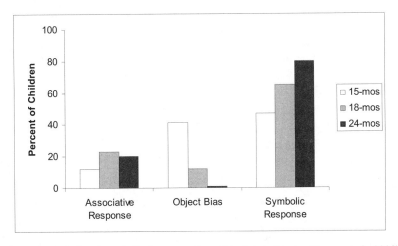

Figure 11–2. Infants' symbolic interpretation of depicted objects. (Ganea et al., 2008).

as the correct target). The number of children who responded symbolically was significantly different from chance (25%) for all age groups.

This study provides evidence that some children as young as 15 months of age interpret pictures symbolically and that children's appropriate interpretation of the referential nature of pictures increases gradually with age. However, in stark contrast to Preissler and Carey's (2004) study, in which *no* children selected the picture alone, some children at every age (2 at 15 months, 4 at 18 months, and 3 at 24 months) selected the picture alone on the Picture–Object Test. These children seem to consider the picture as a better referent for the word than the real object.

One factor that might explain why fewer children in this study gave a symbolic response (choosing the object alone or both the object and the picture) is the nature of the pictures used. In the Preissler and Carey (2004) research, the children learned the novel label in relation to quite small (5 cm × 5 cm) black-and-white line drawings. In the current study the children learned the label in relation to larger, highly realistic color photographs (13 cm × 18 cm). It is possible that the high level of realism of the photographs may have increased their physical salience, thereby making the representational relation more difficult for children to appreciate.

This speculation is consistent with the finding of Pierroutsakos and DeLoache (2003) that infants manually explore photographs more than black-and-white line drawings. The realistic nature of pictures may thus play a counterintuitive role in how easily infants interpret them symbolically, with more faithful representations actually eliciting less mature responses. Future research examining the effects of iconicity on children's grasp of the referential function of pictures will provide important information about the processes involved in the early development of a symbolic understanding of pictures.

Even after coming to appreciate the symbolic nature of pictures, very young children still evidence substantial difficulty negotiating the relation between pictures and what they depict (Callaghan, 1999; Rochat & Callaghan, 2005). For example, before the age of two years, children have problems matching a real-object display with a color photograph of that display (Harris, Kavanaugh, & Dowson, 1997), and even 2.5-year-olds sometimes incorrectly choose which of two objects matches a picture they have just seen (Callaghan, 2000). Young children also reveal a variety of confusions regarding the differing properties of pictures and depicted objects (Beilin & Pearlman, 1991), and the differing consequences of actions on pictures versus objects (Flavell, Flavell, Green, & Korfmacher, 1990; Zaitchik, 1990; Robinson, Nye, & Thomas, 1994).

Learning from Picture Books

With their increasing appreciation of the symbolic nature of pictures, it should be possible for very young children to acquire new information about the world from pictures. Almost certainly, the most common opportunity that very young children have for learning from pictures comes in the form of joint picture-book reading interactions with their parents, teachers, and older siblings. Such interactions are very common in the homes of American children: Most children below the age of three are read to several times a week, and the majority of them participate in daily book-centered interactions (Rideout, Vandewater, & Wartella, 2003). The prevalence of picture-book reading in American homes is at least partly attributable to American parents' belief that books and reading play a positive role in the development of young children (Gelman, Coley, Rosengren, Hartman, & Pappas, 1998; Rideout et al., 2003).

This general assumption has empirical support. There is extensive documentation of positive relations between early picture-book experience and later developments, most notably with respect to vocabulary development. Vocabulary size in preschool children is correlated with the amount of time they spent in picture-book interactions with their parents (DeBaryshe, 1993; Sénéchal & Cornell, 1993; Whitehurst et al., 1994; Fletcher & Reese, 2005; Karass & Braungart-Rieker, 2005).

The relation between joint picture-book reading and literacy skills and knowledge has also been documented. Early book-reading experience is positively related to how much young children know when they enter school about the nature of books and how they are used (Mason, 1980; Sulzby, 1985; Teale & Sulzby, 1986; Adams, 1990; Bialystok, 1995; Bus, van Ijzendoorn, & Pellegrini, 1995; Whitehurst & Lonigan, 1998; Justice & Ezell, 2000; Sénéchal & LeFevre, 2001).

Experimental evidence of the benefits of picture-book reading has come from effective intervention programs with educationally at-risk young children, based on joint parent–child picture-book interactions (e.g., Whitehurst et al., 1994; Lonigan & Whitehurst, 1998; Whitehurst & Lonigan, 1998). The very successful interventions of Whitehurst and his colleagues involve a highly interactive style of reading known as "dialogic reading," which is based on three principles (Arnold, Lonigan, Whitehurst, & Epstein, 1994): (1) using evocative techniques to encourage children to participate actively in reading interactions; (2) providing children with feedback in the form of expanding their ideas and utterances, correcting misconceptions, and praising their active participation; and (3) scaffolding the interaction to maintain a level of book-related input that is near or slightly beyond the child's current level of understanding.

One reason that interventions based on these principles are so effective is that they differ from how most parents interact with their young children in picture-book interactions. For example, with infants, parents spend most of the time simply calling their child's attention to the pictures and providing labels for them: "That's a frog. Oh look, a bear." They rarely relate the pictured items to real ones, even if real objects of the same category as the depicted ones are nearby and visible (DeLoache & DeMendoza, 1987). Parents of two- and three-year-old children typically just read the text in books (Huebner & Meltzoff, 2005).

With older children, parents provide additional information, commonly drawing their children's attention to categorical relationships among depicted items (Gelman et al., 1998). Recent research by Gelman, Chesnick, and Waxman (2005) suggests that parents tend to talk more about categories when referring to pictures than when talking about real objects. Getting information about kinds and categories is especially important for acquiring general knowledge about the world, and picture-book interactions thus provide an opportunity for parents to scaffold this development. Parents of older children also try to orient children to the general theme of a book by, for instance, providing information about the spatial relations among depicted objects and by talking the graphic representations included in the book (Szechter & Liben, 2004).

Clearly, very young children learn a great deal in terms of vocabulary and literacy knowledge from their extensive participation in picture-book interactions. What else is it possible to learn through such interactions? We have recently inaugurated a program of research asking new questions about very young children's learning from picture books. Unlike most previous research, our focus is not on the nature of the interaction or on general learning but on the acquisition of specific information. We are interested in the extent to which very young children learn information from picture books that they then extend to the real world.

The prototype question underlying this research is this: If a toddler learns in a picture-book interaction something about horses—their name, where they live, the fact that they sometimes pull wagons—to what extent does the child extend that knowledge to the first real horse he or she encounters? In other words, what influences very young children's extension of information learned from the pages of a picture book to the real world?

Two primary goals guide this research: One involves increasing our basic understanding of the development of pictorial competence (DeLoache et al., 1996; DeLoache, 2002) by examining the processes underlying very young children's ability to extrapolate information learned about depicted objects and events to real ones. The second goal is primarily practical—discovering more about what can be done to enhance infants' and very young children's learning about the world from picture-book interactions.

Our initial study (Ganea, Bloom Pickard, & DeLoache, 2008) focused on a very common form of early picture-book reading in which the book serves primarily as a mechanism to promote word learning. We examined 15- and 18-month-olds' learning of a novel name for an object from a brief picture-book interaction with an adult. Most importantly, we asked whether they would extend the name from the book to the real object and generalize it to a new instance of it. We also wanted to find out whether the nature of the pictures in the books influenced children's learning and generalization from them. Thus, we used books that contained realistic photographs, colored drawings, or cartoons to teach 15- and 18-month-olds a novel name ("blicket") for one of two novel objects.

The results indicated that, as expected, both age groups learned the novel word for the depicted object from the brief picture-book interaction. Moreover, they extended the name to the real novel object. The older children also generalized it to a new instance (a differently colored exemplar). Thus, by 15 months of age, children apply something learned from a book beyond the pages of the book, providing evidence that early picture-book interactions can serve as a source of information about the real world. Very young children also transfer information in the opposite direction, and iconicity again plays a role. After learning a label for a real object, children more successfully transferred to a photograph than to a cartoon of the object (Ganea, Bloom Pickard, & DeLoache, 2008).

These results for iconicity show that the early application of information between books and the world is quite conservative. The very young children in this research extended and generalized what they learned from a book to the world only when there was a substantial level of physical similarity between depicted and real objects. Similar effects occurred for their identification of known objects depicted in a book.

Simcock and DeLoache (2006) also reported effects of iconicity on slightly older children's learning of sequences of actions from picture books. The 18- and 30-month-old toddlers in this study were better at imitating a sequence of actions with novel objects if it was depicted with realistic photographs than with line drawings.

The fact that the iconic nature of pictures seems to have an important role in children's ability to interact meaningfully with books has important educational implications; namely, that books with more realistic pictures are better for assisting young children's learning.

Another common aspect of books that might affect learning and generalization by young children is the physical complexity of the book in which information is presented. "Manipulative" books are very popular style of book for young children. These are books with features that invite children to interact physically with the book (e.g., pop-up elements, flaps, and tabs). Chiong and DeLoache (2007) found that very young children learn alphabet letters better from books that present information in a simple format than from manipulative books. These results suggest that manipulative books may distract children from the relevant content presented in the book and thereby hinder their learning.

Another set of studies has focused on the processes involved in young children's learning of conceptual information from picture books, with a particular focus on the learning of simple scientific information. We chose the topic of the biological defense mechanism of camouflage to examine three- and four-year-old children's learning of simple scientific information from specially constructed books (Ganea, Ma, & DeLoache, 2007).

The books contained color photographs depicting a type of insect (butterfly) or animal (frog) in camouflage and non-camouflage situations. For example, a yellow butterfly was shown sitting on a yellow flower, making it difficult to see, and then on the bark of a tree, where it was very visible. The accompanying story provided factual information about color-camouflage (without actually using the word "camouflage"). The text explained, for example, why a predatory bird could find and eat the butterfly when it was on the tree but not when it was on the flower.

Before reading the book to the children, we first assessed their prior knowledge of camouflage. The child was shown two depicted animals (a green lizard lying among green leaves, or a red lizard lying on sand) and asked to indicate which one a bird would be likely to eat and to explain why. Then the child engaged in an interaction with the experimenter, who read the story aloud in a natural way.

On the subsequent test, the children were shown two pictures of novel butterflies (same-category items) or two frogs (cross-category items) in camouflage and non-camouflage situations, together with a picture of a bird. They were told that the bird was looking for food and were asked to show which of the two butterflies (or frogs) it was more likely to eat. In addition, on one of the trials, they were asked to *explain* why the bird would eat the particular item they chose.

The results indicated that four-year-olds learned the information about color camouflage from the book and used the concept of camouflage to explain their choices. On the pre-test, the four-year-old children chose the correct target animal at chance (62% of the trials), and justified their choices with camouflage-based explanations on only 5% of the trials (using the idea of camouflage, not the term itself). After reading the book, these children chose the target animal on 75% of the trials. More importantly, the children now justified their correct responses with the concept of color camouflage on 53% of the trials. These results reveal that by four years of age children can learn new conceptual information from picture books and that they are capable of applying that information to novel exemplars. In contrast, the performance of the three-year-olds did not change from pre-test to post-test, either in their choices or their explanations, suggesting they are relatively limited in their ability to acquire conceptual information from books.

A future goal of this research is to examine the effect of presenting scientific information in fantasy formats on young children's learning and extension of information to the real world. It is well established that young children have a tendency to reason teleologically about biological domains; that is, they often attribute purpose or design to natural phenomena (Springer & Keil, 1989; Keil, 1992; Hatano & Inagaki, 1994; Keil, 1995; Kelemen, 1999a, 1999b; 2003). Given that this tendency is already quite strong in young children, it seems likely that presenting scientific information in fantasy formats might make children less likely to interpret it appropriately. In addition to the possibility that fantasy elements might encourage even more teleological reasoning by young children, fantasy might interfere with their interpretation of the reality status of the information they encounter in the first place.

A study exploring the general issue of the effect of different types of pictures and language on children's learning of simple scientific information supports this assumption (Seiver, Greif & Keil, 2003). Kindergartners listened to either fantasy or factual stories about biological (animals and plants) and physical (natural non-living kinds and artifacts) domains. The stories presented simple scientific information, such as how a snake sheds its skin or how a magnet works. The fantasy stories had pictures of inanimate objects (e.g., magnets) that had faces, facial expressions, and limbs. In addition, the objects were described with intentional terms (e.g., as having desires and thoughts). The factual stories provided straightforward factual explanations of the scientific concepts.

Children who had listened to the fantasy stories remembered less of the story content than did children who had heard the factual stories, and they provided fewer correct answers to factual questions than did children who had listened to factual stories. Thus, the fantasy stories seemed to interfere with children's ability to reason causally about the scientific phenomena described in the pictures. This study suggests that books with fantasy context might be detrimental for learning scientific concepts. The use of anthropomorphism (e.g., attributing human reasoning to nonhuman beings) and teleological explanations in children's books might confuse children and prevent them from thinking in a scientific manner.

We have recently found evidence of a generalized effect of exposure to fantasy books in a tendency for young children to extrapolate fantasy elements encountered in books to the real world (Ganea, Richert, Bean, & DeLoache, 2006). Two- and three-year-olds were read fantasy cartoon books in their preschool classroom on two consecutive days. The books depicted animals wearing clothes and engaged in human-like activities. The question was whether children's beliefs about real cats and pigs would be affected by the fantasy content of the books. On the third day, the children were asked a series of questions about what kinds of things cats and pigs do in the real world ("Do cats scratch?" "Do pigs bake cakes?"). The results showed that the children who had recently been exposed the fantasy cartoons were significantly more likely to attribute human powers to animals than were those in a control group who had not recently been exposed to fantasy books. These studies suggest that fantasy formats in books can affect children's interpretation of real phenomena and might ultimately impede their learning of factual information from such books.

CONCLUSIONS

One of the most important advances of the first years of life is the dawning of symbolization, which sets in motion revolutions in infants' and young children's interaction with and ability to learn from people, either directly or from cultural artifacts such as pictures. We have summarized here recent research from our laboratories on the development in the second year of life of infants' ability to comprehend references to absent objects, focusing especially on recent research on the ability to learn new information about an absent referent—a prerequisite to learning from symbols. Our second focus was the learning from another nearly ubiquitous source of information about the world—pictures. The extremely common form of parent–child interaction, joint picture-book reading, is a learning opportunity from which most young children benefit.

A host of research questions springs from our research on very young children's updating of their representation of an absent object. For example, how does the strength of children's mental representation of an object affect their updating ability? Would it be easier to incorporate new information in a relatively extensive mental representation of a highly familiar object? It seems likely that it would be, but one can also imagine that updating might actually occur more readily for less elaborate representations. Is updating more likely to occur with shorter delays between the child's initial experience with the object and the time at which new information is received? Similarly, does the delay between children's receiving the new information and being presented with the choice of altered and unaltered objects affect their performance? These and many related questions will be the focus of future research.

A particularly fruitful topic for future research might be the relation between very young children's ability to understand and update references to absent entities and their ability to learn new information about the world from picture-book interactions. What cognitive abilities are common in acquiring new information without direct experience in these quite different ways? A related topic concerns the relative credence young children might place in verbal information and/or testimony versus pictorial evidence. Would one be privileged over the other?

In conclusion, very young children's learning about the world is based in large part on information provided to them by a variety of symbols—most notably language and pictures. Further research on the early understanding and use of various symbolic artifacts should enhance our knowledge about the role of learning in the development of the infant mind.

Acknowledgments   Preparation of this manuscript was partially supported by a grant to the first author from the National Institutes of Health (HD-25271–19) and by a grant from the National Science Foundation (ROLE 0440254) to the second and first authors.

References

Adams, M. J. (1990). *Beginning to read: Thinking and learning about print.* Cambridge, MA: MIT Press.

Adamson, L. B., & Bakeman, R. (2006). Development of displaced speech in early mother-child conversations. *Child Development, 77,* 186–200.

Arnold, D. S., Lonigan, C. J., Whitehurst, G. J., & Epstein, J. N. (1994). Accelerating language development through picture-book reading: Replication and extension to a videotape training format. *Journal of Educational Psychology, 86,* 235–243.

Beilin, H., & Pearlman, E. G. (1991). Children's iconic realism: Object versus property realism. In H. W. Reese (Ed.), *Advances in child development and behavior* (Vol. 23, pp. 73–111). New York: Academic Press.

Bialystok, E. (1995). Making concepts of print symbolic: Understanding how writing represents language. *First Language, 15,* 317–338.

Brown, R. (1958). *Words and things.* Glencoe, IL: Free Press.

Bus, A. G., van Ijzendoorn, M. H., & Pellegrini, A. D. (1995). Joint book reading makes for success in learning to read: A meta-analysis of intergenerational transmission of literacy. *Review of Educational Research, 65,* 1–21.

Callaghan, T. C. (1999). Early understanding and production of graphic symbols. *Child Development, 70,* 1314–1324.

Callaghan, T. C. (2000). Factors affecting children's graphic symbol use in the third year. Language, similarity, and iconicity. *Cognitive Development, 15,* 185–214.

Callaghan, T. C., Rochat, P., MacGillivray, T., & MacLellan, C. (2003). The social construction of pictorial symbols in 6- to 18-month-old infants. Unpublished manuscript.

Chiong, C., & DeLoache, J. S. (2007). The effect of manipulative features on young children's learning from picture books. Unpublished manuscript.

DeBaryshe, B. D. (1993). Joint picture-book reading correlates of early oral language skills. *Journal of Child Language, 20,* 455–461.

DeLoache, J. S. (2002). The symbol-mindedness of young children. In W. W. Hartup & R. A. Weinberg (Eds.), *The Minnesota Symposia on Child Psychology* (Vol. 32, pp. 73–101). Mahwah, New Jersey: Lawrence Erlbaum.

DeLoache, J. S., & DeMendoza, A. P. (1987). Joint picture-book interactions of mothers and 1-year-old children. *British Journal of Developmental Psychology, 5,* 111–123.

DeLoache, J. S., Pierroutsakos, S. L., & Troseth, G. L. (1996). The three R's of pictorial competence. In R. Vasta (Ed.), *Annals of Child Development* (Vol. 12, pp. 1–48). London: Jessica Kingsley Publishers.

DeLoache, J. S., Pierroutsakos, S. L., Uttal, D. H., Rosengren, K. S., & Gottlieb, A. (1998). Grasping the nature of pictures. *Psychological Science, 9,* 205–210.

DeLoache, J. S., Strauss, M., & Maynard, J. (1979). Picture perception in infancy. *Infant Behavior and Development, 2,* 77–89.

Dirks, J. R., & Gibson, E. (1977). Infants' perception of similarity between live people and their photographs. *Child Development, 48,* 124–130.

Flavell, J. H., Flavell, E. R., Green, F. L., & Korfmacher, J. E. (1990). Do young children think of television images as pictures or real objects? *Journal of Broadcasting & Electronic Media, 34,* 399–419.

Fletcher, K. L., & Reese, E. (2005). Picture-book reading with young children: A conceptual framework. *Developmental Review, 25,* 64–103.

Ganea, P. A. (2005). Contextual factors affect absent reference comprehension in 14-month-olds. *Child Development, 76,* 989–998.

Ganea, P. A., Bloom Pickard, M., & DeLoache, J. S. (2008). Transfer between picture books and the real world by very young children. *Journal of Cognition and Development, 9,* 46–66.

Ganea, P. A., Ma, L., & DeLoache, J. S. (2007, March). *Children's learning and transfer of scientific information from picture books.* Poster presented at the Society for Research on Child Development, Boston, MA.

Ganea, P. A., Preissler, M., Butler, L., Carey, S., & DeLoache, J. S. (2008). Young children's understanding of the referential function of pictures: A developmental progression. *Manuscript under review.*

Ganea, P. A., Richert, R. A., Bean, E., & DeLoache, J. S. (2006). Fantasy picture books and young children's conceptions about reality. Unpublished manuscript.

Ganea, P. A., & Saylor, M. M. (2008). Further evidence for contextual effects on infants' absent reference comprehension. *Manuscript in progress,* Boston University.

Ganea, P. A., Shutts, K., Spelke, E., & DeLoache, J. S. (2007). Thinking of things unseen: Infants' use of language to update object representations. *Psychological Science, 8,* 734–739.

Gelman, S. A., Chesnick, R. J., & Waxman, S. R. (2005). Mother-child conversations about pictures and objects: Referring to categories and individuals. *Child Development, 76,* 1129–1143.

Gelman, S. A., Coley, J. D., Rosengren, K. S., Hartman, E., & Pappas, A. (1998). Beyond labeling: The role of maternal input in the acquisition of richly structured categories. *Monographs of the Society for Research in Child Development, 63* (1, Serial No. 253).

Harris, P. L., Kavanaugh, R. D., & Dowson, L. (1997). The depiction of imaginary transformation: Early comprehension of a symbolic function. *Cognitive Development, 12,* 1–19.

Hatano, G., & Inagaki, K. (1994). Young children's naive theory of biology. *Cognition, 50,* 171–188.

Hockett, C. F. (1960). Logical considerations in the study of animal communication. In W. E. Lanyon & W. N. Tavolga (Eds.), *Animal sounds and animal communication* (pp. 392–342). Washington, DC: American Institute of Biological Studies.

Huebner, C. E., & Meltzoff, A. N. (2005). Intervention to change parent-child reading style: A comparison of instructional methods. *Journal of Applied Developmental Psychology, 26,* 296–313.

Huttenlocher, J. (1974). The origins of language comprehension. In R. Solso (Ed.), *Theories in cognitive psychology* (pp. 331–368). Hillsdale, NJ: Erlbaum.

Huttenlocher, J., & Higgins, T. E. (1978). Issues in the study of symbolic development. In W. A. Collins (Ed.), *Minnesota Symposia on Child Psychology* (Vol. 11). Hillsdale, NJ: Erlbaum.

Justice, L. M., & Ezell, H. K. (2000). Enhancing children's print and word awareness through home-based parent intervention. *American Journal of Speech and Language Pathology, 9,* 257–269.

Karass, J., & Braungart-Rieker, J. M. (2005). Parenting and temperament as interacting agents in early language development. *Parenting Science and Practice, 3,* 235–259.

Keil, F. (1992). The origins of autonomous biology. In M. R. Gunnar & M. Maratsos (Eds.), *Minnesota Symposia on Child Psychology: Modularity and constraints in language and cognition* (pp. 103–137). Hillsdale, NJ: Erlbaum.

Keil, F. C. (Ed.). (1995). *The growth of causal understandings of natural kinds.* Oxford, UK: Clarendon Press.

Kelemen, D. (1999a). Function, goals and intention: Children's teleological reasoning about objects. *Trends in Cognitive Sciences, 12,* 461–468.

Kelemen, D. (1999b). Why are rocks pointy? Children's preference for teleological explanations of the natural world. *Developmental Psychology, 35,* 1440–1453.

Lewis, M. M. (1936). *Infant speech: A study of the beginnings of language.* New York: Harcourt, Brace.

Lonigan, C. J., & Whitehurst, G. J. (1998). Relative efficacy of parent and teacher involvement in a shared-reading intervention for preschool children from low-income backgrounds. *Early Childhood Research Quarterly, 17,* 265–292.

Mason, J. (1980). When do children begin to read? An exploration of four-year-old children's letter and word reading competencies. *Reading Research Quarterly, 15,* 203–227.

Murphy, C. M. (1978). Pointing in the context of a shared activity. *Child Development, 49,* 371–380.

Pascalis, O., de Schonen, S., Morton, J., Deruelle, C., & Fabre-Grenet, H. (1995). Mother's face recognition by neonates: A replication and an extension. *Infant Behavior and Development, 18,* 79–85.

Pierroutsakos, S. L., & DeLoache, J. S. (2003). Infants' manual exploration of pictorial objects varying in realism. *Infancy, 4,* 141–156.

Pierroutsakos, S. L., Lewis, E. N., Brewer, C. J., & Self, J. A. (2004, May). *An earlier look: 4-month-olds' manual reactions to pictured objects.* Poster presented at the International Conference on Infant Studies, Chicago, IL.

Preissler, M. A., & Carey, S. (2004). Do both pictures and words function as symbols for 18- and 24-month-old children? *Journal of Cognition and Development, 5,* 185–212.

Rideout, V. J., Vandewater, E. A., & Wartella, E. A. (2003). *Zero to six: Electronic media in the lives of infants, toddlers, and preschooler.* Retrieved May 25, 2004, from the Henry J. Kaiser Family Foundation Web site: http://www.kff.org/entmedia/3378.cfm.

Robinson, E. J., Nye, R., & Thomas, G. V. (1994). Children's conceptions of the relationship between pictures and their referents. *Cognitive Development, 9,* 165–191.

Rochat, P., & Callaghan, T. C. (2005). What drives symbolic development? The case of pictorial comprehension and production. In L. Namy & S. Waxman (Eds.), *The development of symbolic use and comprehension.* Mahwah, NJ: Erlbaum.

Sachs, J. (1983). Talking about the there and then: The emergence of displaced reference in parent-child discourse. In K. E. Nelson (Ed.), *Children's language* (pp. 1–28). Hillsdale, NJ: Erlbaum.

Saylor, M. M. (2004). 12- and 16-month-old infants recognize properties of mentioned absent things. *Developmental Science, 7,* 599–611.

Saylor, M. M., & Baldwin, D. A. (2004). Discussing those not present: Comprehension of references to absent caregivers. *Journal of Child Language, 31,* 537–560.

Seiver, E., Greif, M., & Keil, F. (2003, October). *Learning science with storybooks: Do anthropomorphic explanations affect learning?* Poster presented at the biennial meeting of the Cognitive Development Society, Salt Lake City, UT.

Sénéchal, M., & Cornell, E. H. (1993). Vocabulary acquisition through shared reading experiences. *Reading Research Quarterly, 28,* 361–374.

Sénéchal, M., & LeFevre, J. (2001). Storybook reading and parent teaching: Links to language and literacy development. In P. R. Britto & J. Brooks-Gunn (Eds.), *The role of family literacy environments in promoting young children's emerging literacy skills. New directions for child and adolescent development* (pp. 39–52). San Francisco: Jossey-Bass.

Shimpi, P. M. (October, 2005). *Infant sensitivity to associated object cues.* Poster presented at the meeting of the Cognitive Development Society, San Diego.

Simcock, G., & DeLoache, J. S. (2006). The effects of iconicity on re-enactment from picture books by 18- to 30-month-old children. *Developmental Psychology, 42,* 1352–1357.

Springer, K., & Keil, F. C. (1989). On the development of biologically specific beliefs: The case of inheritance. *Child Development, 60,* 637–648.

Sulzby, E. (1985). Children's emergent reading of favorite storybooks: A developmental study. *Reading Research Quarterly, 20,* 458–481.

Szechter, L. E., & Liben, L. S. (2004). Parental guidance in preschoolers' understanding of spatial-graphic representations. *Child Development, 75,* 869–885.

Teale, W. H., & Sulzby, E. (1986). *Emergent literacy: Writing and reading.* Norwood, NJ: Ablex.

Veneziano, E., & Sinclair, H. (1995). Functional changes in early language: The appearance of references to the past and of explanations. *Journal of Child Language, 22,* 557–581.

Werner, H., & Kaplan, B. (1956). *Symbol formation: An organismic-developmental approach to language and expression of thought.* New York: John Wiley.

Whitehurst, G. J., Falco, F., Lonigan, C. J., Fischel, J. E., DeBaryshe, B. C., Valdez-Menchaca, M. C., & Caulfield, M. (1994). A picture book reading intervention in daycare and home for children from low-income families. *Developmental Psychology, 24,* 552–558.

Whitehurst, G. J., & Lonigan, C. J. (1998). Child development and emergent literacy. *Child Development, 69,* 848–872.

Yonas, A., Chov, M., Alexander, A., & Jacques, J. (April, 2003). *Actions of 9-month-old infants directed at a real toy, a photographed toy, and surfaces.* Poster presented at the meeting of the Society for Research in Child Development, Tampa, FL.

Zaitchik, D. (1990). When representations conflict with reality: The preschooler's problem with false beliefs and "false" photographs. *Cognition, 35,* 41–68.

12

The Role of Learning in Cognitive Development

Challenges and Prospects

RICHARD N. ASLIN, UNIVERSITY OF ROCHESTER

Infant development is really rather simple—no metamorphosis, no shedding of skin or scales, no shift from aquatic to terrestrial to avian habitats. Moreover, we have a very good description of the end point of development, including the behavioral and mental states that characterize the mature form—the human adult—because it is "us." Why then the mystery, the debates about nature and nurture, the constant searching for the one thing that makes human development different from development in all other species? Surely the answer must come from the fact that we humans do certain things a whole lot better than any other species. We have language (not just a set of signs to express emotional states), we have mental states and the knowledge that others do as well (not just associations between gaze direction or pointing and behavioral outcomes), and we have the capacity to innovate (not just by accident but with the clear intent to solve a previously unsolved problem). These qualities of human cognition in the adult cry out for answers about their origin: Where do they come from, and what mechanisms enable them to emerge?

The field of infant development has progressed through two lengthy periods (each lasting several generations). Phase 1 was all about learning, with internal states (and their neural mechanisms) judged to be largely irrelevant. Phase 2 was all about cognition (i.e., internal states), and subtle behaviors, such as where one looks and for how long, defined the essence of infant competence. Thus, it is timely for the field to reflect on the major issues that emerged at the conference and are reflected in the 11 chapters in the present volume, in an attempt to bring these seemingly related, but often separate, mechanisms of development into some sort of synergy. The final discussion took a two-pronged approach to accomplish this task: raise the set of key questions that the conference organizers posed to each presenter, and answer them by citing the work of the presenters or by challenging them (and the field) to strive to address them. We also took the opportunity to expand on some of these key questions in an effort to raise additional challenges for the field.

IS INNATE (PREVIOUSLY ACQUIRED) STRUCTURE REQUIRED TO EXPLAIN LEARNING?

The simple answer to this question is an emphatic yes. Consider even the most behavioristic account of learning (aka Skinner). The influence of elementary reinforcers—positive (food) or negative (pain)—must be specified innately. No one has ever claimed that reinforcers themselves must be learned. In fact, there are many spontaneous behaviors (sucking, saccadic eye movements, foot kicking) that occur at fairly steady rates and are highly resistant to extinction (i.e., their base rate falls only when negative reinforcement is delivered, not when positive reinforcement is withheld).

If the influence of reinforcement is innate, then what else might be innate (i.e., present at birth)? This, of course, is the question that continues to vex the field, in part because birth is not the earliest age at which learning begins (except for visual learning), and in part because once the newborn is exposed to a rich environment, learning can take many forms. For example, contingency learning is present in newborns' sucking behavior and in slightly older infants' foot-kicking responses. In post-Skinnerian terminology, these are examples of supervised learning: There are clearly defined stimuli and rewards (auditory or visual events) that lead to changes in some motor response. But much of what an infant learns does not occur in the context of any extrinsic reward; rather, most experience (environmental stimulation) is simply available to the infant and has no direct outcome on the infant's interaction with its world. This has been called unsupervised learning because there is no "teacher" directing the infant's attention or providing the infant with feedback about the importance of one type of environmental stimulus over another.

There are several measures of unsupervised learning in infants, all of which rely on a period of exposure to some stimulus events (either before arriving at the lab for testing or immediately preceding the testing phase in the lab). The habituation paradigm attempts to control for some of the individual differences in baseline looking times, whereas familiarization paradigms assume that a fixed amount of exposure brings all infants to an asymptotic level of input. These unsupervised learning paradigms have revealed much about the biases, some of them innate, that infants bring to bear on making sense of environmental input. For example, newborns have preferences, most of which cannot have been induced by prenatal exposure. But clearly most of the information acquired by infants comes from exposure to environmental input. How then does the infant select from this input the information that is most likely to be relevant for successful adaptation to the external world? And what prevents the infant from attending to all the potentially relevant information that turns out to be "noise"?

The answer to these questions is not obvious. But one cannot ignore the likely possibility that infants are pre-adapted to possess those biases, whether sensory, attentional, learning, or computational, that will be minimally sufficient to address all of the information-processing tasks required for normative (species-typical) development. The problem for infancy researchers who care about mechanisms of development is the difficulty in determining whether the time course of acquisition, which is quite rapid in many domains, is best accounted for by an innate set of biases or by the redundant structure of the voluminous input to which the infant is exposed. A slightly biased learning mechanism, such as one that preferentially seeks visual patterns with more contours on the top than on the bottom (see Simion, Turati, Valneza, & Leo, 2006), may be sufficient to account for face preferences in newborns, especially since upright faces are the predominant stimulus available to young infants. In contrast, there may be no initial bias for the downward flight of an object as it is released from the parent's grasp (Hood, 1998), but because objects almost never move upward (balloons are an exception), the gravity bias observed in toddlers may be entirely the product of experience.

What seems lacking in discussions of the origins of cognitive development is the Bayesian perspective on prior probabilities (see Gopnik et al., 2004, for an exception). According to Bayes theorem, the probability that a given instance of environmental stimulation has a particular underlying cause is the product of two other probabilities: (1) the probability of the cause, given the environmental stimulation (which can be partially observed), and (2) the probability of the environmental stimulation (which can be observed). This second term, called the prior probability, indicates that if something is very likely to occur, it enhances the weight that gets attached to a given correlation between underlying cause and observed stimulation. Recall the sniper who struck in Washington, DC, in the fall of 2002. Because several witnesses reported seeing a white van at the scene of the first few shootings, the inference was made that the sniper was driving a white van. However, it turned out that the prior probability of white vans was extremely high, rendering the causal inference incorrect.

The point here, with regard to Bayes theorem, is that prior probability distributions can originate from two sources: innate biases or observation. In the field of language development, specifically with regard to grammar acquisition, the Chomskyan perspective posits very little observational priors (just enough to choose between parameter X and parameter Y). Others, such as the Tomasello perspective, posit a minimal role for innate priors because of the myriad redundant sources of information and their ubiquity in the environment of infants and toddlers. Unfortunately, this debate is likely to be unresolvable because the definitive test would require withholding certain key inputs during early development. As a result, this debate is more tractable in domains such as object cognition, where both humans and animals share the (more or less) same external world, and invasive animal studies can be conducted.

One study demonstrating a strong prior was performed by Needham, who permitted infants to use a spoon as a potential tool to search inside a box. Infants who have experience using a spoon in its canonical way (holding the handle to bring food from the bowl to the mouth) fail to grasp the spoon by its bowl when the handle is the only part of the spoon that can fit into a small hole. In this case, infants do not adjust their manual behavior to overcome the prior (although older infants eventually become more flexible). However, in other cases, such as in studies of symbol learning by Namy, infants can quickly adjust their prior (from a bias for considering words but not gestures as symbols to considering both as symbols).

These are examples of priors established by experience; but what about innate priors? Baillargeon argues for an innate prior (or core knowledge) called the principle of persistence. According to this principle, there is a bias for infants to assume that objects do not change their properties (including solidity, location in space, color, and form) unless there is some obvious external agent (e.g., a change in illumination, a distorting force, or a person that moves the object). However, all of the evidence marshaled in support of the principle of persistence comes from visual fixation measures using the violation of expectation (VOE) paradigm. This VOE paradigm has not been used successfully with infants younger than 2.5 months. Thus, there is an early period of development during which visual exposure is limited but not absent, and a learning mechanism could be an effective means of establishing priors. Moreover, as argued by Johnson, there is empirical evidence in infants younger than 2.5 months using the habituation paradigm for the absence of one aspect of the principle of persistence (in studies of object unity). Thus, the question of how priors in a given domain originate is still a key topic in the field.

WHICH ASPECTS OF THE ENVIRONMENT SUPPORT LEARNING?

The foregoing discussion highlighted the importance of the environment, both because it contains the minimally sufficient structural information required for learning and because it may play a role in setting up priors, which then further constrain the learning process. But what do we mean by "the environment"? It is undeniable that a rich tableau of potentially useful stimulation, both social and physical, is available to any infant with intact sensory systems. However, much of this stimulation has no informational value; that is, it is not structured. For example, every sensory system has internal noise, and even suprathreshold signals from the environment contain many contingencies, but only a small fraction of them are relevant to any task facing the infant. That is, the world is filled with false correlations (also called spurious coincidences) that appear to have structure, but do not. Thus, in the domain of unsupervised learning, there is uncertainty about what we mean by the environment because it is not clear which parts of the potential array of stimulation are relevant for the infant to attend to and learn.

A number of the contributors proposed mechanisms by which infants could extract the "relevant" information and ignore the noise. These mechanisms include comparison (Baillargeon, Oakes), variability of exemplars along some dimensions but not others (Needham, Oakes), attention to components (Baillargeon, Johnson, Needham), priming (Baillargeon, Johnson, Needham, Wilcox), perceptual primitives (Saffran), manual manipulation (Needham, Oakes, Wilcox,

Woodward), learning sets (Adolph), and associative biases (Johnson, Namy). Not to be overly negative, but each of these mechanisms fails to explain why the mechanisms "work" in a given context. For example, comparison requires the infant to fixate portions of two side-by-side visual stimuli. Admittedly, detecting the matching versus mismatching portions of the two stimuli is easier (demanding less memory) when the stimuli are simultaneously present than when they are presented successively. But have the details of this comparison process itself been observed directly (e.g., in fine-grained eye-movement patterns), or have they been inferred from superior discrimination performance in simultaneous versus successive paradigms? Similarly, do we know that increasing variability along a dimension induces greater attention to the non-varying dimensions? And does manual manipulation function solely as an attentional facilitator, or does the grasp itself provide additional discriminative information? And if there is a hierarchy of perceptual primitives, are they associated more efficiently simply by frequency of occurrence or by "stronger" associative links?

In the domain of supervised learning, which includes any overt behavior that has an outcome (consequences) that could serve as feedback, there is the potential for a tighter linkage between stimulation and its underlying cause. For example, in reaching and grasping, there is ample opportunity to receive relatively immediate feedback about the relation between object size and the hand shape required to grasp the object. Failure to anticipate the correct hand shape results in an unsuccessful grasp. Similarly, postural control also leads to immediate feedback, especially when loss of control is catastrophic. But most behaviors have delayed consequences, which extends the time during which any aspect of the prior stimulation could serve as the cause of a successful (or unsuccessful) outcome. By analogy, consider the ups and downs of your retirement account: There is clear (even daily) feedback, but the underlying cause is largely unknown. In most everyday behaviors, the infant is confronted with a similar semi-supervised learning situation. How then does the infant attach the correct stimulus with the observed outcome? This linkage most likely requires a set of biases or constraints on what "counts" as a viable stimulus in the context of a given behavioral outcome. This interpretive dilemma is analogous to the reference problem in language development. How does the infant know whether an adult who views a rabbit hopping across a field and then speaks the word *gavagai* is labeling the rabbit, the act of hopping, the color of the rabbit, the fact that the event is amusing, or any of an infinite number of other possibilities (including the concept of disembodied rabbit parts)?

WHAT KINDS OF LEARNING MECHANISMS ARE PRESENT DURING DEVELOPMENT, AND DO THEY CHANGE?

Many aspects of learning were discussed during the conference, and many different terms were used to describe learning: association, imitation, category formation, context-specific learning, statistical learning, rule learning, priming, learning sets, and habituation. All of these terms have in common the notion that information is extracted from external stimulation and/or self-produced stimulation and stored, in whole or in part, for later use. As discussed above, some forms of learning (supervised) have additional external stimulation that serves as a guide or teacher by providing feedback to the learner. Other forms of learning (unsupervised) provide no such feedback but are examples of learning by mere observation (although feedback may be indirect if there are strong priors and the infant attempts to predict future inputs, thereby noting whether the predictions are correct or incorrect).

The challenge for researchers is to gain a better understanding of the neural bases of learning, which at present posits a very small number of elementary mechanisms (e.g., long term potentiation or Hebbian learning). Is it possible that all of the terms used in the infant (and adult) literatures to describe learning could be reduced to two or three fundamental types of neural circuits? Admittedly, these circuits could reside in very different brain regions that receive inputs from domain-specific sensory systems and send their outputs to domain-specific memory systems. That is a point made by Saffran using slightly different terms. Alternatively, it may be that custom circuits are needed to perform the kinds of neural computations required for specific tasks, and so the domain specificity is present at all levels, from input to output. If so, then brain-imaging techniques may help differentiate among these alternatives.

WHAT IS THE NATURE OF THE INTERNAL REPRESENTATIONS DERIVED FROM LEARNING?

The use of the term *internal representation* raises legitimate concerns. On the one hand, this term has often been used as a catchall for any aspect of cognition that is unexplained. On the other hand, no one seriously considers a return to behaviorism, in which only overt performance served as the object of investigation. At least for humans, even infants, there is a general consensus that there are covert aspects of cognition. But because much of cognition is, by definition, unobservable, it should be characterized using careful language. When we say that an infant has a representation of space, we mean that there are organizing principles that affect the infant's behavior in space, whether that involves reaching responses, anticipatory eye movements, or the duration of fixation to one class of events over another. Whether this representation carries with it internal states such as "surprise" is simply unknown at present, unless we define surprise solely by the criterion of the dependent measure of looking time (e.g., Baillargeon: "a shorthand descriptor to denote a state of heightened attention or interest caused by an expectation violation"). By analogy, we cannot know if the facial expression of "disgust" that follows tasting a bitter liquid is experienced by the newborn in the same way as it is by an adult because the newborn's facial expression has not been validated by another dependent measure (e.g., a verbal label or a pattern of brain activation in the "disgust" region).

What does seem clear is that internal representations are likely to be domain-specific, task-specific, and context-specific. This is because learning must occur, at least initially, over events and not categories. So, the *input* to internal representations is domain-, task-, and context-specific (as noted by Saffran). The question, then, is how these internal representations change with experience. One possibility is that representations simply get more complicated, with multiple levels, each of which can be tapped to solve a particular task. Another possibility is that representations become organized hierarchically with a set of weights (i.e., priors) that determines the ease of access to each level. A third possibility is that the foregoing hierarchical representation has not only passive weights but also active competition between levels so that it becomes difficult, once a given level is "preferred," for other levels to be accessed. Unfortunately, it does not appear that the field has a clue as to which of these possibilities (or others) best characterizes infant cognition. This is the result, in large part, of the heavy methodological constraints that prevent researchers from studying a multilevel set of behaviors whose inputs can be well controlled and whose dominantly active level of representation can be definitively assessed.

Several of the presenters did provide some intriguing evidence that, however internal representations are formed, they are flexible. Bauer showed that reactivation of memories, even if largely forgotten, provides an opportunity for reconsolidation. This is both a good thing because it can solidify the commonalities of the original event and the reactivated event, and a bad thing because it can allow non-central aspects of the original event to become reinforced by the reactivated event, thereby leading to memory distortions. Oakes showed that category formation is a fluid process that depends on the relative stability of prior experiences and the patterning (variability) of the current set of exemplars. In some sense, categories are never stable but vary along a continuum of stability–adaptability that is determined by the strength of the priors and the context in which the exemplars are presented. And DeLoache showed that in toddlers, representations can be updated even when the object itself is absent and is merely referred to by a word or a picture.

One final point needs to be emphasized regarding the origins of domain specificity. The claim here is that domain specificity arises under most circumstances as a result of both a bias to attend to certain types of stimulation and a bias for certain neural mechanisms to preferentially process that stimulation (together these comprise what Saffran calls the "input"). The key point is that small, initial biases at the level of input (pattern of stimulation) and processing (brain mechanism) can lead to a cascade of specializations that might otherwise be devoted to another pattern of stimulation (e.g., if the preferred pattern of stimulation were absent) or to other neural mechanisms (e.g., if the brain were damaged). There is ample evidence for substantial plasticity in both the ability to adapt to new stimulation and to use alternative brain mechanisms, particularly (though not exclusively) in infants. Saffran goes on to argue that the "output" of learning is also domain-specific after domain-specific inputs are analyzed by domain-general computational mechanisms. It may be useful to remain agnostic on this latter point about domain-specific output because one could imagine that the representations themselves are context-specific rather than domain-specific (i.e., they are designed to solve specific tasks, not tasks within specific domains).

WHAT IS THE BREADTH OF GENERALIZATION
FROM LEARNING?

The foregoing discussion of internal representations leads naturally to the most interesting aspect of learning: How does it transfer from one domain, task, or context to another? Learning would be incredibly inefficient if it were to require associative linkages based only on actually experienced events. Here is where we see the largest disconnect between those who study infant cognition and those who study infant motor development. Consider the following extreme cases. A 20-month-old visits the zoo for the first time, sees a tiger, and shouts, "Kitty!" This is an instance of lexical generalization presumably based on the partially overlapping set of perceptual features between a highly familiar object (one or more cats) and a novel object (the tiger). Despite the fact that the tiger was in an unfamiliar context (behind bars in a zoo), the toddler readily extended the name to this new object. Now consider a 13-month-old who is confronted with a gap in a surface of support. As an experienced crawler, this infant has been systematically avoiding attempts to traverse gaps that exceed a certain size. But now, as a cruiser, holding on to a railing, this same infant shows no generalization to the same gap sizes but toddles blithely over large gaps that he or she avoided as a crawler. The only change in context is the locomotor posture of the infant, which seems to an adult to be much less novel or confusing than a very large, striped cat behind bars.

Adolph characterizes the motor domain as a "problem space" within which all the micro-parameters are assembled into a "system" that shows excellent transfer. When the infant is in this problem space (e.g., crawling), there are perturbations in the surface and in the tightness of the infant's clothing, and developmental changes in the infant's limb lengths and muscle strength. Yet despite these variations, within a single problem space the infant shows excellent transfer to novel combinations of these variables. In contrast, when the infant enters the new problem space (e.g., cruising), all of these previously calibrated variables are set back to zero and the protracted process of acquisition begins anew.

Adolph contrasts the slow learning rate and excellent transfer of problem sets to the rapid learning rate and poor transfer of associative learning. Here the infant appears to attend to exemplars over a system of rules, and this same dichotomy has been used by Marcus, Vijayan, Bandi Rao, and Vishton (1999) to describe the statistical learning of exemplar information and the rule learning of underlying structures. The former shows rapid acquisition and poor transfer, whereas the latter shows slower acquisition (perhaps) and good transfer. But in the case of motor learning, it would appear that the entire "space" within which the parameters that are being controlled reside has been explored during the protracted learning process. Thus, "transfer" is really an example of interpolation within this problem space, whereas in cognitive domains there can be examples of transfer that involve extrapolation (e.g., there is no similarity relation between the learned exemplars and the generalization exemplars in Marcus et al., 1999). For motor development, then, how does the infant determine what a new problem space is? That is, what triggers the infant to set the motor parameters back to zero and to begin to acquire new parameters? Perhaps E. J. Gibson (1997) had the right answer: "The question becomes how flexibility is achieved rather than exactly what transfers. What is learned is an ability to assess physical proficiency on-line, relative to the goal and to the environmental supports presently available" (p. 161).

One such example of flexible transfer comes from Woodward's work on how self-produced manual exploration (the "sticky mittens" paradigm developed by Needham, Barrett & Peterman, 2002) influences knowledge of others' reaching responses. Although three-month-olds' experience with sticky mittens led them to look longer at adults who reached for a "new goal" object, this violation of expectation did not transfer from mittened hands to bare hands. Thus, although pre-reaching infants learn from the novel outcome of their own self-produced arm movements to predict the arm movements of an adult, they do not transfer that knowledge to novel contexts.

FURTHER QUESTIONS

The duty of a discussant surely goes beyond the five questions put forth by the conference organizers of the present volume. Here are three more questions: First, if priors are established by early inputs during the learning process, do deviations in the inputs that establish these priors (i.e., rendering their information biased in some respect) create a "conceptual garden path"? That is, can early biased learning recover when later learning provides information that contradicts the early information? Recent work from my colleagues and me at Rochester suggests that in the domain of statistical learning, adults show a first-in bias that blocks later learning.

Second, does development proceed, in part, by becoming more efficient at basic aspects of information processing, thereby creating "excess capacity" that can be used for higher level aspects of learning (e.g., generalization or rule extraction)? That is, might there be an advantage to "over-learning"? This identifies an intriguing path for future research in which the standard habituation phase is repeated several times even though the infant has met a predetermined criterion of looking-time decrement. Infants may well habituate to a superficial level of analysis and encoding of the stimuli and then, after a break of a few minutes or even 24 hours, benefit from further exposure that enables them to analyze and encode further properties of the stimuli.

Third, what can we conclude about the continuity versus discontinuity of cognitive abilities across development? One classic example is the apparent disconnect between what infants appear to know about object solidity (using looking time measures), and what toddlers fail to know about object solidity more than a year later (using reaching responses) (see Berthier, DeBlois, Poirier, Novak, & Clifton, 2000). Have toddlers forgotten what they knew at five months of age? Is reaching so much more demanding than looking that it overrides the knowledge that is present when the task is simpler? Or is the knowledge that infants possess qualitatively different from the knowledge that toddlers possess?

CONCLUSIONS

The goal of this commentary was to summarize and challenge. There is no question that the field has grown remarkably in the last few years as learning and cognition have begun to meld into unified theories of development. But we have a long way to go, and several key questions remain unresolved. Where do the biases, innate or acquired, come from? What is the inventory of environmental parameters to which infants attend? Is there a large or a small set of neural mechanisms that supports different aspects of learning? If internal representations are fluid, then what enables the stability in behavior? Is generalization of learning interpolation, extrapolation, or both? The chapters in this volume, and the stimulation provided by the conference and its participants, will surely encourage the field to tackle these questions and further integrate learning and cognition in infancy research.

Acknowledgments   This commentary is based on discussions that followed the formal presentations of the primary participants at a conference entitled "New Approaches to Infant Learning and Cognition" held on May 21–22, 2005, at Duke University. I am indebted to Rachel Keen who jointly contributed to the final discussion at the conference and provided helpful feedback on a draft of this commentary.

References

Berthier, N. E., DeBlois, S., Poirier, C. R., Novak, M. A., & Clifton, R. K. (2000). Where's the ball? Two and three-year-olds reason about unseen events. *Developmental Psychology, 36,* 394–401.

Gibson, E. J. (1997). Discovering the affordances of surfaces of support. *Monographs of the Society for Research in Child Development, 56* (3, Serial No. 251).

Gopnik, A., Glymour, C., Sobel, D., Schulz, L., Kishnir, T., & Danks, D. (2004). A theory of causal learning in children: Causal maps and Bayes nets. *Psychological Review, 111,* 1031.

Hood, B. M. (1998). Gravity does rule for falling events. *Developmental Science, 1,* 59–63.

Marcus, G. F., Vijayan, S., Bandi Rao, S., and Vishton, P. M. (1999). Rule-learning in seven-month-old infants. *Science, 283,* 77–80.

Needham, A., Barrett, T., & Peterman, K. (2002). A Pick-Me-Up for Infants' Exploratory Skills: Early Stimulated Experiences Reaching for Objects Using 'Sticky Mittens' Enhances Young Infants' Object Exploration Skills. *Infant Behavior and Development, 25,* 279–295.

Simion, F., Turati, C., Valneza, E., & Leo, I. (2006). The emergence of cognitive specialization in infancy: The case of face preference. In Y. Munakata and M. Johnson (Eds.), *Processes of change in brain and cognitive development: Attention and performance XXI.* Oxford, UK: Oxford University Press.

Author Index

Subject Index